GOODBYE BAFANA

GOODBYE BAFANA

Nelson Mandela, My Prisoner, My Friend

James Gregory

with Bob Graham

HEADLINE

First published in 1995
by HEADLINE BOOK PUBLISHING

10 9 8 7 6 5 4 3 2 1

British Library Cataloguing in Publication Data

Gregory, James
Goodbye Bafana
I. Title   II. Graham, Bob
323.11968

ISBN 0-7472-1698-3

Typeset by Keyboard Services, Luton, Beds

Printed and bound in Great Britain by
Mackays of Chatham PLC, Chatham, Kent

HEADLINE BOOK PUBLISHING
A division of Hodder Headline PLC
338 Euston Road
London NW1 3BH

Contents

Prologue

Everywhere were faces I recognised: Castro, Arafat, Prince Philip, Hillary Clinton. All the old lags from prison were there too, Walter and Mac, Kathy and Andrew. Wherever I turned were celebrities. There were kings and princes, sheikhs and dukes, rulers and dictators: the great and the good from the world over.

As I sat watching the impressive line-up, a sense of the ridiculous overwhelmed me: just a few years ago many of these people were considered terrorists and criminals, a threat to our lives. They now mingled with dignitaries from 167 countries, filled with pride yet at this moment all content just to be sharing the same shaded sunlight. Could this really be happening? Memories kept returning of a time when we had been told in no uncertain terms that many of these people were subhuman, animals to be broken until they begged for mercy. But here they were basking in glory.

The old grey mohair suit had seen better days, but I had managed to get into it without a problem. Under the early morning sun it was hot, but I didn't want to take off my jacket – sweat had already soaked my blue shirt beneath. It was not done, in this sort of company, to sit with a damp shirt sticking to a clammy back. Beside me my wife Gloria sat gripping my hand and pointing out the world leaders as they entered the amphitheatre. With all this waiting I decided I needed a leak.

Security was very tight and when I asked one serious-looking young man where the toilet was he was instantly alert, demanding why I wanted to know. I told him that unless he wished to have wet shoes and a very embarrassing scene, then he'd better just give me a simple answer.

It was somewhere at the back, I was told, behind the row upon row of assembled dignitaries. Each step of the way I was accosted by people I had guarded in prison. They embraced me, hugged me, shook my hand, slapped me on the back, told me how good it was to

1

see me, and wasn't all this grand. Some of them I remembered – Laloo Chiba, Mac Maharaj. Others I recognised but could not put a name to even though they were now members of parliament.

As I returned to my seat the over-zealous security man with a wire hanging out of his left ear stopped me, wanting to know where I was heading. I patiently told him. When I showed him my red ticket which sat me in among the special guests he gave me another distrustful look. I could see it in his eyes; he was wondering why a nobody like me was sitting with the somebodies. I smiled at him and told him he was right, I did have the wrong ticket. It should not have been for the special red section, but the extra-special purple section among the even bigger somebodies. 'Ja, ja, ja,' he nodded, 'sure, just go and sit down please.' He reluctantly added the word 'sir', just in case. When I had arrived at the airport there had been profuse apologies: there had been a ticket mix up and I had been allocated a red ticket, was that okay? That day I would have been delighted, no honoured, to get one of the green or white tickets for seats further back. No, I was not going to complain because someone had messed up. I was only too pleased to be here at all.

All around there was noise: screams of delight, people talking loudly wanting to be noticed and the choir belting out their rhythmic songs, in praise of Africa and Madiba. I closed my eyes and just listened.

The call had come through to my home early the previous week. The President, the woman said, requests my presence at the inauguration, and naturally Gloria's. The caller was sorry about the rush, what with the election and everything, but it was pointless sending the invitation by post, it would not arrive in time. Just show up at the airport and collect the invitation. There was a special flight laid on, she added.

'The President requests,' the woman had said. Some request. I would have crawled every inch of the way, through the Great Karoo Desert and over the Drakensberg Mountains on bare hands, to see this day in person. It's not often you get the opportunity to see a birth and a burial in the same ceremony.

At the airport I'd never seen so much security; enough armament to invade a nation. And this was a day when we were giving peace a chance. I had watched all the private jets lining up to be parked: it was worse than a crowded supermarket car park. They told me they gauged a visitor's importance that day on how close his private jet was allowed to park to the main terminal. It was more than an imagined insult to the likes of Arafat that his aircraft was given a spot

2

further from the main doors than the one carrying Castro. It would take many weeks for bruised egos to mend after this show.

Once the ceremony was under way I could no longer see the podium. As soon as he came on, up jumped the small army of photographers and cameramen. I shut my eyes and although I could not see him I could hear that slow, distinctive drawl, to which I had become so accustomed over what seemed a lifetime. When I closed my eyes I could see Robben Island, that Devil's Island prison where we had kept him. I could see the times when he had wanted to be free. I could see the man standing there so tall, so ram-rod straight that he towered above everyone else. I opened my eyes and as I blinked in the sunlight of this inauguration day, behind him, in the distant misty hills, I could pick out the Voortrekker Monument, a symbol of those old Calvinist days that we were here to bury for ever. It is a birthday-cake memorial to the 500 or so Boers who had slaughtered 10,000 Zulus in the Battle of Blood River, but how strangely out of place it seemed now, almost obscene. I wondered if he had noticed it on his way in? I wondered if he had also seen the graves of Hendrik Verwoerd and Daniel Malan. After all, these were the very Afrikaners who had been so convinced that they, and their kind, whites, were superior in every way to the likes of him and his kind, blacks. The echoes of countless appalling acts perpetrated by the white man under the guise of apartheid were never far from any of our minds this day: Sharpeville ... Soweto ... Steve Biko ... Chris Hani ... but today we were seeing the death of the old evil ways of apartheid and the birth of a new nation.

If the man gave any thought to the monument or to the graves of those who had driven him and his people to hell and back it never showed for a moment on his face. I felt a chest-splitting pride in him today. We'd both come a long way together. Not only had we healed the differences between us both as men, one black, one white, but the process had started throughout our land. And here, on this very day, in this very amphitheatre, Arafat, the PLO leader, was actually meeting, and more importantly, talking with Israel's President Ezer Weissman for the first time. It really was a sight to behold. Arab sheikhs were bowing their heads in respect when a rabbi read a lesson from the Old Testament. There were prayers from the Hindu, Hebrew, Muslim and Christian religions. My mind kept playing over and over again that old record about us all coming together in a great big melting-pot: maybe we could.

A week or so later there was a second phone call. The President requests my presence once more. This time for the opening of

3

parliament, and he was sorry the tickets got messed up last time; it had all been such a rush. Out came the old grey mohair suit again.

At the main gate there was the same look of incredulity from the security guards when I presented my invitation. A second, closer examination to make certain it was not a forgery, and this time a seat in the President's personal box. And this time, unlike the last, there was no pomp and ceremony. Now we were down to the emotional stuff.

The band of former exiles, criminals, terrorists and traitors, many of them sentenced to death at one time or another, were taking their places at the head of this emerging nation. Just to stand and watch them striding into the chamber, their heads held high in unquench-able pride, was enough to induce tears.

I watched them, knowing many of them from the cells. They were followed by the men and women of the movement who had been confined to their homes, often for years, cut off from family and loved ones. There were those who had been beaten up, harassed, dumped in prison and had lost comrades in the years of struggle, just because they believed in equality. Now their time had come.

And there, standing head and shoulders above them all and smiling more broadly than anyone, was Madiba, the father of the nation.

At the end I could not move, exhausted by the emotion of it all, Gloria still gripping my hand. Security men were swarming again and they tried to usher us out. But no, we were not leaving, we insisted. There was one more appointment, one more ceremony to go. In the bowels of the parliament building we sat with the man, now President, to drink tea, and toast one another, just as we had so many times in the past.

As we left with a feeling of exhilaration, we were stopped by two men, one of whom I recognised: Kobie Coetsee, the Minister of Justice. He wanted his companion, one of the country's most notable judges, to meet me.

'This is James Gregory,' he said, introducing me. 'You will have heard a lot about him.' The judge nodded his head in perfect rhythm with pumping my hand. 'This is the man who took the hatred for the white man out of Nelson Mandela.'

Chapter 1

My first meeting
with Nelson Mandela

The shaft of light was like a metronome, sweeping the bare walls of the room with monotonous regularity. I would wait for the beam to enter the room from the left, through the curtainless windows and pass along the wall opposite. The windows were wide open to try and catch any breath of air from the ocean just beyond. The window frames cast a shadow on the wall and for a time I would concentrate on their misshapen silhouettes. I played imaginary noughts and crosses on the nine squares created by the shadows of the mullion bars, but still could not force myself to sleep. I tried to use the passage of the light to coincide with the counting of sheep. One ... pause until it reappeared ... two ... pause some more ... three ... pause ... four. Instead of having the effect of sending me to sleep, the beam from the lighthouse on the foreshore had focused my mind and made me more restless for what lay ahead.

Sometime before dawn I set myself a plan. Could I get up, crawl quietly to the door and escape from the room unheard and unnoticed between one sweep of the light and the next? Several times I held my breath, willing my body to move. When, after several false starts, I eventually did move, I'd forgotten the boxes and piles of clothes stacked beside the bed. My first step was within a second of the light leaving the room. It was also a step that ended the existence of a boxed set of wine goblets, a wedding gift. The next movement was more a hop, step and stumble followed by a curse. Gloria stirred, but then fell asleep; she was used to my getting up at an unearthly hour.

In the kitchen I ruefully inspected my foot, now bleeding from the shattered glasses. They were a gift from Gloria's mother. No doubt bought specifically to inflict the present injury, I thought. I could hear the old woman laughing at the thought of the glass splitting my skin. The blood seeped over the old, cracked linoleum. I could not even wash the wound – there was no water in this place. We'd been told it would be piped in tomorrow. There was a smile on the fellow's face as he said it; the sort of vacant, distant smile that means tomorrow could be anytime in the next few weeks.

What on earth had I let myself in for? They had warned me that this was the worst place to come to, the place to be avoided at all costs. And this was no way to start. Even though they'd promised as much time as I liked to settle in, promised a nice house, in fact anything I wanted. I should have known better, should have known not to trust these people who wanted me to look after the main man, the one they called the Black Pimpernel. What was I thinking of when I agreed? Me a twenty-four-year-old nobody from the outback, still a kid really. I had read about this man in the newspapers and heard about him on the radio. I knew it was the prospect of facing him tomorrow for the first time that had kept me chasing the shadows.

I stood in the dismal kitchen, not wanting to switch on the light, knowing its yellowness would only emphasise the drabness of the place which had been empty for weeks before we moved in. The old confusion as to whether or not we should be there returned as I stared out through the window at the lighthouse, watching its remorseless beam coursing the entire area. Over and over again I could hear them trying to convince me that I'd be in control. That the man and his comrades would be the ones with the worries, not me. What the people in charge had told me was that it would be my job to demoralise the blacks, especially him, reduce them to nothing, till they begged forgiveness and admitted they'd been wrong. Well, maybe they'd spent tonight without sleep as well. Somehow I doubted it though. I knew he and his kind were just animals who didn't really care anyway. Maybe they were worse than that. They didn't even deserve to be here. They deserved to be left swinging from the end of a rope for a few days in the high noon heat of the Great Karoo to let the buzzards and insects have a good feed.

This was the bastard who was responsible for the turmoil dividing my country, for stoking up all its anger and bitterness, and for causing us to become the pariahs of the entire civilised world. He was the one who had turned the world against us. The lies he and his kind told to try to get sympathy from the soft bleeding-heart liberals, always looking for a cause to latch on to, making out that we were the ones to blame. They had imposed

6

sanctions against us, trying to starve us into submission. But what had they deprived us of? Big Macs and rust-bucket Peugeots and little else because we found ways around their stupid rules. What did foreigners know anyway? They'd never understood us in the first place, and it was likely they were just jealous of what we had here. This bastard was lucky. He'd escaped the hangman's noose, God knows how, probably by threatening the judge's family I suspected. But now he was going to be in my care. I tried to picture his face, put flesh on the black and white picture I'd seen so many times in the papers. Soon I'd know what he was like in person. I would see his fear.

The moment had come a bit unexpectedly. I was not supposed to be on duty that weekend, having just arrived fresh from the mainland a few days before. I had planned to take a week to settle in and get the house in order. But on Saturday morning the chief warder, a man called Munro, came knocking at the door, all starch and bristle, complaining that they were short staffed. He was pleasant enough, but he made it perfectly clear he expected me to be down at the prison first thing on Sunday morning. Not that it made much difference to me. I was glad to get out of the house and let Gloria get on with emptying the cardboard boxes which seemed to be everywhere. Instead of trying to get everything out as quickly as possible, she opened each one almost as if it were a Christmas present. When I agreed to work, Munro seemed to relax and removed his peaked hat to make his little speech.

'Welcome to the island, Gregory. I'm sure we'll get along just fine.' His voice was clipped and had that note that senior officers always adopt when talking to subordinates, sort of distant and mechanical. He went into a prepared speech telling me how good life was on the island, what with the fishing and open air, knowing full well I'd heard all the rumours to the contrary. I just nodded and smiled, and to be honest I was a little embarrassed that he'd walked in on the mess of the house. Everything was covered in a thick coat of dust from the floor sanding which had been going on for several days. The baby was crying, unable to find one of his toys, and Munro turned his attention to Gloria.

'Mrs Gregory, you'll find this is a fine place to bring up a young family,' he said, the monotone of his voice making it more like an order than an observation.

I think Munro was pleased to make the first meeting as short as possible – he didn't want to get his uniform dusty – so after telling me I had to be at the front gates by 5.30 next morning, he said he had to go and see other families. Just as he closed the front door behind him, he hesitated and popped his head back to say: 'Oh, by the way Gregory, we'll be sticking you in with the Poqo.'

The dreaded Poqo: the band of criminals who had turned our beautiful land into a desperate battleground. Who were responsible for turning black man against white man. Who had made it very clear they wanted what we had, earned by the blood and sweat of our forefathers. They wanted our land, they wanted our jobs and they wanted to kick us into the sea. And, along the way, they wanted to rape our women and destroy everything that generations had worked for and died for as well. I knew all about the ones they called the Poqo. They were from different groups, all with their own fancy title and all of them proclaiming injustice and screaming for freedom. Did they ever stop and think about freedom and justice when they were planting their bombs and killing people? Maybe I'd ask this main man if he could answer that. Let him talk his way out of that one. Let him explain how much the Poqo had done to bring jobs and prosperity to our country. Let him explain how his freedom charter would make life better for us white people and get him to wiggle out of this 'Africa for the Africans' business that we'd started to hear about. All that his bitching and whining had done was to carve open a wound between black and white that was festering into a gaping sore.

That morning I stood there in the kitchen until I was sure the bleeding had stopped, imagining his face and imagining challenging conversations with him. I'd show him who was boss.

The thought of meeting him and the other Poqo, the leaders, brought bile to my mouth. I wanted them to be hanged, for my country to be freed from their evil. As I stood there in the darkness, silently venting my hatred, the confusion streamed back again. Was I up to the job? Could I handle them? The answer was as distant as it was academic. Now there was no choice. I'd accepted the posting.

Gloria had laid my uniform carefully across the back of the old cane chair in the bathroom. Clean grey knee-length socks were draped over the top of the grey-brown safari suit, and beneath the legs of the chair were my brown shoes, polished the night before. But where was the whistle and its green lanyard? To appear on duty without it was a punishable offence. I'd never find it in the mess of cardboard boxes.

The sound of the search, of boxes being ripped open and first toys, then pots and pans, then books being dumped impatiently on the floor woke the baby. And he woke Gloria. She stood in the doorway, hair all tousled and holding the whistle in her hand.

'I suppose it's this you're looking for?' she said, sleepily. 'You should have asked. I left it beside the bed.'

There was pleasure in putting on the uniform, knowing I'd be doing my duty for my people. It was a sort of vague, distant pride I'd felt every day since I started, knowing I'd be making a contribution against the criminals and terrorists who were the blight on the beauty of our land.

It was shortly before the first grey embers of dawn began to appear behind the silhouette of Table Mountain that I slipped quietly out. This time just before dawn was one which, in the coming years, would never cease to amaze me. This moment, a whisper before the darkness receded, was the briefest of times when everything was at peace. The ocean seemed to be hushed, almost resting before it began its daily pounding of the island and Cape Town's distinct shore. The birds were silent and the night crickets had ceased. This was the best part of the day, especially in summer, before the heat snatched away the cool air and made breathing a chore. In winter, it was the opposite. It was this time when the winds and the rains seemed to pause before the main assault of the day began.

The road from the main accommodation area to the town was tarmacked and the kerbs were painted an immaculate white, the result of prisoners' art work. It ran through neat rows of single-storeyed white houses, their gardens trim and neat, the leaves on the bushes covered in a film of sand. I passed a car, falling apart, without doors and a back window, parked beside a house; and a children's playground, slide, swings, a roundabout, deserted and empty. A union flag, the flag of the Republic, hung limp from above the old white-faced church. On a street corner was an old ship's cannon, now painted black.

Outside the main administration building a prisoner had his back toward me, his head deep inside a large black drum. It was an almost comical pose and I smiled at the thought that in any other walk of life there would be a temptation to tip him inside. But this was prison life, and I knew he was emptying slops from the officers' mess.

I asked him where the maximum prison was. My voice, normally soft, was almost shrill and harsh. He was a coloured, most of them were coloured, and when he brought his head around to face me I

9

could see he'd been eating something out of the slops – there was a white mess around his lips.

'Just tell me where the maximum is,' I demanded, sorry I'd spoken to him at all. He just stood there, wiping his hands down the sides of his thin green prison clothes, his eyes filled with the guilt of being caught eating out of the mess slop tin and, I suppose, unable to comprehend me. Clearly he couldn't understand why a prison officer didn't know the way to the maximum. He looked at me quizzically, wondering if I was testing him, or if I was sizing him up for a beating or a kicking.

'Yes baas, I know baas, you new baas, please you go that way baas.' He pointed to his right, down the road, waving his long bony hand backwards and forwards like a snake's head. I walked on and when, twenty seconds or so later I looked back, the prisoner was still standing staring after me, cap in hand, scratching his head, trying to make sense of the encounter, wondering why I'd not punished him for stealing from the garbage drum.

The greyness of the coming day was giving a cheerless, glaucous colour to the bushes and spindly, straw-like grass that covered the sandy earth. Somewhere to the right there was a movement, and I stopped, aware of the acute silence. There, not a spit away from me, stood a springbok, its head raised out of the grass, its long neck turned to look at me. I stood there for an eternity, wondering if this was a superstitious symbol for me. Later, when I thought back at the moment, I remembered speaking to the creature, the national emblem of all true South Africans. 'What have you come to tell me? Is there a message?' It's strange, but in my mind, I thought this bok had been sent to tell me I was doing right, that I was combating evil and wrong. Whatever the reason, I took it as a sign, as sure and positive as the serpent that presented itself to Moses.

I continued to walk. On my left was an eerie sight: a neglected graveyard. Row upon row of headstones, some elaborate, others simple. All of them broken, askew, half hidden in the drifting sand, a bizarre contrast to the orderliness all around. Was this where they dumped the terrorists when they died? It was enough to bring a shiver despite the increasing humidity in the air. Later I learned that this was a cemetery for the lepers who had formerly inhabited the island. I hurried by.

The prison itself emerged out of the greyness, a sprawling mass of low buildings, almost like the cattle sheds I'd known from my childhood. The four gun towers stood out as clearly as the lighthouse, the salient features on the island. In front of the jail, on a patch of straggly straw-like grass, now burned brown, sat a four-wheeled Second World War cannon, neatly surrounded by a row of white-painted bricks. The barrel of the gun pointed out to sea, another relic of the island's history. As I sat on the low wall outside the front gates, waiting for the guards to open up, the first rays of the sun began to reflect off the Blouberg Hills down beyond the small island harbour. I took comfort in the beauty of the mainland hills, in how enticing they must seem to these prisoners. So close, but so far away. Separated by just five miles or so, but by such treacherous waters which made freedom nothing more than a constant tease. I knew that, in all its history, no man had ever escaped. This place was our own Alcatraz, our own Devil's Island. There was only one way off, and as far as I was concerned, for these bastards inside, they weren't ever going to take it. It was sweet irony that they could see the mainland, see the perfect beaches, could watch the growth of skyscrapers signal the affluence of a society they would never enjoy, and they'd never touch them. That was a punishment in itself, to have this view, but never get to be part of it.

Maybe it was the obvious newness of my uniform, maybe my refusal to get up and shake hands or introduce myself, that led to the hostile glances from the dozen or so other warders gathered outside the gate. I was the new boy and not yet to be trusted. Just as I'd heard about the inmates, so I'd heard about these men too. Mean and hard. Completely dedicated to hatred. They hated the Poqo and kaffirs and koolies so that made it okay. I could live with that. As we sat on the wall sizing each other up, the unmistakable reek of stale booze lingered in the air, the rancid breath of two warders too close for pleasantries. I'd get to know them soon enough.

The others had seemed to drift in out of the greyness, but when Munro arrived shortly before 6.00, it was in a cloud of blue exhaust from a *bakkie* that had seen better days. I was told later that the open-backed truck, held together with a combination of wire, string and paint, was government issue. It showed what the government really thought of us. With Munro's arrival the others jumped to attention. No, let me rephrase that: they'd sort of unfolded to their feet into a semblance of a line. I just kept to one side. It was just like boarding school all over again. Line up here, line up there, polish this, polish that. All crap, I'd decided. It was inside a man's own head where you found discipline, none of this must-do stuff.

Behind Munro there was an ox of a man. The others seemed to cower in his presence. I was told later this was Smit, T. G. Smit. He actually shot himself with his own revolver later, but this morning he was the guy everyone was answering to. Munro stayed to one side, disdainful of anything as unremarkable as taking a roll-call. Smit did the name calling. We stood there, now maybe fifteen or twenty of us in all, beneath the flag-pole outside the front gate. Above us the orange, white and blue union flag of the Republic hung limp. I suppose the roll-call was vaguely military-style, eyes right and the stand to attention, eyes front and the rest, but it lacked the sharpness and thrust of the parade ground.

Smit read out the names and when he finished he lingered: 'Any names not on my list?' Can't this square-head count, I thought. I stuck my hand up.

'And just who are you, a blerrie escapee?' Smit wanted to have a little sport before the day began properly, and clearly he had me earmarked as his target. Munro jerked to life and leaned forward to whisper in Smit's ear.

'So you're Gregory?' The line seemed to have melted and I could feel the eyes on me. Someone sniggered. Smit was enjoying this: 'So you're the new guy who's looking after the Poqo? Just remember who they are and what they will do to you, eh? You have a wife and family, eh?' I nodded. 'Okay man, well remember what these kaffir bastards will do to them if you give them a chance. They love white meat. Don't give them a chance, just do your duty.' I nodded again.

It was after this greeting that I became aware for the first time of the prison itself and it was only then it hit me that the moment had come, the reason I had been sent to the island.

'Right Gregory, let's go meet the kaffirs,' Smit said.

Smit took me on a grand tour to each of the sections housing the main criminals, to the sports fields, the hospital section and the kitchens. Later, I could not remember any detail of Smit's tour. My mind was fixed on the men in B Section, the home of the main man. They were cut off from the main sections, segregated in a prison within a prison. These men were the most dangerous.

When the moment came it was as unremarkable as it was forgettable. Smit did the introductions, as blindly unaware that the sweat that stained the entire back of my shirt was as much from apprehension as the heat of the morning.

He stood in the corner of the yard, his back turned to me, talking to a smaller, older man. Beside them two more men stood listening, nodding their heads in agreement. Even from the rear, I could recognise him, his ramrod back and broad shoulders prominent. Smit waved his long muscular arms and bawled out his introduction: 'Right, here he is, your new censor officer.'

He turned round, his eyes fixing me firmly with an aloofness, a detached remoteness I found immediately disconcerting. Every eye was on me, the forty or so pairs of eyes of these Poqo, terrorists and killers, but I could not take my eyes from the main man.

My thoughts were racing. So this is what you look like. At last I see you. You are a blerrie lucky bastard. You should be dead. The judge made a mistake. He should have passed the death sentence on you. Smit began pulling at my arm, aware I was staring at the main man.

'Come man, come meet him, I see you have picked him out.'

He gestured toward the man, standing there in his prison green shirt, shorts and sandals.

'Gregory,' he nodded with obvious disdain for the man, 'this here is Nelson Mandela.'

His voice was as firm and direct as his eyes: 'Good morning,' he said. 'Welcome to Robben Island.'

My reply was unusual. 'Good morning,' I replied. 'I see you.' It was a phrase I'd learned a generation ago as a child, growing up with Zulus, a greeting of friendship. Immediately I caught myself, wondering what the hell I was doing using it for the first time since Ongemak.

Chapter 2

Boyhood at Ongemak

It was the end of the Second World War and while the rest of the world was thinking of rehabilitation, recovery and rebuilding, South Africa, in the minds of its white leaders, was in the throes of planning further destruction and distress. Apartheid was just around the corner, although it would be a long time before it had an impact on my life. At that time, 1945, I had been serenely happy living at Ongemak. The name means 'discomfort' but in reality the farm was anything but that. It was a home where I learned to hunt and fish, to live off the land and to be virtually self-sufficient. It was a home where the troubles of the outside world never penetrated. My country was in turmoil; death and destruction, prejudice and bigotry were ways of life. But those matters never reached Ongemak. I was to learn about apartheid and what it meant only when I was sent away to school. In those early years at Ongemak I received a different sort of education which would one day serve me better than any I was to have forced into my susceptible young mind in a classroom.

Ongemak was my universe. It was the home, according to family legend, given to the Gregory family by the great Zulu warrior Mpande, half-brother of Shaka. At the time Mpande had been the paramount chief of the Zulus, which means 'People of Heaven'. Mpande had conspired to overthrow the despotic tyrant King Dingaan. He gathered an *Impi*, a battalion of warriors, to help him. Mpande also recruited the power and expertise of a number of battle-hardened white commandos to act as his counsel and to advise on military strategy. Among the white recruits was a man called Gregory, one of my ancestors who had taken part in the years of *Mfecane*, the crushing, the time of chaos when fleeing tribes attacked their neighbours who, in turn, fled and attacked other tribes. From the tip of the Cape right through to the central plains of Africa there had been slaughter. King Dingaan had killed the Boer pioneer Piet Retief and many of his Voortrekkers and was intent on continuing the Mfecane, until Mpande stepped in. Together Mpande and his white generals, my ancestor included, defeated Dingaan and secured thirty years of peace. As a reward for their help Gregory and the other white commandos were given land. Hence Ongemak.

While this story was part of our family legend, passed down from one generation to the next, no one had ever tested or challenged its authenticity. The truth was that no one really wanted it to be disproved; it was an intriguing legend to have. It was much the same as the story of how the Gregory forefathers came to be in South Africa. From the earliest days that I could remember, sitting with my father, I was told of how we were all descendants of Rob Roy, the Scottish Jacobite outlaw who lived in the eighteenth century. I can still see my father, an earnest and serious man, sitting telling me the story of how the Gregory clan had arrived on the African continent.

It was a story I repeated many times at school; it gave me great pride. According to my father's version of the legend of Rob Roy, or Robert MacGregor to give him his proper name, he had had a brother named James. It was said both brothers loved the same woman, who was called Stella Jenkins. They agreed that only one could have the woman and that they should enter into an agreement whereby the brother who did not have the woman would, instead, inherit the family estate from their father. By one course or another, and I was told it was on the toss of a coin, Robert won the hand of the woman and James was left with the land. Unfortunately, James could not stand the thought of losing the woman he loved and, broken-hearted, had given the land to his brother and left Scotland altogether. Sometime in the early to mid-eighteenth century he ended up in South Africa, in northern Natal, where he changed his name from MacGregor to Gregory. Whether or not the family legend is accurate mattered little to us. It was always a good bedtime story, and one which I passed on to my children. What is certain is that all the Gregory clan, going back five generations, were farmers in Natal, and my middle name is Jenkins, after the woman my ancestor loved and lost.

The family name was to lead me into many fights in the years when I was sent by my parents to Afrikaner schools. The uncompromising attitude of the Afrikaner boys was to call me a *rooinek*, a red neck or Englishman. As I became the butt of their attentions, with fists as well as words, I struck back. As any person with a drop of Scots blood in their veins will readily admit, it is one thing to be called a red neck, a name given to the red-tunicked British soldiers who fought the Boers, but an altogether different matter to be labelled an Englishman. It led to many fights.

My mother's side of the family was much more sedate but no less steeped in tradition. Born Margrita Susanna May, she was a descendant of the Besters, one of the original Dutch settlers who had come to the southern tip of Africa in search of a new home. The Besters had taken part in the Great Trek of Boer farmers in the nineteenth century and were as involved in Afrikaner history as was possible. The Besters had been one of the beleaguered Boer families who had trekked into the ambush set by Dingaan at the foot of the Drakensbergs. Many died, if not at the hands of the Zulu warriors, then from the sickness and malnutrition which set in after many debilitating battles. Before they all perished their plight came to the attention of Andries Pretorius, a hero of every Afrikaner. He mounted a commando raid to rescue the Trekkers who had gone in search of new lands to farm. Together with 500 men Pretorius vowed that if God gave them victory over Dingaan they would hold the anniversary of the battle a hallowed day and build a church of thanksgiving.

Pretorius, a careful and thoughtful strategist, chose his battle-ground on the banks of the slow-flowing Ncome, a river that would thereafter be known as Blood River. He had chosen well and the Trekkers and commandos set their *laagers*, or camps, in such a way that two sides were protected by the confluences of the river. In the ensuing battle the Boers, numbering no more than 550 defeated 12,000 Zulu warriors, killing 3,000 of them as they launched wave after wave against the laager of white men. Not one Boer life was lost that day and the conviction was born among these settlers that they had entered into a covenant with God, just as He had with Moses and the Israelites. It was a belief that everything they were to do, every course they were to follow, every choice they made, was to be with His blessing. It was the birth of a theocracy that was to have terrible ramifications in the generations to follow.

My maternal grandfather, Paul Gerhardus Bester, and my grandmother, Susanna May, came from a farm near the Natal town of Melmoth. It was the same farm where the most famous of all Zulus, the great Shaka, had lived. Shaka's family had a *kraal* (stockade) on the Bester family farm.

Later, in my school years, when I told my father of the fights I

17

had because I had been called a rooinek, he would laugh it off and explain my proud Afrikaner history. My paternal grandfather Gerhardus Phillip Jenkins Gregory had, after all, fought against the British for the Boers in the Anglo-Boer Wars at the turn of the century. At that time my grandmother was one of the tens of thousands of Afrikaner women who were held by the British in prisoner-of-war camps for two years. The conditions in the camps were appalling and to this day Afrikaners talk of the thousands of innocent women and children who died in those camps. They were kept captive to prevent them running the farms while their menfolk were away from home fighting. The British came and burned their fields and killed their livestock in an effort to destroy the Afrikaners. Ongemak was one of the farms that suffered badly at that time, its land plundered. My father, also called James, was born on 30 June 1900, and he was with my grandmother in the concentration camp.

My grandmother suffered greatly in the concentration camp where misery was heightened by lack of food and decent living conditions. Women were so desperate for firewood that they collected dried cattle droppings to put on their camp fires. My grandmother would wander among the captured cattle skewering the droppings on a stick and collecting them in a bag to take to the camp to dry in the sun. At one time a rumour swept through the prison camps that the British planned to kill all the young Afrikaner male children with their mothers. My grandmother was too terrified to leave my father, at that time less than a year old, alone in the camp. So she put him inside the large hessian bag she carried over her shoulder. She covered him with grass before throwing the dung in on top of him. She cut small holes in the sides and bottom of the sack for him to breathe. Much of the hatred among the Afrikaners towards the British even today still stems directly from the treatment of those women and children in the concentration camps.

Small wonder, then, that when the Great War started in 1914, my grandfather, along with many Afrikaners, refused to pitch in on the side of the British. However, my father did fight during the Second World War and was awarded two medals, the Oak Leaf War Medal as well as the Protea Medal, for Africa Service.

I was born on 7 November 1941, the fourth of five children, following Jean, Gert and Paul. Michael was the youngest. During the war, when father was away fighting, we stayed in Vryheid with my grandparents. It was only after my father returned from battle and we went home to Ongemak that I can recall my life beginning.

Ongemak was in a part of Natal that the concept of apartheid never seemed to reach. Certainly as far back as I can recall there was never any attempt to impose apartheid, or apartness as the word translates into English, on my life. I grew up living mainly as a Zulu child. My main language was Zulu, although I could also speak Afrikaans and English. My whole life revolved around my friends who were all Zulus. Bafana, the Zulu boy from one of the kraals on the farm, was to become closer than a brother. I spent the formative years of my early life living as a Zulu, being taught to hunt and fish as one, to live and celebrate as one. It is a wonder my family ever saw me in those years.

During the day I played with Bafana and our other young Zulu friends; at night I would frequently slip away to sleep in the kraals and be treated as one of the normal children of the Zulu families. It is much to my parents' credit that they did not see anything abnormal about this behaviour. They gave me a freedom which was to influence me greatly in my later life.

Ongemak was huge, or, at least, it seemed so to me. I knew that I could walk all day and never reach its boundaries. There were times when I travelled on horseback, or sometimes by tractor, and the farm just seemed to stretch on forever. Of course, I knew there were neighbouring farms, that there was life outside Ongemak; but to me anything that was important seemed to happen there. It was normal that each farm would have a kraal on it. The number would, naturally, depend on the overall size of the farm. We never measured farms in terms of acres or hectares, but in terms of kraals. Ours was a twenty-kraal farm, an average-sized spread.

The farming at Ongemak was very basic. Only the ploughing was mechanised, using four old Massey Ferguson tractors my father owned. Everything else, the picking of crops, milking or sheep rearing, was all done by hand. The work was seasonal although we never needed to hire outside help with the kraals on the land. Many of the kraals had themselves been on the property for generations.

The farm itself was hilly although there were long, flat stretches, river valley beds, long since dried up, which were fertile and easy to plough. There were high mountains, the Umtlazaiki Range, which seemed to stretch up above the clouds. High up in the mountains there were dense black wattle plantations, where the sun could not penetrate, and it was there that I had some of the best

19

adventures of my early years. My memories of the area are, naturally, clouded and strengthened by my fond nostalgia for them, but I can never recall any thoughts of prejudice or racism. Everything seemed to revolve around the end of the dry season, sometime at the end of July when we would frantically begin summer planting. We would all, my father, the blacks from the kraals and myself, plough non-stop. I can remember sitting at the steering wheel of the Massey Ferguson, barely able to see over the top of the column, never mind the ground in front, ploughing late into the night until darkness fell. When the first rains came a planter was hooked behind the tractor. One section would contain the maize seeds, the other the fertiliser to hasten the seeds' progress.

The maize would grow and along with it the weeds. And when the mielies, corn cobs, were between three and four feet high the girls and women would come from the kraals (because this was considered women's work) and walk up and down the rows chopping the heads off the weeds, and leaving them on the ground to dry and die. They called it *skoffel*, an Afrikaans word. Just before we harvested the crop, in late November or early December, it would have to be sprayed with a solution of worm poison to kill the snywurms, the cut worms which gather inside the cobs; otherwise they would destroy the entire plant.

Mielies were the staple food of the area and throughout much of southern Africa, particularly loved by the Zulus. The maize we would grind in a mill which my father powered by putting a fly-wheel and belt on to one of the tractors. We also had maybe a thousand merino sheep which roamed free about the farm. I think one of my earliest memories is watching the black men shearing the sheep in season. I was always fascinated at how the sheep shearer would squeeze the sheep between his knees and shave the animal in less than two minutes. It was, I told my father, something I wanted to learn when I grew up.

The entire area was subtropical in climate, and was as fertile as anywhere on this planet. Bananas grew in abundance, even in the mountains. Around the farmhouse, at the bottom of the slopes, growing wild, was an orchard plentiful in mangoes, guavas, granadillas, figs, avocados, even grapes. The avocados were fed to the pigs.

The entire area was a self-sufficient community where the word hunger was never heard, never even whispered. Everyone, my family and the Zulus who lived in the kraals, were well cared for.

My father was known as *Nkosi*, meaning 'big boss or father'. It was an affectionate name used by the Zulus that also reflected their respect for him. In those parts he was the first to organise a doctor who would call once a week and hold a surgery for the entire farm, including all the workers. To be honest, I'm certain bringing the doctor to Ongemak was a matter of simple expediency because if any of the workers were sick the nearest town was Gluckstadt, some distance away. By car alone it would take three hours or more. But on foot, or by cart it would take many days, and this meant losing valuable labour at crucial harvesting or planting times.

The labour in our house and in the fields came from the kraals. Every six months each kraal had to nominate two girls and two boys, usually in their teen years, for work. It meant we had anywhere between sixty and eighty labourers. In exchange for the labour, the kraal dwellers were allowed to stay rent-free and given two horses, four donkeys to pull ploughs, two goats and four sheep.

When I was young, by law, a child did not have to be sent to school until the age of six which meant that at Ongemak I did not have to go for three years, a time which I still cherish as the best of my life, a time when my closest friend was Bafana.

Chapter 3

Bafana,
my Zulu friend

Bafana, who lived on one of the kraals, just turned up at the farmhouse one morning and immediately struck a vital chord with me.

His first words to me were, 'Would you like to go hunting?' They were the words I had been longing to hear. As far back as I could remember, I had heard the men talk of hunting, I had seen people trekking off into the bush. I wanted to go too, but I was just a small child and they would not take me, telling me I'd have to wait until I was grown up.

Bafana's words instantly confirmed him as my friend. It never mattered he was a Zulu boy and I was white and we were, according to the emerging laws of our country, supposed to be kept apart. Our friendship just happened naturally. It was a friendship which was to shape the rest of my life.

Two of my brothers were older than me and the nearest contact with someone of my own age and colour was on a neighbouring farm. Not that the question of colour or race ever came into my mind in those days. On a few occasions when we were invited to go to a party or a *braai*, a barbecue, there would be girls and there would be music and most people finished up dancing. As a young boy I would have preferred stroking a mamba, a poisonous snake, to dancing with a girl. So, bored, I usually finished up sitting alone in my father's car and falling asleep. The boys who were there didn't seem to want to do the same things that I wanted to do: fishing and hunting. Not that I was complaining about a lack of friends. I had Bafana.

Although we were the same age, he stood taller than me and I remember he was stronger, so invariably he took the lead in most matters. My parents dressed me the same as the other white boys in khaki pants, shirts and socks. But from virtually the first day Bafana and I were together I saw immediately the sense in dressing as a Zulu, wearing a *beshu*, a cow-skin or ox-skin cloth which covered my front and rear. Temperatures in summer were often in the 90s to the 100s and so humid that it felt like breathing from the spout of an old steam kettle. Even in winter I cannot recall ever being cold. Maybe in the early morning there was a sharpness, but afterwards the sun climbed high in the sky. Most times Bafana and I would run barefoot although when we were in rough wooded areas where there were thorns we wore *badatas*. These were the hardest wearing footwear I ever knew, made from old, disused tyres with slits cut along the side and rawhide hooked through for laces. Just as my father was known by the Zulus as Nkosi, the boss or owner, so I became known as *Nkosana*, literally son of the boss.

Bafana would bring some other young Zulus with him, and we became a gang of usually four or five. They began to teach me how to hunt using a *kierie*, a Zulu throwing stick, then later a *knobkerrie*, a larger stick. We began by hunting *tarantal*, guinea fowl, but soon graduated to *patrys* or grouse. Within a short time we were all expert shots with our kieries. Soon we were imitating the real Zulu warriors, re-enacting the great battles. We usually had a battle following a rainstorm when it was easier to mould our home-made ammunition from the soft clay. The way we would fight was to split into two armies. It always transpired that Bafana was with me, and we would cut down young saplings from the black wattle trees for our weapons. To the end of this small branch we would mould our clay in the size and shape of a clenched fist and allow it to dry. These were called *kleilats*. This, then, would become our throwing stick. It carried a fearsome blow. Occasionally one side would play crooked and mould a few stones into the clay endings.

Bafana and I would pretend to be Shaka and Mpande, the heroic Zulu warriors. Our other gang members were the enemy and we spent days, weeks, learning to fight the Zulu way with knobkerries and light wooden spears called *assegais*. I quickly learned how to choose my kierie from the black wattle tree, or if we could find it, a brandkneukel bush with its long, straight branches, and my shield would be made from several layers of silverleaf bush.

It was almost as if I did not live with my parents. My room was at the end of the *stoep*, the verandah, on the ground floor. Every morning Bafana would be there before dawn and I would wake to find him sitting on his haunches waiting for me. I would ask him why he waited like that and he said he had learned how to be patient. Before my parents were up I would be gone with Bafana on our adventures. It would not be unusual for me to go several days

24

without ever seeing my family. Here I was, a five-year-old child, already learning to live on my own.

Although we spoke Afrikaans in the house, the second and frequently used language was Zulu, because of the workers both in the house and in the fields. English was used, particularly by my father, but it was third in usage. It was, therefore, natural for me to speak Zulu and by being close to Bafana it was a language which I perfected. First came the language and then the culture of the Zulus.

The first hunting trips we took were to the top of the Umtlazaiki Mountains which marked the boundary of our farm. We knew a neighbouring farmer called Pretorius who owned a large dam where he attempted to breed fish. He had many problems with *platanna*, flat frogs, which prevented the fish breeding. He told us he would pay us a *tiekie*, a sixpence, for every frog we caught. To reach Pretorius's farm we had to ride three, maybe four hours by donkey along a narrow ledge. But Bafana and I made sure the journey was well worth our trouble. We spent nearly a week gathering buckets of frogs, counting each and every one and dreaming how we would spend our new-found riches. Just to make the trip truly worthwhile Bafana taught me how to trap fish the Zulu way. We never told Farmer Pretorius. When we returned home I begged my father to take Bafana and me into Gluckstadt where we could spend part of our newly acquired fortune on sweets. It was when we were on this first shopping trip that Bafana taught me a little of the respect Zulus had for their elders by first purchasing a large wad of tobacco. I was, at first, aghast that he should be spending so much of his hard-earned platanna-hunting money on tobacco until he explained patiently to me that it was a sign of respect for his father who had provided him with everything else. It made sense, and it was a lesson I never forgot. I, too, bought some tobacco for my father and when I handed it to him he gaped in astonishment. The platanna hunting became a ritual and we planned it just before my father went into Gluckstadt to stock up on fertiliser or supplies. Bafana and I would make the trek up to Pretorius's farm to earn some spending money.

Wherever we went hunting on the farm, we would cook whatever we caught ourselves. We would always try to find an old, disused ant heap to use as a makeshift oven and hollow it out to build the fire inside. Once the fire was alight the smoke and heat would pour through the thousands of holes left by the ants and would become the perfect oven. If we had captured a bird we would prepare it and lay it on top of the ant-heap oven to cook. Another particular delicacy which I learned to enjoy was a worm called a *ximbi*, which lived on the black wattle trees. The ximbi was long and thick, almost like a large caterpillar. We would strip and behead it before laying it on the oven or skewer it on the end of a stick and cook it in the fire. I grew to love the taste of ximbi, a richly flavoured meat not unlike chicken. Of course none of my family would ever consider touching such a Zulu delicacy, but they saw no harm in me eating it.

Bafana also taught me from an early age how to survive on berries and wild figs in case we were ever stranded; it was an education in survival which was turned into an adventure. He taught me which roots to dig out, which leaves and fruit were edible and which creatures were to be hunted and which were to be left alone because nature needed their presence. For instance, there is a tall, slender white bird which is known as a tic bird. These, together with its smaller, red-coloured cousin, were not to be killed at any cost. These tic birds scurried around, often on the backs of the cattle and goats, eating the tics and flies off their backs and keeping them healthy. On the other hand there was the *muisvoel*, a mouse bird, with its long tail and a sharp, parrot-like beak. These were nuisance birds and could be shot at any time because they would get in among the fruit and crops and eat their way through them.

Everywhere on Ongemak, on the various kraals, Bafana and I were made welcome. Often when we were out we would be caught by a sudden tropical storm and head for the nearest kraal. We would go to the headman's hut, always a beautifully thatched *rondavel*, round hut, and ask his permission to stay. Bafana and I were known to all the kraals and I quickly learned the tradition of formally entering the kraal: it had to be approached via the cattle byre, the central point of any kraal because it was the place believed to be frequented by the spirits. I learned also that the headman's wives would have their huts on the left-hand and right-hand side of the byre, according to their order of marriage.

I was fascinated by the attitudes of the Zulus towards death and by the way my young friends had deep respect for their ancestors as well as their living elders. The religion of the Zulus, like all of the Nguni peoples, is one of ancestor worship based on a belief that when a person dies, he will continue to watch over his people from the spiritual world. The Zulu has a saying: 'According to the power and authority a forefather had in his lifetime, so it is from the place

26

to which he has gone.' In effect it means that after death the person carries into the next world the same influence he had during his lifetime on earth. The spirit of a Zulu king will watch over the entire Zulu nation, for example, while the ancestral spirits of a family will care for that family as well as their cattle, goats and crops.

It became clear from my earliest visits to kraals that the ancestral spirits had to be regularly remembered and offerings were made to them to show they had not been forgotten. At family festivals it was usual for the head of each family to sit beside his cattle byre and pour a little home-made sorghum beer on the ground for his forefathers, before he himself began to drink. A woman would, in turn, take a little bread and place it beneath the eaves of the hut for the old matriarch of the family. I know it was always strongly believed that if the ancestors were forgotten they could show their displeasure by bringing some misfortune on a family. Whenever some accident or misfortune befell a person he would examine carefully not how it happened, but, instead, the events leading up to the incident, to see how he may have possibly offended the ancestral spirits.

Although the religion of the Zulu is centred on an ancestor cult, they nevertheless believe implicitly in a God, Nkulunkulu, the Greatest of the Greats. It was, however, believed that Nkulunkulu involved himself only in major issues, matters of life, death, famine or natural disaster. He was believed to be the creator of everything and from this stemmed the belief that man is born healthy. The belief was simple logic: if He who made all things made man also, how could it be otherwise? Because of this belief, the Zulu cannot accept that accidents or disasters, apart from the most minor, are natural phenomena. How could there be a malfunction in a perfect world in which all things are made faultlessly by Nkulunkulu? If such a malfunction does occur the Zulu believes that someone is trying to do them harm. It was a logical thinking process which, at that age, I was not fully aware of. But the more time I spent with Bafana the more I gradually just accepted it as a fact, as would a Zulu.

When I stayed in a kraal overnight, often with Bafana and his family, other times at kraals where we would ask to shelter, we were both treated with great kindness. Everyone on the farm knew Bafana and myself. I was considered one of them, a white Zulu. Whenever we went to a kraal we were greeted and in return I would greet the inhabitants of the kraal with respect. For instance, in the morning a woman would say to me *Molo umfana,* good morning young boy. I would reply *Molo mama*, meaning good morning to a person who was not quite my mother, but a close acquaintance. It was the mark of respect to an older person.

Even though the farm was enormous, maybe ten miles wide by eight or nine miles across, Bafana and I got to know every kraal on the property as we wandered on our adventures. Bafana's kraal, a collection of ten or twelve rondavels, was about three miles from our main farmhouse. Whenever a kraal was nearby it was always obvious to us because the smell of the fires hung thick in the air. I think that the smell of a kraal will remain in my nostrils forever. Bafana and I got to know what sort of wood was being burned, even from some considerable distance. Bluegum tree logs would have a clean, menthol smell whereas wattle and thorn trees had a sweeter, almost tangy, scent to them. A common smell on every kraal was that of *dagga*, or cannabis, which was grown throughout the mountains in among the black wattle trees. Although I was then too young to understand what the smell was, its sickly sweetness was one I understood to be an adult smell.

When we stayed overnight in a kraal Bafana and I always slept in the headman's hut, as his personal guests. But there was also a ritual to respect as his guests. Before being given food we attended to the chores of the headman, just as he would. We would ensure his cattle were securely in the byre for the night before entering his rondavel. Then we would sit cross-legged in the middle of the room waiting for the food to be brought in by the women. Bafana's father had two wives and they would take it in turn to cook for him, each having a rondavel on either side of his main hut. Again, it was the smells and the sounds which remain deepest in my memory, for as the women of the kraal prepared the food, often a mielie and sour-milk-based food called *maas*, they would sing their beautifully rhythmic songs and chants. Each household had their own huts, but all were spaced around a common ground in the middle, an area of hard-packed ground which was used as the festival area.

It was in these festival areas where I experienced the greatest privilege – being invited to attend wedding ceremonies. These were the best times I could remember as a child. This was party time. Bafana had already taught me how to dance barefoot like a Zulu, imitating the role of a warrior, carrying our knobkerries, assegais and shields. When we knew a wedding was imminent we would prepare our own dances. No matter how good our dances were, they never compared to spending the evenings watching the fabled snake and reed dances by the light of the fires. The young girls' breasts would be bare, and it seemed the most natural sight in the world as they danced and sang. Later on, when I went to school with other white boys, I was always puzzled by their obsession with female breasts. I used to listen to them discussing a girl's breasts and wondered what all the fuss was all about. I had seen bare breasts from an early age and accepted them as perfectly normal. I never spoke about it to the white boys; they would never have understood and I know they would have accused me of going with the blacks. The only time the black girls used to cover up their breasts in those early days was when they worked in our own farmhouse. Then my mother supplied them with western dresses, insisting they wore them.

When I heard white people talking of how Zulus dressed, accusing them of being savages, I often wondered if they really understood the great detail and beauty of the beads and brass decoration they wore. I learned how different beads worn by young women would signify all manner of things, such as when a girl was of a marriageable age. The originality, colour and precision which went into the dress and beadwork was an art in itself. I recall being shown the elaborate beadwork of one woman, strung in beautiful loops because, the diviners said, 'the spirits we call up come and sit on the loops of the beads and speak only to our ears'.

When I stayed in the kraals I had no inkling of race, colour or politics. I never considered myself white or my friends black. We were just friends. In many ways, this upbringing was the foundation upon which friendship developed later.

Just like any young boys we would laugh and joke about many of the traditions that took place. From those early years I developed a strong understanding of the Zulu mind, in which a woman would be subservient to a man in a household. This was not to suggest, however, that a woman of strong character would allow herself to be dictated to. Far from it, but she accepted that her role was to run the household and train her daughters. It was a frequent Zulu phrase that 'men's affairs are men's affairs'. But when it came to the tradition of *lobolo*, or bride price, we would often have great merriment. The custom of lobolo, that is handing over cattle to the father of the bride as compensation for the loss of a daughter, is still common to all black peoples of southern Africa. The number of cattle handed over for a prospective bride would depend on her marriageability, a phrase that we, as children, could never quite comprehend. Sometimes a suitor would give upwards of twenty cattle for the daughter of a chief or a girl of similar social standing, while the average family could only ask for four or five cattle. Sometimes the considerations handed over would include other livestock such as a horse, or household items such as pots and pans, blankets or any items that the parties would agree. Naturally, we as young boys had our own grading system: we never rated any girl worth any more than an old rusted pot. When we knew a young girl was due to be prepared for marriage, we spent hours comparing what we would pay for her, anything from a crippled and ageing donkey to a cracked and holed cooking pot. We finished up rolling on the floor in fits of laughter.

The weddings and festivals were wonderful times when friends from neighbouring kraals gathered. All sorts of meats would be barbecued. The celebration would start on a Friday night and continue for two full days and nights. The sorghum beer was prepared for the elders, and for us a home-brewed ginger beer which we loved. The young girls would dance for hours and they would be followed by the praise-singers who would chant and praise the two families being united by the wedding. They would include everyone from the bride through to the distant relatives. Eventually they would end up with the bridegroom and praise him for being a king, a big man and the bull. It was a chanting praise-song which would be totally impromptu, but with a deep, rich tapestry of Zulu phrases and meanings. There would be two praise-singers from the bride's side and two from the groom's and they would each, in turn, sing the praises of the other side.

Bafana and I were not so much interested in the praise-singing as the feasting. There was enough meat and fruit for Africa. Some of the raw meat was hung up and people would come and hack off a piece to eat. Big bluebottle flies rested on the meat, but they would just be swept aside. I knew that if my mother ever saw a bluebottle on a piece of meat, she would have thrown it away, but not the Zulus; they just cooked the meat and enjoyed it. In those days I always assumed that when I married I would have the same type of festival.

The huts in the kraals had walls of reed and black wattle. In between the wooden framework was smeared a compound called *daga* which was a mixture of soil and clay. It would be packed on both sides of the frame. The floors upon which we slept were dirt which was levelled. The floor was always the source of great pride among the young girls who would make them shine like a polished linoleum. They smeared a mixture of fresh cattle dung and water on their hands and rubbed the floor for hours in a circular motion until it became a glassy, hard surface. There was no smell of the cattle dung and it provided a rock-like, polished surface.

At night we used to drift off to sleep listening to the sounds of the *sonbesie*, the sun beetles. These creatures could be heard for miles and their high-pitched whine, almost a scream, seemed to epitomise the heat and humidity of the kraal. All the kraals were built close to streams or fresh-running water and at night the croaking frogs competed with the sonbesies.

In the morning we would be woken at dawn with a meal of maas which I still cherish to this day. No matter how much my mother tried to repeat the blend of sour milk and mielie at home, it could not be copied. It was an acquired taste, but one which, in time, I realised was an enjoyable acquisition.

The discipline on the kraals was admirable, and I never ceased to be amazed at the way Zulus would treat fellow Zulus if they believed their family, or kraal, was under threat. Often entire kraals, of up to fifty people, would try and settle on our land. But my father never had to chase them away; he left this to the people already living there. It was around the time one group of people were chased away from near Bafana's kraal that he and I sat talking about owning land. I found it difficult then to understand why it was that black people worked on the land, but did not own it. I remember how Bafana sat and his voice seemed to be distant, almost detached: 'But Nkosana, such things are not possible in this life. First we do not have the money to buy the land, and even if we had enough money the government would not give us permission; they say the land is for the white man and we are the workers. That's the way of life.'

Chapter 4

An encounter with the
Medicine Man

Bafana and I were more of a nuisance than the rats that my father tried to keep out of the meat store. Whenever he was away in the fields we crawled through the gap in the store roof, the same way the rats got in, to take our pick of the raw meat and the *biltong* which he had hung to dry. Biltong became a particular target for us, meat cut from cattle or buck, salted, then hung up to dry naturally, uncooked. It is said that during the Boer War the English had to keep stopping to have a brew up, but the Boers, with dried sausage and biltong in their saddle-bags, could continue fighting for days. All they needed was water to wash down the biltong. It comes in a variety of meats, from beef to kudu (a kind of antelope), springbok and virtually any kind of buck.

To say we were very fond of raw minced meat is putting it mildly. So great was our love of it we would gulp down handfuls at a time. When my father eventually found the hole and filled it, we found an alternative supply in my mother's fridge. Many times, after taking a few handfuls, Bafana and I would watch through the kitchen window as my mother went to the fridge to get out the meat to make sausages. When we saw her quizzically looking at the bundle, wondering why it was smaller than she remembered it, we would hold our noses to prevent laughing out loud, then run to the far end of the house to explode in hysterics.

Sometimes my mother would mention her suspicions to the girls in the kitchen: 'Lizzie, you know I am certain there was more than this when I put it in the fridge last night.' It was not so much an accusation of Lizzie or her other helper Manda, more a puzzled expression as though she did not trust her own memory.

Eventually she discovered the reason for the missing meat when I went down with severe stomach pains from a tapeworm. I suppose the seriousness of it convinced me that I was being punished for being dishonest with my parents.

I woke one morning in agony. Bafana had already arrived, and was sitting out on the stoep waiting for me. He heard my groans and came in.

'Maitulela, what is wrong? Why are you in such pain?' There was a fear in his eyes. It was the first time he had seen me ill. Bafana ran to fetch my mother from the kitchen. (I had been given the Zulu name Maitulela, meaning the person who keeps to himself or the thinker, and was only called Nkosana when white people were around.)

Mother's remedies, the epsom salts and stomach powders, failed to work and two days later she took me to the doctor. He diagnosed the tapeworm. When he asked if I had been eating raw meat, I glanced quickly at my mother. She saw the look and instantly knew she had found the solution to her missing meat. Looking at the doctor I nodded, knowing that a hiding would follow when I got home.

The beating from my father's stick was nothing compared with the increasing pain of the tapeworm which defied the doctor's modern medicine. A week later, I was unable to get out of bed; the lack of food and weakness had begun to take its toll. Bafana sat all day beside the bed. His eyes were wide with worry. Often, during the day, all he would say was: 'Maitulela, I'm sorry, it's my fault you are dying.' I don't think I knew about dying, just that it was not too good because everyone seemed very sad. And it certainly felt pretty rough.

This news about my tapeworm spread through the farm and one morning, early, Manda, the girl from Bafana's kraal, the one whose job it was to make father's coffee each morning, announced, 'The old man, the *sangoma*, he is here.'

I think Manda was apprehensive, maybe even fearful, as all the blacks were because the appearance of this old man, the medicine man, was possible trouble for everyone. They all believed he could have been there to cast a spell for some misdeed, imagined or real. No one knew for sure.

My father stood on the stoep to confront the sangoma. He was clearly unwashed, and his wispy beard fell down around a jacket that looked as if he had not taken it off in years. He squatted Zulu-style on his haunches six feet in front of the stoep. Just looking at this sangoma was scary enough; he had a wild-eyed look of a crazy man, and anyway I'd never seen anyone this old before. He was more wrinkled than the face of a pug dog, all hollowed and wizened by his lack of teeth and he wore a cloak of civet skin and monkey hide. Around his neck were the tricks of his trade, the pig's bladder and necklace of baboon's teeth, while a string of bones, claws and birds' beaks hung from his coat buttons.

When he spoke, he did so without obviously moving his lips. 'I see you, Nkosi.' It was the Zulu greeting of respect. 'I heard the young man, Nkosana, he is sick.' At that he unwound a small leather sack from behind his back, walked to the edge of the verandah and placed it at his feet. My father seemed to know what to do, how to handle this strange visit, and knelt beside him. The sangoma tipped the sack to reveal a root, the size of a sheep's head, dark and partially covered in soil. It was even more wrinkled than the old man's face. I could not hear what my father and the old man were discussing; they were in whispered conversation, the old man holding the root in his hands, playing it from one to the other. Eventually my father stood up and I heard him confirm, 'The water must boil, yes?'

The old man nodded and again there was his voice, without movement from his lips. 'Make sure he drinks it, because the taste is awful, and give it again to him the day after, before he eats or drinks anything else in the morning.'

So it was organised. The next morning I was summoned from my room, and I knew I had to drink the old man's medicine. Before I reached the kitchen I could smell it, a pungent, gagging smell. I'd never experienced anything like it before or since. My father saw my hesitation at the doorway and grabbed my arm before I had a chance to disappear. He thrust the mug into my hands. I yelped in pain: the boiling water had turned the metal container into a scalding weapon.

'Come on man, just drink it and get it over with.' My father was impatient; he had no time for cries of protest. I still remember the taste today. It was the most vile, sickly taste, worsened by the steam rising out of the thick, yellow liquid which filled my nostrils with the stench. I know the first cupful came back immediately. My father poured a second and that went the same way. Then I think I knew my father would keep force-feeding me this stuff until it stayed down, so I somehow decided to try not to throw it up.

Sometime later in the afternoon, I was in severe pain, of a type I'd never experienced before. It doubled me up, forcing me to cry from the cramps and ache in my stomach. My father came and told me to be a big boy; it was getting better. In my head I cursed him for

35

his stupidity: how could it be getting better when the pain was worse than ever? Next morning I got another dose of the stuff. This time I'd learned that the best way was to drink quickly and get it over with. We needed just one mugful. Within two hours I had been to the toilet and the worm had gone. That was not just the end of it. I never had stomach trouble again. I have no idea what the root was, and certainly my father never knew because I heard him telling another farmer he wished he'd asked the old man what it was.

My father asked the workers on the farm where the sangoma was, where he could be contacted. The workers' fear of the old man surfaced again and they told my father that if they needed him they went to the mountain and shouted for him, hoping he would hear. My father said that he wanted to reward him for bringing the medicine which had cured me. Sometime later I know he heard from one of the cattlemen from a kraal that the sangoma had asked my father for a little bit of meat now and again.

So it was agreed. Whenever we slaughtered a sheep a leg would be left in the rondavel, the building where the milk was separated from the cream. Once every couple of weeks the meat was put in there inside a cold box, and next morning it was gone. We knew it had to be the old man because no one else would have dared touch it for fear of a spell being cast on them. I often tried to watch for the sangoma as he came for his reward, but he proved as elusive as Santa Claus.

I was young and the whole concept of magic and the power of the sangoma fascinated me. When I spoke to Bafana about it, he told me that it was a serious matter, and anyway, didn't I know that in our kitchen we had an *umlimo*, a white witch, working for us. Naturally, not wishing to let Bafana know that I was unaware of this information, I nodded and wondered what he was talking about. A short time later I was to discover when one of my father's prize lambs vanished.

My father was furious and threatened to get the police in to investigate the matter. The workers suggested that instead of having the trouble with the police, the best method to find out who had stolen the lamb was to ask the umlimo. It was said she would have the knowledge.

In the quiet of the house I asked my father who or what an umlimo was. He told me, 'To become an umlimo it must be a girl who is considered totally pure and will remain a virgin all her life.' I nodded sagely, not knowing for a moment what on earth he meant by a virgin. However, he continued, 'Then she is taught all the knowledge of a great seer which is added to the gifts of knowledge with which she has been born.' It all seemed very mysterious, but also very impressive.

So that day, instead of summoning the police, my father asked all the workers to gather outside the house. They all sat against the wall wondering what on earth was happening until the umlimo came dancing out of the stable, dressed in traditional clothes, waving her horsetail whip, cracking it in the air and wailing. I was entranced.

She skipped and danced, twirling around in a trance-like state. Suddenly she stopped and looked at the people who sat with fear in their eyes. Then she began to dance again, this time directly in front of the workers. She halted in the middle of a gyration next to one of them and pushed the horsewhip towards him. She did it on several more occasions with other workers and each time the whip sprang backwards away from the person, almost as if it had a mind of its own. She continued, on and on, until she came to one young man, a newcomer to the labour force. As she thrust the horsetail whip towards him, instead of springing backwards, it snapped forwards and struck this man across the face, a stinging blow. The man cried out in pain and collapsed in a heap at the umlimo's feet. He eventually confessed that he had been the thief and took my father to an area where he had buried the skin and bones.

I was so fascinated by all this magic that I asked her how she did it. Bafana recoiled away in horror, telling me I should never ask an umlimo how she got her powers. But I did.

She was affronted. 'I did not do it. It just happened automatically. The man who was slapped in the face was not slapped by me; the whip was guided to him by my powers.' When I protested that this could not be so, she challenged me. 'Go, take three of your toys and hide them and wherever they are I shall find them.'

Together we went to an area close to one of the farm rondavels which sat on one side of a stream. She told me, 'You hide the three toys inside the rondavel and I shall walk straight to them and pick them out for you.'

Bafana, who was terrified of what I was doing, was forced to stay outside and keep watch on the umlimo while I went inside the rondavel and hid the toys. Later, without searching the hut, she walked to each toy.

As she handed them to me she said, 'Now, perhaps you will

believe it is not me, but something else which took my hands to them.'

It was soon after this incident with the sangoma and the umlimo that Bafana saved my life. Every day our gang of four or five would head off to an area near the Umfulosi River where we knew the fishing was good. It was several miles from the main farmhouse, where the river stretched to maybe fifty yards wide. There were deep rock pools and we knew there were plenty of *geelvis*, yellow fish. Although the geelvis were small, they were tasty and easy to cook. It was an area we knew well and where we loved to swim in the cool, clear water.

The dry, cherry-red earth paths through the fields were well marked, often from centuries of being padded flat by Zulus, although in places overgrown with calf-high grass. We walked in single file, swinging our fishing tackle over our shoulders as we talked. In one hand we carried our knobkerries.

My bare left foot stepped on something round, and then slipped off to one side. It felt as if I had stood on a person's arm. As I struggled to regain my balance I knew instantly: I had stood on a snake. I never worried about snakes on the farm; they were a natural, constant hazard that was a part of my everyday life. I always knew to be particularly careful on hot days because snakes, once they have found a shady spot, tend to lie still even when they are aware of someone approaching. Despite the massive numbers of snakes in Africa, it is still unusual to be bitten by one. A mamba, for instance, would not normally attack. The vibration on the ground of an approaching person is enough to warn them and they would head to a quieter area.

As my foot slipped I cried out, *'Injoka!'*: snake. I felt the tell-tale sting burn through the skin on my left leg. I leaped away to one side in alarm. Instantly Bafana and my other two friends knew what to do. It was essential, possibly even a matter of life and death, to find the snake and kill it so that a doctor would know which snake had bitten me and be able to administer the correct antidote.

'Let's catch the injoka,' Bafana cried, leaping straight into the long grass, ignoring the obvious danger to himself. The snake which had been disturbed had been stood on and had bitten once. Now it was at its most dangerous and could strike again. Regardless of the danger Bafana thrashed and smashed away with his knobkerrie, clearing a path through the grass until he exposed the snake. A beautifully marked diamond-backed black and yellow puff adder, one of the most deadly of all snakes, was uncovered.

Like a demon he attacked the snake, battering it to death. Instead of holding it aloft as a prize, he tossed it to another of our friends and told him, 'Here, you must carry this back to the farmhouse.'

I was in increasing pain and the realisation that I had been bitten by a puff adder began to sink in. I knew, just as Bafana knew, that I needed medical treatment. And quick. Although the poison of a puff adder works more slowly than that of, say, a mamba, it is nonetheless potentially fatal. Even though we were both young boys, then no more than six years old, we knew there were two important rules which had to be obeyed. First, I had to get treatment quickly; without it I would die. Secondly, I had to stay off the leg to ensure blood did not rush through my veins and carry the poison through my body to reach my central nervous system which would become paralysed. We knew, because we had been told by my parents, that once the poison reached the central nervous system it relaxed you. Sleepiness followed, a sleep from which there was no awakening. This was going to be touch and go.

Bafana was practical and insistent. 'Come, Nkosana, climb on to my back. I will carry you home.'

It was at least two miles to the farmhouse. I shall never forget as he hoisted me on to his bare back and trotted the entire distance. Bafana's breathing was shorter and more laboured than mine by the time we reached the house.

The two other Zulu boys, one carrying the dead puff adder, had run ahead to warn my parents of the snake-bite. As they ran we could hear them in the distance, screaming, 'Injoka, injoka, injoka...'

One of the maids rushed out, saw the commotion and ran for my mother, who grabbed the medical kit and came to meet us.

My mother was calm and asked Bafana to carry me to the wooden verandah. She injected me with a serum, but said it was important to get me to hospital as soon as possible. The serum she had given me would merely slow down the progress of the poison. She said I needed proper hospital attention. My breathing was becoming shallow and I felt sleepy. I turned to Bafana and told him he must talk to me, he must keep pinching me so that I would remain awake. I was terrified of falling asleep; I thought I would not awaken. My father fetched his car, a black V8 Ford, and laid me out on the back seat for the two-and-a-half-hour drive to hospital. My last memory of the trip is holding Bafana's hand as he burst into tears; he could not keep me awake. He, too, thought I would die.

I was to learn later that the doctors said I was close to dying. If

Bafana had not carried me back to the farm so quickly for the initial injection, I could have died.

The incident had a deep effect on me. It now meant I owed my life to Bafana. My father, naturally, thanked Bafana by summoning his father from his kraal to the farmhouse. As a reward for Bafana's quick-thinking my father gave his family an ox and a heifer.

Chapter 5

The loneliness of school

I always knew that one day my parents would have to send me away to boarding-school: Ongemak was a remote place, too far from any community. Whenever my parents talked of school, it was almost as if it was a threat, that they would send me there unless I behaved. When, eventually, I did begin my school days, I realised just why they had taken such an approach. These were to be the loneliest days of my life. It was an experience which was to shape my character, and life, for ever.

The Lucas Meyer School was in the town of Vryheid, a predominantly Afrikaans town, nearly four hours' drive from Ongemak. The meaning of the word *vryheid* is 'freedom', although it meant anything but that to me. Freedom had been about my life with Bafana on the farm, but this school was worse than a prison.

For my first days at school I stayed with my grandmother who owned a house in Vryheid. She was a severe, strict woman, who kept me inside all the time. I was not allowed out to run and play the way I had been used to. Her attitude was that children were to be seen and not heard.

That first term was as miserable as could be. I missed Bafana and I missed my home. When I was not at school I had to sit and be quiet. My grandmother employed two black girls in her kitchen and when I sat with them to talk, asking if they could get me news of Ongemak and Bafana, she became angry. I wanted to establish a communication between my home and school, especially Bafana. But before anything came of it my grandmother stormed into the kitchen and scolded me for talking to blacks. I was confused more than angry, not understanding why I should not talk to blacks when I had done so all my life until then.

On one occasion I got my own revenge on my grandmother. She rented out a two-bedroomed flat at the back of her home to another old lady who was as miserable as she was. When my brother Paul came to stay he convinced me this woman was a witch because she was always dressed in black, with long dresses and a shawl, no matter that the temperature outside was unbearable. At the back of the property were the toilets, detached from the main house. This old woman had two cats, both entirely black, and wherever she went both cats followed, their tails stuck straight into the air. Paul insisted the reason for this was that the cats were the witch's *katstert*, her evil omens. I lived in mortal fear of this old woman until one day Paul told me how to break any spell she might cast on me. He said he would even pay me five shillings, at that time a fortune to me, to do it. I was hooked.

At the rear of the toilet was a flap through which the night soil bucket could be taken out for emptying. When the old lady was in the toilet I had to lift the flap and throw in a fire cracker. This I did and ran away as the laughter of Paul filled the air. The old woman came rushing out, her skirts around her waist and the cats following her, their fur standing on end to match their tails. My grandmother gave me a thrashing which hurt for several days, but the sight of the old woman made the pain more bearable. I also believed I had broken her witch's power by letting off the cracker.

I think it was a combination of that incident and my grandmother's total intolerance of me which led to me becoming a boarder at the Vryheid School. If I had been miserable at my grandmother's, worse was to follow at school.

When I arrived at Vryheid, my head was filled with all the stuff from my parents about how much I would enjoy being with my own sort of boys. I knew from the start that was not true because the school forced me to dress in short pants, long socks, black shoes that always had to be polished, a grey woollen jersey and a jacket that I had to wear even in summer in temperatures of more than 100°F. I was used to wearing just an old cloth around my middle and running barefoot, and in winter, when it did get a little colder, an old shirt. And the boys at the school were not at all like me because they didn't want to talk about hunting and fishing, or about planning a trip to the mountain to pick berries or catch frogs. They only wanted to talk about rugby and cricket.

They were all older and bigger than me, or so it seemed. Most had been at school for two years when I arrived. The first thing I remember was the talk of initiation. It was organised by the big shots, the group of boys who pushed me from one to another calling me a farm boy and a rooinek because my name was Gregory and I was not an Afrikaner. When I asked them, 'please, what is a rooinek', they laughed and pushed me some more, yelling that I was an Englishman bastard who didn't even know he was English.

I had to run the gauntlet from the bathroom to the dormitory, and I heard they'd hit new boys with belts and empty their tuck-box, filled with goodies from home. They wanted the biltong and the biscuits for themselves. I also heard from the other new boys how these big ones would also fill your shirts with newly cut grass, then make you run round the fields until you were soaked in sweat and the grass acted like itching powder. Sometimes, they said, if they really didn't like you, they would take you to the toilets and push your head down into the bowl. If they really hated you they would take it in turns to pee on your head. And apparently they hated all rooineks.

That kind of nonsense, I declared, was not going to happen to me. No blerrie way. It was in the first week, after the rumour had got around the new boys, maybe a dozen of us, that this initiation business was going to happen. I remember there were about ten of us in the dormitory on the first floor and when we went to the bathroom to prepare for bed, one of the big shots came in and picked on me, demanding my tuck-box.

I was scared but I was not handing it over. 'No, you can't have it, I'm not listening to you.' As the guy, who must have been nine or ten, started pushing me into a corner, beside the wash-basins, I threw down my face flannel and laid into him, all arms and fists. Although I was smaller I had learned well from Bafana and my Zulu friends. They had developed within me a talent for fighting using a natural quickness. But whereas the scraps with Bafana and my Zulu friends were always fun, this was now serious. It may have been this boy was taken by surprise, or maybe he'd never been challenged before, but I caught him a good few shots in the face and nose. I was not content to whack him to his knees and make him cry. I was steaming, really angry, and wanted to know who had sent him to bully us. He told me he'd been sent by a boy named Westerhuizen, who was two years older. I don't know what was in my mind by now, but a cold anger had taken over. I remember the look of the other new boys as I stormed out of the bathroom, leaving my dressing-gown on the hook beside the door, down the passageway and into the third dormitory where the older boys slept.

I marched straight in, wearing just white underpants, saw this boy sitting on his bed with his pals, and headed directly for him. As a punch it was more of a slap, but it had the desired effect. His

43

tooth flew out of his open mouth. I was later to discover it was a false tooth that had been screwed in. At that moment I didn't care what sort of tooth it was. I wanted to remove more, but was grabbed by several of the boys. I hadn't even spotted the teacher who had been standing at the back end of the dormitory.

'Gregory, you boy, what do you think you are doing?' he cried.

My reply is one which was repeated time and again by the others who retold the story, using their own less than accurate versions of what happened to describe how the tooth not only flew out of Westerhuizen's mouth, but also out of the open window.

'I'm going to kill him,' they all agreed was what I told the teacher in a quiet, flat voice.

Of course, there was immediate retribution from the school. I was given six cuts of the cane by the headmaster. What I never really understood was why he thrashed me first, then as I stood on his carpet, in front of the huge oak desk nursing a stinging backside he demanded, 'Now tell me what happened?' I just assumed this was the way of the grown-ups, to beat someone first and ask questions later.

When I started to go into the business about the first fight in the bathroom, and how I'd got Westerhuizen's name from his gopher, the head held up his hand and declared he'd heard enough. He gave his verdict. 'Clearly you're a trouble-maker. I'm going to get your father here. Anyway, he's going to have to pay for the broken tooth.'

My father never came, but in tears I told him on the phone the whole story. The headmaster was then informed by my father that whatever happened to this Westerhuizen's tooth, he'd deserved it, and as far as the Gregory family was concerned the matter was closed. There was nothing the school could do really, other than to brand me as trouble. Not that it bothered me; it meant I got left alone by the older boys who seemed to shy away from taking me on because they knew the story of Westerhuizen's tooth.

The teachers also soon branded me a trouble-maker. Worse, I had become a target for other boys of my age who, knowing my reputation, wanted to make a name for themselves. It led to many fights. I was always scrapping, which merely confirmed to the teaching staff their early opinion of me. Initially I was angry that, having been picked upon, I was the victim in the entire situation. It meant I had few friends, but that did not bother me. Later, I just grew to accept the situation.

I think that was how the loneliness started. I was ignored by the older boys and it had a spin-off effect of creating fear within boys of my own age; they just didn't want to be associated with someone who was considered a hard case. Or else, they just wanted to fight me. Sometimes, when I saw another younger pupil being bullied, I went out of my way to make friends, sitting next to him in lessons, walking with him, but it never seemed to last. I might have stopped him being bullied for a time, but somehow the friendships always seemed to peter out. Maybe it was me as well. Once I knew this little guy didn't need me beside him anymore, that he wasn't going to be bullied, I left him alone.

The school went from standard one to standard five, ages between eight and thirteen. I was only there two years, standard one and two, but they were years that still have a haunting effect on me.

I should have guessed that when the headmaster phoned my father to complain about my fighting that first time, and my father didn't come to stand beside me, there was a problem about the distance from home. I never thought about it then. It was only later – that first weekend – when everyone seemed to pile off home. Just before the third weekend, on a Friday night before wash-time, everyone was busy packing their suitcases in the dormitory. I knew it was not the end of term, although I wished it was, so I copied them and did the same. I only had one large suitcase whereas most of the boys seemed to have a large one and a smaller one as well as a tuck-box. They used the small one for these weekends and seemed to be throwing in their ordinary clothes as if they were heading off somewhere. I didn't have a small case, so I piled mine into the large suitcase. I didn't know why, but something had to be happening.

Next day, Saturday, there were normal lessons in the morning, and instead of having lunch and then an afternoon of sports, everyone headed off to the dorms to collect their cases. Well, I guessed it was time to go home, so I followed. It was clearly a good time because everyone was laughing and being friendly, so I assumed my parents were coming to pick me up.

We all scrambled down to the front drive, beside the massive iron railings and gates, where cars and trucks were already beginning to arrive. There were hugs and kisses and mothers embracing their sons. I stood with a group of boys from my dorm, inside the gate, swinging our cases and whacking one another with them playfully. Eventually, as the numbers dwindled, those of us

45

who were left soon tired of the battering of the cases, so we sat on them. Finally, I was left on my own, sitting on my case, waiting. No one bothered to say a thing to me. So I sat all afternoon, watching the cars that passed by the gates, waiting for my father's Ford truck to arrive. At dusk a teacher, who had been out in the town, walked through the gate and asked why I was waiting. I was convinced my father had been unavoidably detained on the farm, or his truck had broken down. Fords, I told the teacher, were always breaking down, and for some reason or other my father would only buy Fords.

A little later the same teacher came back to the gate. It was now dark and he said I should come in and have some supper. I said ja, it'd be a good idea.

That night I was the only one in the dorm and it was spooky. I sort of missed the others, even the ones who cried themselves to sleep.

The next weekend everyone was going home, I repeated my preparations and went to the gate again with everyone in the dorm. This time, however, I didn't sit on my case too long. Just until the last person had left, and I went back to the room and slammed the case against the wall, letting its contents spill over the floor. I felt my parents had abandoned me. They'd dumped me in this place telling me a bunch of lies. The boys they'd said were like me were very different. And they'd deprived me of being with Bafana while he was having fun.

Nobody came for me and nobody phoned to explain why they'd not come. After that second occasion I stopped packing. I just stayed in the dorm, lying on my bed all afternoon. When it got dark I would drag my bed from its place inside the door to the window at the far end of the room. I'd pitch it so I could look out in the direction of Ongemak, my home. And I would pray and pray they'd come to fetch me home. I prayed so hard I cried myself to sleep on many nights.

That really confirmed my isolation and loneliness and shaped my character. It also made me very bitter and I grew distant from my parents. Occasionally they'd arrive at the school on a weekend and say they were taking me home, but I'd play it all very cool. I'd not forgiven them for leaving me those early times so I never showed my gratitude.

I knew that I could not stay at home all my life, that I had to attend school, because that was the law. But I was filled with a fury that I had been abandoned by my parents who didn't seem able to give me affection. Without ever consciously turning my back on my parents, a void developed between us which grew wider as the years went on. I vowed then that if I ever had children I would never abandon them in a boarding-school.

At Lucas Meyer School there was a large oak tree in the main grounds. At break time when everyone headed out to play sport, I went to the tree and sat either on the ground beneath it or up in the branches, eating my sandwiches and missing my friend Bafana. My body was at school, but my mind was back on the farm. Many times, during lessons, I was in trouble with teachers who caught me staring out of the windows day-dreaming about Ongemak. I wondered where Bafana was, how many fish he had caught, how many frogs or birds he had hunted that day. I missed him and home.

At half-term and the end of term, Bafana knew I was heading home to Ongemak and would be waiting for me at the front gates. We would embrace as two brothers and I would immediately dump my school clothes for a beshu and head off into the bush, never stopping to greet my family.

At times like this Bafana and I would sit quietly discussing school. We were both convinced that I was being punished by my family's spirits for some reason.

'What, you have to wear a long-sleeved shirt, thick sweater and socks?' he used to ask, incredulous at the demands of the school uniform.

'Man, it is worse, much worse,' I would tell him. 'Sometimes when it is the hottest part of the day the teachers tell us to put on our jackets, and we must wear a tie.' The concept of why we wore a tie wrapped tightly around our throats was beyond Bafana. He fell about laughing. 'Man, they are trying to hang you, that is how they reward you,' he cried.

The harder he laughed the more I tried to explain what went on. He asked about my shoes. 'Ja well, we keep them on all day and only take them off at night when we go back to the dormitory to sleep.' More laughter.

I tried to explain athletics to Bafana, how we had to run inside two long white lines.

Bafana was serious for a minute. 'Nkosana, we do that here, we run alongside the river; we do not need people to paint white lines on the grass.'

When I told him of having to sit in hot, crowded rooms to be taught, and then how we had to spend each evening doing more reading and writing after school, his face turned suddenly very earnest.

'Nkosana, my family tell me it is important to get an education, that to be without education is punishment. But now I'm not so certain who is being punished, you or me. I think I am better not going to school if they treat you this way.'

Bafana made an assessment of my school. 'It sounds like a jail, like being locked up as a wild animal. If you were, say, a large healthy bull and they tried to cage you in a kraal, you would go crazy. I know of a bull who once killed one of his keepers, it gored him to death against a wall, because the man was trying to imprison the animal in a kraal. That bull, Nkosana, is like you. You are being kept prisoner just like the bull and one day you will break out.'

Chapter 6

Ongemak is sold

The first hint I ever had of the existence of apartheid was when Bafana told me there had been trouble on the farm while I was away at school. A group of Zulus had arrived on the farm one day demanding my father allow them to set up a kraal. He chased them away with the help of the existing kraals who didn't want any newcomers. When Bafana told me of the incident we spoke of why it was black people did not own land.

'Nkosana, don't you know that black men cannot own land, that all the land is owned by white men who are better at fighting.'

This concept puzzled both of us because we both knew that when it came to fighting there was no one better than a Zulu. Weren't we the best example of that, we could defeat any person.

But Bafana was serious. 'No, Nkosana, it is so. The black man does not have the money to buy land. He is given his money by the white man, but just enough to buy his cattle and his food and his clothes. He cannot buy more than that, no land and no motor car.

'Even if all black men put their money together and had enough to buy land the government would not allow them.'

'Why Bafana? Why will the government stop black men owning land?'

'Nkosana, it is because black men used to own all the land and the white men came and wanted it. In order to get it they had many battles and many people died. They think that to give the black man land again would lead to many battles and many people would die.'

The explanation was simple. It was without antipathy, merely an acceptance of the life as we knew it. We shrugged it off as the natural way of things which was not going to affect our friendship.

I also began to feel the pressure of apartheid and of politics at school where boys would argue over loyalty to the National Party. Until then boys of my age would argue over which type of car a family owned. I was classified as a Ford boy because my father always chose Fords. Other boys were Chevrolet owners. In basic, infantile ways this was a simplistic form of gangs, split into whichever car a family owned. At school, with the rise of Nationalism, it soon divided into party lines. Those who supported the apartheid ways were all National supporters, the others were for the United Party. It led to many very serious fights where the Nationalists battered hell out of the fewer United boys. Most, if not all, the teachers were National Party supporters and had little sympathy that the United Party boys were being frequently beaten up. Although my father was a National supporter, I often began to side with the United boys because I felt they were being picked on and bullied. My introduction to the world of politics was at the end of someone else's fist for not supporting the views of their parents. It was all very silly really, fighting over matters of which we had no understanding.

During one holiday I returned to the farmhouse at Ongemak late one evening and heard my mother and father talking about selling the farm. It was a prospect that had never bothered me, a matter I had never even thought possible. It had been in the Gregory family for generations. It seemed natural that that would always be the way of things. I also assumed that if they did sell the property we would move to a larger one, and not only our family, but my friends in the kraals would come also, including Bafana.

Over the next few weeks many people, prospective buyers, came to view the farm and it was fun showing them the entire area, taking them to the corners of the farm where Bafana and I had explored and knew well.

Then one night the phone rang and when my father put it down, he said simply that Ongemak had been sold. He said he would have to go into the bank in Gluckstadt the next day to make arrangements, but that we should prepare to move.

I was initially excited at the prospect; a new farm to move to, bigger than Ongemak, somewhere new for Bafana and me to explore. It was then my parents explained fully to me that selling Ongemak also meant leaving Bafana behind.

I was beside myself with rage. I stormed off to my bedroom at the end of the stoep. I lay on my bed crying, wanting the whole business to stop. Wanting my parents to change their minds about selling. I went out that evening to find Bafana, to talk to him and see if we could find a solution to the sale of the farm. I went to his kraal and his father was surprised when I arrived; it was already dark and unusual for me to arrive so late. He said Bafana was not in the kraal, but would return next morning.

However, by dawn everyone on the farm knew about the sale. When I got up, the heads of the kraals were waiting outside the main house. They wanted to speak to my father to find out what would happen to them. With my family owning the farm there had never been a problem over their presence. They wanted to know if the sale would suddenly change that situation. They were all worried men, telling my father they feared the new 'baas' would chase them from Ongemak. He might bring his own labour with him, and there would be no room for them.

My father had not even considered their worries. He was awkward with them, uncertain what to say. He said that if there was a problem, he would promise that every kraal would be found a new home on another farm. We had a cousin, named Craig, who farmed in the Swart Umfulosi area and he promised to help relocate every displaced family.

That morning Bafana came to find me sitting on the stoep.

I could tell he had heard. He sat beside me on the steps and said, 'Nkosana, we must think of this as going to school. We will see one another all the time. You will come back and see me or I will come to you and we will play as before.'

I was more cheerful now. It didn't look as bleak. 'I can take my bicycle or maybe a horse and ride over here. We will play the same as before.'

The move happened quickly, that holiday, and I remember Bafana and I had said we would meet on the day of us leaving the farm. But somehow it didn't happen. As we left in my father's car I can still recall how my face was stuck hard against the window, searching for my friend. I was not crying because I believed that I would be back at Ongemak soon to play.

How wrong I was. It took a little time for the full impact to sink in. We were moving a considerable distance from Ongemak to a larger property many hours away. When I returned to boarding-school I was more withdrawn and lonelier than ever. I suppose this was my form of rebellion against my parents, for taking me away from the one friend I had. I was always in trouble with the teachers for repeatedly forgetting to do homework. For weeks I was thrashed and beaten as punishment. It merely gave me the physical pain I was already feeling inside. When the headmaster beat me with a cane I never cried. It would be wrong to say I didn't care, but it was close to the feeling.

Eventually, sometime around the mid-term, a teacher called Pienaar began to talk to me, asking me why I refused to do the school work. At first I would not talk to him, I refused to explain anything. He persuaded me to talk, and the story of Bafana and leaving Ongemak began to emerge. He told me how, when he was young, his parents also farmed in Natal and how he too had a friend on the farm. One day they had to split up because Pienaar had to go to school, then college, and his friend, who was black, could not be with him.

'James, that is the way of the world; sometimes you will leave friends behind.'

I sat, refusing to accept his words. He continued: 'It doesn't mean you have to leave everything. Even though you have left your friend behind at Ongemak you still have a memory of all the things you did together and you must remember all the things he taught you. He taught you the Zulu way to survive and live and those things you must put into practice now.'

Gradually, over several weeks, Pienaar's kindness and understanding began to break through my depression. The story must also have got around to the other teachers because the punishments lessened and eventually stopped. I began to start doing school work again. Although I did not take a full part in the social activities by playing with the other boys, at least I was beginning to accept that my friendship with Bafana was a chapter that was now over and one that I could not change.

I resolved the problem by telling myself repeatedly that when I was older I would return to Ongemak myself and find my friend. Of course, it was the promise of a little boy and never became a reality.

Chapter 7

A new farm
and a new school

The new farm was called Trapani, near the town of Mkuzi, which was about an hour's drive away from the Indian Ocean coastline at Sodwana Bay and about an hour's drive south of the Swaziland border. It was a farm three times the size of Ongemak. I know that it was so big that I never reached any of its boundaries. My father told us the reason for the move was that this property was a much better financial venture than Ongemak and we should be grateful that he was thinking of our future. I did not say a thing, thinking only of how he had forced me to leave behind my one true friend.

The farm was so vast my father had to employ a manager, a German called Marx who helped him look after the place. Unlike Ongemak there was a greater variety of produce: maize and cattle as before, but also thousands of acres of cotton and sugar-cane. The wildlife on the farm was also very different; all kinds of buck and baboons everywhere. My parents told me, however, that they would have to send me to a new school, and for the first time in many weeks I began to feel hopeful that I might not have to return to boarding-school. My hopes did not last long because within a few days they took me to see my new place of learning, three hours' drive from Trapani at Nongoma. It was a school run by the provincial administration, which had both day boys and boarding facilities. If I disliked my first school, this was even worse. The worst year of my life.

I was only ten years old and already had an attitude problem. I would not be bullied by older boys and certainly would not do anything they told me. These boys were as old as seventeen, so there was clearly going to be conflict.

The majority of the boarders were teenagers from the sugar-cane farms. The boarding-house was a ten-minute walk from the school grounds and when I returned to the house each evening I was in permanent fear of being beaten up by the older boys. I had seen them picking on other boys of my age, beating them with sticks and laughing. It was cruel, unnecessary bullying; no other words for it.

When I reached the boarding-hostel I often heard the beatings going on in the dormitories. I would creep into the cloakroom and hide among the coats, praying I would not be spotted. Many nights I stayed there for an hour or more, waiting to hear the meal bell sound, when I would suddenly emerge.

There was little use complaining. The older boys from the farms seemed to be friendly with the teachers and I soon discovered why. At weekends, when they returned home, they invariably invited teachers to join their parents on hunting and fishing expeditions. There was a group of boys and teachers who seemed to have formed a club, a mutual admiration society. I hated them beyond belief. When I told my father he scorned me and told me the experience would make a man of me. The anger I felt at being separated from Bafana was intensified by being dumped in this torture chamber of a school. And my father's attitude towards my fears worsened my feelings for him. My mother never involved herself and I could feel I was drifting further and further apart from my parents, resenting them at every turn.

At school meal times we had a senior overseer, one of the older boys, who would have his cabal of friends around him. The monitor or overseer seated at the head of my table was a bull-nosed, bull-necked boy called Schmidt. He would tell us younger boys what we could eat and what we couldn't, keeping the best food for himself and his friends.

On the first occasion he told me I could not have custard with my pudding. As the jug passed me I grabbed it and poured some. Schmidt was livid and ordered me to scrape it off my plate back into the jug. I was terrified because this boy was huge and played in the rugby team. I refused and began to eat, which was against the rules: it was forbidden to start eating until every person at the table had been served. I thought Schmidt was going to pick me up and throw me through the windows, but I kept eating, as quickly as I could.

He exploded. 'Gregory, you have just signed your death warrant. Tonight you will die.'

The hooded, ominous looks from the other boys at the table confirmed my worst fears.

The period before bed was purgatory. I was wetting myself in fear, knowing Schmidt planned to hurt me. When the lights went out I tried to control my fears by crouching into a ball. I could hear him coming and kept my eyes tightly shut.

For the next three hours I actually believed I was going to die. Schmidt beat me through the bedclothes until my body ached. He did it in such a way there were no bruises. He then covered my head and sat on me, smothering me. I cried so hard that eventually I passed out. When I awoke next morning I ached so badly I could hardly climb out of bed. But I was alive.

The next day was Sunday. Throughout the service in the chapel I never looked once at my fellow pupils. There was a hatred growing within me for them: they had all watched me getting beaten and kept quiet. I prayed in the service for all sorts of bad things to befall Schmidt.

I had trouble walking straight, but I was not going to show these blerrie bastards they had me beaten. After chapel I went out across the school fields and stayed out until dark, missing lunch. In the evening I returned to the dinner table, to be confronted with Schmidt again.

When the custard jug was passed round again, Schmidt hissed, 'Gregory, none for you.'

I looked him in the eye and poured the custard on to my plate. I didn't care what he said or did. I was going to defy him the only way I could. There was a gasp from the other boys and a silence seemed to descend over the entire room. Several teachers swung round to see what was happening. Schmidt backed down and, instead, ordered, 'Gregory boy, for eating your food when others had not been served you shall be punished. Eat the custard with your fork.'

I did so, taking enormous time and pleasure doing it. And I savoured every drop, knowing that each time I put the fork into my mouth it was like a dagger into Schmidt's pride. My only problem was keeping the smile off my face. I had beaten him and the others knew it.

Alongside the hostel was a craft centre, where we made clay pots and plates. I enjoyed working there until I found out that the older boys were taking everything that was made into the town of Nongoma and selling it to a black trader who, in turn, sold the things along with carvings in his market.

The first weekend I was able to go home was about the fourth into the term. My parents came and asked me how I was enjoying school. When I told them I hated it they laughed and said, 'Same old James, never satisfied. You'll get used to it.'

Without Bafana I dreaded holidays almost as much as I dreaded school. When I returned to Trapani I was lonely and began to explore on my own. Sometimes I went on horseback, and occasionally, when I was within close range of the farmhouse itself, my father allowed me to drive the tractor. It was during one of my explorations on horseback that I met another Zulu boy. He just came out of the bush and began stroking the horse's mane. He talked to me and when he realised I spoke Zulu began to open up. Would I like to go and see the places where the crocodiles were? Would I like to go fishing? They were dangerous places, but he would gladly show me. Would I? This was the way my friendship had started with Bafana and it was how a friendship, although not so close or long-lasting, happened with another black boy. He was called Dali.

Dali lived on one of the kraals and was actually one of the workers in the farmhouse, cleaning the area. Sometimes, when he could take a break from working, we would sit on the verandah where we had four large leather chairs. He told me of areas on the farm which were good for hunting and fishing. I told him I was home for just a short time because I had to attend school, but that if he could show me where these good places were, we would be friends. Soon he took me to a small dam, near the house, where we swam. We laughed and played all afternoon, diving and splashing. It was the first fun day I'd had in a long time.

The joy of the day was heightened the following morning when my father came in, a sombre look on his face.

'A croc has taken one of the heifers,' he declared as he marched into breakfast. This was excitement, but more was to follow.

We all wanted to know where it was, and when he announced it was in the dam where Dali and I had been the previous day, I almost choked on my food. I kept quiet, believing it the sensible policy to adopt. I couldn't wait to get out to tell Dali.

My father knew that many of the rivers in the area dried up in the heat of the summer and the crocs often travelled overland to find water in places such as the dam. He had to get rid of the croc and eventually, after three days, he managed to kill it. Later, when my father had more experience on Trapani he would buy donkeys cheap at auction, take them into the bush and shoot them near dried-up river beds. These were left as food for the crocs to entice them out so that they could be killed.

The day after my father killed the crocodile in the dam, he was approached by the head of a kraal, asking if they could have the dead creature. It was greatly valued. They could sell not only the skin, but also the liver, fat and nails, even its brain. They were highly prized by the *Muti* men, who were a type of medicine man. They used the various parts to brew strange concoctions and herbal remedies.

56

When I told Dali about the croc being in the dam his eyes went wide in fear, then he laughed and kept laughing. I joined him.

We decided then we needed to have a method of ensuring that anywhere we went swimming was croc-free, so we devised a scheme. I asked my father if we could have a couple of dogs. He agreed, believing that I wanted them as pets. To a certain extent we did, but Dali and I used the dogs to swim in the water before we entered. We reasoned that if they were not snaffled by a crocodile then we would also be safe.

It was around this time that I also began to have other sorts of pets, particularly baboons. My father considered them a nuisance, a pest because they caused damage in the cotton fields. The cotton bush produces a green bud and the snow-white fluff of cotton is contained inside this bud. They are considered ready for plucking when they pop open. However, they are also considered a great delicacy by the baboons which roam wild in their hundreds through southern Africa. They could destroy a complete row of plants as they scavenged for food. Often they would only eat a few buds, but break many others as they did so. My father was angry and decided the only way to deal with these pests was to set bear traps in the fields. It was left to two black labourers to find out which areas the baboons were targeting and to set the traps to kill them.

It happened at times that the baboon killed in a trap was a female with a baby clinging to her. I told the labourers that if they found the babies to bring them to me and I would look after them. I would take care of these young baboons on the verandah, which was close to my room. My parents largely ignored me and with the help of one of the kitchen workers I began to look after many of the young baboons. I used baby bottles, the type girls use for their dolls, to feed them with a watered-down mixture of lukewarm fresh milk. By caring for the baboons, I won admiration from the Zulus who believed my father's method of killing them was both cruel and wrong. They believed that these creatures could have been kept off the crops in a different way.

There was one little baboon who was just a few days old when I first got him. He took a fancy to me and, I suppose, it meant a lot to me to ensure he survived. I fed him all the time, and eventually when he was old enough he would run with me everywhere. At times I would be sitting cross-legged on the verandah and he would come charging round the corner and leap on to me, hanging on with feet and legs. He would hold tight and look at me as he made strange guttural noises. I suppose he thought I was his mother.

I called him Kehla, after an old man who lived on the farm. He had a face so old and wrinkled that his cheeks and eyes were sunk into the pit of his skull, and a small, thin grey beard. The baboon had the same type of face and the same wispy hair around his chin. When the baboons got to the age of four months, big enough to begin to fend for themselves, I would take them out into the veld and let them go. I knew they would be adopted by a herd and grow up normally. But Kehla was not like that, he would not go.

At night-time he would sleep in my bed at my feet and many times I woke up and felt my foot warm. He was wetting my bed. My mother must have known this, but she never once mentioned the bed-wetting to me, and I never told her that Kehla was staying in the room, so heaven knows what she thought.

My room was at the end of the passage and since it was closest to the verandah I could climb out of my bedroom window and be on the verandah without disturbing anyone else. Kehla lived in mortal fear of my mother. I think that at some time she must have beaten him with a broom, and thereafter the baboon stayed clear of her. The floors were all wooden and creaked at the merest hint of movement. So when someone was walking down the passage to my room I knew several seconds before they arrived: I could hear their footsteps. So also could Kehla. Now, when my mother approached, Kehla was up and out of the window faster than you could say speeding baboon. Yet, when it was another member of my family or one of the kitchen girls, Kehla just remained there, never bothering to move.

Another pet was a brown owl I had found as a young owlet on the farm. He was clearly orphaned so I took him home and fed him as I did the baboons. Eventually I got a cage for him and he, too, stayed in my room. It was so hot and humid at Trapani that we never closed windows. At night I would open the owl's cage and the gauze doors that covered the windows and he would fly out. In the early morning, by the time the stars were fading, he would be in the huge old fig tree at the front of the house, hooting. He was signalling to come in. If I was asleep he would continue hooting until someone opened the gauze around the verandah to allow him to fly in. He would then return to his cage in my room. He would just sit in his cage all day until darkness returned. We called him Dracula because he always went hunting after dark. Dali and I often caught mice and small rodents from the fields and threw them into his cage. Although Dracula was tame, he would nip pretty severely if an arm strayed into the cage.

My first year at school; I am in the front row in the centre

My horse Kolbooi, on the Ongemak farm where I spent my childhood

Wearing the blazer of
Vryheid High School

Nelson Mandela as a young man
of nineteen (*Mayibuye Centre*)

Gloria and me with Zane, our first child, in 1964

With my son while I was working as a traffic policeman

The house where
Nelson Mandela
lived from the
1920s to 1939
(*Mayibuye
Centre*)

Mandela burns
his pass book
(*Mayibuye
Centre*)

Kehla loved red jelly. Whenever my family went shopping in Mkuzi I would buy packets of red jelly with my pocket money for him. I would often have five or six jellies setting in the fridge for the baboon. I had tested him with other flavours, green and orange, but he ignored them, preferring only the red. One day my brother Paul came home with some older pals and told them about Kehla and his love of red jelly. That afternoon they mixed up a jelly and added in a half-bottle of brandy. I only discovered what had happened when I heard them all roaring with laughter as Kehla stumbled drunk around the yard. I was furious, but they simply laughed harder. Eventually Kehla clambered up the big fig tree opposite the house and refused to come down. When I climbed up close to him he bared his teeth and I knew he was suffering with one hell of a *babalas*, a hangover. At one stage he covered his eyes with his hands as the brightness from the sun hurt him. Eventually as the babalas wore off, Kehla recovered and came down from the tree.

Whenever visitors came to the house I was always careful with Kehla and took to chaining him up beside the fig tree. The chain allowed him to climb the tree, but not roam too far. But I should have known the pet baboon would become an attraction for visitors, particularly other farmers' children. They would tease him, often throwing sticks at him. I would warn them that if they hurt Kehla he would get mad and attack them. By this time, he was six months old and well on the way to being fully grown. His teeth were sharpening, and just as he had bared them to me in the fig tree, so when he became angry, he would show them like an angry dog.

Kehla became the focus of attention for one particular boy, who came one day with his parents for a braai. He also brought his girlfriend and, I suppose, thought he would show off by teasing the baboon. He kept poking a stick at Kehla who, at first, ignored him. I sat back watching this, saying aloud that he should stop. The boy ignored me as well. Eventually Kehla's patience snapped and he bounded down the fig tree and headed straight for the boy who panicked and ran. He got about two yards when Kehla tackled him, in perfect rugby fashion, around the ankles and brought him to the floor. Kehla then sank his teeth into his foot. I knew immediately this was the end for my pet baboon.

Next morning I got up early to try to take Kehla back to the wild. Dali and I walked him many miles before letting him go. When we tried to leave him Kehla just followed us home again. I was in tears of frustration, knowing that unless the baboon stayed in the wild my father would have to shoot him. I knew the rule was that once the baboon had bitten someone, he had to go; he could so easily do it again, under the slightest provocation.

My father waited until I returned to school before getting rid of Kehla. First he tried taking him into the remote bush and setting him free. But within a few hours Kehla was back again. When he could not get rid of him that way, he eventually, reluctantly, shot him.

I came home two weeks later and my father did not say a thing. He let me believe Kehla had been left out in the wild. When I asked Dali what had happened, had he helped my father take Kehla into the bush, he told me the truth. Once again I had this depressing feeling that I was destined to lose any person or thing that I cared for.

It was on Trapani that Dali also taught me to appreciate the cane rats for eating.

When the sugar-cane fields were to be harvested my father let it be known among the kraals that he needed sixty workers to cut down the cane. At harvesting time the fields were dense, virtually impossible to walk through. The leaves at the bottom of the cane were dry with a very fine thorn attached. To be scratched with these thorns was painful; first there was an itch which eventually festered and turned into a boil. In order to get rid of the dry leaves, you had to set fire to the area and allow the direction of the wind to control it. There would be up to eight men in a line along the edge of the field, each standing a hundred yards or so apart, and they would systematically set fire to the field and watch as the flames rushed through the cane, burning the leaves in a whoosh, as if they were covered in petrol, leaving the stalks of cane untouched.

When I knew this was to happen I would get three or four boys from the kraal and wait at the far end of the field. As the fire rushed through the cane, the rats would flee in panic and run out through our end. With our knobkerries, we would be waiting to smash the rats, the size of terrier dogs, across the skull. We would then take them, skin them and eat them. Usually rats are considered dirty animals, but these creatures lived entirely off the sugar-cane and were considered very good to eat. Each of my friends would take bundles of the dead rats back to his kraal as a present, while I would take mine home to braai.

Chapter 8

The school that taught me to hate

At the end of the first year at Nongoma School I confronted my parents. I was not, I informed them, returning to that school after the Christmas break. They could try any trick to get me to return, but I would run away. It would not have been my threats but the school report, which labelled me as unhappy, uncooperative and, basically, a waste of time, that persuaded my father he should seek an alternative.

My parents chose another school in Vryheid, this time the high school. I suppose life was a little better there, but that was because I had begun to learn to look after myself and avoid trouble. I was now in standard six, aged around thirteen. There were initiation ceremonies for new boys, such as myself, but these were less cruel than at the previous school and were more a matter of fun: during the evening study session, from 7.00 until 9.00 when we read our books for homework, newcomers had to sit with a piece of soap on their heads. The soap was not allowed to drop, which meant sitting with the head held very upright and very still. If the soap fell at all during the two-hour session, the initiation had to be repeated the next night. It took me four nights before I mastered the technique.

It was at Vryheid that apartheid began to impinge on my mind. The indoctrination process was started by the teachings at school. The teachers were almost entirely Afrikaners, who were intent on placing their own interpretation on what was happening in Africa. Each morning in assembly we would start with a prayer for the Afrikaner people and for peace, our peace. In our neighbouring African countries there were uprisings. The Mau Mau rebellion was sweeping through Kenya. Our history and geography teachers told us how 'those damn kaffirs' were intent on driving the white man into the sea.

'Look, see how they mutilate, kill, torture and rape the white people,' the history teachers would tell us. 'See how grateful the kaffirs are to the white man. We bring them the wheel and we bring them civilised ways and how do they reward us? Ja, they kill us.'

In Ghana, President Nkrumah was demanding independence. In Nigeria and Tanganyika the war drums were as loud. In Rhodesia and Nyasaland the rumblings of discontent from the blacks were being heard in Vryheid.

'Look,' we were told. 'Look at who is behind all this killing and savagery. Ja, it is the communists from the Soviet Union. The Western countries, America, Britain, Europe are tired after two world wars and they don't want to fight. They have lost the will to be powerful. The colonial powers are dying and the Cold War is handing the initiative to the communists.'

The teachers would get documents and read them out to us, claiming they were the writings of the South African Communist Party and the African National Congress. These documents purported to claim that the day of the white man in Africa was almost over. They quoted text from the Pan African Congress manifesto, reading out the belief that Africa was a black man's continent.

I remember that in one lesson a teacher sat reading to us about life in a communist state. Children spied on their parents, parents spied on their children; children were taken from their homes without reason, taken for experiments. We were told about Siberia: once a person was sent there, that was it for life. Any crime was against not only the state, but all its people. People had little or no food: all money was spent on the army. For holidays people worked on state farms. It was a way of life which was to be avoided at all costs. The teachers, who gave us our only real exposure to politics, told us how this was what the ANC wanted to bring to South Africa.

Geography was about the way black states were taking the lands of the white man and how the commies were infiltrating the civilised countries of the world for their own political ends.

History was about how the Afrikaners had been dealt a rough hand by the British when they arrived in South Africa. How they were cheated and lied to at every turn and how the British had always taken the side of the natives, the blacks. The teachers were adamant that the only government that had an answer to the *Swart Gevaar*, the Black Peril, was the brave South African parliament of Nationalists. They had a vision to prevent all future troubles, built on keeping races apart, rather than allowing them to integrate and squabble as in the past. Ja, the teachers cried, the great vision of our

62

leaders was misunderstood worldwide. We were not driving a stake into the heart of the blacks. No way man, we were actually helping them create the homelands that they had always craved for. We were giving them peace and security. This was all based on a principle of *kragdadigheid*, a strength to do and achieve.

'The troubles in other African states were caused by British colonialism gone sour,' we were told. 'The Brits come here and impose their will on us. They take our lands and kill our people. They set the blacks against us and they stir up constant trouble. Whenever we find riches in our country, diamonds and gold, they come and steal it from us.'

We examined in detail the Mau Mau uprising in Kenya. We concentrated at length on the mutilation of whites by the blacks and on the ritualistic torture practised by the 'savages'.

We were told how the entire uprising was devised by the communists in Moscow to unsettle the entire African continent. The eventual aim of the killings was to burn all the crops, slaughter all the cattle, steal every firearm, rape every white woman and child and kill every white man.

The tales of barbarism from Kenya filtered down through the newspaper reports and these only reinforced the teachers' views. We heard how Mau Mau were ordered to kill and mutilate their own family members. We read how they severed the heads of their victims and drank their blood.

The teachers took great pains to ensure we had read the Mau Mau oath, which sent us all into shivers: 'If I am ordered to bring my brother's head and I disobey, this oath will kill me. If I am ordered to bring the finger or ear of my mother and I disobey, this oath will kill me. If I am ordered to bring the head, hair or fingernail of a European and I disobey, this oath will kill me. If I rise against the Mau Mau, this oath will kill me. If I betray the whereabouts of arms or ammunitions or the hiding place of my brothers, this oath will kill me. When the reed-buck horn is blown, if I leave the European farm before killing the owner, may this oath kill me. If I worship any leader but Jomo Kenyatta, may this oath kill me.'

We read and heard graphic details of massacres of entire communities, decapitation, mutilation, new-born babies' heads cut off in front of their mothers, heads sliced off with pangas, pregnant women hung from trees and their stomachs sliced open for the foetus to fall to the earth. Body parts hacked out. Hearts, livers, brains. Then dried and eaten by the savages.

In history lessons, the Battle of Blood River and the day

commemorating it, celebrated by all Afrikaners, the Day of Covenant, was used as a rallying point. That day, we were told so many times, was the perfect illustration that God was on our side. It was the day when all Afrikaners were given a sign that by standing alone and proud and winning a victory over the black savages, we were carrying out God's will. Which meant apartheid was right and justified. That, too, was God's will. We were putty in the hands of these skilled teachers.

The bitterness that every Afrikaner feels towards the British about the injustices of the Boer War prison camps all came tumbling to the fore, and because my father and grandmother had been in one I was susceptible. It was a further way of justifying apartheid.

The teachings were, looking back now, so predictable: 'Look at how those British used a scorched earth policy, our Afrikaner women, mothers and their babies dying in concentration camps. They complain loudly of the Nazis during the war and the persecution of Jews, but they remain silent about the British and what they did to our people. We are now in power, on top. We have a right, we have earned a right to remain on top. We have built our laager, as we did at Blood River, out of our own steel. It is called apartheid and it is our strength.'

To justify our apartheid, our apartness from blacks and other races, there was a frequently used phrase: a sparrow does not mate with a swallow; a goose does not mate with a duck; a cow does not mate with a buck. A sparrow sticks to a sparrow, a goose with a gander and the cow with a bull. There is one exception, the horse, who mates with a donkey and creates a mule; and we all know what stupid animals the mules are. That, it was said, was nature's law, God's law. It was why white should breed only with white.

To justify the existence of apartheid further, our teachers talked of how the only possible way of controlling communism was through apartheid. Without it, there would be chaos. With pious glee the teachers pointed to the Bantu homelands and how the Nationalist government of South Africa was being fair to the blacks and offering them the goal of self-government in their own territories. On the other hand, this was contrasted to the communist way which was one-party rule.

To achieve this aim the Soviets needed to create chaos throughout Africa; they needed a continental blood bath in order to seize power. The commies wanted our gold and our diamonds. They wanted to control the Cape sea route. With that in their grasp, they would then control the whole of Africa. Today Africa, tomorrow the world.

In sport we played harder because it was demanded that we prepare ourselves for battles ahead. It was important we were tougher and faster than anyone. When we were ostracised from the world, cut off, we were told it was because the rest of the sporting world was afraid to play us. We were too good.

At first all this anti-black propaganda was too hard for me to take in. These were the very people I had grown up with through the early years of my life. I had learned to love and appreciate them. There had been Bafana and his family and the families on the kraals who had treated me as a son. These people had never once threatened my life or that of my family. Had not Bafana saved my life? Had it not been a sangoma who made me well when I was sick? These things I knew, but the daily pumping of propaganda was as effective as the drip, drip, drip of a water tap on the sanity of a prisoner. Eventually it took effect.

One weekend, when I was one of the few boys left at school, again abandoned by my parents, a teacher took me to a political rally in town. He said it would be good for my education.

The rally was in a hall in Vryheid, crowded, smoky and the mood of the gathering very angry. There was barely room to stand, but I remember they were talking about how close to Vryheid a white family had been killed by panga. They had been chopped around badly.

'See, this is the work of the kaffirs,' cried one man as he stood up to support the National Party. He won roars of approval.

Another stood to proclaim: 'We should all arm ourselves and be prepared to stand together as our forefathers did at Blood River. We must be prepared to stand and defend our land and our children.' More roars.

When one man stood to try to give rational argument on behalf of the black workers who had never been any trouble, he was heckled and shouted down. He was booed and spat at, and called a *kaffir boetie*. It was a term I had heard before, knowing it meant the lover of black people. It was a term I didn't realise then would be applied to me many times in the years that were to follow.

The meetings broke up in a storm of insults, and a fight between several men. One man had said he thought that apartheid was wrong and was the curse of the devil. Before he had even finished the sentence, he was set upon by three or four men who pommelled him to the ground. It was frightening stuff for a

65

thirteen-year-old schoolboy to witness. It was also very effective in convincing me that what my teachers said was right. Here, after all, were hundreds of grown-ups who believed passionately in all this stuff about blacks wanting to kill us whites. They knew a lot more than I, they had wisdom which I did not. I was well on the road.

The indoctrination also took place in subtle forms. By this age I was turning into a good 100-yard sprinter. But the school coaches would rile me by telling me that a kaffir could out-sprint me.

'Come, Gregory, would you want to be beaten by a blerrie kaffir?' The sportsmaster knew how to get me going faster.

Without knowing it, my life had been moulded, un-moulded and remoulded. It was a chipping, chipping, chipping process which eventually led me to being as bad as the rest of them, turning into a teenager who had the same racist beliefs as my fellow whites.

One afternoon I was in town with a group of boys from my school, planning to visit the cinema. We spotted a small black boy wearing a green and yellow striped school blazer. It was our school blazer which had obviously been handed on to the boy's mother, probably a maid in one of the white homes. The jacket was pretty shabby and was worn out. But when one of my school colleagues spotted it on the back of a black boy he was immediately furious.

'Look, a blerrie kaffir wearing our blazer,' he cried.

A group of the boys who had been queuing outside the cinema, waiting for it to open, rushed over to the boy and ripped the jacket from him, swearing and cursing the bemused child who must have been three or four years younger than they.

A group of white adults stood on the pavement watching this. They also stood idly by as the white schoolboys then proceeded to punch and kick the black boy, yelling at him that he should never wear our blazer again. Just who the blerrie hell was he to wear our colours? I confess I stood and watched this without any guilt. I had been indoctrinated.

When I went home, either at holidays, or when my parents bothered to take me at weekends, politics was the main subject now in our house. My father voted for the National Party. My grandfather voted for the United Party and I would hear the furious debates between the two men.

My grandfather tried to reason that the relationship between the black man and the white man had always been one of common purpose, of living side by side in a hostile land which, together, they had learned to conquer. Look at how well we had lived at Ongemak and at Trapani where we had many blacks living on the land working with us.

My father would storm back, 'Ja, but these are kaffirs we control. They need to work for me because without that work they would starve and have no place to live.'

He would point with some relish to repeated attacks on white farms at that time, spread throughout the country. Without us realising it, these attacks were particularly highlighted by a white-dominated press, determined to milk every ounce of propaganda from these killings.

'Look, man, look how they are gathering at our borders. They are gathering, preparing to take over our lands,' he would rant. 'Look at these ANC people, look at how they preach sharing and living together, but practise killing and terrorise with their bombs and bullets.'

When I listened to the radio, it was the same theme, white farmers, murdered. Their wives raped and then killed. Blacks building up secret armies.

Terrorism was coming to the fore and I heard then of the ANC armed brigades, the Umkhonto we Sizwe, the Spear of the Nation. At that time, the name Nelson Mandela never really registered in my young mind. I was not to know then that he was one of the key people behind the movement; I only got to know his name years later when he was arrested and appeared on trial for treason.

Buildings were being blown up, electrical installations destroyed, there were all sorts of terrorist activities having a severe effect on our everyday lives. When the bombers hit such installations it was often weeks before full supplies were restored.

These incidents were themselves blown up, out of all proportion, by our teachers who spoke of them in assembly.

'Look at how we white people build these installations for the benefit of everyone, black people and white, and how these terrorists destroy them,' they would preach. 'Look how grateful they are to us for providing services and skills. If the whites had not come and provided these things they would all have died of starvation and sickness. See how grateful they are to us. This is how they say thank you.'

Until that age I had always subconsciously retained my belief that black and white were equal. This was the belief I had learned as a child and my own experience showed me I had little to fear, rather there was much I could learn, from my black friends. Now, I was changing. When the school asked for volunteers for the cadet force my hand shot into the air. Being a member of the force meant you were a member of a quasi-military organisation. You were at the first step on a path which headed to the defenders of our nation. That is, the white nation.

Vryheid High was a big school, up to 1000 pupils, and the teachers tested every boy as a marksman. I was a natural, having been shooting guns from an early age on the farm. I was immediately installed as a sergeant in the cadet force and the school shooting team. It was a new-found status where I started to be accepted as an equal by other boys. I was in from the cold, at least for a short time.

Two of the teachers were given the honorary rank of lieutenant colonel and every boy in the cadet force had a military uniform. It had a very macho effect on us, dressing in khaki army uniforms and parading around like real soldiers. Twice a week, Tuesday and Thursday, we gathered for drilling, left turn, right turn, march, wheel, all that stuff. We learned the correct methods of handling a gun. The officers barked at us that we were the young men our country needed to depend upon to protect our families and our heritage from the coming black onslaught. It was all very powerful stuff.

I recall one incident where I was not drilling properly, slightly out of step. I was hauled out by the officer.

'Gregory, boy, come here.'

I marched out in front of the other cadets.

'Gregory, do you realise that when you pass Matric and you go into the army to protect your country that you are going to have one hell of a bad time?'

'Yes, sir,' I barked back.

'Ja, Gregory, you will have such a bad time because you cannot drill properly. If you can't drill you can't be in the army and if you can't be in the army you can't defend your family and your country. So what will happen to you, boy?'

'I'll be killed, sir.'

'Correct, boy. Now get back in line and do it properly.'

'Yes, sir.'

It was a fear that was instilled into every young boy, whether they liked it or not. I'd read in magazines how the North Koreans indoctrinated their troops by playing military tunes day and night in their camps and how the Chinese troops were bombarded with the thoughts of Chairman Mao twenty-four hours a day. This was the same type of brain-washing. Indoctrination at all costs.

On Tuesdays and Thursdays I suddenly found myself feeling great pride in being part of the cadet force. On with my brown shirt and trousers, my khaki socks and shoes. I was a sergeant, a cut above the rest. Ja, man, now I was a somebody. I carried a gun and I had power. I did not have any friends at the school, I was now a confirmed loner, but when I put on my uniform I had control over other boys. That gave me a sense of power I'd not experienced before. Naturally, I accepted the teachings that went with this indoctrination.

I was also gaining a confidence I'd never had before. I also began to notice girls. A shy, coy smile. An interest. It was happening. But I was quick to learn that girls also meant trouble.

I was in standard seven, walking on my own to the boarding-hostel from school, when I was smashed in the middle of the back with a school case. I stumbled, shocked, and turned around to see what was happening.

There stood one of the boys from standard nine, two years older than me. Bigger and stronger. He was seething as he looked at me. I was bemused and more than a little scared because I had no idea what this was about.

'You're charfing my girlfriend,' he accused.

I was completely dumbfounded. Not only was I not charfing, or chasing, his girl, but I did not even know who he was talking about. Maybe I had smiled at her, maybe she at me, I had no idea.

I told him, 'You're wrong, I have no idea what you're talking about.'

'You're a blerrie liar, Gregory.'

I faced a problem. This guy was bigger and stronger than me and if I turned my back chances were he would set on me. There were other boys around and now, if I did walk away, my name would be ridiculed. He came closer and slapped me, his hand half-clenched. I was straining to retain my composure, knowing I was probably in for a pounding.

I took the matter in my own hands. 'If you want to fight then I'll meet you after study time at the back of the field.'

That satisfied him and he went away grinning, looking forward to his shindig with a younger boy. News went round like wildfire and by the end of study time a large number of boys had gathered for the fight. I was not actually scared. Instead, I began to psych myself up for this, telling myself I could beat him. I decided to stay out of his reach and box him by moving constantly on my toes. I'd be like a cobra, darting in and out again, stinging and whipping myself away again.

A couple of hundred boys or more had gathered. This boy, his name was Joubert, made the mistake of rushing me from the start. I stepped aside from his flailing arms and peppered his head then withdrew to a safe distance. He was stung and taken by surprise. He repeated his move and I did the same. This time I drew blood. The roars and cheering of the watching boys subsided for they had come along to voice their support for Joubert, expecting he would whip my hide. By the time the fight was over Joubert was cut to ribbons, his face a mess. I shall always remember walking away from the fight, wanting to cry because no one had said a thing to me. I was left on my own. I suppose that hardened my own resolve.

A few days later, when news of my victory had swept the school, I made friends, at least on a temporary basis, with another standard seven boy who was constantly being beaten up. He was small and wore thick-framed spectacles. His hair was bright red and his body thin and weak. They used to rag him silly. Many times I saw him sitting beside the school wall, curled up in tears. He became my friend for several weeks, until the other boys left him alone.

I changed school again. I was sent to Voortrekker High School in Pietermaritzburg, even further from my home at Trapani. I was only there for one year before I was again in a fight, this time with the principal's son.

The problem was that, despite having accepted the racist belief that the blacks were trying to slaughter all the whites, there was still within me a part that remembered my past, at Ongemak. I could not entirely leave it behind. My time at Voortrekker was marked by a success in swimming, where I was chosen to represent Natal. I was happiest in the water, doing lap after lap, cut off from the rest of the world, in an existence of my own. At the new school my attitude hardly changed towards other people and I remained a loner. As I studied for exams I wandered through the school fields, reading my books on my own. I would sit in the grass and prepare. As I walked I frequently came across black labourers, weeding the flower beds or cutting the grass. There was a school instruction that forbade any pupil speaking to the black workers. But, as usual, I ignored such things. I would speak to them, a greeting in Zulu, and they would reply. Sometimes we had a conversation, maybe about where they were from or if they knew

70

places I also knew. It was civil enough. The trouble was the headmaster's son got to hear of it and it led to a fight. He was a year older than I and wanted to dictate matters. I was not having it. In the fight I cut him badly. A teacher was called and my father was telephoned. Although I was not formally expelled, it was felt expedient that I should leave at the end of the year.

Another year, now standard nine, when I was sixteen, and another school. This time Ermelo High School, even further from my home, in Transvaal. It was a bastion of the National Party. It was considered one of the country's top schools and attracted boys from all over South Africa. To me it was just another excuse for my parents to get rid of me. By now I no longer cared where they sent me. Another year, another boarding-school, another period of suffering. New names, new faces, new teachers, but the same old situation. I would be alone against the rest of the world and I was going to survive and get it finished with as soon as possible.

My first day at the boarding-house, Huis Veldsman, was a good indication of what it would be like; perhaps my reputation had preceded me, I don't know.

I was given a room with a boy named De Wet. He had not, yet, arrived, and as I unpacked my clothes, shirts, socks, underpants, trousers, all neat, military fashion, I could hear the other boys talking. They were all enthusiastic, calling one another and gossiping about how their holidays had been.

I was on my own and I heard them asking one another if the trouble-maker from Voortrekker had arrived. Ja, he's in the room with De Wet, they said. The talk was of how they would teach me a lesson. I sighed, knowing this was to be the same as before.

Within days I'd had my first fight. Some boy tried to push me around and I would not be pushed. Then came another fight, this time at night in the dormitory. It was a small group of boys who were friends of my first opponent. This led to teachers being called. The headmaster, a man called Slabbert, read the riot act, warning me that with my reputation, one more incident would lead to expulsion.

The other boys knew I was on a last warning, so once again I became a target for them. The teachers knew also that I was now a target, and when several fights followed, they took my side, merely caning me for fighting.

One night I was walking in the darkness to the boarding-house after the Sunday evening church service when, out of the dark, came two boys. I saw something coming towards me and ducked.

It ripped my ear and as I screamed the two people ran away. At the time I was walking with another boy, Basjan Laing, and he saw the attackers. They were two boys in our dormitory. By the time I got to the house my shirt was covered in blood from the ripped ear. I took off my shirt and marched straight for the attackers, smashing one in the face. I knocked him out.

This was big trouble. I was taken to hospital to have my ear lobe stitched and summoned before Slabbert.

'Why didn't you just report the first attack to the teachers?'

'Sir, I was angry at the cowardly attack.'

'But Gregory, you cannot take matters into your own hands all the time. I think I shall have to expel you.'

I was furious. 'No, sir, I do not accept that. I want my father called, I want the police called and I want everything about this to come out. It was me who was attacked. I merely defended myself.'

I was shouting. I demanded further: 'And I want money now to get my shirt and suit cleaned.'

Slabbert saw the sense of this, knowing my family would make a fuss if I was expelled. He agreed to try to calm the situation down and speak to the other boys who wanted to antagonise me. I was left even more alone.

Then came Sharpeville and, after it, Langa. March 1960. The names of little-known townships were now making headlines around the world. The death toll was put at sixty-nine in Sharpeville, but in real terms it was much higher. From now on the struggle between whites and blacks would attract the attention of the world. We'd heard how this was all about a passive-resistance campaign, against the pass laws. We'd heard how the white policemen had opened fire. We were schoolkids, confused and not a little frightened for our own lives. Maybe this was the beginning of the black uprising that had been predicted. We asked our teachers what had happened. The teachers were certain and told us, as if they had witnessed it themselves. They told how the blacks had demonstrated and that, instead of being peaceful, had been intent on causing trouble. They would not do as they were told and even had guns which they were going to turn on the police.

We were all agreed, the blacks got what they deserved. They want trouble, then we're ready for it. Ja, for sure.

We knew about the pass laws because each evening an alarm hooter sounded throughout Ermelo. It was the signal for any black in the town boundary to leave and go to his home. Anyone found on the streets after that sound could be arrested. When I'd first heard the hooter I questioned this law, reasoning that if a man was visiting his girlfriend or was doing some late work, he had good reason to be out of his home. No, the teachers told me, if a black was in a town after 9 o'clock when the hooter sounded, he was only looking for trouble. He was either looking for a place to break into or to kill a white family. So it was fair then; the only way to control them was to make laws which were strict. And if they didn't like it, too bad.

In 1961 I completed my standard ten, or matriculation year, and passed all my exams. My parents wanted me to go to university, but I'd had enough of teachers and places of learning. I wanted to work. I applied to join the Department of Justice, a safe job. At that time when a white boy came out of school without a trade, he either went into the Department of Justice, the railways, the police or the army. This was government service and it was a job guaranteed for life. I was on my own road to Robben Island.

Chapter 9

The road to
Robben Island

My choice was limited, but I was determined to make my own way. I was not going to be a farmer like my father. The resentment towards my parents which had festered within me for a decade or more was still eating away at me. I was going to do it my way.

Three days after leaving school I began work as a messenger boy in Vryheid Court. I was the boy who everyone told to go do things. Go hang out the flag from the pole. Go get the sandwiches. Go carry the files. The job in Vryheid was temporary, until the results of my matric exams were published in late January. When I knew I had passed, the Department of Justice made a decision which changed the course of my life for ever.

The chief magistrate called me in and congratulated me on my exam success.

He continued, 'Young man, we would like to transfer you, to start you off on the road to promotion.'

I nodded and smiled.

'We'd like to send you to Windhoek.' He glanced at me to see my reaction.

The smile was gone and I frantically searched my mind to place Windhoek. In South West Africa, now Namibia. In the middle of a desert. What was this? I'd be stuck in a place which I'd hate. South West Africa then was also a farming community and the towns and communities little different to the type in which I had spent my early childhood. I wanted something different.

The magistrate saw my hesitation and asked, 'Is that a problem for you, young man?'

'No, sir, not really, but Windhoek seems to be in the middle of a desert and I'd prefer somewhere different.'

The magistrate hummed and hahed and stroked his chin. Then he said, 'Leave it with me. I'll see what I can do.'

Two days later he called me back again.

'Young man, this is good for you. I have a position that the Department of Justice want filled in Cape Town. Would you like to take it?'

I did not hesitate. 'Yes, sir, please.' Cape Town was at the other end of the country, but I'd heard of its beauty and it felt as if I was burying my school life in the appropriate manner. The further away the better.

'You must understand that this is a long way from your home and with you being so young you may need help finding somewhere to live.'

I was quick to tell the magistrate that my sister lived in Cape Town, her husband worked as a medical superintendent at the Groote Schuur Hospital.

The magistrate nodded and said he would write to my parents and tell them of the opportunity.

He added, 'You must remember that you have a lot to learn. If you want, there is a future for the rest of your life in the Department of Justice. It is a good, sound job and prospects for a young man like you are excellent. I suggest you take a correspondence course at UNISA, the University of South Africa, and study for a BA Law degree.'

My heart was pounding. I was overjoyed. Here I was, within weeks of making my own decision about leaving school and getting a job, getting an opportunity which sounded wonderful.

I had £10 in my pocket when I climbed aboard the train at Vryheid for the two-day journey to Cape Town, stopping at Ladysmith on the way. The departure from my parents was unemotional: no tears, no fond farewells, the same sort of departure I'd been used to when I returned to boarding-school.

My father gave me £5 and my mother made up a parcel of food. When I went to the train compartment, there were five grown men already in it. My mother took me outside the carriage and told me to be careful with my money, these men could steal it. I slipped it into my underpants for safe keeping. As the train pulled out of the station I looked back to wave goodbye, but my parents had already left the platform. I was on my own. Again.

The journey was filled with interest, new scenes and places. And I never touched the food my mother had prepared for me; it was dumped to one side. Every time one of the men in the compartment decided he was going to the dining car to eat, I'd get an invite. 'Come, kid, come and get some food, you're a growing lad.'

When I arrived in Cape Town I was tired. But my sister met me and told me I had two days' rest before starting in the Cape Town courts. I felt I was no longer a boy. I had joined the adult world.

When I went to the court I was taken to the chief magistrate, a man called Bestbier. He was a pleasant man who told me that if I ever needed help in any way, I could approach him and ask. He then put me to work with a man named Fischer, to learn the job of being a court clerk.

Fischer showed me in a sombre manner the court files, large ledger books in which all records were kept. Names, case numbers, bail amounts, fines, everything. It was my job to ensure they were properly kept. I also had to monitor all the court fines and issue receipts. I was working ten hours a day and was still falling behind with the workload. I stayed until 10 o'clock at night. I spent Saturdays going in to try and prevent the backlog. The security staff knew me and told me many times I was working too hard, that as a young man I should be out having fun with people of my own age. But I was happy enough. I now had a job and I was absorbed by it; I was determined to do it as well as I could and if that meant working long hours then so be it.

The court, the old building, was in the centre of Cape Town, next to the police station in Buitekant Street. There were ten courts in all, listed from the letter A to J. The first five were criminal courts, including the traffic courts, the others juvenile courts. I was working in the criminal side and got to know the group of interpreters who were there. The chief was a man called Mr Oosterhuizen, a white man, who worked with four blacks. I was working closely with these men and got to know Mr Oosterhuizen – 'please just call me Oosie' – and one of the black interpreters, Billy Mama. I started by calling him Mr Mama, but after a while he knew I could speak Zulu and Xhosa and told me, 'James, man, you just call me Billy.' These two men looked after me, making sure that I knew what was going on. We shared the same office, and when they were not busy Billy and Oosie sat talking to me.

At lunch-times, when the court closed, Billy Mama would come in, close the door and say, 'Right, James, lesson time.' He knew my Zulu was good, but my understanding of Xhosa was weaker. He was determined to help me improve it. It was the first close contact I'd had with a black person since I'd left Ongemak and Bafana. Although the two African languages are closely related, they were different and I was constantly making mistakes in Xhosa. Billy set out to correct the mistakes, telling me that one day I'd make good use of them. Neither of us were to know just how prophetic that comment would turn out to be.

Billy prepared written work for me and when we were together we spoke only Xhosa. Gradually, my mistakes lessened.

I had been in the courts several months when I realised there was a problem with the administration system. There were long delays for people who had been dealt with by the court and had been fined. Under the existing system, they could not be released until bail bond had been paid and a release warrant had been signed by a magistrate. So I went to Mr Bestbier, asking to see him. His secretary, sitting in her darkened room, was severe and strict. 'I'm not so sure the chief magistrate can see someone as junior as you. Make an appointment.'

I made an appointment and when, eventually, I got to see Bestbier, he agreed that a change was in order to prevent the long queues which cluttered the corridors of the court. Eventually, they instigated a system which allowed for payment and a release warrant issued by a court official called the prisoners' friend.

Within six months I knew the job inside out. I was getting bored. I was studying in my spare time at UNISA for a BA Law degree. I was working hard, but having mastered the system in the criminal courts I went to see Bestbier and asked for a move.

'James, don't you like the job?'

'Sir, it's not that. It's that I now know this job and find it boring. I don't want to keep doing the same thing, I'd like a change to another department.'

Bestbier agreed to transfer me to the civil court department. Six months later I went to Bestbier again. He moved me to the maintenance department, dealing with maintenance payments. Then on to the juvenile department.

In the middle of my first year in the courts I met Gloria, a trainee hairdresser who lived close to my sister in Plumstead, a quiet suburb of Cape Town. We married in January 1963.

I had been in the department a year when Bestbier called me into his office.

'James, in the new year we are sending four young men from Cape Town's magistrates courts to Pretoria to be trained as prosecutors. You are one of those I have nominated. I'm telling you this now because I want you to be prepared to travel. Is this okay with you?'

I was overwhelmed. 'Ja, sir, for sure. Thank you.'

Bestbier told me the course was to last six months, but before that I had to sit language tests, Afrikaans and English at higher grade. To qualify for the prosecutor's course I had to pass both. I studied hard and gained both with a top grade one pass. At the same time my quarterly results from UNISA came through and I was passing all my exams. At the end of the first year of university exams I had top marks.

In the new year I was again summoned to Bestbier's office. I expected to be given details of the prosecutor's course, the times and locations. I was excited as I sat in front of him for I was also celebrating the birth of my first son, Zane, in January 1964.

'James, I'm sorry to tell you I have changed my mind about the course. As you know, the other three people going on the course are more senior than you. And I have just employed a young man who has two years of law studies under his belt. I'm sending him instead of you. Your turn will come in time.'

I remember feeling as if I'd been struck by a train. I could not believe what I was hearing. I sat in the bail office unable to speak to anyone. People were queuing and shouting at me. I was unable to move.

Oosie came in and asked what had happened. I told him and he sat beside me. 'Man, this is wrong, he promised this to you.'

Oosie went to Bestbier to plead my case, but the chief magistrate would not be swayed.

I reacted badly, no longer working late to ensure the work was completed. Bail bonds were not filled in. I stopped my law studies and began looking for another job. Without telling anyone, including my own family, I was determined to get out of the court job.

At the time my pay was £30 a month. In the Cape Town *Argus* I saw an advertisement for trainee traffic officers. The wage was £64 gross a month. I applied and got the job.

The day I resigned Bestbier was livid.

As I sat in his office, my resignation on the desk in front of him, he told me, 'James, you are being stupid. You have a bright future here. Don't take this business about the prosecutor's course badly; your turn will come. You have done well since arriving; don't spoil it all by throwing it away.'

I was determined and angry. I told him, 'You broke your promise to me. If that's what you do this year, what will it be next year. No, sir, I'm going.' As I sat in front of him he telephoned my sister and told her what I had done. I'd kept the entire matter quiet and my sister burst into tears. My father was called to try and persuade me to stay.

79

I said no, I was going to be a traffic cop. It was my life and I would not be dictated to. My parents were constantly on the phone telling me I was wrong. My sister told me I was wrong. The only person who backed me was Gloria.

I joined the traffic department and for three months went on a training course, studying road traffic ordinances, motor vehicle insurance, public relations, criminal law, practical training and a variety of traffic tests. When I qualified they sent me on foot patrol in Claremont, a nice leafy suburb, about a mile long. I walked one way up the pavement, and back on the other side, issuing tickets for parking, loading zone violations, double parking, anything at all. It was monotonous. I broke up the boredom by helping a Sergeant Rainie train the motor-cycle squad. From an early age I had ridden a motor cycle and was very skilful. When I asked the chief inspector, a man named Dowd, if I could transfer to the bikes he was firm. No way, not until I had completed my two-year stint pounding the pavements in Claremont.

I went to Dowd a second time to plead my case and when he refused again I was off on my travels once more. This time I'd seen an advert for a grade one traffic cop in Worcester, in the Boland. I applied by letter and got the job.

The job in Worcester was, at least, more interesting. Sometimes I went on foot patrol, sometimes I would take the motor bike, either a BMW or a Harley. If it rained there was a car or a bakkie. In the town was also a prison, Worcester, and through my job I began to get to know a number of the local warders.

The man in charge of the small traffic department was called Loubscher and one day a few weeks after I arrived he called me into his office.

'Ja, man, howzit?'

I was a little hesitant, knowing he wanted something. 'Fine, man, just fine. I'm enjoying being here.'

We sat drinking coffee and the subject turned to five tickets I issued to a local farmer, a man called De Wet from Rawsonville. I'd picked him up because he'd overloaded his lorry transporting fruit to the markets. It was a common problem.

'Ja, but James, these people are farmers, people like us. We need to use discretion. If you want to issue tickets there are other, easier targets. For instance, whenever you see a taxi driven by a black stop him, they are easy targets. Test them for everything. There is usually something wrong. If you want to hand out tickets, do it that way, man. But not the farmers, some of these people are our friends, they are like you and me, man. We help them, they help us. It's survival in this country now, man.'

I knew exactly what Loubscher was saying. I supposed he was getting gifts of fruit, vegetables and meat from the farmers he called his friends.

I told him, 'No, I'm sorry, if I see an offence I'll ticket them, whether they are black or white.'

I was known as a strict cop. If I saw a driving or traffic offence I ticketed the person. But I was also known as being fair. I targeted whites as well as blacks although I knew the black taxi drivers were easier targets.

During the night-time patrols, waiting for the drive-in movies to empty, I got to know a number of prison officers. They would come and speak to me as I sat on my motor bike or in the car, waiting.

I was also becoming more aware of this man called Nelson Mandela, hearing how he was the one behind the plan for the blacks to kick us into the sea and take our land. The Rivonia trial had happened, and I read every word that was in the newspapers about it. This stuff affected me and my future. Many times I sat with the other traffic cops jawing about what a brilliant piece of police work the arrest of the terrorists had been.

I read about how these killers had all the arms and explosives stashed away, prepared for the onslaught. They were just waiting for a signal, which they said would be broadcast on Radio Free Africa. But, of course, it was all stopped by the arrest of the terrorists at Rivonia, just outside Johannesburg. The leaders were all caught red-handed. Ja, great police work. I read it. They quoted experts from the FBI in America and Scotland Yard in Britain, that this was police work of the very highest calibre.

This all happened at a time when lonely white homesteads were being attacked, white farmers being butchered. Maybe these things were purely criminal, but to white South Africans, they were perceived as political, the foretaste of the slaughter that the blacks were threatening.

So Rivonia was a great coup for the police. Although Mandela was already in prison at that time, serving five years for other offences, he was said to be the main man, the leader. Until then I had only been vaguely aware of his name; I must have read it or heard about it. But after Rivonia, we all knew this man was the man who was the power behind the terrorists. When he appeared at court we had this ridiculous spectacle of hundreds of blacks showing up shouting *Mayibuye Afrika*, may Africa return. And they would chant *Amandla*, *awethu*, the power is ours. Well we showed them who held the power and that we would not be intimidated. I read every scrap on these people because it had a real bearing on my life. These people were my enemies, trying to take away what I had earned and what my forefathers had earned with their blood and toil. I was angered by what I read, that these people would try to win power at all costs. My views, I believed, were shared by the majority of ordinary, white South Africans. We all believed that this black threat had to be stopped, and when these people were brought to trial it was a great victory for law and order.

When they were found guilty we all hoped they would get the death sentence. We hoped Mandela and his gang of killers would hang. If they were not stopped, the blood of all white people would stain the land. And if we only locked them up and released them later, they would start up all over again. When we sat together talking there was unanimous opinion: these bastards should hang. We were united on that.

During my evenings on patrol I got to know a prison officer called Tiekie Van Stittert. One evening, as we drank coffee together, he put the thought in my mind. 'Man, why not come and join the prison department. The scope is unlimited, good money, good accommodation and good prospects.' I shook my head saying I was happy as a traffic cop. However, the idea began to grow within me and when I found my path for promotion blocked in the short term I decided to apply.

In June 1966 my application was accepted. I could join immediately.

Within two months I was sent to the training establishment at Kroonstad and then returned for my first job at Worcester. With the job went a house and I was in need of it because by that stage Brent had been born.

Several months after starting work at Worcester I was called in by the commander, Terri Blanche.

'Gregory, we have a special job for you. A very special job for you. On your record is the fact you speak Zulu and Xhosa and can write both these kaffir languages perfectly, is that correct?'

'Ja, that's correct, sir.'

'Right, man, we need someone of your special skills. On Robben Island. Will you go?'

Robben Island, the place I knew they'd sent Mandela and his fellow terrorists. I'd heard all about it.

Chapter 10

Robben Island:
our own Devil's Island

It could so easily have been a holiday resort, less than four miles from the sandy beaches of the Bloubergstrand coastline which each summer attracts sun lovers in their thousands. Towering like a protective barrier less than seven miles away to the north of the island is Table Bay Mountain, a view known the world over. Robben Island itself is a windswept outcrop of land just over a mile wide by three and a half miles long. When I was told I was being sent to *die Eiland*, a mixture of pictures flooded into my mind of the small island, the one-time leper colony, which now housed the most dangerous terrorists in the world. How many times had I stood in the middle of Cape Town and narrowed my eyes to view it in the distance, just a tiny outcrop of limestone poking its head out of the clear-blue water? How many times had I imagined how it would be living on the island, knowing those animals were being held there? I knew its history, a cauldron in summer and a chill-box in winter, caught in the wash of the icy Benguela Current which drifted all the way from the Antarctic. I'd heard about the wonderful fishing, the solitude and the remoteness; you were cut off from the rat race of ordinary life. I'd also heard rumblings of the brutality and beatings and of the drunkenness and fights.

At home Gloria was delighted. She had heard of its reputation for brutality and desolation, but for her an island had a sense of romance, and it was an escape from the sort of life we had then. We were struggling financially with two young children. Zane was four and Brent just two. We could not afford a house, and lived instead in a tiny flat in Worcester. Gloria had to work long hours as a hairdresser, leaving the children in a crèche. Neither of us wanted that sort of life, we wanted to remain a close family with Gloria being at home to care for the boys in those vital, early years. We both knew that whatever the reputation of Robben Island, it would provide us with a house of our own.

I also knew of Robben Island as the home of the Poqo. Although that was the name given to all the political prisoners, the name was a misconception. Poqo was, in fact, the military wing of the Pan African Congress, an offshoot of the ANC. But in the vernacular of the warders, or *volksmond*, people's talk, Poqo was the collective term for terrorists.

I knew all about Mandela, Sisulu, Kathrada and the rest. Like so many people I had read every word printed in the newspapers about the Rivonia trial. These guys were splashed all over the front pages for weeks on end, men who wanted to overthrow the government by violent means, not caring who they killed to achieve their aims. I'd been primed by years of apartheid indoctrination to believe these men were terrorists who planned one day to wipe out all white people in South Africa. I was white so, naturally, I was one of their targets. They wanted to steal our lands, to rape and butcher our wives and families and to kick us into the sea, off the end of Cape Point.

These men had been convicted of treason against the state, and, I believed, should have been hanged. When the death sentence was not passed it caused a wave of anger and revulsion among whites, but they were reconciled by the fact that these men were sentenced to life imprisonment. And life imprisonment meant being banished to Robben Island where the stories of hardship were becoming legendary. This was at least a crumb of comfort.

When the prison authorities assigned me to Robben Island they said it was because I could speak Zulu, Xhosa and both Afrikaans and English. I knew I was going to be the censor, the person who was going to have a say in what these terrorists could read and write, how they would be treated during their life sentences.

I was new to the prison service and when men talked of the island they did so with a mixture of fear and reverence. Many warders talked of how they would resign if ever they were transferred there. Stories of how brutal it was not only for the prisoners, but also for the warders, were widespread. Occasionally I heard of warders who volunteered to work on Robben Island, where, they said, the fishing was good and where, if you did your job, there was a freedom which did not exist in other prisons.

There were also stories circulating among the warders of how these Rivonia terrorists were different from the common criminals. For instance, if an ordinary criminal gave you trouble, if he would not do his work or he was rude, he simply got a hiding and that was the end of it. No complaints, no troubles. But these people were said to be very different. They were arrogant and difficult, always trying to cause trouble. They would push a warder as far as they could and, if there was any violence, they would make official complaints. Even if they were put on a charge of breaking prison regulations they always fought the case, hiring attorneys and making big scenes out of small incidents. It was a vastly different ball game with these Poqo.

When I left the police traffic department my salary dropped by nearly fifty per cent. But I could see that the prison job, although initially paying less, offered me better prospects, particularly because of the accommodation that went with the job on Robben Island. It would allow us to save for a home of our own. There was also a bonus which every warder received for working on the island. They said it was because of the hardship of being cut off from the mainland. I was soon to learn that this extra thirty rand a month was immediately taken up with buying shampoos and toiletries to combat the brackish water, the only supply on the island.

We went to the island just before Christmas 1966. It was a glorious day when there was hardly a ripple on the water as we sailed out on the prison ship the *Diaz* from the harbour front. It was one of those days when the sea was calm and the seals were everywhere. The journey from Table Bay Harbour to the island's one working jetty at Murray's Bay, named after a nineteenth-century whaler, took just under an hour. As we sat on the upper deck of the *Diaz* the island began to emerge more clearly: we could see the white-painted lighthouse, its scarlet red dome and railing visible from the moment we left the Cape Town harbour. It was the tallest point on the island and one we knew well. Slowly we closed on the island, the rocky shoreline on the northern side looking deceptively inviting. The old jetty was now disused and crumbling, battered by the icy blasts which started somewhere a thousand miles distant out in the South Atlantic. It was a small town with an Anglican church. The white-walled buildings shimmered in the sun. Sweeping into the harbour we came upon our first sight of the prison. Sitting just behind the entrance wall it seemed to make a statement: this was the prison and this was what the island stood for, imprisonment. Above the archway which led to the prison – and which was the only entrance to the rest of the island – the motto of the place was inscribed loud and clear: *Robbeneiland, Ons Dien Met Trots*, Robben Island, we serve with pride.

A warder, his name was Frikkie Steyn, was waiting for us, with an old beaten-up, rusted heap of a car at the jetty. I had known Steyn from Kroonstad, the training establishment. He'd heard I was coming and was planning a welcoming braai.

'Come, Greg, let me take you all for a spin past your house. I think the workmen are still there.'

Indeed the workmen were still busy at the house, a low, flat bungalow-type square box, with white walls and a red door. It was number T38. Who had devised such a number and why had long been forgotten. I was once told the homes had been occupied by the naval department during the war and the numbers related to craft numbers. The sound of sanding machines greeted us, along with clouds of dust emanating from the front door. Gloria, clutching Zane to her, looked dismayed. She was clearly worried about our furniture which had been shipped over ahead of us. We went in and began to realise with a sinking feeling that this was no South Seas holiday island. Dust was everywhere. It covered our furniture and possessions. There was no escaping it. I pacified Gloria by telling her it was better to start off with the wooden floors well sanded before we decorated the house to our own taste and style. The desolation of the place had sent her into tears. This was not how she had imagined her new home.

Steyn was spirited: 'Ag, man, don't worry about the blerrie mess, you'll soon get the place the way you like it. No problem. Come, stay at my place for the next few days, until they get your place cleaned up enough to live in it.'

We had little choice. T38 was virtually uninhabitable in its present state. Steyn lived three doors away and we stayed with him for two nights while the floors were finished. Each day we went to see the progress of the sanding which was being carried out by inmates in their olive green prison garb.

Gloria was unhappy, she wanted to move into her own house as soon as possible; no matter how kind the Steyns had been, we were still lodgers, and the houses were too small for two families to live in harmony. Any more than a couple of days and we would be at one another's throats.

That first weekend was a long holiday weekend, but my thoughts were fixed firmly on getting the house in order, to get rid of the dust which seemed to be everywhere.

Christmas was just around the corner, but we hardly gave it a second thought; our only concern was to get into our own home. Steyn's house was bearing in on me; it was like a vice being slowly

86

closed. I needed to be outside, breathing the fresh air of the island, feeling its isolation. Steyn's bike was against the back wall and it offered the perfect solution. I rode up the main street, between the rows of neat little white-washed warders' houses. I saw a wife pushing a pram, another couple strolling, inmates working on the lawns, or what was left of them in this summer heat. I continued up past the Anglican church we had seen from the boat as we arrived, along the road further. A plethora of buildings I would get to know so well over the next few years were spread around on both sides of the road. I rode on. The only conversation I'd had so far on the island was with the Steyn family. I didn't stop to speak to anyone and there did not appear to be any inclination from anyone to halt my progress.

The heat of the summer had already turned what little grass that grew on the island to straw. With the exposed limestone and sand, it gave the entire area the appearance of a semi-desert. The only colour, apart from the buildings, came from the trees, bushy Port Jacksons with their crisp yellow flowers. My mind was coming to terms with the island. I'd heard of its reputation, but I'd expected it to be different, to be more ... alive. This place seemed to be as lively as a morgue. Everyone I'd seen, the inmates as well as the warders or the families, almost seemed like zombies, wandering as if in some trance. I rode on to the end of the road, on to the limestone path that had been carved out of the scrubland, to the spot where I could sit on the rocks and stare directly at Cape Town. The gentle motion of the waves played with the mass of seaweed which struggled for life in the icy currents. The long strands curled like snakes from the sea-bed. The gentleness and solitude of the seashore convinced me I had made the right decision; this was a peaceful setting and no matter what they threw at me in the prison service I felt certain I could handle it.

Perhaps it was the seaweed, knowing it was plucked from the sea to be used as fertiliser by the inmates, which turned my mind to the prison and to the ANC leaders whom I knew would be under my charge. The thought of Mandela and the memory of the Rivonia trial was still fresh in my mind.

The bitterness returned, along with a feeling of anger and frustration: he, of all the group, should have been hanged.

I had followed the trial closely in the newspapers and on the radio. The trial had started out as the State versus the ANC High Command and others. Over the weeks, it gradually came to be known as the State against Nelson Mandela and others. And why?

Because he was an arrogant agitator who showed no respect for the very institution of the courtroom. Every time he came he thrust his arm in the air and sparked cries of *Amandla*, and *Ngawethu*, power to the people. Was that any way to behave? And hadn't he been the one who had refused to be cross-examined in the witness box? Nelson Mandela wanted to make political speeches all the time. He didn't want to face the truth of cross-examination and he called himself a lawyer! I knew all about his sort of lawyers! Communists who wanted to end civilised life in South Africa. The words he had used had been like an invitation to the judge, Mr Justice de Wet. I'd read it over and over: 'During my lifetime I have dedicated myself to the struggle of the African people. I have fought against white domination and I have fought against black domination. I have cherished the ideal of a democratic and free society in which all persons live together in harmony and with equal opportunities. It is an ideal which I hope to live for and to achieve. But, if needs be, it is an ideal for which I am prepared to die.' The man had used those words to trumpet his own cause. Mighty fine words for a man who refused to be questioned about the killings carried out by the Umkhonto we Sizwe, the armed wing of the ANC, which he had started. As I sat remembering the emotions over the Rivonia trial, and the verdicts which were greeted in stunned outrage by many white South Africans, the anger returned. He was found guilty, he had refused to answer the court's questions and he should have been hanged. He'd survived to come here, to this very island. Well, we'd see just how brave Mr Nelson Mandela was now.

Sitting there on the foreshore helped clear my mind of the frustration of the unfinished house. As I returned Gloria was walking to the Steyns' house, a smile on her face. It was the first time I'd seen her smile in days.

'James, come, they have finished the floors, they say it's all right to move in now.'

She was happy because she had her house. It would be weeks before we would get the house straight and the dust out of every crevice, but at least it was home.

It was shortly after we'd thanked the Steyns and closed our own front door that the chief warder, Munro, called to welcome us to the island.

As it was a holiday weekend Munro apologised for disturbing us. He made his greetings as short and sweet as he could politely manage before springing on me the real reason for his call. Could I start work the next morning?

When I agreed, he sprang his little surprise. 'Oh, by the way, Gregory, we'll be sticking you in with the Poqo.'

I was to come face to face with Nelson Mandela.

Chapter 11

Finding my footing

He seemed to stand taller and straighter than any of the others with an aura that made a statement. 'I am a leader. You will not intimidate me.' Even in his drab prison clothes Nelson Mandela was different. As I stood to one side of the yard in the shade, just watching these men, the Poqo, I could feel his inner strength. I knew this man would be a difficult one to overcome.

This was the prison within the prison which was officially called the Solitary Block. It was designed specifically to separate the leadership of the Poqo from the militants and rank-and-file members of each of the organisations. It was a purpose-built one-storey rectangular structure surrounding a solid cement courtyard, a little larger than the size of a tennis court. The grey, soulless centre had cells on three sides; the fourth, a twenty-two-foot high wall, was topped by a catwalk which was patrolled by German shepherd dogs.

Standing in the shade of the wall, on the western side, I felt their eyes flicking towards me and away again, yet in the moment of contact they penetrated me, trying to figure me out. Lengthy direct eye contact was rare; these men were sitting mostly in ones or twos, although occasionally in larger groups, while others were walking, strolling around the courtyard.

The three lines of cells were known as sections A, B and C. Mandela and the rest of the Poqo were in section B, which lined the eastern side of the quadrangle. The other two sections were solitary confinement areas, largely left empty. I looked across to the line of windows, seventeen in all, tiny square double windows, with their four bars cemented into the walls on the inside. The windows had been left open to allow what little breeze there was to take away the stench of incarceration. In total the entire section contained ninety single cells. I had been told it was known to the rest of the prison population as *Makhulukutu*, after the leader group. In prison jargon, the Poqo were known as 'The *Makulu* Span', the big team.

I was aware of an unease among the inmates, a change. Small groups who had been sitting cross-legged on the courtyard began to stand up, there was a buzz about the place; something was definitely happening. I soon realised it was the sudden appearance of Vosloo, one of the senior warders in the prison. The Poqo were at once alert. It was the first indication of their in-built radar and network which warned them of visits before they occurred, before any senior officers actually showed up in their section.

Vosloo took me into B section which housed the Poqo.

'Come, Gregory, come see where these kaffirs and koelies live.'

Inside the corridor the heat and smell hit me. Disinfectant, mixed with the unmistakable stench of sweating bodies and urine. The unforgettable smell of incarceration which was to remain with me for much of the next three decades.

'Go, have a look for yourself,' encouraged Vosloo. 'Familiarise yourself, see where we keep these animals. See how well we look after them; better than they deserve, man. Better than what they have come from.'

The floor of the corridor was bare, grey cement, but it was polished as a mirror, the way the Zulus had polished the inside of the huts in their kraals. The row of fluorescent tubular lights down the middle of the corridor which were always left on glistened off the floor and pale-green gloss-painted walls. Slowly, I paced out the line of thirty cells, looking at the names above each door. Here, first inside the barred gate at the entrance, on the left-hand side, was Motsoaledi, an ANC terrorist. At the far end of his cell, through his barred windows, I could catch a glimpse of the harbour and beyond, the enticing beaches of Bloubergstrand. That was nice, to let him see the forbidden fruit, I thought. Slowly down the corridor, fourth on the right, Mandela. His details were listed on a card which at one time had been white, but was now yellowed with age; he had already been here two years. It bore his details: N. Mandela. 466/64. It told me he had been the 466th prisoner to be admitted on the island in 1964. Not for him the benefit of a room with a view. No, his barred cell looked out on to the courtyard.

The cell was sparse, neatly cared for. The *sisal*, or straw mat, used as a bed, was rolled up inside the right-hand wall, the three thin, grey blankets neatly folded beside it. In one corner was the rusted iron bucket known as a *balie*, which was used as a toilet. It had a porcelain lid which was invariably turned upside-down to contain enough water to allow them to shave or wash their hands and faces. Beside the folded blankets were two strips of old, grey fraying cloth. I was later to discover one was a face-cloth, the other a towel. This was a man's possessions.

Vosloo talked mechanically of the daily routine. 'They are awakened at 5.30 each morning, and they must prepare themselves to be ready for cell opening at 6.45.

'They must have their cells neatly ready, mats and blankets rolled and folded. And they must take their balies and wash them in the bathroom and shower area.

'Then they must go out into the courtyard and wait for their breakfast, which they don't deserve. Man, these kaffirs are never happy, they are always complaining about the food. They don't know how well off they are. They eat better in here than they ever did at home.'

I wasn't about to argue with Vosloo, but I already knew the food was not the sort I would feed to a dog. It was unpalatable and looked disgusting. The breakfast of mielie pap was wheeled into the courtyard and slopped into metal bowls that were often dirty from the day before. The coffee which accompanied it was a revolting swill of black liquid, unlike any coffee I had ever seen before. This was a mix of ground-up maize, baked until it was black, then boiled.

I wandered into Mandela's cell wondering how such a tall man could stretch out along the narrow space. Years later Mandela would tell me how, when the men from the Rivonia trial were brought to the section, the floors and walls were still running with water; they had been built hurriedly and the cement had not yet dried. When they had complained of the damp, the commanding officer, called Wessels and one of the old, hard school, had told him that their bodies would absorb the moisture. Inside the cell the window looked even smaller, perhaps one foot square, at eye-level. The view on a dull day would have been a scant scene of the courtyard and the grey stone wall opposite. This day it was just a blinding mass of white light from the unforgiving sun which shone through his barred window.

Each cell had a second window also barred, facing into the corridor, and two doors: an inner, five-barred metal grille gate and a second, outer door of solid oak. I paced the room in my size ten shoes. It was almost square, three steps by three steps.

Slowly, absorbing the feel of the section, I wandered down the line of cells, the homes of the Poqo, men I had been taught to despise: Mhlaba, Mlangeni, Kathrada, Sisulu, men I thought I already knew from the infamous deeds I'd read and heard about.

At the end of the corridor the stench of the area increased: the toilet and shower area, a lower, flat space, its puce-coloured walls chipped and flaking.

Vosloo walked slowly behind me, inspecting cells, flicking and poking with his stick. At the bottom of the corridor we turned right into the isolation area; it was darker, more sinister.

'This here, man, is where we keep Tsofendas.' The name was etched larger in the hearts of Afrikaners than any other: this was the madman who had taken a knife to Hendrik Verwoerd and stabbed him to death.

Outside the cell a guard sat, a notebook on his lap. 'We watch this madman twenty-four hours a day. We write down every word he says; they're the orders from Pretoria.' I looked through the window and saw the killer sitting hunched up in the corner of the cell, his knees drawn tightly up to his chest. His eyes were shut and he was gibbering to himself.

Vosloo was beside me again: 'Come, man, that's the end of the tour.'

I was still uncertain of what my job was here in the B section. I asked Vosloo, 'What precisely do I do?'

'Nothing, just keep a watch over the Poqo. It's easy, they are kaffirs.'

Outside in the sunshine, the prisoners were walking, lapping the courtyard on their oval route to nowhere, their faces either staring at the ground or straight ahead. It was an eerie sight. I went over to another guard but he shied away. 'No, keep away, we are not allowed to stand together and talk. Vosloo doesn't like that.'

I began to walk, bored and confused about how I was best to spend my time. Several times I cast a glance at Mandela, but he was deeply engrossed in conversation. Three laps of the courtyard and I could feel the sweat coming, so I headed for the shade of the verandah, close to the bathroom and toilet corner. The prisoners simply ignored me.

This was a weekend and the prisoners were excused work; I had imagined they would at least do something, exercise or play a game of volleyball, something. But not this.

My eyes were drawn back to Mandela as he stood talking. I could pick out his compatriots from the pictures I had seen. Walter Sisulu, Mac Maharaj, Ahmed Kathrada and Laloo Chiba. They walked their laps of the courtyard, always animated until they reached within ten yards of where I stood and then ... silence. At noon the food was wheeled in, a mixture of mielie rice and ground-up mielies called *samp*. It was supposed to contain vegetables although they were as rare as an ice-cube in the Karoo Desert. There was also a drink called *phuzamandla*, meaning drink of strength, made from powdered mealies and yeast, which is stirred with milk and served as a thick milkshake-type drink. However, the concoction wheeled into the courtyard was a thin, weak variety which looked like dirty water.

The prisoners knew the routine well and took their food and headed for their own cells. There was almost silence as I walked into the corridor of B section although occasionally as someone spoke it echoed all along the hall. I closed each of the inner metal-barred grille doors with hardly a glance from the occupant. At Mandela's cell his back was turned to me. I went on to the next.

As I closed the final cell I handed the keys to a warder at the end of the area and headed off for my own lunch, an enjoyable two-course meal of meat and vegetables followed by good strong coffee. I smiled at the difference between the food I had seen dished up in the B section and the food I was served. That's what serving a life sentence should be about: punishment of the stomach as well as the mind.

At 2 o'clock I unlocked the cells again and let them wander out into the courtyard, where I had picked my spot again beneath the verandah in the shade.

The afternoon was an almost dreamy time and I felt myself drifting off in the heat of the day; it was hard to concentrate, watching this endless stream of prisoners strolling around the courtyard. At 4.00 a shrill whistle sounded which made me spring to attention, suddenly awake again. The prisoners lined up to be counted, their eyes forward, refusing to focus on Vosloo as he counted them. As they were dismissed they headed again for the cell area where they were allowed half an hour to clean up. I watched Mandela carefully and observed how he was the centre of so much activity. As they walked around the courtyard he was frequently joined by other prisoners who walked with him then departed again. As they walked from the count-up and inspection, he was again the focus of attention from his colleagues. Several times they would approach him, ask a question or tell him something, and he would stand and nod or shake his head, often talking earnestly. It was clear this man was the leader of the group.

The sun had cast a shadow over the entire courtyard as they filed away to B section for their own clean-up period. The walls seemed to close in on the smell of forty bodies that had been in it throughout the day. It was the locker-room smell of sweat and toil, intensified by heat and humidity. The shadow of the walls closed the entire courtyard as I stood at one end listening to the songs now emanating from the bathroom area.

I walked slowly down the line of cells, outside the windows, listening to the sounds of the Poqo as they sang of their homes and sang of their struggle. It was the nostalgia and harmony which reminded me of the kraals when the Zulus would sing. I had learned as a child, and I realised again as I stood listening to the prisoners, the songs of the black man contained more than just melody and words, they were the African way of conversing, of commenting, of observing. I knew there was so much I could learn from listening to these songs.

Vosloo and the other guards had vanished for half an hour, but reappeared suddenly at 4.30 when supper was delivered in large metal containers. I wandered over to the meal area and watched as the same mielie pap porridge was delivered on the plate with a slap. I thought again, if the courts had not carried out the death sentence by hanging these terrorists, then to spend the rest of one's life being served this kak was a punishment in itself. There were pieces floating in the pap which I was told were vegetables, carrots or beetroot thrown in and occasionally meat. But they looked like burned kernels of corn to me.

I had read the regulations carefully and knew there was a distinction between the food served to black prisoners and the food served to the coloureds and Indians. Now I was seeing it first-hand as the few coloureds in the area were served with a small hunk of bread and a dollop of margarine, half-melted and close to becoming rancid. The bread was known as *katkop*, cat's head, after the shape of the bread when it was hacked into quarters. Whatever it was, the blacks never received any. They were treated differently from other races, even in prison.

As with lunch, the food was eaten in silence. By 5 o'clock Vosloo gave me my final task of that day: to lock up, count the numbers and to fill in each form to ensure everyone was accounted for. As I walked through the corridor of B section, I looked in at each prisoner in their cramped cell. Not one bothered to look at me, their eyes busy elsewhere, averted. I was a nonentity, part of the enemy that they had avowed to defeat. As I closed several doors,

Mandela's and Sisulu's among others, I remember from that first day, their deep voices came from behind it with a simple 'Good night'. How strange that a courtesy should be extended in such circumstances.

Vosloo and the other officers were anxious to get away and, as the junior warder, I stayed locked into the corridor area until the night-shift showed up.

Now, with the disappearance of Vosloo, the talk started in the cells, from one prisoner to another. It was an invaluable insight into the thinking of these men. Not for them pointless complaining about their situation; they were intent on conversing about higher matters – religion, social issues, concepts in physics and chemistry, literature and art. That evening just listening to them was a beginning to my understanding of how different these men in B section were. It was a group of men unlike any the people who trained us at Kroonstad had ever mentioned. I'd expected something very different.

The night guys came, with their flasks of tea and coffee and packages of sandwiches. I had not met them and when they saw me they were hesitant, distinctly cool. I was a newcomer and I had a specific role to play, that of censor, so I was, therefore, a man to be wary of. That evening the look from the night guard was one of disgust.

Without being introduced, he started on me. 'Man, why do you let these kaffirs make so much noise? They are breaking the rules, there should be silence.'

The night warder stormed up and down the corridor, yelling in Afrikaans: *'Stilte in die gang!'* Quiet in the passage. I felt very much the junior warder, being reprimanded.

'You must keep them quiet. They want to talk, but it is not allowed.' I said I was listening to what they said, that some things were interesting.

'Ag, that is just kaffir and koelie talk. It's just nonsense and it's not allowed.'

I was to learn later that there was no call of 'lights-out'. The forty-watt bulbs in each small cell would burn all night long, as they did through the days.

As I walked slowly home that evening, the sun setting in the hills behind Bloubergstrand, I went over the day and how strange and almost dreamlike it had all seemed. What had I expected? What had I been told to expect from the people at Kroonstad? These blacks were terrorists and they wanted to kill me. But here they were in my control now, and they were just ordinary people. When I had been introduced they responded politely. My mind was spinning; this was not what I had expected at all. They were different.

I was back in the cell area again next day. Just as I had locked them in the night before, so I unlocked them. More surprises; from each and every man a polite 'Good morning'. That was it, no more: just a civil greeting. One of the earliest lessons I had in warder training school was how I should be on my guard when prisoners tried to engage in conversation. The instructors said that this was always a tactic and something else was behind it. They were trying something on perhaps. To gain confidence, to win special concessions, special favours, to ignore a breach in rules. These things always started small, always insignificantly, but before you knew where you were, you were in trouble. These terrorists had snared you in their trap. They were looking to entice you into friendship and then blackmail you to make their own lives easier. Consorting with the prisoners was dangerous. But then my mind turned to my initial assessment: these people were different from what I'd expected and, even, what I'd been told to expect. These Poqo, they all bade me a good morning and got on with their tasks of preparing for another day in prison.

As I had done the day before, I stood in the shade beneath the verandah with the prisoners in the courtyard. Several times Vosloo poked his head into the yard to check where I was and disappeared again. The sheer boredom and monotony of standing watching the prisoners began to seep into me. I knew that I could not spend the rest of my life like this; this was also a life sentence. I, too, began to walk around the circuit of the yard. At first there were glances from the prisoners, then an approach from one of them, a coloured man.

I remembered his cell, near the top of the corridor on the right, perhaps the last one.

'Good morning, sir, my name is John Ferris.' It was a surprise, audacious almost. I was immediately on the alert, wondering if this was what the instructors had warned me about. I was certain this was a ploy to gain my friendship, so my natural wariness took over.

'I understand you're from Worcester.' How the hell did he know? He smiled, a twinkle. I'd heard the bush telegraph within the prison system was better than any letter or telegram system. But this good? There was little that these people missed. They'd told me that as well at Kroonstad.

Despite the warnings from the instructors I saw little danger in entering into conversation. I knew that to be in section B, Ferris had to be a senior member of the ANC or PAC, a Poqo, and I reasoned that it would help me understand those under my care better and that as long as I was careful about what I said, there would be no breach in regulations.

'Ja, I came here from Worcester, just a few days ago.'

'Man, I'm from Worcester as well; they actually arrested me at my home.'

I told Ferris that I'd been a traffic cop in Worcester and watched how his brow furrowed. I could see his mind ticking over and before he could ask how I'd finished up on Robben Island, continued, 'I then transferred to the prison department because there was better opportunity for advancement and they asked me if I would come here.'

His eyes went wide. 'You mean you actually agreed to come here?'

I smiled. 'Ja, no problem. I saw it as a South African version of Hawaii.'

He laughed aloud and drew looks from other prisoners around the courtyard. 'Man, that is the first time I've ever heard of someone actually volunteering or agreeing to come here. Have you not heard how bad it is for the warders as well as the prisoners?'

I was puzzled by how much he knew about the living conditions. Ferris was open and talked of how the political prisoners in B section – the ones we called the Poqo – had heard many times from the prisoners on the criminal side of how many problems there were among families and warders living on the island.

'Those ordinary prisoners, some of them work down at the warders' houses as monitors, doing the labouring work, and they hear and see things. It gets back to us.'

I nodded and Ferris continued. 'We hear when there are fights or when a warder has a bust up with his wife. It's just common knowledge and gets around here like a bushfire, man.'

Ferris went into detail about one warder who threw his wife out after finding her in bed with a junior warder, a single guy.

He laughed. 'Man, we could have told him his wife was playing around. It was the gossip in here long before the husband found out.'

I was fascinated by the depth of his knowledge and allowed Ferris to continue. 'It is just human nature that we are all living on a small island and everything that happens will be found out by someone else. The people in here,' he swept his arm around the area, 'we just make it our business to hear things. We have little else to do, so we hear.'

Ferris shrugged. 'We know you are the new censor officer, we knew even before you arrived. We'd heard about you and how you speak our languages. That tells us a lot about you because to be able to speak and read Zulu and Xhosa you must have had an interest in us as people and our culture.'

So that was it. They wanted to test me to see how sympathetic I was to their cause. They wanted to know if I'd be a soft touch for them, if they could pull me in to do favours for them. I jumped in: 'Ferris, get it straight, the reason I speak and read Zulu and Xhosa is because I grew up with the black languages, not because I sympathise with terrorist causes.'

At this, Ferris was quick to respond. 'I was not suggesting anything other than the fact that to speak the native languages you have to have an understanding and that's all we ask, understanding.'

We walked on in silence and as I stopped again beneath the shade, Ferris stopped also. We spoke more about Worcester.

'Do you know the coloured section?'

'Ja, of course. I was always in there on my motor bike or sometimes in the car.' I laughed. 'As a traffic cop it was always easy to be there because of the problems from the coloureds. The world's worst drivers.'

Ferris himself smiled and told me where his parents lived. When I asked about his family I knew there had been a subtle change already. He had enticed me into wanting to know more about him.

Just before lunch as we stood in the shade, he turned and said, 'Mr Gregory, you coming here is a welcome sight for us because of your reputation.'

I was puzzled. 'What reputation? I am new to the service.'

'Already you have a reputation from Worcester where you worked as a traffic cop. Although you booked many coloured people and many blacks, they all said you were a fair man. They say you also booked white farmers as well and that shows you are a man of fairness. That's good enough for us.'

It had been a strange second morning. And over lunch I was deep in thought, trying to remember what Ferris and I had said to one another. What was his motive? Was I being targeted as an easy touch? My mind was spinning again, rushing over the consequences. Was I also being watched by the prison authorities for my reaction to this conversation from Ferris? Would they want to report it? I was certain Ferris had been testing me, to judge for himself and the rest just how sympathetic I would be. They had obviously selected him because of my connections to Worcester.

During evening lock-up when I went to Ferris's cell at the end of the corridor, he again spoke about Worcester.

'Do you ever go back there? To make a visit or see friends?'

'No, my only reason for being there was to work, and now I'm here.'

There was a wistfulness in his eyes. I knew he missed his home and his family.

My walk home again that evening was filled with the thoughts of John Ferris and already, subconsciously, the first changes were taking place in my way of thinking. I was only to realise the extent of those changes many years later when I reflected back on the Robben Island years. I had not cast him aside as a terrorist to be ignored. I had not told him to mind his own business when he asked about Worcester and my background. I had not brushed him aside, knowing he was testing me, calculating my reactions. This whole business was more complex than I had imagined. I laughed and said out aloud, 'Ja, not a matter of black and white.'

It was another long weekend, a holiday, and on the Monday Munro asked me again to work in B section. It was the same greeting as before, a simple, polite good morning and good night. Before the end of the third day Munro called me into his office, in the administration block, the first offices inside the front gate, and informed me I was to start my assigned duties as a censor officer next morning.

'I must also tell you that it is the practice here on Robben Island that every second weekend you must work as an ordinary warder here in B section.' When I raised my eyebrows in surprise, he continued: 'Ja, Gregory, it is normal practice here, but I feel that as the censor officer dealing with these people, you should not be booked at a particular post or anything. I would like you to handle any visits these Poqo have. Just be there in case you are needed.'

I nodded and realised that I was to be treated differently.

The main correctional services offices were located, not at the prison itself, but a mile away, close to the small town which is the warders' community. Here were the main administration offices and facilities such as single warders' accommodation, officers' club and restaurant.

I was to share an office with two other men, Pogard and Jordaan, like me, censor officers. As I entered that first morning I was greeted by Pogard who said, 'The CO wants to see you first.'

The chief officer, Colonel Piet Badenhorst, I heard later was nicknamed 'Kid Ruction' by the prisoners. I was to learn that Badenhorst was a man who represented the toughest and most extreme views towards both his warders and inmates alike. The only time he dealt with a prisoner was when he meted out his punishments: isolation, loss of food, strait-jackets, loss of privileges, strip searches.

The CO's office was across the small verandah and at the end of three similarly sized offices. As I entered, he was sitting, staring out of the window.

I was introduced by his secretary who went out, leaving the Colonel and me alone together. He sat, leaning back in his chair, almost sniffing me, looking me up and down.

After several minutes he began. 'Gregory, welcome to *die Eiland*.' There was a smirk across his face. 'I, too, am new here, so we will learn this job together, eh?'

I stood, hands clasped behind my back, staring ahead, military fashion.

He continued. 'You know what your job is.'

I was uncertain if it was a question or a statement, so I replied, 'Yes, sir, I do.'

'So what is it?' There was a hiss from his voice.

'Censoring, sir.'

'No, Gregory, your job here is to demoralise these people. Go and do it for our race, for the white people whose country this is.'

'Sir, what do you mean?'

The snarl. 'You know exactly what I fucking well mean. You may leave.'

Chapter 12

Brutality

The holiday was over. Pogard, the warder in charge of the censor's office, was an irascible Afrikaner who hated not only blacks and coloureds, but virtually everyone else with whom he came into contact.

Each day the mail would arrive by boat from Cape Town and we would open and read each and every letter. It was the same with letters being sent from the prison. We had to read every one. The difficulty, as I saw it, was despite having done my stint at the training centre at Kroonstad, I had not been instructed in censorship.

I knew life was not going to be easy from the first morning when, after introducing me to my colleagues, Pogard just nodded his head and carried on working. Jordaan, at least, had the courtesy to shake hands and invite me for a cup of tea. I had also been told by Munro that Pogard was due for retirement and that was the reason why I had been recruited specially for the job.

'Don't mind him, he's just a miserable old bastard who won't be here much longer,' Jordaan told me. 'He's got a chip on his shoulder about the world, so it's not something against you personally. Just ignore him.'

But it wasn't easy ignoring someone who was to be my supervising officer, the person who would, supposedly, teach me my new job.

When I was given a desk and chair, complete with telephone, I waited for Pogard to take charge, to give me instruction.

Eventually I had to take matters into my own hands, having sat staring into space for more than half an hour.

'Ja, excuse me, Mr Pogard, can you tell me what I should be doing please?' A fair enough question I considered, given the circumstances.

The reply was barely above a snarl. 'Read the blerrie Bible.'

I was nonplussed. 'Excuse me?'

'I told you boy, read the Bible and don't come back asking me about anything more for the next two weeks. Then I'll ask you questions about it and heaven help you if you get anything wrong.' He continued to mutter to himself as I spread my hands wide in questioning wonder towards Jordaan who was sitting watching this bizarre interchange with a sly smile.

Jordaan came to my rescue when it became clear Pogard had no more to say. 'He means the B-orders, we call them the Bible in here. You'll have to sit and read them all over the next two weeks.'

'Where is the Bible, sorry the B-file?' My heart was sinking faster than my enthusiasm for this place.

Jordaan pointed it out, a thick, brown-covered file containing thousands of papers, each of them clipped inside.

'Here, man, welcome to the Bible. Enjoy the reading. The plot's a bit thin, but you'll welcome getting to the end.' Jordaan was enjoying his fun at my expense.

The Bible, or the B-orders book, was a thick manual which was continuously updated by addendums from Pretoria which either increased the existing orders, or rescinded them and replaced them with a new order.

The manual was split into four different sections, A to D, dealing with personnel, discipline, finances and logistics.

Jordaan told me that I was required to know all about section B, the area dealing with discipline, particularly where it related to censorship. I went through every file, reading and re-reading the orders. Many of them I had read before as part of the written examinations taken at Kroonstad. Three days later I'd had enough.

I turned to Pogard on the fourth morning, the Friday. 'Look, I have been through this book so many times now. What is for me now?'

Pogard had just come in and was caught off-guard by this request. His view was that a newcomer was there to be spoken to, not to ask questions and put his own views across. Typically he had come in his normal miserable self without so much as a good morning to Jordaan or myself. He was standing beside his desk, unpacking his pack of sandwiches – we called them his 10 o'clock sandwiches because on the strike of 10 every morning he put the first one into his mouth.

'Read them again. And when you've finished read them again. If you have any questions read them again and keep reading them until you have answered all your own questions. I said two weeks reading them, I mean two weeks.'

When a letter was written by a prisoner it was recorded on a file index, as were all letters received. It was a system similar for visitors where each prisoner's visitor was logged: name, date and time. It meant that the many complaints of letters going astray were dealt with immediately. We could say if, and when, a letter was received or written and what had happened to it.

The procedure in the office was very simple. The letters came, they were censored, that is either cut or blackened out, they were recorded and they were either posted or handed over. There was nothing complicated about the job itself; the only complication was in deciding what should be in a letter and what should not. And when there was difficulty, we referred to the B-orders which stated clearly that politics and news from outside was strictly forbidden. I was to realise the thinking behind these orders: to keep these Poqo isolated, from their homes, from their families, from the outside world. This was isolation. As I read the B-orders, I considered them more than fair. It was right these people should be punished this way; they were terrorists. I was to spend years following this path blindly, cutting and ensuring that the isolation was as complete as I could make it. If there was news from outside, or if a prisoner tried to write anything about conditions in the prison – treatment, food, clothing or that type of thing – I simply deleted it. At that time on Robben Island, they were allowed one letter every six months, but later on conditions improved. For instance by the time Mandela got to Pollsmoor in 1982, he was allowed five letters a month, in and out and, if he did not receive a visit, he could have two extra letters.

At that time Pogard, Jordaan and I were responsible for all the political prisoners from the various groups: the ANC, the PAC, Swapo, the Black Consciousness Movement and the Black Liberation Movement.

Each prisoner was classified by the prison service as belonging to one of four categories: A, B, C or D, with A being the highest classification which allows most privileges and D being the lowest with the least privileges. When prisoners first entered the system they were all classified as D category, it did not matter who they were or what their crime was, and so all political prisoners, or what Pretoria then described as 'security prisoners' were all automatically classified as D on admission. The privileges affected by

105

such classification included visits and letters, studies, where they were kept and the opportunities to buy groceries and any personal items. I knew the prisoners' attitudes to the classification process: they hated it, claiming it took years before they earned the A classification. Certainly, as I got to know the Poqo better, I realised they wanted a prison system with just one category.

Every six months a prisoner was called before the prisons' institutional board which reviewed all classifications. The board was meant to assess the individual behaviour of each prisoner and consider them for an up-grading of their classification. However, with the Poqo, the reality of the situation was that the board was a political tribunal which tried to get information out of each prisoner about their own particular group.

By the time I arrived on Robben Island Mandela and the other men from the Rivonia trial had already served two years of their life sentence. Their pattern of existence, for that was what it had become, was already well set. They had formed themselves into their own internal organisation as the leader group. I learned over a number of years that the group was sometimes referred to as the High Command or the High Organ. It consisted of the most senior ANC leaders on the island, the men who had, at one time or another, been on the ANC National Executive: Walter Sisulu, Govan Mbeki, Raymond Mhlaba and Nelson Mandela. Although the High Organ could no longer have a direct effect upon the ANC's external policy since it was so far removed from its grass-roots, it still played an influential role in the life within prison. It was a role which continually grew as the numbers of ANC activists and members imprisoned swelled. The High Organ was to play a large role in encouraging and helping young ANC men, many of whom had been without formal education, to spend the years of incarceration studying for higher education, diplomas and degrees. In the years that followed, Robben Island was often referred to as either 'the university', or 'Mandela's university'.

I was also to learn of how the composition of the High Organ – Sisulu, Mbeki, Mhlaba and Mandela – was a source of controversy among the black ranks. All four men were of Xhosa background and it encouraged the growing accusations, particularly from other black races within the ANC, that the leadership was almost exclusively Xhosa-dominated. It was the reason why, in later years, Ahmed Kathrada, a member of Durban's Indian community, popularly known as Kathy, was drafted on to the High Organ, as was Laloo Chiba of the PAC.

In the role I played as censor officer I was to have more contact with the Poqo than virtually any other person within the system.

As D category prisoners each was entitled to have only one visitor and write and receive only one letter every six months. This was the single most controversial aspect of their incarceration for the prisoners. They all viewed it as an inhuman rule, which affected not only their own psyche but also their families. Visits and letters were restricted to what was described as 'first-degree' relatives, and herein lay a problem, for the Afrikaner meaning of 'immediate family' differs greatly from the African sense. African family structures are larger and more inclusive with anyone who claims to come from a common ancestor deemed to be part of the same family.

The mail call took place once a month and as the day approached I could see a change in prisoners' attitudes. Even though a person could only receive one letter every six months their own personal anticipation increased as each month went by until they had missed five in a row. It created an unnecessary tension which I firmly believed only made looking after them more difficult.

The treatment of the prisoners was harsh. I knew it would be. I'd heard all the stories before I arrived. Although I did not have daily contact with them I would ride down from the administration office every day to pick up the mail. At the time I had an old bicycle, falling apart: it was barely two wheels, a saddle and frame. It did not have brakes and in order to stop it I had to put my shoe against the side wall of the tyre to slow it down. I had the bike painted a gold colour. Each day I would ride from the administration building in the centre to the prison. Knowing the High Organ were among the prisoners assigned to work in the quarry, sweating as they were forced to dig the limestone, I would take a detour and watch them. I was always fascinated by the leader group, this High Organ, as they worked. In the old days the blacks had short moleskin trousers and sandals with a khaki shirt. Later, in winter, they were also given a moleskin jacket and shoes.

I'd heard the stories of the brutality and maybe it was a morbid curiosity that drew me to the quarry. It was situated towards the middle of the island, about ten minutes' walk from the outer walls of the prison. My appearance would often attract the attention of the other warders who were patrolling the perimeters, all of them heavily armed, several of them holding their large dogs on leashes. The noise of the quarrying, the chipping, smashing and grunting, rose from what was literally just an open hole in the ground. The limestone dug out each day was used to build the roads and paths around the island. The quarry acted like a large echo chamber and, as I rested from my bike ride, I would hear the Poqo singing songs of protest in their own language which went way over the heads of the Afrikaner guards who had no idea what the words meant. Initially I found it disconcerting, but soon I came to be amused by the ingenuity they showed as they sang. They ensured that whatever the demands placed on them by the warders, some of whom were still appallingly violent, they would only ever work at their own pace. I could hear from the songs they sang in Xhosa how they would help everyone in the quarry to work at a consistent pace. One of their songs translated into English as 'The white man's work is never finished, hold your knees, hold your knees'. The meaning of 'hold your knees' was to go slower.

Each day the leader group was paired off in the prison section and chained together by the ankle before being marched off to the quarry. Although the distance was little more than 600 yards, it often took more than fifteen minutes for the slow shuffling span to reach it. Once inside the quarry the shackles were removed for the day's work. The sound most often heard from the quarry was the voices of the guards. 'Werk, man, werk,' they cried in Afrikaans.

Often when I stopped in the quarry after my ride, I would be perspiring from the heat. Down there, stuck in that hole in the ground, however, the temperature was even more intense. I was always thankful I never had to go into that hole, a veritable furnace. In summer the walls deflected any cooling breeze sweeping in off the ocean. Not only were they being burned from above by the sun, but also within the quarry where the sun's glare rebounded off the white stone, reflecting into their eyes and burning them. Years later the effects of the quarrying would leave virtually every one of them with impaired or damaged eyesight. All the warders working in the quarry wore dark glasses. The prisoners were not allowed them, although they demanded them on a regular basis. The lime was soft, but in between there were hard layers of rock. The prisoners had picks and they had to chip and hack their way through the hard layers to reach the limestone. As the lime was chopped out, it was carted to another area of the quarry where other workers used hammers to smash it into smaller powdery pieces. I think they worked for two or three days with the pick before changing over to the hammers to smash the lime. It was hard labour, but at that time I had little sympathy for these men; my attitude was firm and unyielding.

For a time, when there were severe staff shortages on Robben Island, I was ordered to work at the stone quarry every Monday and Tuesday as well as every second weekend. It did not matter that I was attached to the censor office. We all had to take our turn at weekends, but these extra two days a week were additional. I was invariably attached to the guards who took prisoners to the stone quarry. The inmates assigned to this quarry were all those classified as D or C, except for the leader group who were, of course, always classified D.

At the time there were two warders, Du Plessis and Delport, who had terrible reputations for the way they treated the prisoners.

Many times I witnessed verbal abuse; swearing and shouting at black prisoners. 'You blerrie kaffir, you're a lazy fucking shit, your mother is a bitch.' It was the language of every day. The work was heavy and demanding. Whenever a prisoner stood up to stretch his aching back he was subjected to the most appalling verbal abuse.

On one occasion when I was guarding the quarry Delport was in charge. He had already taken a dislike to me and whenever I was sent to the quarry to help him guard it, he virtually treated me like a prisoner, confining me to a guard post all day long. Once when I was thirsty I climbed down from the post, about twenty feet, to get a drink. Before I had taken two sips of the brackish water from the tap, Delport was on me, shoving and pushing.

'What the hell do you think you're doing,' he demanded.

'I'm thirsty and need a drink,' I replied.

'Fuck you, you're as bad as the kaffirs here. Get the hell back to your post or I'll charge you with insubordination and leaving your post without permission.'

I returned, angry at Delport's attitude. On another occasion after he had been screaming and swearing all day, he refused to allow the prisoners to finish at the normal time of 4 o'clock.

'No, fuck all you kaffirs, you're all lazy. You haven't done enough work today. You'll stay until I decide you've done enough.'

It also meant that the guards had to remain as well while Delport sat watching the prisoners for a further four hours' toil until it grew dark shortly before 8 o'clock.

The route from the prison to the quarries was along a narrow pathway which was covered over with a high-wire tunnel. Some of the warders walked along on the outside of the tunnel, carrying their rifles. Behind the prisoners came the dog handlers with the snarling, snapping German shepherds. Once the dog handlers ordered the prisoners to run to their cells, but their heavy ankle shackles impeded them. The warders shouted they should run or face the dogs. Inevitably in the haste of trying to run with chains several people fell, and this in turn pulled down others, so that it led to a number of people being trampled. Those who did not run were set on by the dogs, and badly bitten.

An outrageous incident that happened just before I arrived on the island went around the entire prison service within days of it occurring. It was considered a great joke by the other warders. The story went that the warder who was working in the quarry area – the older of the two Kleinhans brothers – was approached by a prisoner, Guni Gunglovu, who asked if he could have a drink of water as he was very thirsty. Kleinhans began by berating Gunglovu and ordered him to dig a hole five feet deep in the ground. Once the prisoner had completed the hole, Kleinhans then told him to stand in it as other prisoners filled the hole with soil, up to Gunglovu's neck. At that point Kleinhans then urinated on the prisoner's head, and laughingly told him, 'Here, you said you were thirsty, drink that, it's the finest whisky.' It was disgusting and degrading, but Kleinhans laughed and jeered as he did it.

There was a bull of a warder called Opperman, who was always beating prisoners. When prisoners stopped to have something to eat at lunch-time, he would stand beside them and urinate, splashing his urine into their food, then order them to continue eating.

Night-time searches took place frequently during the winter when temperatures plummeted to way below zero. The cold was worsened by the driving winds which whipped off the ocean and the damp which invariably accompanied it. Whenever searches were ordered, it was usually close to midnight. Everyone would be ordered out of their cells, stark naked, and made to stand against the wall. The warders would deliberately take their time searching each and every cell, looking for scraps of paper or written notes. Sometimes the prisoners would have to stand for several hours, not daring to move for fear of being beaten up.

At the time any complaints from Mandela and the others fell on deaf ears. All complaints went through the commanding officer,

Colonel Piet Badenhorst, the man I'd met when I first arrived. Badenhorst had a fearsome reputation for being one of the most brutal and authoritarian men in the entire prison service. According to tradition, the commanding officer was supposed to visit the prison at least once a day. We hardly ever saw Badenhorst at the prison; he was off doing his own thing. Badenhorst had a hatred of blacks and a contempt for the job. Many times I watched him standing in the bar getting drunk, cursing all the 'fucking kaffirs', and in the same breath cursing the government and the prison authorities.

'I don't give a fuck what they think in Pretoria,' he often proclaimed. 'I don't need their fucking job.' According to Badenhorst, his family were wealthy and owned several farms.

'If those fuck-heads in Pretoria want to sack me, let them. I couldn't care less.'

Badenhorst gathered around him all the hard-heads and extremists who wanted to turn the clock back to the early 1960s, the worst days of violence on the island.

Just after he arrived he had a confrontation with Mandela, who was working in the quarry at the time. I heard about it later. The day of his arrival he pulled his car up at the entrance of the quarry and, knowing of Mandela's reputation, bellowed out at him: 'Mandela, jy moet jou vinger uit jou gat trek.' It meant, 'Mandela, pull your finger out of your arse.' I was told that the phrase incensed Mandela who started towards the cackling Badenhorst, who then turned on his heel and drove off in his car.

Within minutes of leaving the quarry, Badenhorst had ordered a lorry to the work-site, to pick up the prisoners and transport them back to the cells' area where they were to be lined up in the courtyard.

There, they were confronted by Badenhorst, pacing up and down, swiping his swagger stick against the neatly pressed uniformed trousers. As usual he was swearing: every sentence, every phrase contained invective and oaths. His favourite phrase, which was repeated a hundred times a day, was 'Jou ma se moer', your mother is a moer. Moer was a term for a potato seed as well as a colloquial term for an intimate part of a female's anatomy.

In his guttural voice Badenhorst told the prisoners he had been disgusted at the laziness he had observed at the quarry and, as a result, he was arbitrarily dropping all classifications by one notch. A number of the men already in the B section at that time had been designated C category, allowing them to begin studies, a valued privilege not permitted to D-category prisoners. When I heard about the incident later it was clear to me Badenhorst had deliberately sought out Mandela at the quarry and was looking for the slightest provocation to dish out his own brand of punishment.

On one occasion I was with Badenhorst when he visited B section. He ordered every prisoner to be locked in his cell as he prowled the passages of the section. I watched him wander down through the cells, picking on prisoners and giving each a blast of his favourite phrase, knowing he would always get blacks to react when their mother's name was insulted.

'Jou ma se moer,' he would say. And, invariably, he would get a reaction and order further punishment, a loss of meals or privileges. He would then turn to the two or three warders who were with him and boast, 'See, what did I tell you, man, these fucking kaffirs haven't got the sense not to respond. I tell them their mother is a moer and it's enough to set them off.'

Badenhorst was to provide his own downfall in early 1972 after he had a series of meetings with the leader group who had threatened work stoppages, go-slows, even hunger strikes to try to prevent the harsh withdrawal of all privileges. Badenhorst had just laughed in the prisoners' faces, telling them that he didn't care what they threatened, he was the boss and he was not prepared to listen to them. But at this time a delegation of judges had arrived from the Cape Provincial Division of the Supreme Court. Justices Jan Steyn, M. E. Theron and Michael Corbett accompanied by the Commissioner of Prisons, General Steyn, arrived to inspect the facility. Knowing the high-powered delegation was expected, Mandela had been selected by his colleagues to address them about the prisoners' concerns. At first the three judges asked Mandela if he wished to speak to them in private, but Mandela, standing upright and assured, told them it would not be necessary.

He spoke clearly in his stern voice. 'In fact I shall be only too pleased to have both General Steyn and Colonel Badenhorst here as I address you on some of our concerns. As you might expect, many of our complaints relate directly to the general state of our imprisonment here and it is only right they should be here to reply to those criticisms.'

The statement from Mandela was surprising and Badenhorst and General Steyn looked at one another in astonishment.

Mandela recounted a number of recent assaults in the general section as well as the unfair loss of privileges in B section. He mentioned a number of beatings and how the viciousness was

112

often covered up by brutal guards. He turned to Badenhorst and added that whenever prisoners tried to complain of the brutality, the commanding officer refused to listen.

Badenhorst was fuming and, ignoring the presence of the three judges as well as the commissioner of prisons, demanded, 'Mandela, have you ever witnessed any of these assaults in the general section?' The question was as ridiculous as it was invalid, knowing that Mandela was in a different section.

Mandela retorted: 'No, I have not, as you well know. However I am certain they have occurred because I have been told of them by people I trust to tell me the truth.'

Badenhorst was now sweating and I almost expected him to use his '*Jou ma se moer*' insult. Instead he went up and stood very close to Mandela and thrust his finger in his face and hissed, 'Be careful, Mandela. If you talk about things you haven't seen you will get yourself into trouble. You know what I mean?'

Badenhorst had fallen into Mandela's trap this time. Ignoring the threats, Mandela turned to the judges and said, 'Gentlemen, you can see for yourselves the sort of man we are dealing with as commanding officer. If he can threaten me here, in your presence, you can imagine what he does when you are not here.'

Judge Corbett suddenly spoke up and declared, 'The prisoner is right. Now we shall listen with fresh ears to whatever complaints you have.'

Mandela had achieved a great victory and began listing all the complaints about diet, work and studying as well as loss of privileges. Within three months Badenhorst was removed from his post.

There were others, men who had apparently joined the prison service because it gave them an opportunity to vent their racist anger on black prisoners. Not all were Afrikaners. There was a British guy, a man called Suddaby who had, at one time, been in the Royal Navy. By the time I arrived on Robben Island Suddaby had been there many years. He was one of the old school who believed in violent means to contain prisoners. When he was duty officer, one of his roles was to interview each prisoner to ask if they had any complaints. I was on duty in B section on several occasions when he was the duty officer. His arrival was announced by a ringing of the bell, a signal for every prisoner to prepare for inspection, almost military-style. At the entrance to each section the warders stood, rigid to attention, waiting for Suddaby. He strolled in and asked the warders if the 'kaffir prisoners' were behaving themselves. Invariably the warder, falling in with Suddaby's attitude, replied that they were not. Suddaby then shouted out, 'Three meals'. It meant that everyone in the section lost their next three meals. No reason given, just an arbitrary punishment on a whim.

When he went to the office to listen to individual complaints Suddaby had every prisoner line up in the passageway. I was usually with him as he sat in his office. One day I recall he lost his temper and ordered me out to 'tell those kaffir bastards to keep quiet'.

I went into the passage and told them, 'Captain Suddaby says you must keep quiet, you are disturbing him.' I returned to the office.

Once again the sound of talking came up from the line of waiting prisoners. It was normal chatter, not exceptionally loud. The next moment he jumped up and stormed into the passage.

'Listen, you lot of black bastards. You can't do as you are ordered. You should have been shot, all of you, and your damn parents should have been charged for the bullets.' I was shocked at the insult and was not surprised that the line of forty men simply turned their backs and filed out of the passage; their complaints could wait. Whenever they heard Suddaby was the duty officer in charge of listing complaints they never again appeared before him. He was now being snubbed.

Chapter 13

The beginning
of knowledge

The process of getting to know the men in B section had started that very first weekend when John Ferris had spoken to me about my time in Worcester. It was deepened first through reading the letters which passed through my hands and then, after the first few months, through the weekend work when I was assigned to the section. In many ways it was these weekends which were to be the important building blocks for later relationships. There were times when the harshness of working in the quarries was slightly more relaxed and times when the prisoners wanted to engage in conversation. It was clear from the very early stages that every one in the section knew my role was that of censor. It was a controversial role which had caused more anger than any other fact, even the brutality. The prisoners' letters were a contact point with their families and loved ones. To have them ripped to shreds was as dehumanising as it was unfair.

After Pogard left the censor section, we were joined by another new man, Kernekamp, who came to us from the Eastern Cape.

Initially my contact with the leader group was through Ferris, but then, gradually, they each came and greeted me.

Initially my contact with Mandela was intermittent. I knew who he was, just as I knew the other prisoners who had been highly publicised. In the beginning we had a passing contact.

Whenever I showed up in the section at weekends there was always a polite, 'Good morning, Mr Gregory'. I always returned the greeting and found myself giving the Zulu greeting, 'I see you'. Over weeks, months, the greeting became more, a smile, a gesture, in the evening on departure, a farewell, 'Have a good night's rest'.

Often the prisoners would challenge me about a letter, asking why they had not received one. It would not be unusual for a person to claim during a visit his visitor had told him that he or she had written three letters, none of which he had received. I always promised to investigate the claim and get back to them. From those early days I endeavoured to ensure that any letter which came was properly logged: I did not want to be accused of throwing away letters or not passing them on. So a system was started of logging every letter, when it was posted, when it arrived, who sent it and whom it was for. There was also a notation against any censorship. If a letter was considered too political it was logged as 'kept on file'. If that was the case I ensured that the prisoner who had been due to receive the letter was informed of the decision to keep it on file.

I soon realised that many of the visitors were not always telling the truth about writing letters. They claimed to have sent a letter, sometimes two or three and they never arrived. For whatever reason those letters never reached Robben Island. Either the letter had been intercepted by the security forces or the person was not telling the truth.

Prisoners in B section would also ask if I'd received a request for a visit from a family member. During my lunch period I would go and check against the list for an application. This always opened me to ridicule from the other warders who felt I should not tell the prisoners anything. And certainly never in my own time. It was doing the kaffirs a favour, and it wasn't our job, they argued.

'Greg, man, let those kaffir bastards wait,' they would say. When I ignored the warders, they laughed and told me I was becoming the prisoners' houseboy. I tried to reason with them that keeping an accurate record of what was going on was making my job easier.

It was recommended in the rules that the only times we should talk to the prisoners was when we wanted them to do something. Social contact was not recommended. But common sense prevailed; there was no reason why I should not be civil to these people. I had expected something very different from what I was experiencing. Maybe, in my head, I'd expected terrorists coming out of the bush with a spear or gun in their hands. I expected them to be snarling and cursing me. I was wrong, as wrong as was possible to be. These men were educated, more educated than we whites who were guarding them. They had degrees coming out of their ears. More than that, they were polite and they were, despite the appalling conditions in which they found themselves, remarkably good-humoured. I was never treated as 'the enemy', or as a white man who had to be punished. I was the prison officer who happened to censor their letters and visits, and when I gave them truthful, honest answers they accepted them.

The more I realised that these were cultured people, the more I was drawn to Mandela, so obviously the main man, the leader of the ANC. This was the man I had considered to be the most terrible terrorist of all not long before. It was not as if I'd had some 'road to Damascus' conversion, it was more a simple fact that my preconceptions were wrong. It did not take me long to figure that out. And once I'd accepted that my preconceptions were wrong, I had to replace them with ideas which were realistic. Take away a man's beliefs and they must be replaced by new ones; there is no place for a vacuum inside a mind.

The weekends spent in the prison gave me access to these Poqo and I was determined to understand them. I spent my time, much as my first days, walking round the courtyard, lapping it, as a long-distance runner would a track. Sometimes I walked with Mandela, sometimes Sisulu, Ferris, Mac Marahaj or Kathrada, sometimes alone.

With Mandela I was always curious. 'How can you behave like this when you're facing a life sentence?'

'What do you mean?' His voice was always the same; deep, resonant with a slow awkwardness that almost seemed to suggest he was picking his way carefully through the language.

'This.' I would indicate the yard and the men in groups, some talking, others smiling and engaging in conversations. 'This, here, where it is obvious your morale is high and your support for one another is total. Even joining me here to talk. You show no hatred, no animosity. How can this be?'

Mandela began to examine what I had expected, and delved into my preconceptions. When I told him my feelings – that before I arrived I believed that they were all terrorists who should have been hanged – he considered this view.

He would spend hours discussing the merits of why he should have been hanged and why he should not. He never once told me I was wrong and that my preconceptions were wrong. Instead, he directed his conversation to the processes which had led me to those feelings. Often we would talk all morning and I would hardly notice the time had flown by. I was actually now looking forward to the weekend duty to spend time talking with these men. On occasions we would go into his cell, or to the office. Whenever we went into the office I invited him to sit down. He expressed surprise the first time, saying that he had never before been invited to sit down in the office.

Walking in the yard he explained, 'A life sentence is not a matter

117

of curling up and dying. We are not criminals, we are here for a cause. That cause is to free our people and to free our country.'

I would always argue, 'Yes, but with violent means.'

We would range back to Sharpeville in 1960, which was the first point of contact I'd really had with the violent struggle. Mandela asked me what I knew of Sharpeville. I told him what our teachers had told us: the blacks were coming in revolt, that they wanted to overthrow the government, but the police got to hear of the plans and shot the trouble-makers. We never had arguments about our different perceptions. Instead, we would listen to one another's beliefs, first mine, then Mandela's.

Over the weeks and months I have to admit I found the time in their company illuminating. Mainly it was Mandela. He would say: 'When you consider the position of the black man in South Africa you have to try and imagine how you would feel if you were in our position. It is not a matter of rolling over. Ask yourself how you would deal with the position if you were black.

'We are not criminals, we have a cause and we believe that cause is to free the country of persecution.'

We would talk of the pass laws, the curfew laws, the Bantustans. 'Those are the things that make the blacks angry; that is why we are in here now.'

We discussed the history of the ANC, how it had started in 1912 and how it was entirely peaceful. 'Our people went to the government and pleaded with them to talk and come to a fair settlement of the problems that were afflicting us all, the land rights and so forth. We wrote letters to the government, to the State President, but never got a reply. We were ignored, snubbed. We always sought a peaceful solution.'

Mandela began to direct my thoughts back to my childhood. 'Remember when you were young, growing up with blacks, did you ever see them as warriors or as people who wanted to live a decent life where they had enough food and property to look after their families?'

I considered the question often and talked of how I believed the Zulus I had known were fundamentally peace-loving, interested only in providing for their families. The only time in their history when they became warriors was when they were threatened by rival tribes, be they black or white.

Mandela continued, 'So, consider the problem of the ANC, who started as long ago as 1912 asking for equality and an equal voice.

118

From 1912 to 1960 is a long, long time and they were dealing with a white government which was heavily armed and becoming more extreme with each passing year. They had introduced laws which discriminated against all blacks. We were no longer free men in our own land, they didn't want to give us the time of day. What course was left to us?'

I would always argue the white point of view. 'Ja, but we were told, and we could see, that the blacks wanted a revolution, they wanted to overthrow the white government. We, as whites, were facing an increasing onslaught where terrorist acts were being carried out, people were being shot, bombs set off, killing innocent people.

'At school our teachers told us that the plan of the ANC was to destroy the white man. If there was a bomb blast in Port Elizabeth or Johannesburg or Pretoria, they would explain that it was part of the black tactic to take our land, the land earned by the blood of our forefathers.'

This argument went over and over again, but centred on this one theme, our differing interpretation of history.

I then decided to seek outside opinion, to research the question myself. When I had a day off I would catch the ferry to the city and head for the main library in Wale Street. I needed to know what the history books stated in relation to the ANC and the blacks and how Mandela had interpreted them. I had to know the truth about the motive behind this argument which I had heard. What was driving these people? I had to know who was right and who was not. I knew I had to face these people, I had to understand them. It was a decision which would begin my conversion and change my life irrevocably.

It was usually on a Friday, every second week, when I took Gloria and the children to the mainland where they would go shopping or visit my in-laws. I would excuse myself and head for the reference library where I wanted to read many of the books which were banned from sale in ordinary shops. I explained to the librarian that I was a prison warder from Robben Island studying for a history degree and that was why I needed the books.

The library was typically quiet and frequented by a number of young university students. The more I read, the more I was fascinated and intrigued. I began to delve into the background of the ANC, reading first their Freedom Charter. As I read it I wondered how many other whites in South Africa had actually taken the time to read it. It read:

We the people of South Africa declare for our country and the world to know:

That South Africa belongs to all who live in it, black and white, and that no government can justly claim authority unless is it based on the will of all the people;

That our people have been robbed of their birthright to land, liberty and peace by a form of government founded on injustice and inequality and that our country will never be prosperous or free until all our people live in brotherhood;

That only a democratic state can secure all their birthright without distinction of colour, race, sex or belief.

And therefore we, the people of South Africa, black and white together, equals, countrymen and brothers, adopt this Freedom Charter: The People shall govern!

Every man and woman shall have a right to vote. All national groups shall have equal rights!

All apartheid laws and practices shall be set aside: The People shall share in the country's wealth!

The mineral wealth beneath the soil, the banks and monopoly industry shall be transferred to the ownership of the people. All other industry shall be controlled: The land shall be shared among those who work it!

All the land shall be re-divided to banish famine and land-hunger. All shall have the right to occupy land wherever they choose: All shall be equal before the law!

No one shall be imprisoned, deported or restricted without a fair trial: All shall enjoy equal human rights!

All shall be free to travel from countryside to towns and from South Africa abroad; pass laws, permits and all other laws shall be abolished: There shall be work and security! The doors of learning shall be opened! There shall be houses, security and comfort! There shall be peace and friendship!

Let all who love their people and their country now say as we say here: Those freedoms we shall fight for, side by side, throughout our lives, until we have won our liberty!

I read and re-read the Freedom Charter and while I thought there were a number of areas which were naive or economically flawed, such as nationalisation of industries and occupation of land, I could identify its fundamental fairness and thought it was a sound tenet for the future.

Each time I spent a day in the library I would return to the island

120

even more intrigued by what I had read. I was developing an appetite to learn about this part of my country's history. When my family asked me where I had been I made an excuse, telling them I had been to the bioscope, the cinema, to see a film. For some reason that I could not explain to myself I was coy about my research and what lay behind it.

Over the coming weeks I read about the Bantu Authorities Act, the law which had resulted in indirect rule from the government in Pretoria through subservient black chiefs who did what they were told. I was astonished to read that the Bantustans represented only thirteen per cent of the country's whole area. Tied into this legislation was the Group Areas Act whereby eighty-seven per cent of the country was given to less than twenty per cent of the population. I began to see Mandela's point, that this was a cynically unjust law. There were no two ways about it.

I read about the Suppression of Communism Act. Commies were every white person's fear: along with the invasion of blacks would come the commies. How many times had I heard of the South African Communist Party and the ANC being lumped together. Without one there was no other. They were both hell-bent on taking over the country. As I read the Act I began to detect the authorities' paranoia which seeped into every sentence.

I read, too, that the concept of apartheid claimed not to have the intention of generating racial strife and hatred. It used fancy terminology: 'Separate Development, Plural Democracy, Self-Determination'. But whichever phrase was used to describe it, there was no getting away from the fact that apartheid was simply a vehicle for creating division and hate.

Then came the Native Urban Areas Act, the legislation which allowed enforced removal of blacks into locations outside towns: the birth of the shanty towns, the squatter camps, the appalling mile upon mile of cardboard, flattened tin and shacks – a natural breeding ground for discontent and crime.

This was followed by the pass laws, the method of controlling labour. What other country in the world would insist that its citizens could not go out and look for a job without the permission of some petty official? And a white official at that? I sat reading the law, shaking my head in disgust. How on earth could our politicians have passed this law and expected it not to have created anger? I wished then I had read it thoroughly before. This was the law which told a black man that in order to get work he needed a permit, a pass. This piece of paper would only be valid for fourteen days and if, in that time, he had not found work, he had to return home. If he did not he faced being jailed. What utter folly, what a waste of time and resources.

There was further madness: the Population Registration Act, the Prohibition of Mixed Marriages Act, the Immorality Act, all legislation which was crudely designed to engineer a nation's population and racial mix. Wasn't that what Hitler had embarked upon? The Separate Amenities Act kept blacks away from the white man's benches, playgrounds, beaches, railway coaches, public buildings, cinemas, bars, hotels, restaurants, libraries, buses – even toilets.

In the history books, which I noted were mostly very dusty and clearly unopened for years, I read with growing distaste of the concept of *Baaskap*, the white man's belief in bosshood, his certainty that he was superior to the black man. I was fascinated by the 1952 Defiance Campaign when hundreds of thousands embarked on Gandhian civil disobedience to throw the government into confusion – for months we had thousands of protesters defying apartheid and curfew and pass laws so as to invite arrest. It led to chaos.

In the Promotion of Bantu Self-Government Act, the legislation talked of a 'higher morality', for the policy of 'Separate Development'. There had been much fanfare at this legislation which was designed, it claimed, to diminish hardship and problems. It proclaimed that this act would provide black homelands for self-government and eventually total independence. This was supposed to be the 'benevolent science of Separate Development'. It sounded fine, but tied in with the population numbers was a crude attempt to shovel more than eighty per cent of the population into thirteen per cent of the land, which in turn was made up of the poorest territory with least potential in terms of natural resources. It was a mirage which any fool could see would merely increase tension. This was not social improvement, it was social cruelty – heartless, callous and downright wrong.

Each time I went to the library I returned more angry than before, angry at being cheated by politicians who lied.

I remembered that as I was growing up there had been a fierce debate at school just before the bloodshed of Sharpeville. It was at the time of the visit of the Prime Minister of Great Britain, Harold Macmillan, to South Africa. I vaguely recalled how he had upset the government of Verwoerd. I sought out the speech.

Macmillan's speech had been a warning ignored. 'The wind of

change is blowing through the continent. Whether we like it or not this growth of national consciousness is a political fact. We must all accept it as a fact. Our national policies must take account of it.'

The third world of emerging nations was trying to choose between the models of the first, free world of the West, and the second, communist world of the East.

He continued: 'We reject the idea of any inherent superiority of one race over another. Our policy is therefore, non-racial. I have thought you would wish me to state plainly and with full candour the policy for which we in Britain stand. It may well be that in trying to do our duty, as we see it, we shall sometimes make difficulties for you. If this proves so, we shall regret it. But I know that even so you would not ask us to flinch from doing our duty. You, too, will do your duty as you see it.'

I then read of Verwoerd's reply, given without notes and impromptu. He made a defence of the white man's right as a European in the minority on the black continent and presented apartheid as a policy 'not at variance with the new direction in Africa, but in the fullest accord with it' – because he was going 'to grant independence to the black homelands, exactly as Britain is doing in her black colonies'. It was a quick-witted, sharp reply which, at the time, white South Africa cheered wildly. I can remember even cheering as we discussed the matter in school. But it had missed out the one aspect which altered the picture radically: it failed to do the simple mathematics which proved the homelands too small for its ever-burgeoning population.

I studied and read until I was certain: I had been deceived in the years of my education. I also felt that these men, Mandela and the others, were possibly right. I would only commit myself then to a possible acceptance. I believed only time would tell.

When I returned to the island I began to see a different man from the one I had met that first time: not a terrorist animal, but a black man with a genuine grievance.

Chapter 14

Letters and visits

I was in a turmoil as I struggled to sort out my confusion and anger. Yes, I had been lied to and deceived, but that had happened before in my life, when my parents had sent me to school. I resolved that I would handle this situation as I had then. I would seek out my truth.

My conversion had begun slowly, prompted by the discussion I'd had with the leader group when I worked in B section, but it was hastened now by my own research. These people I was guarding, these people I'd regarded as terrorists and enemy, were actually telling me the truth.

I began to call Mandela by his first name, Nelson. It seemed less harsh, if not friendly. Then, with a belief that we were no longer enemies, I began to accept him and his ANC comrades without actually realising it.

Each time I returned from the library I was anxious to meet Nelson or any of the other leader group: I was, after all, set on my own educational learning curve.

On my weekend duty I would invariably invite Nelson into the office and begin straight away: 'Tell me more about the ANC, what is the attitude to the Bantu Authorities Act?' I would listen, occasionally asking questions and Nelson would speak, without putting over a heavy political dogma, but with conviction and rational logic. Without ever admitting it I knew that my barriers, built up by years of indoctrination and hatred, were being demolished by sound good sense and truth.

I never set out with a determination that I would bend the prison rules or allow the prisoners favours which were at variance with my duties, but I subtly began to discover that the rules were themselves open to interpretation.

As I have said, one of the most sensitive areas in the prison was letters. So, whenever I received a letter from a prisoner which had

125

to be posted to a family member and I saw it contained material that would have to be censored, I would withhold it until I was back on duty at the weekend and meet the person who wrote the letter. At first they would be angry that the letter had been delayed.

'No, man, don't be angry. I have done this to assist you,' I explained. I would then point out the section or passages which would have to be censored.

I would tell the prisoner to rewrite the offending paragraph or passage and to leave out certain parts and it would be posted. I always knew that the security services were almost certainly monitoring the letters once I had posted them, so I had to ensure that I did not allow blatantly political material to slip through. Often, in the early days, there were those who would refuse to change the letter by rewriting it and I would shrug my shoulders and tell them it would not be posted, but would be placed on file. Often the rewriting of letters took several days and I would spend my lunch-times in the section. It was the same with letters I received for the prisoners. If a letter was to be heavily censored with the majority of it being cut, I would, as a courtesy, go and see the individual prisoner involved and explain the situation. I would tell them, 'If you want you can have the letter, but it will be badly cut, perhaps almost all of it. If you prefer, the letter can be left on file and maybe, at some time in the future when things change, you can have the letter in its entirety.'

Many of them simply told me, 'Go ahead and cut it. I would like to receive whatever is left anyway.' That response always saddened me because I knew that with a maximum of one letter every six months they were desperate for virtually anything from outside. If a letter was placed on file I always made sure that the prisoner knew who the sender had been. I knew the rules were inhuman, and I was trying my own way of getting the best out of the situation. I have to admit that it was not really viewed that way by the prisoners who all felt anger at the censorship.

I knew the censorship laws were harsh and wrong. I could see little harm in allowing in a lot of the details which were supposed to be cut. But, equally, I also knew that the longer I stayed in the job the more I would be able to manipulate it to my own way of thinking. I often felt that the best way was to have the letter placed on file and for the prisoner then to begin a campaign of applying to, or even pestering, senior officers, up to the commanding officer, for the letter.

When I first arrived on the island I found the other censor

officers actually throwing away letters which they deemed to be against the rules. I watched on several occasions one of the others reading a letter which had come in and when they got to a part which was at all political, they would crumple the entire letter and throw it away.

That angered me and I had several rows with the other two censors, Jordaan and Pogard, pointing out to them that they were breaking the law. I went to the commanding officer, at that time Colonel van Aarde, and suggested we fully review the system.

It was agreed that we would, instead, cut out every word that had to be censored and keep them stuck to a separate sheet of paper.

Part of my duties as censor officer also included being in charge of the visits. It was the way I got to know Nelson's family as well as anyone could. Now, not only was I reading all their personal letters, I was also sitting in on most of the meetings they would have over the next two decades. It was inevitable that I would share their secrets, their emotions, their disputes. I became the fly on the wall of the Mandela household for the next twenty-four years.

The way visits were handled was that there was always a written request to the commanding officer from a member of the prisoner's family, which would be passed on to me. Some people would ask for a specific date, some would ask for a visit in a particular month, others when it would be convenient. Most needed a date some time in advance to arrange their own accommodation in Cape Town. Invariably these people were travelling from points all over the country and I knew were going to enormous trouble and expense to get to Robben Island. I also knew the International Red Cross had allocated twelve rail tickets to Cape Town to each immediate member of a family annually. I tried to arrange for a visit to be allowed the day after a person arrived in Cape Town, to give them as much time as possible to get across on the ferry from the mainland. Then, having agreed a visit, I had to write out a permit, allowing the person to travel from their home to Cape Town.

At the time there was in existence a prison department form which was pretty rudimentary and failed to include many important details, such as times when visitors had to report to the harbour to catch a ferry and the ferry timetable as well as maps and directions. I know that, on one occasion, June Mlangeni, Andrew's wife, had arrived in Cape Town at 7.00 in the morning after a train journey from her home in Soweto which had taken two nights. She was very tired, and began walking from the railway station to the harbour front to catch the ferry. By the time she arrived at the harbour the only ferry had gone. She had wasted her trip. The same thing happened to other people many times. So I redesigned the entire form, and included all information about permits, directions and timetables.

The new form contained a section which countered any banning order. Often many of the family members, such as Winnie Mandela, were subject to banning orders which restricted them from leaving their homes. Now this form I sent to them, approving a visit to the island, allowed them to leave their home to travel for the visit. I always advised Winnie that because of her frequent banning orders, she should take the form to the local magistrate who could then inform the local security police about the forthcoming visit.

My feelings were changing. I realised that the government was now using racial hatred to keep themselves in power. I decided I would do what was within my power to help these people who were opposed to the government. I was not a subversive, more a laid-back sympathiser. I did not talk directly to Nelson about this, or my feelings, but they knew from my actions.

My relationship with Nelson was growing closer. No longer would we be content with a polite 'good morning', or an enquiry, 'how are you?' Now we would stop and have a proper conversation. He knew about my family, about my wife and children. After all, I knew from his letters and later from their visits all about his family. Nelson would now ask about my family and inquire about their welfare. At first I assumed he was being a little obsequious, asking for the sake of it; later I was to learn it was a genuine politeness, one which never left him. Nelson had an encyclopaedic memory for names and detail. He remembered everyone and never failed to ask about them. When I spoke about my family he took time to listen and showed concern. He was also aware that I was getting to know his family well.

Visits were still very rare, and when they did take place I knew that Winnie was always harshly treated by the authorities. In small, spiteful ways they did everything they could to make her journey from Johannesburg as difficult as possible. In the two years before I arrived on Robben Island Winnie had been stopped altogether from visiting her husband. The entire way she was treated was, to my mind, unjust and despicable. It was little wonder that as a result her attitude had become as anti-authority as could be. I learned that after her first visit to Nelson, in 1964, she was constantly harassed. Her home was searched time after time and her own family, brothers and sister, was forbidden to live with her. It was not enough that the authorities had deprived her of her husband, sentenced to a life imprisonment; they were also determined to punish her in any way they could. It was clear to everyone that the name of the game against Winnie was humiliation. The regulations governing her trips to Robben Island, when they were allowed to resume in 1966, were difficult. The authorities insisted she travel only by plane from Johannesburg, barring her a cheaper route by road or rail. Once she had arrived at Malan Airport in Cape Town she was ordered to take the shortest and quickest route to Caledon Square, the Cape Town main police station, where she had to sign various documents. To ensure she complied with this order, there were always several security police officers tailing her every step of the way. After her visit to the island, Winnie again had to return to Caledon Square and sign still more documents. She then had to head straight back to the airport, not stopping to speak to or visit anyone.

On the day of a visit, be it Winnie or any of the other relatives of the B section prisoners, I would be waiting at the harbour for the boat to dock at 8.30. I always ensured that the visitor was on the boat, by a simple radio call to the captain, before arranging for the prisoner to be brought from his cell to the main waiting area: I was always conscious that if they had been brought to the waiting area and their visitor failed to arrive, the disappointment would be heightened.

The visiting room was down by the harbour, a low single-storey brick-faced building which looked out over the harbour and ocean. In any other location it would be considered a desirable residence with wonderful sea views. On the lawn outside was a magnificent flowering manotak tree, which provided waiting families with plenty of shelter from the sun's harsh rays. But, here on Robben Island, the building was no more than a cold, dark shed-like building which echoed to the cries of broken families. The building was divided into two sections, a waiting room with a few tables and rickety old wooden chairs and a long, impersonal visiting room which itself was split into nine cubicles, each one a visiting booth. Whenever Winnie would come to see Nelson she was always perfectly behaved, arriving immaculately dressed and carrying herself with a fierce pride which challenged anyone. I was to learn over the years just how much Nelson was in love with this

129

strikingly beautiful woman and how he treasured her visits. I was to hear and read of the controversies which always seemed to be close to Winnie. But, in all those years, a lifetime to many, Winnie behaved impeccably and with great decorum and dignity, despite the often outrageous treatment meted out to her. In the years that followed Nelson's eventual release and his ultimate success as a politician, he would be criticised for defending his wife in the face of evidence which damned her. I was never surprised that he stood by her as he did; she was the stalwart who had stood by him through all his years inside and she was frequently the inspiration behind his burning desire to succeed.

On the days when I handled the visitors there were usually no more than three or four using the facility: this was a day reserved for the B section and then, because of the category restrictions, they would only be allowed one visit per six months. I would space them out along the corridor, made even more dingy by the décor of faded, painted white walls which had the bottom half panelled in a black plastic cover. There was a time, before I had arrived at Robben Island, when the scene was bedlam with the place filled with visitors, separated only by wire and each shouting to make themselves heard. It was my view that the fewer people in the area at any time, the more privacy could be gained by each family. In effect, the visiting area comprised two separate rooms; one for prisoners, the other for visitors. On the prisoners' side was a round wooden seat, like a bar stool. They would sit on it and stare through the one-foot by one-foot, inch-thick glass panel which distorted any view on the other side. It was like seeing life through a 1950s black and white television screen. In the early days there was a hole in the cement wall which allowed each side to speak to one another; it was pretty useless and led to people spending most of their time straining to hear one another. Eventually, this unsatisfactory system was replaced by a three-way telephone, one for the visitor, one for the prisoner and the third for the warder who was listening in just behind the prisoner. It was the regulation that each and every visit had to be monitored with a guard standing beside the prisoner, preventing them speaking about politics or such matters. I was invariably with Nelson and on each of the early visits I would tell him, 'You know the rules and regulations of the visits. Confine whatever you want to talk of to family matters.' Later this was unnecessary; he knew the rules.

Visits were always emotional times. It was, to my mind, one of the cruellest aspects that loved ones who had not seen one another for months were given thirty minutes in less than satisfactory conditions, to speak of their entire families.

They would go over and over the family matters that were natural: 'How are you? Are you okay at home? Have you got enough food and clothing? How is the family? Tell me about each one.' Nelson was always concerned about Winnie, desperate to hear from her about the harassment and the banning orders, the police raids and the arrests. Was she okay? How was she coping after being fired from her job?

It was inhuman to expect two people to conduct their family lives in such confined space and time. Often it was in an atmosphere of extreme emotion, with tears and sadness.

Once again I was the proverbial fly on the wall, knowing I was there, but not wishing to be so. I could feel, from their words, the appalling abject despair, the loneliness and longing. I would watch Winnie, the woman with a pride as fierce as any lioness, with tears rolling down her cheeks. More than any other factor I felt the intrusion of listening in to their conversations was the worst part of it all. Certainly I knew the authorities' thinking behind it; they wanted to stop any communication with the outside, to cut off the leader group from any outside political activity. But the mere thought that this would be furthered by preventing the families having privacy was utter lunacy and, to my mind, naive. Many times I wanted to throw the phone down and tell them to discuss anything they wanted. Frequently I was tempted just to hold it to my ear and ignore what was being said. In many ways that is what I did, I closed my ears, shut off my mind, not wishing to intrude. Once the emotion got to me and I could feel my own tears welling from the sadness of this married couple. I just shut down.

After each visit, Nelson would always like to walk back to his cell and sit and remember each and every word that had been said. He would normally not say a word to me as we walked back together. On one occasion he came out of the visiting area, into the bright sun and I could see he was blinking the tears of regret in his eyes. He wiped them with the back of his large hand and looked away from me, not wishing me to see his emotion.

I said to him: 'Come, let's go back to the section and don't worry; the lump in my throat was bigger than yours.'

He looked surprised and turned to me. 'What lump?'

I just nodded and said, 'The lump in my throat, come...'

We walked on in silence, his head fixed on the limestone gravel of the pathway.

131

Several of the other prisoners had visits which ended up in fights, with the woman accusing her husband of deserting her.

'It is your damned fault I am suffering, it is your fault the children are hungry, it is your fault I can't send them to school. It is all because of you and this damned cause.'

Sometimes whispers would reach the ears of the prisoners who would then accuse their wife: 'I've heard you've been with someone else, you've got a boyfriend.' The woman would invariably get angry and storm out.

The situations were fraught with tension, emotion and stress.

In all the years I was with Nelson I never saw him fight with Winnie. Sometimes there was a difference of opinion, sometimes some questioning of one another; these were two people strong-willed and determined. That was inevitable. But through all the years of incarceration Winnie remained firm and strong in her commitment to the one she called *Madiba*. Nelson, in turn, called her *Namzamu*, her family name of *Zami*, occasionally *Nubantla*, family terms of endearment.

There were times when Winnie would visit and, although she was required to speak in English, she would break into Xhosa. When this happened with other visitors being handled by warders who could not speak the language, the visits were ended prematurely, but I always knew what Winnie was saying and accepted that as part of her culture; it was natural for her to want to use Xhosa.

Just before the third Christmas when Nelson was preparing for a visit from Winnie he asked me for a favour.

'It is something a little special,' he said.

'Okay, well tell me, what is it you wish me to do?'

'I have a chocolate, one which I have been given by another prisoner. I have been saving it as a special present for Winnie for Christmas. Can I give it to her?'

I knew that to acquire the chocolate in the first place had taken all sorts of ingenuity: it would have come into the section from the main prison and illustrated to me just how good the smuggling system was. I knew also it was meant as a present for Winnie which would mean a lot to both Nelson, in giving it, and Winnie in receiving it.

I considered the situation, knowing the risk I was taking, exposing myself to a reprimand, possibly even the sack if caught.

'Look, you know I cannot allow you to hand it over personally, but if you agree, I will give it to Winnie.' It was agreed. The chocolate was wrapped in a typical shiny foil and when he handed it over he insisted, 'Please unwrap it and look inside to ensure I am not handing over anything illegal.'

At the end of the visit, as Nelson walked back to the cell area, I returned and hastened Winnie to one side. The temperature was already in the 90s and the chocolate had become soft in my pocket.

As I pulled it out it looked a sorry, insignificant sight. Yet I knew it had carried great meaning for these two people. I held it out in my hand and told her, 'Here, this is from Nelson. He says it is his Christmas present to you.'

Winnie was choked up, immediately understanding how difficult it had been for her husband to get hold of this sweet.

'Thank you,' she whispered. 'You are a kind man.'

I thought no more about the incident until two days later when the Cape Town Afrikaans newspaper *Die Burger* and the English-language paper the *Cape Times* carried a large article about Winnie Mandela having had 'a picnic' with her husband on Robben Island.

The article claimed the two had sat beneath a tree on the island, spread a cloth on the ground, eaten bread and cheese and had a cool drink. Not only was it incredibly ill-informed, it was filled with the type of naive stupidity which I would get used to from the media. Not only were the articles ignorant of the fact that the Mandelas were still not allowed contact visits but they were filled with the type of information which even a child would have known was not possible.

When I read these articles I knew there was trouble on the way. Within a day a Captain Aucamp from the security section in Pretoria was on the island, demanding to see me in the commanding officer's office.

'Well, Gregory, just how do you explain this blerrie situation,' he demanded.

I knew there was only one way to handle the situation and that was by telling the truth. I explained about the chocolate and told him I saw little harm in the situation; it was, after all, Christmas time.

'Christmas, blerrie Christmas, what the hell has that got to do with the situation?' Aucamp was raging. 'Do you now realise what blerrie effect this ... this ... this stupidity of yours has caused?'

I gave him my best furrowed brow look and shook my head. 'No, sir, I cannot see how this could lead to trouble.'

'Well, Gregory, think, man. Think of how we are trying to

demoralise this blerrie terrorist, trying our best to isolate him from his family and here you are playing blerrie Santa Claus, handing presents from Mandela to his blerrie wife.

'Didn't you think that this chocolate could have some sort of message inside, man?' Aucamp stormed around the room, thumping his fist into the palm of his hand. He was now talking to himself. 'Yissus, I cannot believe of such stupidity.'

I waited for the rage to subside and added quietly, 'Sir, I should let you know that I unwrapped the chocolate and examined it first before handing it over to Mandela's wife. There was no message inside.'

Aucamp huffed and puffed before turning on me once again and directing his finger at me. 'You're lucky this time, Gregory. I'm not going to take any action against you. But if you ever allow this sort of thing again, you'll be up on a disciplinary charge before you can even think the blerrie name Nelson Mandela. Now get out of here.'

Within a couple of hours the prisoners' telegraph system knew of my trouble. The next time I was in B section Nelson came up and was filled with anger. 'Mr Gregory, let me apologise for this matter. When I asked you to give Winnie the chocolate I never imagined it would result in this trouble for you. I'm so very sorry.'

Despite the ticking off from Captain Aucamp, I was philosophical about the situation and could still see little harm in handing over the chocolate.

I told Nelson, 'Listen, man, forget it, it's not a problem. It was no big deal and only others wanted to make it a big deal.'

It was not long after this incident with the chocolate that Nelson and I had our one, and only, row. It followed the arrest and detention of Winnie. She was picked up in the early hours of the morning of 12 May 1969 and detained under the wide-sweeping powers of the Terrorism Act.

Although news of what was happening in the outside world was deliberately kept from the political prisoners, this was one occasion when in sly ways the security forces made sure that Nelson was kept well informed about Winnie's situation. Normally any news of what was happening, particularly politically, was kept strictly from the leader group in B section. It was part of the isolation policy that the authorities had adopted, to keep them ignorant of what was happening as much as possible. In fact they usually did find out, one way or another, but this was purely through the astonishingly complex network of intelligence they themselves started in the prison. But when Winnie was arrested and detained, there was a concerted effort to ensure Nelson knew everything that happened to his wife. Her detention was in itself used as a weapon to place additional strain on him. When he returned in the early evenings from a day of slave labour in the quarry Nelson would find a newspaper cutting tucked neatly beneath his sisal mat. The authorities were determined to undermine his confidence and resolve.

The raid on Winnie's home had been part of a nationwide crackdown on ANC members and sympathisers in which several hundred people were detained. I could see how the situation was affecting Nelson. He was looking tired and I was told how he was spending most of the nights just lying on the cold floor of his cell, unable to sleep. I know he was worried not only about Winnie's fate but also his two daughters and who was looking after them. I knew from him that he had many good friends and family in the Orlando area, but not having any direct news was getting to him. During one weekend I told him that if I saw anything in the newspapers referring to his daughters I would let him know about it.

The commanding officer at the time was Brigadier Aucamp who allowed Nelson to send extra letters to his family, to ascertain what was happening to Winnie and the children.

Then one day, in the middle of the crisis with Winnie, Nelson had a go at me, accusing me of holding back letters from her and about her which would have told him everything he needed to know.

It was during a weekend duty when he came up and accused me: 'You're holding back letters from my wife. I've been told they've been sent and you have not given them to me.'

At first I was taken aback, but my reaction turned to anger. I hit back at him, 'You're wrong. My conscience is clear on this matter.'

I was going to turn away and leave him standing when it occurred to me the problem could exist elsewhere. 'Look, Nelson, Winnie is detained in Pretoria Central Prison and I suspect that any letters she has written to you have been stopped there rather than anywhere else. I'll try and find out.'

I didn't tell him, but I also felt that the extra letters he had been allowed to write were not for Winnie's benefit, but for the authorities who would use the extra allowance for finding out any information.

It took about two weeks but we were able to determine that the letters written by Winnie had been held up by the censor officer in Pretoria.

When we found out Nelson came again and apologised. 'Mr Gregory, accept my apology. I should have known better than to accuse you of holding back three letters. I was hasty.'

I was a little embarrassed by the situation and told him to forget it: it was a mistake any person could make and understandable in the circumstances.

Chapter 15

Deaths in the family

Something was troubling Nelson. He should have been thrilled to learn of the coming visit of his mother Nosekeni, together with his sister Mabel and two of his children, but he was not. I knew, from our regular discussions walking together in the yard, how much this old woman meant to him. When he spoke of her and of his family, it was with a reverence which I admired. It was, therefore, such a surprise to see he was apparently less than thrilled at the coming visit. Maybe it was the prospect of the elderly woman having to travel on the ferry from the mainland at a time when the sea had been heavy for weeks. I knew the family had to travel a long way, 700 miles or more from the Transkei on the east coast, by bus and train. It was a journey that would take two days in each direction, in conditions which were, at best, basic. Maybe he felt degraded by his mother seeing him behind bars. I could not figure it out. And certainly it was not a subject I could discuss with Nelson; I was beginning to learn that a direct inquiry about such troubles would have been an intrusion into his privacy. If he wanted to invite me into his thoughts and worries, then he would do so in his own way and time. Just as I would do so with him. Without realising it, this had become our way, a trust had developed. We never delved into one another's personal lives, unless invited. But this coming visit was troubling him; he had withdrawn into a quiet hermitage, a deep corner of privacy I had not seen before. I knew this was the first time Nelson had seen his mother and the children, his son Makgatho and daughter Makaziwe, since the trial. Nearly three years. He should have been excited, but was not.

Whatever the root cause of Nelson's troubles, it certainly was not the weather on the day his mother visited. The notorious spring south-westerly had blown itself out. The storms which had lashed the island for a week on end had abated and the ocean was like a mill pond. The crossing from the mainland could not have been smoother.

The visit itself was conducted in the usual style and dignity I had begun to expect with Nelson. With the children there was concern about their education, questions about what they were doing. There was laughter and compliments for sister Mabel. He told her, 'You look the same as ever; you have not aged a day.' I began to sense the root cause of his troubles when he asked Mabel about his mother. His voice went almost to a whisper. Nelson knew the rules of visiting: whispering was against the rules and could terminate the visit immediately. But, as I stood behind him, to the right of his visitor's box, I knew this was not some subversive plotting manoeuvre. This was a man worried about his mother's health. 'She has lost much weight, she has aged many years and her face is old and haggard.' It was not so much a question to Mabel, more a statement of fact. His sister only nodded, unable to speak or give an explanation.

Although the visit had been extended by half an hour, it was an occasion when, for the first time since I had been looking after his visits, I wanted to tear down the wall which separated this man from his mother. At that moment I felt a welling of anger against a system which had not only sentenced this man, and others like him, to the island, but had condemned him to such inhumanity. The in-built cruelty and deprivation of the prison itself was a system we had been prepared for. Now, as I stood behind Nelson, watching him communicate with his elderly mother through the small, thick glass frame, I understood the full meaning of what the authorities were trying to do: 'to demoralise'. The very word the commanding officer had used the day I arrived on the island. 'It is our job to demoralise these people,' he had said. 'It is your job to demoralise these people.' It hit me then that this entire system had been set up to punish in a way that was totally unacceptable. It was not enough that this old woman was only able to speak to her son through a microphone which turned his words into a metallic squawk; when she put her bony hand to the glass to stroke the face of her son, all she felt was the cold of the inch-thick glass which separated and distorted the view. When Nelson turned his head to place his cheek against the glass his eyes were tightly shut.

On the short walk back from the visitors' block to the main prison, beside the harbour wall, we did not speak. It was the first time I had seen this tall, proud man, bowed. His chin nearly rested on his chest and the shoulders were slumped more than I had seen when he returned from the quarry after a day's hard labour digging in the limestone. It was not unusual for us to be silent on this walk; I knew these visits were precious times, and Nelson, like any other prisoner, was now recalling every detail of the conversations and visions in his mind. He would store them now for recall later. But this day it was different. Now I saw a man troubled by the sight of his mother. I knew and he knew what was going on.

The telegram, when it arrived many weeks later, was no surprise. It was as short as it was impersonal: to inform Nelson Mandela his mother was dead.

It was early afternoon and when I arrived with the telegram, Nelson was already in his block, standing in the corridor, talking to several others. As I walked in, he turned to face me, and it was as if he knew I had something for him. Leaving the company of the others, he walked toward his cell and stood aside to let me enter first.

I declined and held out the telegram, watching his face, now beginning to gauge his mood and reactions from the slightest changes. He looked directly at me, into my eyes, then down at the brown envelope I was holding out to him. I think I nodded, I'm uncertain, but I know it made the reading of its contents unnecessary. I knew and he knew. We had known from the day of the visit.

A hush descended over the block; the others knew also. A death in a prisoner's family affects everyone, it is a moment they all dread more than any other. It is more than the inability to prevent the person dying, it is a double remoteness that being in prison creates; an inability to be there to comfort and console, to take responsibility and shoulder the burden.

The next day Nelson's request arrived on my desk. He wanted permission to attend the funeral. I closed my eyes and I could see the visit several weeks before, when the smiles of greetings between mother and son were washed away by their shared knowledge that they were then possibly saying their last goodbye. I knew what the answer to the request would be. It had to be sent to the commanding officer, Badenhorst, and to Pretoria for approval, but it would be a firm 'No', and without explanation. Just 'No'.

Later, when we walked in the yard, it was Nelson who brought up the request, trying to explain why he had asked. There was no anger then, more a frustration that the prison authorities had, once again, totally failed to understand him.

'They could have sent me alone to the funeral, or in the company of a warder, in your company,' he explained. He shook his head. We walked slowly around the yard, side by side, not speaking.

Nelson was withdrawing into himself, his explanation to me, but not meant for me. He knew I understood. 'I am not a criminal, I am here for the cause. I would have gone and come back. They are foolish to think otherwise.'

The explanation given by the commanding officer to Mandela was superficial. 'Mandela, while I know you are a man of your word and would not try to escape, I cannot trust your own people and we fear they would try to kidnap you.' It had the distinctly hollow ring of either ignorance of Mandela and his movement or of the man himself.

The depth of Nelson's feelings about his mother's death began to sink in weeks later, as we probed one another's past. We were sitting in the office, sheltering from the heat of the day as we entered into a discussion about my early days. We both enjoyed these moments, both of us laughing and chuckling as we spoke a little of our past. It was the first time I had mentioned my own childhood as I wistfully told him of my days at Ongemak. But his mood changed when I told him of the bitterness I felt toward my parents when I felt they abandoned me at boarding-school. His mood became very serious and I felt a lecture was on its way.

Instead, he began to talk, about Nosekeni, his mother, telling me about how she had been the third of four wives to his father, and how she had brought him up.

But the gentle memories of the early years were contrasted with the difficulties which followed, as Nelson followed the path he had chosen. It was a choice, he said, which forced his mother to follow a path of hardship and neglect.

We sat there together in the small, box-like room, its pale-green walls impersonal and cold, a contrast to the heat of the afternoon outside. Across the bare table Nelson wanted to talk of the woman I had seen on just the one occasion. 'When I came to prison, I knew I had abrogated my responsibilities as a son. I gave up the responsibility of being able to help her through the difficult years of ageing. She needed my attention and I was elsewhere, I had gone.'

I spoke earnestly: 'But, man, you must understand we cannot be our mother's sons for ever. We have to strike out on the course we have chosen. That is what they expect of us; they don't want us clinging at their tails.'

I knew Nelson was struggling with the concept of choice. We

both knew that it was acceptable to be independent. Where he was struggling with his conscience was in deciding if his decision to fight for the cause of equality had been at the cost of neglecting his immediate family. In trying to create a family of South Africans, was it at the cost of the Mandela clan? I could hear him now searching for the answer. 'She had difficult years, times when she struggled as all people struggle with poverty. She was my mother and, as such, became a target for the racists who ruled. Many times I have tried to explain to her that I was not neglecting my own family, that in committing myself to the struggle, I was committing myself to finding the solution for my own family. I'm not sure she always understood.'

His frustration was obvious. 'My choice became their choice, whether they wanted to be part of the struggle or not. My involvement inadvertently penalised them.'

I then knew how desperately Nelson had wanted to attend his mother's funeral. He had wanted to explain these things to her as she was laid to rest in the Transkei dirt where he had been born.

But worse was to follow; a deeper, more painful blow that was to cause a wound within Nelson which I never believe properly healed.

The message came in a telegram from the Mandela family one cold morning in July 1969. It was just a sentence long and said simply that Madiba Thembekile Mandela, Nelson's first and oldest son, the father of two young children, had been killed in a motor accident. He had smashed into the side of a bridge and was killed instantly. Immediately I felt for Mandela. Before I handed over this telegram I had first to confirm it with the authorities, to ensure this was not a cruel joke. But before I had an opportunity to pick up the telephone its shrill ring pulled me out of my trance. It was Pretoria with the confirmation about Thembi. They added few details. I knew Nelson was down in the cell block and that I had to tell him personally, that I was the only one who could do it. I rode my bike from the administration block. I had difficulty seeing my way; several times I kept clouding up. At some stage I dismounted and stopped to compose myself, trying to pick out the words I would use. I knew how it would hit him. This man was already becoming close to me, already I cared for his feelings. I tried to picture what he would be doing when I arrived: would he be standing talking to Walter and the others or would he be in his cell? I resolved that if he was with the others I would ask to see him alone; that would not be unusual. The ride is a hazy memory for me; usually I can remember

141

incidents or details such as the weather, but that day is like a thick fog where I cannot recall a thing.

When I got there Nelson was standing in the passage talking to Walter. He turned and smiled at me, a greeting. He looked into my face and knew something was wrong. I could hardly speak; there was a thickness about my voice. I wanted to clear my throat with a glass of water. I said quietly I had to see him alone. I invited him to the office at the end of the corridor. I still had not worked out how I was going to tell him; I couldn't just blurt out that Thembi was dead. Somewhere in the back of my head all sorts of thoughts were rushing around, everything from the security forces being involved in the death to how Winnie and the other family members would take it. We went into the office, small, crowded by the desk and two chairs, and yet empty because of its lack of decoration. The faded yellow curtains were drawn to keep the sun out; it seemed to be appropriately sombre. I closed the door and as I stood with my back to him, Nelson asked anxiously, 'What is it? What is wrong?' I turned and faced him, but I had to turn away. Later I was to examine this moment in detail and realise how much worse this made it for him. He was always expecting something bad to happen to his family on the outside, maybe Winnie being arrested again or the children being harassed. But at that time I was filled with confusion. I faced him again and opened my mouth, but said nothing. He came towards me and asked, 'Mr Gregory, what is wrong?'

By then we had begun to know one another's mood changes. I said as quickly as I could, 'Your son Thembi is dead, killed in an accident. He died instantly. The explanation I was given was that he drove into the side of a bridge. Maybe he lost control of the car, but I don't know any more details. I shall try and find out. I am terribly sorry to have to tell you.' In his eyes I could see the sternness I was to recognise when he struggled to maintain self control. It was a distancing from me and from others, and in some ways his face receded into a fixed expression, tight lines around his mouth. Those lines always went deeper the more worried, sad or angry he became. At that time, he simply said, 'Thank you, Mr Gregory,' and walked away.

I sat down on the chair behind the desk and rested my head in my hands. What a thing this was, how cruel and wrong it was because I knew then that he would apply to go to the funeral of Thembi, his eldest son, the boy who he would have wanted to inherit his place. I also knew that the authorities would not allow it just as they had not allowed him to go to his mother's funeral nine months before. I wanted to scream out that they were fools, ignorant idiots, who had failed to understand the man they had incarcerated. This was someone who was here because he believed in his cause. The authorities could have treated him like a human being and allowed him the dignity of attending a funeral. Nelson said he would have gone with prison warders as guards to ensure he would return. I knew then that the authorities could have let him go on his own and the man would have returned of his own volition.

Outside in the corridor I looked for him. The others were walking around, some standing talking, some walking. I could not see him so I headed to his cell. He was just standing there, looking out of the window at the fading sky. I wanted to go and put an arm round his shoulders, to offer him a cup of tea, to ease his shock. But I also knew this was not the time to say anything to this man. He first had to absorb the entire situation. One of the others, I can't remember who, came to me and asked what was wrong. It was not Nelson's nature to ignore them and walk past them when they spoke to him. But this time he had. I said nothing and turned and walked away.

I went to the duty office and saw the guy in charge, an officer called Hougaard. I asked him to let the night-warders know that I had given Mandela bad news, and that they should keep an observation on him. I said I wanted to know how he was, if he requested anything. The next morning Hougaard phoned me and told me Mandela had spent the night standing by the small window looking out at the sky. He did not sleep, he did not eat, he just stood there, not moving. It is anybody's guess what was going through his mind. In those days, if there was a car accident involving someone prominent in the ANC there was an instant suspicion that it had been deliberately set up by the security police or that somehow they were implicated. I know that a number of the others in the block thought that. It is anybody's guess what Nelson thought as he stood there by the cell window. He stood there for two nights, unable to move.

The next day I went to his cell again and I stood beside him. At first I wasn't sure if he even knew I was there. He just stood, his eyes fixed on the sky. 'If you want me to go, I shall,' I said. There was the merest shake of his head. 'No, stay,' he said.

I continued, 'I can't tell you how deeply sorry I am because I don't know the depth of sorrow you are now feeling. I also have children, I have two boys but I can't even begin to pretend to know how you are hurting. Many people will come to you now and tell you how they understand how you are feeling. Those people are talking through their hats, but each of them genuinely feels for you without understanding.' I think I rambled for a good few minutes about the lack of comprehension, and also the sympathy that many people were feeling. I know I wanted at that moment to write him a letter, but that it was forbidden by the prison system. If it had been found in one of the many searches of the cells I would have been punished for it.

By the next morning Nelson had written a request which came to my office. It would, and in my opinion should, have touched even the hardest heart. He said that, as a father, he had a responsibility to ensure that his son was laid to rest properly and that his spirit would rest peacefully. He explained that, if necessary, they could send a security cordon with him to ensure he returned to prison. I felt strongly about this and took it to the commanding officer, Colonel Badenhorst. Normally, I would have to make an appointment to see Badenhorst, but that day I marched straight in. He was taken by surprise and looked up at me. 'What's up, Gregory man, problems?'

I went straight to the point, already beginning to feel anger rising. 'You know Mandela's son has been killed?' He nodded. 'Well, he has asked for permission to attend the funeral, to go with a guard, if necessary.'

The contempt was clear in Badenhorst's eyes as he looked at the letter lying on the desk mat in front of him. He didn't bother to pick it up or read its contents. 'He must be mad, blerrie crazy, man.'

That was his own personal answer, but the request still had to be sent to the prison headquarters in Pretoria.

Their two-word reply spoke volumes: 'Permission denied.' The reply was sent to Badenhorst, who called me into his office.

'Here, man,' he said, shoving the telegrammed reply to me. 'Take it and tell him the answer is no.'

I was angry again and for the first time I argued Mandela's cause. 'But sir, this man has made a very valid point. He is not a criminal, he will not run away, I know he won't. He is here in prison because of the cause for which he is fighting. For him to run away and not return here would hurt his cause. It would be safe to allow him out.' It was, perhaps, naive and ill-timed, but my anger was intense. I had seen Mandela's pain.

Badenhorst was taken aback and sat bolt upright in his chair. He was unused to having junior ranks questioning any decision from head office, let alone his own judgement.

His voice was almost a hiss. 'Gregory, let me give you some good advice. Advice you'd do well to remember. Let me ask you: are you deaf, man?' I shook my head. 'Well, then,' he continued. 'You have your answer. It is no. You got me? Now just get out of here. Go.'

So that was it. I then had to go and tell Nelson the decision. By this time, he had left his position beside the cell window and was in the main corridor. In his eyes there was the tiredness that comes from nights without sleep. Again we went into the small office. I invited him to sit for a time.

'Look, man, I'm sorry, but the answer to your request to attend the funeral is no. I'm sorry because I know you would have come back here.'

Nelson was stiff, all business-like, and merely asked for permission to write more letters to family members. There was also a request for a special letter which would be read at the graveside.

Years later, when we sat talking about our families, Nelson brought up the grief he felt over the loss of Thembi, and how at the time of the death he again felt the guilt of committing himself to the ANC cause at the cost of his family life. I recall the lung-bursting pride when he recalled the boy. 'One time when I was working underground, I had to say goodbye to him and the boy stood up, tall and straight and told me not to worry, that he would care for the family while I was gone.'

Nelson's anguish continued for several weeks. I could see he was keeping a very tight rein on his emotions. There was the hard, set face, a coldness that was different from the friendly smile he would normally give. He was also cutting himself off from the other ANC people. I noticed that when they were in the yard Nelson did not walk with them in the usual manner. I understood him wanting to be alone. That ability just to let your mind drift, almost in a trance, was something I knew and recognised within the black man. It was a patience, the sort of patience I had been taught by Bafana when we waited for the python. It was an ability to wait without getting anxious.

The other factor I recognised that was important to Nelson at that time was the way people spoke to him. Often when people die there is a tendency to offer condolences. Often these things are said because they appear to be the appropriate things to say. They are meant to be words of consolation, but so often make matters worse. That did not happen with Nelson; I think everyone kept words to a minimum. It was why when I went and stood beside him in his cell, my silence meant more to him. Because it was the unspoken comfort.

Chapter 16

Robben Island,
a prison for prison warders

Robben Island was more than just a prison for criminals and subversives, it was also a place of hardship for the warders. Being assigned to *'die Eiland'* was seen as a punishment transfer or the place where the prison department sent young recruits to judge how they could handle themselves. Initially, when I was asked if I would go to Robben Island I had been swayed by all the benefits, the fishing, the freedom from living in a city or town, being out of the rat race, being permanently close to my family. It certainly did live up to all these expectations. There were, however, many hardships in being on the island: its isolation, its inaccessibility other than by the daily boat, and the small community mentality which eventually enveloped all aspects of life. It was always considered that the normal length of duty on the island was three years. I was to stay on the island for ten because of the involvement I had with Nelson and the rest of the ANC men.

There were many warders transferred to Robben Island who could never stand the place and either were transferred again quickly or left the job if they were refused a transfer. Life on the island was often brutal among the warders themselves. It was riddled with men who had severe drinking problems or developed them while they were there, because of the isolation. It was cruel on many young warders who were cut off from normal social life on the mainland and it was often harsh on families. On the other hand it was a veritable paradise for children, growing up in an environment which, paradoxically, was safer than on the mainland. Here they were, surrounded by men considered to be the worst of the country's criminals, yet they were never in any danger. Many of the common criminals worked outside the prison boundaries, in the gardens, fields, roads and even in the homes of the warders around the island. There was never once a problem with these criminals harming or even approaching a child. It was a carefree atmosphere for the children similar to that which I had experienced when I was growing up on the farm. They would wander off into the bush and build their little dens, huts and hideaways. Parents never had to worry about traffic, drugs, amusement arcades or any of the problems which began to appear on the mainland.

The only difficulty for children was that the only school on the island was a primary school, catering only to the age of eleven. Then children had to move on to schools on the mainland, mostly boarding-schools. It was the dilemma over my own children's education which eventually led to me leaving the island. Remembering my own bitter experience at such places, I refused to send my children to boarding-school, and determined I would leave the prison service rather than allow them to suffer in the way I had. It was a case of being transferred back to the mainland or I would leave.

From my earliest days at Robben Island there had been a noticeable reticence from many of the warders to associate with me. At first I assumed it was because I was new to the community; later I began to accept that I did not fall into line with the way the majority of them treated the prisoners – as little better than animals. It was an attitude I had experienced before in my life, during my school days, when I was frequently shunned, and it never really bothered me. I could live with it. In those early days the social life on the island consisted of spending most of the nights in the warders' club, propping up the bar and drinking. It was inevitable that there were cliques and groups which stuck closely together. I always seemed to be on the outside of these groups, as I had been years before at school. And just as the school days had been the breeding ground of the bullies, so Robben Island was the adult equivalent.

Any new, young recruit became a target for the bully brigade as I termed them, the older warders many of whom were a throwback to the violent days at the prison. Many of them had elected to stay longer than normal on Robben Island knowing that their behaviour would not have been tolerated elsewhere. Many times I saw younger warders picked on.

'Right, tonight we will be in the bar at 5 o'clock. We want you to be there and we want you to pay,' they would tell the new man.

If the new man refused to play along with the game he was usually beaten up. The drunken session became almost like a ritual

148

for the new men who arrived. Stories got around and many new recruits arrived already terrified as to how they were going to be treated. Many accepted it as an initiation ceremony, others refused and paid the penalty of being beaten up. I knew several who had refused to play along and, instead, would go to their rooms in the main single warders' block, soon after supper. They would wait until dark, then take their blankets and slip out through the windows and sleep in the bush to avoid being confronted by the bullies. The young warders would then return to the dormitory block before first light to wash before going to work.

One of the first victims I knew personally was a young warder who joined my staff in the censor office. I'd picked him when he came to the island from the training facility at Kroonstad. Nick Kennedy had graduated with a good report and was clearly a bright young man. I considered he would be a good acquisition for the office. When he arrived I was immediately concerned for him as I met him at the dockside. He was small and I could tell he was the sort who would become a target for the bully boys.

As we walked from the dockside to the administration office Kennedy's fear poured out. He'd heard about the bully antics.

'Mr Gregory, what will they do to me?'

I was faced with a problem. Should I tell him what I believed was a probability or should I try and calm his obviously nervous disposition?

'Look, just play along with them for a few weeks and you'll be okay.'

'But, sir, I don't drink and don't smoke. In fact I've never had a drink and I don't want to.'

'Ja, but you've asked what you should do if these guys ask you to join them for a drink. I think you should go along with them. If you don't you know it will only cause resentment and they'll take it out on you.'

Kennedy was scared and did not want to go to the club. Even though he did not drink or smoke he was also short of money. I knew that after he paid for his room and board he kept a few rand for himself to buy items in the shop and sent the rest to his mother, a widow on the mainland.

'Look, Nick, if you're short of cash I'll give you some to go tonight to get this thing over and done with.'

The young man's eyes were hard set and I could see he had made his decision. 'No, thank you for offering, but I'm going to be firm on this. I'm not going.'

I tried to change his mind, but Kennedy was having none of it. I knew what would almost certainly follow.

Shortly before 10 o'clock that night there was a knock at my front door. Gloria was in the bedroom and one of the children was crying. When I opened the door, Kennedy stood before me, the light from inside the house glistening on the wet blood that covered his face. His clothes were saturated. His hands were clasped to the side of his head.

'What in hell's name has happened?' It was a question, but I did not need an answer. I knew this had been coming.

Kennedy could hardly talk. He was shaking and I told him to sit down while I called for medical help and gave him some tea.

I examined the wound to the side of his head; in fact it was to his ear.

'I was sitting on my bed, reading the newspaper,' he said. 'Then I could hear them coming. I could hear their footsteps and their shouts. They were saying they were coming to get me to buy a drink for them. They said I owed them. They kicked the door in and one of them saw me sitting on the bed and threw a dagger at me.'

The knife, it appeared, had penetrated Kennedy's ear and ended up embedded in the pillow. The young man had got out through the window and headed for my home.

'Man, you're lucky this was not an eye or maybe worse. Those bastards are just crazy drunks.' I knew the bullies would continue until they got their way and Kennedy bought the drinks for them.

It was bizarre that the medical officer who came to see Kennedy and sew a dozen or so stitches in his ear never once asked what had happened. The news had got around quickly. There was no inquiry, no questions asked, no punishments. Within a few weeks Kennedy left the service, frightened out of it by the bullies and their methods.

In many ways I was no better than the rest of them. Boredom set in and I found myself drawn to the club and the heavy drinking. It started with a casual beer after work. The officers' club was in the main guest house and the warders' club was close to the rugby field in the centre of the town. It had an enclosed verandah where wives, girlfriends and children often sat at weekends. But they were never allowed inside the club itself: it was a haven for men only, the rough, tough types who gloried in the art of standing by a bar and consuming enough alcohol until they could no longer stand.

At first I would head home, to change out of uniform and to tell Gloria I was having a quick drink; I'd be back in half an hour or an hour at the latest. Then I stopped going home from work, heading straight to the bar in uniform to drink, to talk, play darts and drink some more. Then before I'd know it, the time had gone, it was 9, 10 o'clock. Drinking gave me a release unlike anything I'd known before. When I was at school and faced the bullying and loneliness I had to contain my anger inside, although on occasions it would burst out when I would get into fights. Now, once more faced with isolation and bullying, I could hide in my own deep well of drunkenness and recklessness.

There were, of course, other factors. The very nature of the island made it a form of isolation which merely intensified my own feelings of being separate from the rest of the warders. There was also intense boredom. At first I'd go fishing for abalone or crayfish from the harbour area. Then I'd go out in a little boat and do a little line-fishing. But there's only a limited amount of fishing a man can do. Then I headed to the bar. At the bar I never talked about work, about my relationship with Nelson Mandela and the other ANC men. I wanted to escape, to drink and forget. It was a place where we were all together in one sense, that of looking after the Poqo, and many of the warders were extremely racist and prejudiced in their views. Fucking kaffirs this and the fucking kaffirs that, black bastards and shit-faced koelies. This was more than just drunken bar talk, this was the normal language the warders used for these people. Eventually I got to the point where the words just passed me by; I could see their lips moving, but I never heard a word.

The bar was a long wooden bench, the replica of bars the world over. In the middle was the till and on either side were two standing areas. It became like two drinking teams, on one side the loud-mouths, the warders who were racist, foul-mouthed and always out for trouble, on the other a second group intent on drinking to forget. At weekends when there was a rugby match or a sports event we would be standing three, four deep at the bar.

I usually stood with the group who were drinking to forget, to obliterate anything to do with the island. Frequently there were fights between both groups and on many occasions I was confronted by accusations from them of being a 'nigger lover' and 'kaffir boetie'. I lost count of the times I would walk in and be accused: 'Here's the kaffir boetie man.' They would poke fun and make accusations, but normally I let it wash over me. I'd had years of training to ignore this type of abuse when I was at boarding-school. Whenever they called me 'kaffir boetie', I replied with a phrase which the blacks themselves used with the white man of *'ja boertjie'*, yes Boer man, that's right.

My lack of response angered the antagonists even more; they wanted a response, a confrontation with me. Mostly they failed to get it; however, there were several incidents where we did come to blows. On one occasion I had been in the bar for several hours and had been drinking heavily. Just before I was due to leave one of the group came to me and whispered in my ear. 'Be careful, one of them is outside waiting for you on the step. He's going to attack you when you step outside.' Again, a throwback to the boarding-school days. The person who told me had also warned that the attacker was carrying a chain to slash me. I immediately began to sober up, the adrenaline replacing the alcohol; I was aware that this evening would end in violence.

I waited for a group to leave and I tagged on behind them, the last person out of the doors into the darkness. In the shadows I could see the man hiding in the doorway, a chain hanging from his fist. The would-be attacker was a nasty piece of work called Kap. I took what I considered to be a pre-emptive strike; I laid into him without asking questions. I took from him the chain he had in his hand. There was a large metal padlock on the end of it and I knew that one crack over the skull from it could have left me dead or badly injured. By the time I had finished Kap was lying on the step covered in blood. I went home and washed myself down, seething about the cowardly way he had been waiting for me in the shadows.

Next morning I again took pre-emptive action and went straight to the administrative officer. I marched in, threw the chain and padlock on to his desk and told him, 'There was a fight last night and I beat up Kap. I think he's in the sick bay at present with a damaged face and jaw.'

The admin officer looked startled by my action and I could see the grin disappearing from his face. He had been one of the group who had been standing with Kap the night before in the bar.

I indicated the chain and padlock and added, 'I took this weapon from him and I want this matter investigated properly. He could have killed me with this blerrie thing, it's a weapon.' I turned away and stormed out, slamming the door firmly behind me. I never heard about the matter again, and just as had happened at school, the taunts and the baiting died away.

The violence was bad. Shortly after I arrived, a young warder vanished. He was found dead two days later near the old jetty which was down on the northern foreshore facing Table Mountain. An autopsy said he had died when he had fallen off the jetty and banged his head on the rocks beneath. He had been in the water for two days so by the time he was discovered, all the fleshy, soft parts of the body had been eaten away by the crayfish and crabs. There was a police investigation, although I think not as thorough as it might have been. At the time of the death there were rumours that the young warder had been in the company of some of the rougher bullies. Certainly I know that when many of the warders were interviewed they all agreed to stick to the same story. Although it was never certain, there were many who felt that the young man could have been the victim of a drunken spree with some of the rougher characters and he had had some sort of accident with them. Was it murder? I don't know. But I do know there were many rumours around at the time and the behaviour of many warders was both violent and careless enough to suggest it could have happened.

The stories of appalling conditions for young warders became well known and it was not uncommon to see their parents show up with them from the mainland on their first day. They all wanted to inspect the living conditions. Many times I heard them gasp with surprise at the lack of hygienic facilities. I often heard it said that the conditions inside the prison were better than for the younger warders. The fallout rate from new warders sent to the island was high. The first weekend they were allowed off for home leave was often the last we saw of them. If they did not have good reason for not returning they faced being arrested and brought back on a charge of being AWOL. However, rather than face a growing tide of young warders being forced to work on the island, a number of the cases were never dealt with.

One of the most serious problems at the time was the number of warders who drank so much they were actually drunk on duty. They would often head off for lunch and reappear several hours later sozzled. Many times they were so drunk they had to be hidden away in areas of the prison where there were no inmates – places such as the arsenal – to allow them to sleep off the effects of the alcohol.

There was one officer who was often in charge of the prison at weekends when I was on duty, a chief warder named Du Plessis who developed a serious drinking problem. When I showed up on Saturday mornings, my first duty was to take a bakkie, a pick-up truck, and drive to his house. More often than not his wife would tell me he was out cold and she could not wake him. I would take the keys for the office and fill in, taking the early morning parade of other warders, fill the books and ensure everything was working. This procedure went on for months and the only danger of being caught was if the weekend duty officer ever showed up early for the morning duties.

It was inevitable that one day Du Plessis's luck would run out. It happened one morning, a foul winter's day when the rain was lashing the island making life as miserable as was possible. We were all in a bad mood when the duty officer arrived for the inspection.

'Where's Du Plessis?' he barked, looking left and right for the missing chief warder.

I stepped forward. 'Sir, he's had to return to his home. I understand his wife called to say there was a problem with the prison monitor.' The monitor was the prisoner assigned to work doing odd jobs at the house.

The senior officer accepted this explanation for Du Plessis's non-appearance. However, two weeks later the officer arrived early again, I suspect because he had heard the rumours about the drunken chief warder.

'So, Gregory, where is Chief Warder Du Plessis this morning?' he demanded as I again stepped forward to make the excuses. 'And this time don't lie or you will be on a charge yourself. Show me the journal and tell me where he is. And before you say anything remember I know your handwriting and the handwriting of Du Plessis.' I had to admit the truth, that the chief warder was at home, he was not very well.

'Not very well,' the duty officer raged. 'Everyone knows the bugger is drunk all the time; no wonder he's not very well. He's pissed out of his brain.'

It was Du Plessis who was responsible for setting the patrol dogs on a group of the prisoners, an incident I described on page 110. The group included Nelson and the other ANC leaders. Du Plessis was as drunk as a coot and became agitated at the length of time it took for the prisoners to walk the distance. The harder he shouted and bawled the slower they walked. Eventually he lost his temper and, in a drunken stupor, ordered the guards to turn the dogs on 'the kaffir bastards'. He told the guards they should apologise to their dogs for only allowing them to attack 'black meat which is poisoned anyway'.

Nelson Mandela's marriage to Winnie in 1958 (*Eli Weinberg/ Mayibuye Centre*)

Nelson Mandela outside Westminster Abbey, London, in 1962 (*Mayibuye Centre*)

Nelson Mandela
in his cell on
Robben Island
(*Jürgen
Schadeberg*)

A watch tower on Robben Island (*Jürgen Schadeberg*)

Prison guards standing in front of the section which housed the main body of political prisoners (*Jürgen Schadeberg*)

Du Plessis's drinking became so bad he was released from the service. He ended up as a tramp wandering the streets of Cape Town and later the beaches of Muizenberg where he was eventually found frozen to death. He had fallen into a drunken stupor and died of exposure.

About half of the officers on the island were married, the other half single men, often young; in their early twenties. The social life for these young men was non-existent and it was inevitable there would be problems. These young men wanted women and there was no ready supply on the island. Gossip soon spread when a married woman was carrying on with a younger warder. It was virtually impossible to keep such a thing quiet. It also became well known among nearly all the warders that several of the married women were encouraged to become prostitutes by their husbands to earn extra cash. I knew two who admitted it openly. 'Look, man, she's no good to me other than to earn extra money for me to drink.'

The arrangements were always made in the bar. One of these warders acted as his wife's pimp, telling prospective clients, 'Right, I have booked myself on the night-shift for the weekend. The old woman is available for fifty rand a go.' It was a common occurrence that two or three of the young warders would spend the weekend at the home of the married warder with his wife while he was working.

Official permission for a prostitute to live on Robben Island would never be given. Some married women that way inclined would get some woman friend who was also that way to come and stay with them. General Willemse stopped this. Willemse had only been on the island a couple of weeks when he called me to his office.

'Greg, I want you to go to the house of the woman who is selling sex and tell her she has two hours to pack her things to catch the ferry. She is banned from the island from now on.'

I looked puzzled. Then he added, a grin on his face, 'I'm not suggesting you have used her, which is why I'm sending you to get rid of her. Just tell her to ply her trade elsewhere, not here on Robben Island.'

The behaviour of the majority of the married women was exemplary and it became well known who the cheating wives were. They were identified quickly because they were never invited to the ladies' monthly club, known as the *kekkel en kraai* club. Kekkel and kraai is the Afrikaans expression for the noise made by hens when they gather. The club was run by the wife of the commanding officer. It was a tea club, all very demure and proper, which used to meet once a month or so where the eighty or so wives would gather and have a good gossip.

From the early days Gloria and I discussed at length the problems of the island and in particular using convicts as servants. It often appeared that many of the wives would forget that these men were both male and criminal, some of them having been convicted of terrible crimes, including rape and murder.

We understood the rules that before the prisoner arrived to help out, be it in the garden or with odd jobs around the house, Gloria would be fully dressed. Because the prisoners arrived for work shortly after 7 o'clock, it meant an early start. But we both agreed it was the safest way, rather than being seen wandering around the house partially clothed in a night-dress or dressing-gown which could have been interpreted as provocative.

The matter was brutally reinforced one day when we had been on the island several years. A woman who lived four doors away from us was the victim of an appalling attack.

The woman's husband was sent with a group of prisoners to the mainland and was away for the entire weekend. She made the mistake of trusting the convict, allowing him to arrive each morning and make her coffee which he would deliver to her in bed. She made the added mistake of telling the prisoner that her husband was visiting the mainland for several days. The convict hid that afternoon beneath the bed. He was not missed at roll-call back at the main prison; a frequent occurrence where roll-calls were not considered particularly important because of the difficulty in escaping from the island.

It was not until the next morning that the man was missed. I was on duty when the siren sounded from the main prison to indicate that a prisoner was missing. A search had to be organised and the families in the main town warned to stay inside their homes.

I rushed home to tell Gloria. 'Stay inside. Lock the doors and keep the children in until we have recaptured him.'

Within a couple of hours the convict was found hidden inside the church belfry.

But by then, his appalling eighteen hours of horrific abuse of the woman had been discovered.

Shortly after darkness he had emerged brandishing an axe. He threatened to kill the woman's two young children unless she

156

submitted to him. Throughout the night the woman was repeatedly raped. The convict fled before dawn, taking with him a bottle of booze and a bottle of sleeping-tablets. Whether or not he intended to take an overdose is impossible to say, but when he was discovered in the church he was completely drunk, unable to stand. The man was eventually hanged for the attack.

Life on the island always seemed to mirror the seasons. Unlike the mainland where the seasons ran through the annual cycle and where life had its many idiosyncrasies and subtle changes, here it was either a blistering summer or miserable winter, with no in between. In winter the north-westerly blew almost permanently, frequently to gale force. It was remarked that the high seas which whipped up the Benguella stream and the high winds had come all the way from Antarctica. Heavy rain often combined with the wind to make conditions cold, wet and miserable. When the north-westerly blew it was too rough to take the boat out; it meant that often, for many days on end, we were stuck on the island without physical contact with the mainland. At the opposite end of the scale, when the wind did not blow and the mists and fogs came up, we were equally stuck, not trusting the navigation in the treacherous waters across to the mainland. The sound of ships' foghorns, the dull, penetrating bellow reaching into the gut, signalled misery for us and still haunts me, producing waves of near desperation from the memories it evokes. To wake up to the sound of the foghorn when it was a day off, the only day in two weeks when a trip to the mainland was possible, was sheer frustration. For the sound meant two more weeks without any contact with the mainland and the outside world.

When we were stuck it increased tensions all round. In 1968 the island was lashed by a storm for two weeks non-stop and we were unable to get fresh supplies from the mainland: no bread or milk. Army helicopters tried to land carrying fresh produce, but to no avail. Flour and supplies were soon sold out from the shop as everyone began to stock up with items in case the weather closed us in longer.

I think the desperation from many weeks spent on the island without a break led to me behaving stupidly with a gun.

Each Wednesday there was a gun inspection and the more senior officers were allowed to keep their rifles, FN automatics, at home under secure lock and key. I therefore had a rifle at home. When the rifle was issued we were also given a magazine of fifteen bullets, although I had several hundred more from my involvement with the prison shooting team.

Before the gun inspection I had spent the Tuesday cleaning the rifle; inside the barrel there was a hair or thread trapped. The more I tried to get it, the further it slid down and became stuck. Gloria and Zane were on the mainland, visiting the bioscope and her parents. I was alone and in my frustration with the rifle decided to put it aside and head down to the bar for a drink. Half a bottle of brandy later I was back home, again trying to get the barrel clean. I finally decided the best way was to shoot it out. I turned off the house lights, opened the back door and took aim at the dustbin which stood at the end of my path, gauging that behind the dustbin was a sandbank into which the bullets would pass.

I let fly with a complete magazine, firing automatically. The noise was intense and my next door neighbour, a man named Cilie, came rushing out to find out what was happening. At the end of the street was a warder, Gerber, a known tattle-tale. Within minutes the island security officer was at the front door.

'Gregory, I understand you have been shooting off your rifle.'

'Who says,' I countered.

'We have an eyewitness, Gerber, who confirms it.'

I laughed aloud. 'Hell, man, everyone knows Gerber is a liar and is always trying to kiss arse.'

The security officer, a man named Roelofse, was insistent. 'Okay, just let me have the gun. I'm confiscating it.'

He headed off to the main arsenal to store the gun and to prepare the charges against me for improper use of the firearm. I knew I'd made a mistake, but was determined not to let the matter rest. I rode my bike down to the administration building where I saw the duty officer. I asked two questions: had Roelofse examined or smelled the barrel of the gun. I was told he had not. I went and got a friend who had worked in the arsenal and explained what had happened. We both went to the arsenal which was inside the prison and cleaned my rifle. We oiled it and returned it to the locked area. We then went back to my house and got hold of the dustbin which was riddled with holes. We took it to an area where I knew the sea was deep. I loaded it with rocks and left it to sink. We then returned to the island cricket club where I knew I could get hold of a replacement dustbin, a new one, which was one of several sitting outside. The last part of my little subterfuge was to dig the sandbank where the shells had fallen. I counted out fifteen and threw them away. My cover-up was complete.

Next morning I was summoned by the commanding officer, van Aarde. He was ready to haul me off on a charge. I denied it all, claiming Gerber had a personal grudge against me. The commanding officer then examined the rifle and realised it did not have the appearance of a gun which had recently been discharged. He then visited my house where he examined the dustbin. Unmarked. Then he asked to see my shells, the fifteen I should have had issued. I pulled out instead several hundred. Van Aaarde was still suspicious and placed me on a charge. Later, when the case was tried against me, a brigadier was brought in from Pretoria, Hennie le Roux, who agreed with me there was no evidence to convict. I'd escaped. But later the truth began to emerge and over the years became a standing joke. It was said throughout the service that I had a magic dustbin which when shot through had the ability to change appearance overnight.

The one person who did not treat the matter as a joke was Nelson. The truth of what had happened spread throughout the island, even among the prisoners. It was a subject which I had assumed he had either not heard about or had dismissed when, several years later, he brought it up in conversation.

'Everyone thought it was a huge joke,' I told him.

As I spoke I glanced at him and could see he was wearing his serious face. 'It was irresponsible, unworthy of you.'

I tried to justify it by explaining the frustration and boredom, but he scolded me as a father would a child. 'You were lucky. You should have been more restrained and sensible.'

It was his own form of a lecture and I nodded, agreeing with him.

Chapter 17

Nelson's family

Through the years I knew Nelson Mandela he had ample opportunity to express regret or remorse for having chosen the path which led him to prison. His incarceration was to last twenty-seven years. It had been a close-run thing that the trial judge had not ordered the Rivonia men, including Nelson, to be hanged. When the judge pronounced a life sentence, it really did mean a lifetime to be spent behind bars. There was never any thought at the time that this punishment could ever end in quite the way it did. In the conversations I shared, the letters I read and the times I listened as he talked to others, there was never a moment when he spoke of regret. Perhaps, in many ways, this was the quality which I most admired in him, his emphatic determination that his chosen path was to carry his people to their destiny, a promised land of freedom and equality. The only thing Nelson ever expressed regret over, either in his writings from prison, or to me, was the precious time he missed spending with his family and in particular his children.

Makgatho was Nelson's second son, born to his first wife Evelyn. He was named after Sefako Mapogo Makgatho, the second president of the ANC from 1917 until 1924. My first impressions of the young man when he visited his father on the island were not good. It was in the first year after I arrived as censor and I did not like the boy's attitude. I was later to read how he sided with his father after Nelson had divorced Evelyn. As I read it my reaction was that this was rubbish: he had always sided with his mother. Perhaps I am being unkind to the boy; he did after all have to live with the Mandela name. It was not easy for him, but I still feel he never worried too much about his responsibilities.

On one of the early visits Makgatho arrived drunk. The group of visitors was anxious to get off the ferry and under cover quickly to escape the drizzling rain. I watched in amazement as Makgatho began walking very unsteadily towards the prison, ignoring the rest of the group, and the visitors' hall itself. He was going in the wrong direction. I had to summon one of the warders to grab him and gently steer him towards the visitors' section. I told him he should not wander off, but I knew my words had not registered. His eyes were glazed over and his breath reeked of alcohol. Just before he was allowed in to see Mandela, to took out a half bottle of brandy. A warder saw it and told him it would have to be left in the waiting room. When the boy was told he could not take it into the visiting room he laughed and tipped the contents into his mouth.

Nelson would never openly discuss his family although I knew from his letters he was extremely worried about what he described as 'Makgatho's waywardness and sickness'.

In the letters he was always exhorting his family to use their influence on the young man, to encourage him to study and get a better education. Makgatho had left school at fourteen, but Nelson pleaded in his letters and emphasised during the visits that his son should return to school. Throughout the Robben Island years Nelson never stopped trying to persuade him to return to full-time education, but without great success. The more Nelson tried, the more Makgatho resisted and the less inclined he was to follow his father's directions.

By the mid-1970s Makgatho, to the initial despair of his father, married and fathered a son. At first the situation exasperated Nelson, but it turned out to be a blessing in disguise, for Nelson grew close to his new daughter-in-law Rennie, and his grandson Mandla. Rennie, a determined, intelligent young woman, followed Nelson's advice and returned to complete her own education.

In those early years on Robben Island Makgatho displayed an attitude of indifference during his few visits. In the conversations between father and son Nelson repeated many, many times, 'Make use of your opportunities, go back to school, get an education.'

Several times Makgatho promised to return to school, but each time the promises were empty. But gradually he began to listen. He sat his exams, but failed. And once again he complained he wanted to spend his time minding the shop owned by his mother, Nelson's first wife Evelyn, in the Transkei.

But Nelson tried again. 'That is not enough for you. You must not waste your life by spending it tending a shop. You can become somebody.'

It was a long, hard haul for Nelson to convince his son. I could see the boy was not anxious to follow his father's advice. I also realised that now Thembi had been killed, Makgatho was the person through which the Mandela clan line would flow. In letters to family and friends Nelson was anxious to push his son's cause.

Nelson despaired even more when the marriage between Makgatho and Rennie began to sour. Although the family blamed Rennie, Nelson remained neutral about the matter and in a letter to Zindzi, one of his daughters, wrote:

I have taken no sides in this dispute, firstly because I have not heard Kgatho's version. Even when the impossible occurs and Kgatho writes, I will lean towards an amicable settlement. I will think of both parties as well as Mandla who will certainly suffer far more than any other person when his parents break. Imagine, darling, just what our reaction would be if someone urged Mum to pack her belongings and find a new home because of my faults. You are the product of the love and affection of your parents, and throughout your life you have drawn strength and hope from that love and security. Destroying that love and home, for whatever reason, would be like a beautiful rose whose tender roots are exposed to the frost.

Makaziwe was the oldest of the three children Nelson had from his first marriage to Evelyn, a sister to Thembi and Makgatho. He had two other daughters, Zeni and Zindzi, from the marriage with Winnie.

Maki, as she was known to her father, was a child of eight when Nelson was first sentenced. By the time she visited Robben Island, in the company of Nelson's mother and sister Mabel, in 1968, she had grown into a lovely young woman. As with Makgatho, Nelson, when he first saw her, treated her as the child he had left behind all those years before, lecturing her as if she were still eight years old. It was a mistake Nelson was to make on several occasions, although I could see it was for the right reason. He was as insistent with Maki, as he was with Makgatho, that school and education came before anything else.

His lecturing initially had the desired effect. Maki was the first of the children to matriculate, an achievement which pleased Nelson. Then to his disappointment, she married and had two children. It was a marriage destined to fail. Nelson always beseeched his children to pursue their education as far as they could and after the failure of the marriage he again persuaded Maki to go back to her studies.

Maki's own determination later helped her graduate from university. She then took a job as a social worker. Even then Nelson was not satisfied, and he wrote to her of how he wished she had gone further with her education.

In one letter he wrote to Maki:

I am sorry to discover that despite all my efforts and in spite of your promises you have chosen to condemn yourself to the status of an exploited and miserable social worker of moderate academic qualification who sadly lacks the ambition and drive that motivate the more serious-minded youth of today. Many of your mates of the fifties are now doing senior degrees – MAs and even doctorates at overseas universities while you remain shut up in the backveld and unable to give meaningful assistance to the people you would so very much like to help.

Nelson's stern attitude again persuaded Maki to go further and with the help of family friends, Ismael and Fatima Meer in Durban, was able to enrol at the University of Natal. She later completed her honours degree in sociology and won a Fulbright Scholarship to the United States.

The two daughters Nelson had with Winnie, Zenani and Zindziswa, were both born within a year of one another and by the time he was sent to prison the sisters were still very small. It created a vacuum of unimaginable proportion in his life: he had two daughters but he had only held them as babies; he had not seen them grow up. It became part of his inner conflict: between the path he had chosen to follow and his neglect of his family.

Through many of the early years Nelson was deeply troubled by the way the authorities treated his family. There were long periods, in the late 1960s, when Winnie was frequently harassed by the government and, in particular, the security police.

It was in the early hours of 12 May 1969 that Winnie was hauled out of her home in Soweto and detained under the Terrorism Act. The full details of that arrest and the subsequent detention without charge only emerged months after her release. It spoke much about Winnie's incredible resolve that she was able to survive in the way she did. When arrested she had to leave her two young daughters, both under the age of ten, at the house. They were cared for over the months by family friends. It was then that Nelson decided the best option for the girls was to send them to boarding-school in Swaziland to complete their education away from the constant police harassment of Winnie.

During the seventeen months Winnie was held in solitary confinement, she was denied bail and visitors or any communication with Nelson. These details we only learned later, although I could see throughout this period how Nelson worried himself sick at what was happening to his family and how the lack of real information was continually eating away at his own confidence.

Within two weeks of being released from prison, Winnie was served with a five-year banning order and placed under house arrest. It was becoming harder to follow the continual hounding of Winnie. She was being arrested, banned, tried, released, banned and arrested again. The cycle seemed never to end. During one of Winnie's periods of freedom, when Zindzi was old enough to visit her father, they both came to the island and Zindzi saw Nelson for the first time since she was a toddler. At the time the prison authorities were told Zindzi was sixteen. I was to learn many years later we had been well and truly duped by Winnie and Nelson who had modified the birth documents. Zindzi was in fact only fifteen. But, even had I known, would I really have denied him access to the daughter he had not seen since she was a baby? I somehow doubt it – already I was coming to know him too well.

On the day of the visit Nelson was more nervous than I had seen him for a long time. Although he kept his firm self control in most situations, there were always little signs I began to pick up which told me he was either angry or excited. I knew he had not seen Zindzi since she was three years old. I noticed his preparations: his fresh shirt and carefully combed hair. Clearly he wanted to show his daughter that he was still a handsome man.

The visitors were brought from the boat as usual by other warders. I went through the steel adjoining door where Nelson was sitting waiting impatiently.

'Is she here, is she here?' He was anxious in case there had been a last-minute problem, that perhaps Zindzi and her mother had missed the boat. Because of the security police harassment Nelson had not seen Winnie for over a year and he knew, and I did, that it would have been typically cruel of the authorities to have halted this trip at the eleventh hour.

I confirmed Winnie was with Zindzi and they were here.

'Are you sure? How can you recognise her?'

I smiled. 'Nelson, you only have to look at Winnie and Zindzi together to know they are mother and daughter; they are each as beautiful as the other.'

'Can we start now?'

I knocked on the outer steel door and Winnie and Zindzi walked in on the other side of the divide. There was an immediate explosion of emotion which the thick walls and the inch-thick glass separating Nelson and his wife and daughter could not diminish.

The moment was too much for Zindzi as she saw her father for the first real time. She could not remember the man who had left her as a three-year-old, she only knew the stories of his selfless exploits. Now she burst into tears. In the forty minutes she managed only a few words, but Nelson kept directing his conversation to her, trying to calm her.

He told her all the things he had stored in his mind, preparing for this moment. 'You are a beautiful young woman, as beautiful as your mother. Now you are old enough to visit, you can come more often and we can get to know one another properly.'

In order to put her mind at ease in the prison situation, Nelson turned to me as I stood behind him.

'Look here, Zindzi, this is Mr Gregory, he is my guard of honour.' I smiled at his humour.

Zeni was the daughter I always considered to be level-headed and sensible. Where Zindzi followed in her mother's footsteps with her quick temper and explosive temperament, so Zeni took after Nelson; she was more thoughtful.

In 1977 Zeni announced she was to marry Prince Thumbumuzi, a son of King Sobhuza of Swaziland. They had met while Zeni was in Swaziland attending school. The thought of Zeni getting married troubled Nelson. At the time Zeni was under the age of twenty-one and required Nelson's legal consent for the marriage. Nelson was aware of his traditional duties as a father: to determine *lobola*, the customary bride price which is paid by the groom to the bride's family, and interview the prospective groom and assess his future prospects. Naturally Nelson could not fulfil these obligations, so instead asked his legal adviser George Bizos, the advocate who had represented him at the Rivonia trial and who had also become a close personal friend, to stand in for him. Mr Bizos carried out the instructions, interviewing the Prince and passing on his observations during a visit to the island. The visit was seen as a family matter and not a legal one, and was therefore not private. Mr Bizos, however, queried my presence in the room.

Nelson turned and explained how this visit was seen as a family matter before adding, 'Anyway, I have no secrets from my guards.'

Mr Bizos reported to Nelson how the young couple were clearly deeply in love and how their future together looked bright. As a

166

future son-in-law the Prince was more than acceptable and his father, King Sobhuza, an enlightened traditional leader, was also a member of the ANC. When the lawyer went to some pains to point out that the prospective groom was a Swazi prince, Nelson countered, 'George, you make sure the young man understands he is getting the hand of a Thembu princess.'

The marriage held great significance for Nelson because under prison visiting rules, when Zeni married into the Swazi royal household, she was immediately granted diplomatic privileges and could visit Nelson any time she wished. It was after the wedding and after the birth of their baby daughter that Zeni and her husband came to see Nelson. It was to be the first time in his imprisonment that Nelson had been allowed a contact visit; five years before he was allowed such a visit from Winnie.

On the day it was obvious Nelson was nervous and we again went through the same routine as before.

'Where will the visit be conducted?' he asked.

I explained that I planned to use the room close to the normal visiting area which was used for legal consultations.

'Yes, yes, that will be perfect,' he agreed. 'Will we be left alone?'

I knew that this moment would be deeply personal and emotional for everyone concerned and apologised that a warder would have to be inside the room.

Nelson was not taken aback and insisted, 'Well then I would wish you to be there rather than anyone else. You would be best for that.' It seemed strange that this was a compliment which I felt privileged to have received. It was almost like an invitation to a private family function.

Nelson ensured he had a fresh shirt and trousers. He spent a long time over his personal appearance, a trait I recognised as his own vanity. There was nothing wrong in wanting to look his best.

The moment I opened the door and allowed Zeni holding her baby and her husband Muzi into the room was one I treasure from those dark years. I had already taken Nelson into the room and left him sitting on one of the hard wood chairs. As Zeni burst in, Nelson sprang to his feet, his face a picture of absolute joy. He held his arms out to the daughter he had not touched since she was a baby. In those brief moments father and daughter simply stood facing one another. Suddenly Zeni rushed forward, passing the baby to Muzi. She fell into her father's arms.

This was my first experience of having to handle such intensely personal moments and I tried my best to drift into the furthest corner. A window looked out towards the southern shoreline. I stood with my back to the family group, shutting off my mind to what was happening in the room. I knew this was no place for me although the rules said I had to be there.

Nelson was introduced to his new son-in-law who then handed over the baby. There was laughter and a sense of merriment in the midst of the emotion.

'It has been a long, long time since I was called upon to hold a baby,' Nelson said solemnly. 'I hope I can remember how to be gentle. We don't get much practice in here in looking after babies.'

I laughed and told them, 'Nelson, I just hope the baby does not fill her pants. I'm not sure you could manage that.' We all laughed.

There was a particular reason for the visit at that time. It was customary that Nelson, as grandfather, should help in selecting a name for the newborn.

They decided on the name Zaziwa, a name which means 'hope'. Nelson became serious for a moment and I knew he was speaking from the heart when he told Zeni and Muzi, 'That name means a lot to me for through all my years in prison hope has never departed from me and I know it never will.'

As I have said, Winnie was in and out of prison so many times I had trouble keeping track. I was always informed with a telephone call. Whenever the call came through I demanded details so that I could give Nelson as much information as I could. It was when I had to break this news that I saw the steely hardness that would set in his eyes, the expression so deep that it was impenetrable. At this time I had never discussed with Nelson how he felt about these matters, but I knew from the letters which he wrote, which had passed through me, of his feelings. Later he told me that this was the path they had both chosen, knowing it would be strewn with pain and heartache. Even before Nelson and Winnie married they knew what their situation would be. Nelson was already committed to the ANC and Winnie knew that in marrying him she was also choosing a course which would mean hardship and harassment. Their strength was often sustained by the letters. In one, written in October 1976, Nelson told his wife:

I have been fairly successful in putting on a mask behind which I have pined for the family, alone, never rushing for the post when it comes until somebody calls out my name. I also never linger after visits although sometimes the urge to do so becomes quite terrible. I am struggling to suppress my emotions as I write this letter. I have received only one letter since you were detained, that one dated August 22. I do not know anything about family affairs, such as payment of rent, telephone bills, care of children and their expenses, whether you will get a job when released. As long as I don't hear from you, I will remain worried and dry like a desert. I recall the Karoo I crossed on several occasions. I saw the desert again in Botswana on my way to and from Africa – endless pits of sand and not a drop of water. I have not had a letter from you. I feel dry like the desert. Letters from you and the family are like the arrival of summer rains and spring that liven my life and make it enjoyable. Whenever I write you I feel that inside physical warmth, that makes me forget all my problems. I become full of love.

Whenever Winnie was detained Nelson would write to her, giving her strength to carry on. 'This is the path we have chosen for the cause, for the freedom of our people,' he would say.

The sheer emotion of the situation affected me. I would play over and over in my mind the personal sacrifices these people were prepared to make. Initially I had brushed it aside, but the more I learned of how they were right in the things they said, the more it burdened me. It reached a stage when Winnie's detentions or bannings would upset me. My thoughts turned not so much to how it would affect her and Nelson, more the children.

I knew I could slowly apply my own standards to the censorship. I also knew that after I had passed a letter the probability was that it was read again by the security police or other members of the intelligence services. I knew that I had to have an answer if they ever came back to me querying my decisions on censorship.

My argument was always that I would allow mention of the arrests, detentions and the bannings. I was content that everyone knew Winnie was in jail. They knew her attitude to the system she saw as unlawful, they knew she was defiant and they knew she would be overtly political. I passed the letters which came to me, reasoning, 'These are the sentiments which any human would convey to his wife or receive from his wife if the roles were reversed. I would write the same and my wife would write the same.' I always used the phrase, 'Encouraging your family through the darkness of uncertainty is not political. It is common sense.'

At the time I did not see the white regime as unlawful, although my attitude was gradually becoming more critical. Finally I became completely opposed. Initially I saw them as elected by the people, although I accepted that blacks did not have the vote. Through my

169

months of research in the Cape Town library I knew that this was a system which was wrong, but until it was replaced it was still the law. I knew I could not change it. I could just adapt it as I saw fit in small ways which could be to everyone's benefit.

In June 1976 the uprising which began in Soweto, the protest of school children against the enforced use of Afrikaans in all schools as a method of sustaining segregation, triggered much wider protest. It was to last a year and would eventually leave more than 600 people dead. In the aftermath of the Soweto uprising Winnie became involved with the Black Parents' Association, an organisation of professionals and church leaders who acted as a guiding hand for the protesting students. It was virtually inevitable, given the attitude of the authorities, that Winnie would be harassed again. Just two months after the uprising she was arrested and detained under the Internal Security Act and imprisoned without charge in Johannesburg for five months. She emerged from jail in December, but within six months was being hounded again by the authorities. This time the punishment was an internal exile: she was banished to a remote township in the Orange Free State called Brandfort. It was 250 miles south-west of Johannesburg, close to Bloemfontein, an area which was unknown to her.

Life in Brandfort was ridiculously hard for Winnie and Zindzi, who accompanied her mother. The three-roomed, tin-roofed shack was known as house number 802, Brandfort. It was in a desperately poor area where the local people were ruled by local white farmers. It was a traumatic time for Nelson who heard about the banishment second hand. Later, as letters began to arrive from Winnie, I was also to learn of her situation, of the lack of heating, toilet or running water. Whenever I read the letters I continued to have admiration for Winnie's personal defiance. She brought a smile to my eyes when I read how she refused to pay for the water, the lights and the rent. She argued, in her letters, that this house, number 802, was not her home, it was a government jail, so why should she pay. That was Winnie, she would not take any nonsense. I silently applauded her. Winnie's fortitude eventually won over a number of people in the Brandfort area including some sympathetic whites. She set about supplying food to starving black people in the township through her Operation Hunger programme, as well as starting a crèche and a medical centre for the township.

When I read Winnie's first letter from Brandfort I became angry about her suffering. She described the house: 'When I opened the front door there was a mound of dirt in the living-room, most of the windows have been knocked out and the toilet is outside.'

Nelson, pragmatic as usual, replied, 'I realise conditions are bad, but that is the course we have both chosen, we must make the very best of it.'

By now Nelson and I were on friendly terms. He would always inquire about my family and I would also ask about Winnie and the girls, although it was really a stupid question for I already knew from the letters. Nelson would give me a rueful smile and often reply, 'Well, you know where she is; she is as well as can be expected.'

In all the years I knew Winnie we never had a serious cross word, which, considering my role as her husband's jailer, was remarkable. Whenever we met in the company of others we were formal, Mr Gregory and Mrs Mandela. When we were alone we dropped the formalities and used first names although I would not go so far as calling her Zami or Nobandla, the names Nelson used. When we discussed Nelson we always referred to him as Madiba, the leader of the clan. It seemed the natural thing for me to do for I, too, respected him as his own supporters and friends did.

Whenever Winnie arrived for a visit I took precautions to ensure she was treated with respect by the crew ferrying her between Cape Town and the island. I always gave instructions to the boat's coxswain that Winnie was to be left alone inside the boat; she was not to be disturbed or approached. I was concerned on two fronts: that as white men, many with known right-wing views, they could insult her; there was also the problem that Winnie was often under house arrest and the terms of the order were that she was forbidden to talk to outsiders. I heard later that Winnie complained she was being locked inside the boat, but that was never the intention. I tried to ensure that she was left in an area on her own and when it was raining and cold she could use a cabin. It upset many of the warders' wives who were refused use of a cabin.

On one occasion Winnie had arranged for two visits, one in the morning, one in the afternoon. At lunch-time I inquired if she wanted a meal and where she wanted to go. It was agreed that she would remain in the visiting area and I would arrange for a cooked meal to be brought from the warders' kitchen. I explained that I was going home to get some lunch and asked if she would be all right.

'It's no problem; nothing can happen here. If it does I can scream and there are plenty of people nearby who can hear me.'

I was anxious for Winnie's welfare and locked the outer door of the visiting area. When I returned, Winnie smiled and said she'd sat reading her book.

Within two days I was in big trouble. I was hauled in before the commanding officer, Badenhorst.

'You,' he yelled, pointing his finger at me, 'are in serious trouble. Deep kak.'

I was bemused. 'Well if you tell me what it is then perhaps I can understand what is happening.'

'Pretoria has been on the phone. They have had an inquiry from a firm of attorneys asking us to produce our warrant of arrest for Winnie Mandela. I wanted to know what they were talking about. I told them I didn't know of a warrant.'

I shrugged and asked what the matter had to do with me.

Again Badenhorst pointed at me. 'You locked her into what they are calling a cell-like building. Now Pretoria wants to see the warrant of arrest that gave you the right to lock her into the room.'

I was in a corner and suggested Badenhorst come with me to the visiting area where I would show him what had happened.

I took him to the room where Winnie had waited. I suggested he count each window. Six in total.

'Now count the numbers of bars on the windows,' I suggested.

'There are none.'

'Now measure how far the windows are from the ground.'

'Two feet,' he replied, puzzled by what I was doing.

'Okay. Well how can I have detained Winnie Mandela in a room where there were six open windows each within two feet of the ground? At any time she could have climbed out of a window.'

Badenhorst accepted the explanation and told Pretoria the suggestion of Winnie being imprisoned against her will was wrong. The matter was dropped, although it had always rankled me. Years later I discussed the matter with Nelson and we treated it as a joke. He explained it was a minor incident which would have been used to create a fuss, not designed to criticise me, but to criticise the general prison system.

I should have been angry with Winnie, but it was impossible. I felt too much respect and admiration for her strength. Her determination to complete what she had set out to do was, on occasion, an uncomfortable experience.

Another weekend she arrived at the harbour in Cape Town to visit the island. It was the end of June and midwinter. A north-westerly was howling; the sea was impossible. At the time I was based on the mainland and arranged to meet Winnie at the harbour. When I saw the weather I knew the trip would have to be cancelled. However, when I met Winnie she thought otherwise. There were times when I wanted to curse this hard-headed woman.

We turned to a man called Gus Basson, the captain of the boat, the *Diaz*, and he confirmed my view.

'There is no way I'm taking the vessel out in that storm,' Basson shouted, struggling to be heard above the wind.

Winnie, as always, was beautifully dressed. She smiled and spoke in her normal voice, 'I have not come all the way from Johannesburg to be turned back by a bit of wind and high seas. I have come to visit my husband and I shall.'

I tried to explain. 'But, Mrs Mandela, please listen to this man, he knows the sea, he knows the dangers. When he says the trip will endanger lives we have to accept it.'

Winnie shrugged and flounced off, the dress swirling around her. I assumed she was heading for a hotel to wait for the storm to abate or even heading home. I did the same and went home, pleased to be out of the storm.

I had barely reached home when the phone was ringing. It was a guy at the harbour telling me, 'Get back down here, the boat is going out. Mrs Mandela has got her way.'

I returned to the *Diaz* to find a very disgruntled crew preparing for the trip across to Robben Island.

'This is madness, we shall all go down in this blerrie weather,' was Basson's angry remark as I arrived.

I asked what had happened to change his mind.

'I didn't change my mind. It was changed for me by some big name in Pretoria who says we have to take Mrs Mandela over to the island or face the wrath of bad publicity.'

Basson said he would take the boat out, but on one condition, that the crew numbers were cut to a minimum, just the deck crew, an engineer, himself as captain, as well as Winnie and myself.

'I told them that if they insisted on me taking out a full crew I would refuse because it was dangerous already and I was not willing to endanger more lives than was absolutely necessary,' Basson added.

Even in the harbour the boat was rolling and rocking more than I'd ever experienced before. Once out into the main Benguela Stream, beyond the breakwater, it was a nightmare.

173

Winnie and I went into the cabin and as we left the safety of the harbour I looked across at her. She looked back at me, tossed her head back and laughed out loud. I thought it was a gesture to cover her own fear. This was more than we had bargained for.

Normally the trip would have taken forty-five minutes. This day, it lasted what seemed a lifetime. I lay stomach-down on the wooden bench, my arms wrapped tightly around the bench to keep me as still as possible. Winnie did the same on the other side of the cabin.

We were skewing and twisting, being tossed around the ferocious seas. The sounds I could hear above the roar of the wind and seas was the sickening thump as the waves hit the hull as we lurched into a trough followed by a scream as engines were reversed to lessen the next slam of waves. Occasionally I imagined I could hear the rivets holding the hull together popping and pinging. My eyes were tightly closed but as we reached the other side, inside the safety of the island harbour, I heard a squeak from the communication pipe. It was the signal we had arrived. I tried to stand, but my legs buckled. I looked across at Winnie and swear to this day the green hue on her face was not a reflection from her dress. She was as violently sick as I was. The next hour was agony as I spent the entire time being sick. Somehow Winnie managed to see Nelson, but it was a visit the details of which passed me by.

Nelson later told me that midway through the visit I had dropped the telephone which connected the three of us. I had dashed outside to throw up.

'I have never seen a person as ill as you were that day,' he said later. He told me how I needed to sit down on a chair and that several times I toppled to one side. I could remember none of it.

It was then I heard the worst possible request from Winnie: 'I now want to return to Cape Town.' I could not believe she wanted to repeat the journey in the same weather. She could have remained the night on Robben Island, staying at the guest house. But no, Winnie wanted to go back.

I phoned to the mainland and tried to get the air-sea rescue to send a helicopter. They tried to land, but said it was too dangerous. The only way back was on the *Diaz*. When I told Captain Basson, I thought he was going to throttle Winnie or myself. The return was worse than the outward journey. At the harbour I had to be lifted out of the cabin.

As I staggered from the boat I turned to Winnie and got the satisfaction of seeing her as ill as I was.

174

'I just hope you're satisfied now,' I told her through lips that felt like rubber.

Many times we were both to take the same journey and, each time, just before we were about to sail Winnie would roll her eyes skyward and tell me, 'Mr Gregory, I just hope the sea is not too rough today.' I knew what she referred to and just smiled.

Winnie's own strong will and the controversy she created was used on a number of occasions by the authorities to undermine Nelson's confidence. Whenever rumours appeared in the South African press, suggesting she was having an affair with another man, Nelson would always find that a cutting from the newspaper would be left in his cell.

In 1974 after Winnie and a family friend Peter Magubane lost an appeal for breaking a banning order, it was suggested in the Afrikaans press, in effect the unofficial voice of the government, that they were having an affair. The reality was very different. Magubane was a long-time family friend: there was no affair between him and Winnie. The security police were watching both Magubane and Winnie twenty-four hours a day. It angered me to see how such rumour and innuendo was being used to get at Nelson. It was his one Achilles' heel.

Winnie's behaviour over the years had always been at odds with the authorities and led to frequent clashes. However, many of the things she was involved with left her open to criticism. After she returned to Soweto in 1985 Winnie had determined she would be the voice of the grass roots. There was a groundswell of opinion that on many issues the ANC itself had become distanced from the many people it represented: its leadership was either imprisoned or exiled, certainly not experiencing the day-to-day problems of the townships and squatter camps.

With her background in social work Winnie had been deeply concerned with the numbers of youths who wanted out of the townships, young men terrified of the violence who needed refuge. She had taken responsibility for them and arranged to provide them with shelter, board and schooling. The group became known as the Mandela Football Club. In reality these youths were no sportsmen, they were a gang of young thugs, a private army who surrounded Winnie and acted as her guards. Matters came to a head when the gang kidnapped a group of teenage boys, beat them and murdered one of them, a fourteen-year-old named Stompie Seipei. The gang leader, Jerry Richardson, was sentenced to death and Mrs Mandela was given a six-year prison term for being involved in the kidnapping. It was reduced to a fine on appeal.

The incident and the growing numbers of stories about Winnie and the gang members were causing considerable damage to the family reputation.

At the time I could see Nelson was struggling to come to terms with the incidents involving Winnie.

Whenever Nelson discussed the matter with his wife there was a clear clash of wills: two people with very firm ideas on what should happen, neither willing to shift. He stuck to his position, that his wife should turn her back on the Mandela Football Club, the gang members, and Winnie, that she would not abandon them.

At the time of the incidents we were at Victor Verster Prison and Nelson read of several incidents involving Winnie in the newspapers. His anger was barely contained as he instructed me, 'Please phone my wife and tell her to be here tomorrow. We must talk.'

When Winnie visited and they discussed the death of Stompie Seipei and how the team members of her soccer club were collecting money, Nelson was emphatic: these things were wrong and had to stop.

'These boys are a bunch of hooligans and they are using the Mandela name to raise money for their own use,' he would explain.

There would be a row, but neither would raise their voices; it was civilised, but a very powerful clash of wills and attitudes. When they argued they ignored me; it was as if I was not in the room, although both knew that by then I was more informed about their lives than any other person.

On one occasion there was a story in a newspaper that Winnie had whipped the boys with a *shambok* (a large, rawhide whip). The next time she visited, Nelson asked her directly about it and she laughed. 'Why would I do a thing like that?'

Nelson replied, 'That is not an answer to my question.'

'You of all people should know that you cannot trust what you read in the newspapers. You know how they twist and bend each and every little fact. How can you sit there and look me in the eyes and tell me you believe the newspaper and not me? How can you?'

Nelson was exasperated and he would reach a decision. 'Just get rid of these people around you. They are bad for you, this is poor judgement to have them near you, to surround yourself with them. You must get rid of them.'

176

But Winnie was adamant. 'No, these are people, young boys who have been rescued from the streets. They need help and I am providing it. I cannot abandon them; they have already been abandoned once in their lives.'

The arguments were increasing between the two of them. Earlier, on another occasion, Winnie was having a new house built for her in Orlando. She brought the plans to show Nelson when he was in Pollsmoor Prison. There was a conference room with enough space to seat eight people around a table. But after she showed them to Nelson for approval she changed the specifications and enlarged the area to seat twenty people.

I received an irate telephone call at the prison from the builder who claimed, 'We've got problems. Mrs Mandela ordered changes to the house, and we carried out the changes and now we are out of pocket to the tune of about 300,000 rand. We want to know who will pay this because Mrs Mandela says she does not have the money.'

I went to Nelson and repeated the conversation. He was clearly angry. 'Just get her to come here as soon as possible.'

Three days later Winnie swept into Pollsmoor and they had a heated conversation, the closest they came to an open row.

'You were here. The plans were agreed, then you went and changed them. There is more money to be paid out and where on earth will it come from?'

Winnie played innocent. 'I do not understand what is wrong with these builders. I didn't order the changes; they did them without asking.'

It was a debate which would clearly not be resolved so Nelson arranged through his lawyer, Mr Ayob, to have the extra money paid.

Whenever we had brief discussions about Winnie he went on the defensive: 'She has committed an error of judgement.' In the latter years of his imprisonment those errors became so frequent that their separation soon after his eventual release was an inevitability.

Chapter 18

My escape

By 1973 I'd had enough of Robben Island. I felt as if it was me and my family who were serving the sentence and after seven years, my time was up. I applied for a transfer, putting the request in writing. The reply from Pretoria was off-hand: 'Inform the member his request is refused. His duties are needed on Robben Island.'

The feeling I had to get away began to gnaw at me. The isolation was getting to me and the date when Zane finished the junior school and needed to be sent to high school was fast approaching.

Nelson was now the one friend I had on the island. We discussed a lot of family matters and I confided in him my dilemma.

'The problem is that next year Zane will have to go to high school on the mainland and unless they allow me away from here it will mean he will face boarding-school.'

As usual our conversation happened in the main yard as we walked around the perimeter. Nelson knew my feelings about boarding-school, my own personal experiences when I was a boy and how I was against sending my own children to them.

He kept his counsel, muttering just a considered, 'Mmmmm.' I was not asking for his advice, and he knew it; he was allowing me to talk.

'Yissus, I've already asked for a transfer and they've refused me; they tell me I'm needed here.'

Nelson pre-empted my next thought. 'We'll be sorry to lose you. We'll all miss you. Every person has a right to get on with his life as he sees best.' I turned to look at his face, wondering how he'd read my mind. We continued to walk.

'Ja, you're right. I have little choice. If they don't allow me to transfer, then I will leave. I will not send my children to

179

boarding-school after the bitter experiences I've had.' He nodded and we walked on.

In 1974 I went to see the commanding officer, at this time Colonel Roelofse. He could not understand my reason.

'So what makes you think it is wrong to send your children to boarding-school?'

I tried to explain to him, telling him of my own experiences at boarding-school.

'Ag man, forget those days, they are long gone. My children are in boarding-school and they are happy. Do you think your children are better than mine or something?'

Clearly Roelofse was not listening and I tried again to explain. He sighed and said he would put the request to Pretoria, but well ... he shrugged and held his hands apart palms facing upwards. It was clear he had little sympathy and I would be likely to meet with refusal.

Pretoria again replied in the same impersonal manner. 'Inform the member his request is refused.' Now I was getting angry. In mid-1975 I again applied, knowing time was running out and I'd have to move my family to the mainland and find alternative work if I had to resign.

The situation was beginning to dominate my thoughts and I continued to speak about it with Nelson, the only person who I knew felt sympathy for my problems.

His one concern was where I would find work and how I would care for my family. He was concerned. 'You must be careful; you have a family to support. You must make the right choice that ensures you can take care of them.'

I was touched by his concern. 'I think there is plenty of work in Cape Town.' I was tempted to add, especially for white people, but knew he understood anyway. 'But if I can't get a job I shall return to the farm. I have already written to my family explaining what is happening, asking if I could return to work on the farm.'

Nelson knew that a return to my home would mean eating a lot of humble pie, but he changed the topic. 'You know, I'd like to go back to the places where I grew up, to the spot where I was a herd boy and see all the things I remember.' We drifted off into conversation about our childhood, a topic we enjoyed exploring.

When the request was again refused I took the only course I considered open to me: I quit. After handing in the letter Roelofse confronted me with it, waving it before me. 'What's this, then?'

'That's my resignation, one month's notice.'

Roelofse sneered at me, waving the letter some more. 'And where do you hope to get a job?'

The steam was beginning to rise as I replied, ignoring the fact I was talking to my commanding officer, 'That is now no longer your blerrie concern.'

I turned on my heel and stomped off, leaving the commanding officer to do whatever he wished with the letter. Several hours later I was considering an early lunch when the telephone rang. It was General Frans Visser, a senior officer from Pretoria. I'd never met this man, but I knew of his reputation, that of a hard but fair man.

Now he was being friendly. 'Ag, man, what's the problem? Isn't this something we can sort out to everyone's satisfaction?'

I took a deep breath and explained the difficulties with schools and my desire to get away from Robben Island. I added, 'General, you know there is a saying here among the prisoners, that they were sent here by a court order, but the warders are here of their own free will. Yet when it comes time to leave, none of us has the choice to leave.'

General Visser tried to calm me. 'Look, Greg, don't be hasty on this matter. You're considered invaluable to our job. Help us train some more people, young officers for the censor office, in the way you conduct the job, and I'll give you my word you can go anywhere in the republic you wish. You choose the transfer and you shall have it.'

I agreed, and said, 'Okay, sir, I shall take your word for this. I'll withdraw my resignation and instead ask for a transfer tomorrow.'

The following day I saw Nelson and related the conversation with General Visser. As we stood in the middle of the passage outside the cells, he suddenly burst out into a booming laugh. A number of the others from the section were gathering around and Nelson explained what had happened. I actually stood to one side, nodding my head in agreement. They all saw the funny side as Nelson clasped me around the shoulder and told me, 'It looks like we're not the only ones not wishing to lose you, even Pretoria wants to keep you here.'

The laughter subsided as we all began to realise the implication: that I was a prisoner as much as they were.

Nelson then asked, 'So where will you ask to be transferred?'

I replied quickly, 'Fort Glemorgan, somewhere near East London.'

'Why there?'

I too began to laugh: 'Because it's about as blerrie far away from this place as is possible.'

Over the next few weeks Pretoria sent me four new recruits to be trained in the censor office. I remembered how, when I had first arrived, Pogaard had insisted I read the B-orders, what he called the Bible, the rules and regulations relating to censorship.

I knew they would have been well briefed so I suggested they take the B-orders and study them in their own quarters at their leisure. A few days later I called them back and said, 'Right, you have all read the letter of the law, how the censor laws are laid down. Now I'll introduce how you actually operate it, the reality of applying rules which are too rigid.'

I was insistent. 'You must have a flexible attitude when dealing with these people; try and put yourself in their place and consider how much a letter means to them. Try and imagine what it would be like cut off from your families for years on end, with no contact, and how much you would value a letter.'

They wanted to know what they should do when they came across material which should not be in the letters being written by the prisoners.

'I have found the best way, the easiest way, is to take the letter to the person who has written it and outline to him the area which you believe will cause a problem. Then ask him to change it. In fact offer your own suggestions on how best he can write it and still get the same message across.'

It took less than a month to train the new warders. I was looking forward to leaving, to getting back to civilisation and normality. It was now late November and I went to the prison to say goodbye to the men. My final day with them was to have been a Sunday when there were several visits in the morning. Shortly after noon I went to the B section cell area to say goodbye to them. They were gathered in the passage way outside their cells, standing in groups, waiting for the cells to be locked. Nelson, as usual, was standing talking to a small gathering outside his cell and I caught his eye as I walked in.

I walked up to him and extended my hand. 'I just want to say goodbye. And thank you for teaching me so much that I did not know about before.'

The prisoners crowded round us and we were all now shaking hands wishing one another well. My emotions were mixed: I was delighted to be getting off the island but also saddened that I would be leaving behind those I had come to regard as admirable men and, in some cases, friends.

From the far end of the passage Walter Sisulu and Mac Maraj poked their heads out of their cells, asking what the fuss was about.

Nelson spoke to them. 'Chaps, come say goodbye to Mr Gregory. We're losing a friend.' I shook every hand and thanked them. They all did the same, although in some cases I received strange looks when I thanked them. They could never know how my attitude had changed, how I had learned so much not only about them as black men and fellow human beings, but about my country and myself. If I could feel this way, then how many more? As I walked away from the prison, back to my house to continue packing our belongings, I considered just how far we had come. Back in 1966 I had started out by hating these men, by wishing they'd been hanged. Now I genuinely admired them and enjoyed their company. Perhaps I could not change my country or my government, but I was determined to have an influence over my children, to teach them the lessons I had learned on Robben Island.

The following morning we were packed and I needed to get my transfer papers, my official route orders from Pretoria. When I arrived at the administration block I was handed an envelope. Inside was a shock: I was not being transferred to Fort Glemorgan as I had requested, but instead to Pollsmoor, the prison on the outskirts of Cape Town. As I stared at the orders I could feel my anger rising. General Visser had made a promise and this was breaking it.

I threw the papers back on the desk and the startled clerk hurriedly looked up.

'What the blerrie hell is this?' I demanded. 'General Visser promised me I'd be going to Fort Glemorgan and now they're pushing me to Pollsmoor. What's going on, man?'

The clerk just shrugged and stood up. He obviously did not care a jot. He'd been told to give me the route orders and that was all he knew. He leaned back against the filing cabinet and smiled. 'Hell, man, why worry, you're out of here anyway. I'd be pleased to get a transfer from hell and not complain about it.'

I knew there was little the office clerk could do. I had to accept the situation, for now at least.

I went back to the house where Gloria and the children were preparing to leave. When I'd discussed getting away from Robben

Island Gloria said she was relieved to be going. Although she'd enjoyed our ten years on the island, it was time to get back to the mainland to allow the children room to expand their lives both at school and socially.

Gloria saw my face as I walked up the path to the house. 'James, what's up? What's the problem?'

I went inside the house and threw the route papers on top of a packing case. 'Those bastards have not kept their word,' I told her. 'It's not Fort Glemorgan we're going to, it's Pollsmoor.'

Gloria looked as dumbstruck as I felt and she began shaking her head. I thought she was about to cry and I put my arm around her. 'Let's not worry, at least we're away from the island, and we'll be close to your family here still. The best part is we'll never have to come back here.'

I was to look back on this moment and rue those words. Little did I know the government had other plans for me.

Pollsmoor is a massive expanse of purpose-built prison spread across the southern Cape Town suburb of Tokai, set in some of the most beautiful scenery in the entire Cape province. My first duty was to report to the commanding officer, so while the furniture was being delivered and Gloria set about sorting the new flat, I headed to the administration block, an imposing brick-built edifice in the centre of the complex.

I was told that the following Monday I would start duty in one of the prisons inside the complex, the Medium A.

I set about finding schools for Zane and Brent. For Zane, Zwaanswyk High School and for my younger son the junior version, Zwaanswyk Primary, less than three minutes from our house. It was perfect.

Initially we were able to take the children to school by car, but as the unrest which had started in Soweto spread through the townships and spilled over into many white suburbs such as our neighbouring community of Tokai, so we arranged for them to be bussed in each day under armed guard. During that period of unrest when murder and mayhem became the order of the day, white school children became a target. The children of prison warders were even more vulnerable as we too became targets for violent attacks.

On the Monday I started a new job and although my mind kept drifting back to Robben Island and the men I had left behind, I was content. I liked Pollsmoor and when I was given the job as an investigator, looking into incidents in the prison, I accepted that perhaps, after all, this was better than being posted to Fort Glemorgan.

For the next nine months, as violence flared throughout the rest of the country, sparked by the riots and shootings in Soweto, I stayed well clear of politics. My nose was firmly stuck into the investigations unit. Occasionally I would read an item in the newspaper or hear something on the radio, a mention of Nelson Mandela or one of the other ANC leaders. As the violence continued unabated I began to wonder more about my old friends, how they felt about this violence. Although they had been members of the Umkhonto we Sizwe, the armed wing of the ANC, I knew they were not men who believed in violence. They were peace-loving people. They wanted peace for all. I considered just how this violence now affected me. In the past I would have condemned it out of hand, calling for those involved to be arrested and hanged; now I understood it and felt a sadness for us all. We were all blighted by it, both perpetrators and victims.

It was in the middle of an investigation into an incident at the police recreation club in Pinelands that I was asked to go to the Roeland Street Prison in the centre of Cape Town: the commanding officer wanted to see me. I assumed there had been a break-out or a fight and it would need investigating.

When I arrived at Roeland Street I went straight to the office of the prison head, a man named Stassen.

As I entered, he had a rueful smile across his face. 'How's it feel, Greg?'

I was wary. 'How's what?'

'Ag, man, you must have heard. You being transferred back to your first love. Robben Island. Sorry if I've spoken out of turn, but I thought you'd heard.'

Stassen was enjoying this moment, my obvious discomfort at news he knew would anger me. I was determined to stay cool.

'Ja, no problem, man, you know how it is, we do our best to please and all that...'

Stassen made a feeble excuse that he had wanted me to pick up a parcel for Pollsmoor. In reality he wanted to have a laugh at my expense. I left Roeland Street and drove to Pollsmoor in a state of confusion. What was going on now?

I went straight to see the commanding officer, Brigadier van Rensburg. As I burst in he was sitting in his office armchair, drinking tea with a newspaper on his lap.

He smiled in an attempt to diffuse my obvious anger.

'Ah, Greg, good morning, man. How's the runaway?'

'I'm sorry, sir, what do you mean?'

'Well, I'm told you are running away again. You've been transferred back to Robben Island because those guys you trained for the censor office have all left. They couldn't stick it.'

Van Rensburg was an officer who was feared throughout the service for his discipline, but at that moment I cared little for his reputation. I was livid.

I stood in the middle of his office, pointing directly at him, and as he told me I was being transferred back to the island I shouted, 'No, I'm not, you can go, but I'm not.'

The commanding officer stood up and glowered, 'Get the hell out of my office.' He was swearing at me in Afrikaans as I told him, 'The hell with you. Don't worry, I'm going.'

I returned to my office, furious, knowing this had been the hidden agenda all the time. I'd not been transferred to Fort Glemorgan as I'd been originally promised because Pretoria had recognised all along there was a danger that the new recruits could be a problem.

I sat in the office, shaking with anger, before deciding what to do. I headed into the nearby Cape Town suburb of Wynberg, just ten minutes from Pollsmoor. I knew where I was going, the military camp. I was going to join the army rather than return to Robben Island. I knew one of the senior officers and discussed the situation. He agreed that I was eligible and would qualify for a family house in Wynberg. The problem was that I was already in one government department and was, effectively, transferring to another government department. A transfer was out, he said, so the best way was to resign and then join the army. There would be no problem, he said.

The next morning I went to see van Rensburg to quit. I was told to wait outside his office. One hour, two hours. I was getting mightily fed up.

When I was eventually allowed in van Rensburg remained seated, his mood icy. I decided to take the initiative.

'Yesterday you told me I was to be transferred back to Robben Island. I want to know what's going on. Why?'

'Gregory, you're going to Robben Island.' He was unbending as he made it sound like a prison sentence in itself. 'You can't refuse. I have the orders straight from Pretoria.'

I was prepared and my voice went low. 'Right, sir, you may now telephone Pretoria at my expense. Tell them that from this moment

I am giving you twenty-four hours' notice and I'm gone. You understand, gone.'

'What the hell are you talking about? Where will you go?'

I smiled, although inside I was churning. 'Don't you worry about where I shall go. At 5 o'clock this evening an army lorry will be here from Wynberg military camp to pick up my furniture. I've been appointed a staff sergeant in the army.'

I turned and walked out. Behind my back I could hear him spluttering and I even managed a smile as I heard him bellow, 'Get out, just get out.' He wanted the last word.

I was walking out on a career which had now spanned almost twelve years, but I felt this had become a matter of principle. They were not going to send me back to Robben Island and force me to split up my family. Halfway along the corridor, Van Rensburg's secretary came rushing up, out of breath.

'Mr Gregory, please can you come back. The commanding officer wants to see you again.' I shrugged and agreed.

Again he kept me waiting and from behind his closed door I could hear he was talking earnestly on the telephone.

Eventually I was ushered into the room, but gone was the formality of saluting. No politeness now.

Van Rensburg was equally angry. 'Right, Gregory, you've got your way. Pretoria has agreed you can be transferred to Roeland Street where you can handle all the letters and visits to certain people on Robben Island.'

I decided not to provoke him any further and said that as long as it was agreed I would not be returning to Robben Island, I would withdraw my resignation.

Van Rensburg said he was arranging to have my family moved to Roeland Street and a different flat next day. I again hesitated, knowing that would affect the children in school.

'Whoa, hold on a minute, sir. I feel that would be unfair on my family. I feel the children should have an opportunity to complete this year at school before being moved. It's almost the end of the school year and a few weeks will not make much difference. In the meantime I can handle the Robben Island business from here.'

Van Rensburg knew he was beaten. He was now very sarcastic. 'When you feel you are ready to move go and tell the logistics department and pester them with your bullshit, I'm tired of hearing you. Now get out.'

I saluted and as I walked out began to laugh. I didn't care that he heard me.

When eventually I moved back to Roeland Street, at the end of the year just before Christmas, I saw the prison commander, Stassen. They gave me an office and left me entirely to my own devices. All the mail from Robben Island was gathered in a sealed bag and brought to me. I had effectively moved my censor office from the island to the mainland. It had been almost a year since I'd last seen the group and within a few days of the New Year I was to return on the ferry, this time to supervise a visit for Nelson.

As usual I had arranged for Nelson to be brought to the visitors' area where he would be waiting. I went in to see him first. He stood and held out his hand, his face beaming: 'Man, am I glad to see you. I heard you were coming back. We'd all like to extend a very warm welcome.'

We shook one another's hand and I could feel the massive softness, but also the strength in his hands.

'What did you guys do to those young warders?' I joked. 'You clearly frightened them away; they lasted less than a year.'

'Man, are we glad to see you; we have missed you. You thought you were going to escape from here, but you're not. I hope you've missed us.'

I nodded and said I'd heard there had been problems. Letters were being withheld, unnecessarily cut, delayed, all sorts of problems.

Chapter 19

Pollsmoor Prison
and the 'penthouse suite'

1982. With the New Year came the news that I was being sent to
Pollsmoor Prison. There was a call from the personnel department,
with a dismissive comment that it would be made official in a
letter from the commander. If I was being moved, then was it
likely that Nelson could be moved as well, I wondered? Next
day I went to the office at the harbour and cleared out my desk.
I had decided to take a drive out to Pollsmoor. Usually when a
transfer is handed out, a reason is given. On this occasion there
was none.

The prison is a twenty-minute drive out of Cape Town. It is set
in glorious countryside, sitting between the imposing mountains
of Constantiaberg to the north, and the thousands of acres of
vineyards to the south, which continue down to the ocean. The
area is one of the richest in the entire African continent, less than
five miles from Constantia, where some of South Africa's richest
live. It was also particularly convenient for me, being only a ten-
minute drive from my own home in the middle-class area of
Plumstead which adjoins Constantia.

The drive out from Cape Town along the M3 motorway passes to
the east of Table Mountain and follows the line of the Twelve
Apostles, the string of hills which help create the haunting beauty
of the city. To the west the view of Table Bay is left behind as the
plains sweep away in the distance out towards the hills of
Stellenbosch and Franschoek. When the wind sweeps across this
plain the sands create a dust storm. When it is still, a heat haze or a
screen of pollution covers the entire area. It is only in the early
morning, soon after dawn, that a clear and magnificent sight of the
far mountains, some eighty miles distant, is captured. Leaving the
city behind, the M3 cuts through Constantia and the white suburbs
of Newlands, Wynberg and Bergvliet. By rights, the motorway
should run straight through to Cape Point, but for some reason it

comes to an abrupt end at Tokai as if government road-building funds ran out. This is the point where the Pollsmoor grounds border the motorway. But the M3 probably ends at such a place because this is also the location of the Silvermine Military Base, a massive underground nerve centre of the South African Defence systems. It is said that the base extends far into the Muizenberg and Steenberg mountains which also look down on Pollsmoor.

Having decided to go to Pollsmoor, I thought I would stay off the motorway, find a scenic route through the wine-growing district, and enjoy the time of year when the vines were in full leaf. I had often been out to Pollsmoor along the motorway. This time, I would find a route that I could use every day from home. The prison emerged; a solid mass of new sandstone and brick amid a plethora of signs and fences. It seemed out of place among the gentle hedgerows, shrubs and trees.

I was to see the commanding officer, Brigadier de Vortier, but he hardly gave me a glance before dispatching me to the head of the maximum prison, Major van Stittert. This was the same man, Tiekie van Stittert, who some sixteen years before had persuaded me to leave the traffic cops in Worcester and join the prison service. At least his was a face I knew.

I walked into his office and was greeted with a smile.

'Howzit, Greg? Come in and join us. I told you you'd have a good time.'

I smiled. 'Major, nice to see you, man. I've got you to blame for all this. I'd have been better staying as a traffic cop in Worcester. Your recommendation has led me into this mess.' We shook hands and he took off his cap, telling me to drop the rank, and call him Tiekie. We sat drinking tea and he turned serious. 'Hey, man, I've followed your career. You've become a big name in the service, looking after the ANC leaders. But why have you come here, why this transfer?'

I shrugged my shoulders, though I nursed a suspicion that Pretoria planned to transfer Nelson and the others to the mainland (I certainly hoped so: it would mean an end to all those ferry crossings to the island). Maybe something else was planned. I decided to keep my thoughts to myself.

'Tiekie, I have no idea why this transfer.' I decided to turn the conversation to a lighter vein. 'Hey, man, maybe they've sent me out to clear up some of the problems you've created out here.'

We began to talk about the prison itself, and the different areas. After the open spaces of the island it was a maze of corridors and buildings, a mass of high concrete walls.

'Greg, the best thing you can do is just wander around and familiarise yourself with the entire place,' he suggested.

'For what?'

'Look, man, if Pretoria has any special plans, then they haven't let me into the secret, so I can't tell you. I just know you've been transferred here with no specific job. So just enjoy the time you have now.'

I nodded and left, determined to get to the bottom of why I had been moved.

For two days I wandered the corridors and areas of the prison, through the maximum security section, through the two medium security areas, known as Medium A and Medium B, then through the female and minimum security prisons, five sections in total. It was different from the island, no doubt about that, but the faces were the same. The inmates with the same dull watchfulness, the eyes that followed the newcomer everywhere, hooded looks from heads bowed low; occasionally a stare of hatred. There were prisoners on their knees in corridors, polishing and buffing the cold concrete floors until they could see the reflections of their own faces; long corridors with the same remorseless strip lighting, walls painted as I'd known in other prisons, the bottom two-thirds in a pale grey, the top in what should have been white, but, through lack of sunlight, had quickly turned to a lighter shade of dirty eggshell. As I wandered, unchallenged and ignored by the other guards, I simply watched and listened, two qualities I had learned were invaluable to warders. I became detached from the prison, wandering as if I were in a tunnel, the echoes of conversations drifting through the honeycomb of corridors.

I went back to see van Stittert. 'Man, you've got to find out why I've been sent here. I've walked through every inch of this prison and now I know it better than anyone.'

'Greg, I've asked the same blerrie question and the answer comes back from the commanding officer that he doesn't know why you're here. All he says is you're trouble. I tell him you're okay, but he won't have it. He says you've been sent from Pretoria to spy.'

'Yissus, Tikkie, you know that's not me, you know I'm not that sort.'

'Ja, but look at it from his view. He sees you coming in here on a special transfer and for no good reason. You're ostensibly the censor officer for those guys on Robben Island and then you're sent

191

here. We have enough censor people here, we don't need you. So why are you here? You want to know, I want to know, the old man wants to know. So when you come and ask me, I've got to say I'm as much in the dark as you.'

'Ja, okay, Tikkie, but at least give me something to do; let me do some work because now I'm getting bored.'

'Greg, why not go into the censor office and see if they want any help. At least that way you're in an area where you know the routine.'

So I went to the censor office which had a staff of three, headed by a Sergeant Andrews.

I introduced myself and there were hasty looks between the warders: Andrews, who was in his mid-forties, and two younger officers. Immediately there was tension. They were polite enough, but holding back, uncertain. There were three desks and my appearance meant someone had to do without somewhere to work; four into three didn't go.

Andrews spoke up, an awkwardness in his voice. 'Sir, have you come to take over? Do you want my desk or one of the others? It's your choice.'

'No, you just carry on. I've been transferred and at the moment the commanding officer has not been told of the plans for me. I've only come in here because I've spent two days wandering the corridors getting to know the place and I have nowhere else to see.'

That seemed to ease the worries of Andrews, who was clearly upset at the prospect of losing his position of seniority in the censor office.

Then, after four days at Pollsmoor, circumstances changed. Brigadier de Vortier, the commanding officer, was told he was to be transferred and replaced by Brigadier Munro, the man who had originally welcomed me to Robben Island when he was the chief warder in 1966. He was now a high-flyer in the service. I was immediately pleased; here was a man I could talk to.

On the following Monday morning Munro had barely got his feet under the commander's table when I knocked at his door. As my head popped around the door, he jumped up and grabbed me by the hand.

'Greg, great to see you. Howzit? How's the kids and Gloria?' It was good to see a friendly face and for fifteen minutes we chatted about families and reminisced about Robben Island. I explained that I'd suddenly been transferred to Pollsmoor and was uncertain why. He said he'd also suddenly been transferred and was going to try to find out what was behind it all. We looked at one another, and without saying anything, we both knew the reason. Neither of us voiced our thoughts, but I was now convinced Nelson was to be transferred.

'Listen, Greg, I'll make it my business to talk to Pretoria and find out what's behind it all. Just stay loose and don't say a thing to anyone.' It was agreed.

Two days later Munro called me in. 'I'm sure both of us have a good idea what is going on.' I just nodded. 'Mandela and three others are coming here. They've just told me, but this is just between you and me for now. It's your job to find somewhere for them to stay which is both secure and safe, somewhere away from the main population.'

Munro and I agreed that I would continue to play the role of wandering around the prison, but now I had a purpose. I was looking for an area where Nelson and three others would be kept. At that stage I was uncertain who the three would be to accompany Nelson, although I assumed two of them would be Walter Sisulu and Kathy.

We then got down to basic requirements: location, equipment for the area, staffing.

Munro was decisive. 'Greg, you decide where the best place is for them to be, tell me what you need and make a list. I'll sign the inventory. There'll be no questions asked and no answers given. Keep this all quiet for now, until we have everything in place. If anyone wants to give you a hard time refer them to me.'

So that was it. We'd be back together again, just like old times. I went back to wandering through the corridors, now with the purpose of finding the safest place for the four ANC men. I now knew the prison well and was aware that they had to be segregated. I walked every corridor again. On the first floor there was an area, but it was small and tight and was too close to the main population. The second floor was out, no hope there. I decided the only possible place was the third floor, on the roof, a veritable penthouse of Pollsmoor. Nelson and the three others would be the only prisoners on the top floor.

The roof area was sealed off by a steel door; once it was locked there was no way anyone could get either in or out. On the roof was a single cell area. For some reason or another there was a number above the door. Number 99. I was told this was once the area where thirty-five prisoners were kept. Now it was empty, and the ideal spot for my purposes. On another side of the roof was a second area where there was a long row of single cells, once used for prisoners on spare diet isolation, where besides being isolated they also received reduced rations. These, too, could be sealed off by locking one steel door. So there were two large areas, connected by the roof area, part of which was under cover, and part exposed, ideal for exercise and growing plants which I knew would be important to them, especially Nelson. The exposed roof area, L-shaped, was overall about half the size of a football field, covered in a black rubberised matting which would be fine for exercising. I was not to know it then, but the heat on the roof area in mid-summer, with the sun reflecting off the white-painted walls and soaked up by the black matting, would become unbearable. But, for now, I considered the entire area, which could be sealed off by locking two doors, to be perfect. The only problem I could foresee was the huge change in scenery from Robben Island to here at Pollsmoor. No longer would they have the beautiful views of the mainland, Table Mountain, Bloubergstrand, the ocean, the changing seasons and the shorelines with the myriad of wildlife. This was as remote and clinically cut off as could be. The only glimpse of the outside world was a partial sight of the nearby Steenberg Mountain which overlooked the prison. It could be seen over the top of the wall, but even then it was as desolate and grey as could be.

The place where I decided they would have their main sleeping area was large. I measured it out: twenty-two paces long by sixteen paces wide. The room itself was spacious, the ceiling higher than normal, perhaps twelve feet or so, and lines of windows along the top, ten in all. At the back end there was a separate section with a toilet, urinal, two basins and two showers. The wall dividing the two areas was only five feet high, but I decided it should be built to the ceiling, to guarantee personal privacy to the four men who would be sharing this area.

I went back to see Munro and told him the area would be perfect, just what we were looking for. He went with me to inspect it and agreed.

'Now, Greg, just let me know what you need in the way of any changes before they arrive, as well as furnishings, beds, tables, bedside tables, anything down to soap. Just let me know.'

As Munro spoke, I couldn't help but think how different everything now was from the early days on Robben Island when I had first walked into the B section and looked into Nelson's cell to see his only possessions: the neatly folded, threadbare blankets, the rolled up sisal mat and the toilet bucket. Things had certainly changed.

Out on the roof area I began to plan the rooms that I thought the four men would want. Outside the main cell, on to the roof, turn left and there was the area, part under cover, which could be used for exercise. Further around the L-shaped roof were two rooms, number 97 which could, I decided, be turned into a library, and a second room, number 95, which could be used as a study area.

I began to make a list of everything that would be needed: beds, study tables, bedside tables, cleaning materials, new bedding, pillows. I wanted everything brand new, no second-hand stuff. I returned to see Munro.

'Okay, now we have the area and the list of items which we shall need. All I need to know is when are they being transferred?'

Munro looked at me and shrugged his shoulders. 'They haven't given me a time or date; it's all still a big secret.'

I had further questions. 'What I also don't understand is why they are only going to be transferring four. There are more than four in the High Command, or the High Organ as they are known, so why only four?'

'That is another question they haven't answered for me. I have been told that it is Mandela and three others, but which three is still a mystery to me as well.'

I was not to know then that long-term thinking was beginning to change towards the ANC and that this transfer to Pollsmoor was the first, crucial step in the eventual decision to release them entirely. That thought never entered my mind; instead I believed that the authorities thought that keeping them on the island was more of a problem than it was worth.

It was clear to me, as it was to others who listened to the inmates, that Robben Island was now known as 'the university' for young ANC men in prison alongside their leaders, men such as Mandela. These younger ANC men were often less educated, some had no education and under the tutelage of Mandela and the leaders, received the first formal education of their lives. More than being alongside the very men who were the God-like figures at the heart of the black freedom movement, they were also being schooled in the fundamentals of freedom. So by removing Mandela and three other leaders, was this a crude step to block their education? If so, I somehow doubted that it would succeed. I was certain that whatever the authorities did to try and stop that process, they were always doomed to failure.

So there had to be another reason, and at that time I was more convinced the entire change was one of convenience. They had detained Mandela and the other Rivonia men for nearly two decades on the island. They had failed to break them, either physically, spiritually, or in any other manner. If anything, these men, particularly Nelson, had become worldwide cult figures. His very imprisonment and the way he was held was now giving him a status which the South African authorities had never imagined.

I had come to believe that, faced with the inevitable conclusion that they had not been about to break these ANC men, the authorities realised there was little point in keeping them on Robben Island. Worldwide publicity was already focusing on the harshness of life on the island, particularly during the brutal early years. Even though these conditions no longer existed to the same extent as before it was still a harsh punishment for men such as these. By removing them from the island, the authorities were effectively negating another source of criticism.

I was soon to have as much time as I needed to think of every possible reason for why they were being moved. I had a fall and broke my leg.

At the time my family were living in a double-storey house owned by the government close to the Roeland Street prison, close to the centre of Cape Town. For months the paint had been peeling off one corner of the wall. I could have got the public works department in to complete the repairs and paint the area, but decided to do it myself. After all, I lived in the house.

As I began work one morning I slipped and fell, knee first, on to the tarmac below. The result was one badly shattered knee and a leg in plaster for five weeks. I was out of commission for six weeks. I was on crutches and each week the prison department picked me up from home to get me to hospital to find out how the leg was coming along. By the beginning of March I was craving to get back to work. The six weeks at home had left me desperate to get off my backside and on with the new preparations at Pollsmoor. I knew from various telephone calls with Munro that a date had still not been decided for the move of Nelson and the three others. We still did not even know who the other three were to be. At one stage I was told that the whole transfer had been delayed by my fall and injury.

I returned to work at the start of March, still unable to walk without the aid of the crutches. I went to see Munro.

'Greg, still no word, and when I know, you'll know.' I hobbled around, ensuring that the rooftop area was now well prepared. Although everything I had ordered was in place, there was much curiosity among the others as to the reason for the special preparations. Several asked me directly if it was for Mandela. I'd said no, we were preparing a special section for a number of extreme right-wingers, members of the neo-Nazi Afrikaner Weestandsbeweging (AWB) who had recently been captured and I had been brought in to prepare the area because of my experience with the ANC leaders on the island. This excuse seemed to be accepted. But to allay any further suspicions I returned to the censor office for a couple of weeks, until the leg began to strengthen again. But once again I ran into the paranoia of Sergeant Andrews, who was still convinced I had been brought in to replace him. I know he was worried about being taken away from his censorship job and thrown back among the main prison staff, a job which he had said he didn't want.

I tried to reassure him. 'Look, just don't mind me. I'll only be in with you a few weeks before moving on. As soon as I am able to walk properly I'll be working in a different area.' When I offered to help out censoring letters, Andrews was abrupt, saying the office was fully up to date. I was back to square one, twiddling thumbs, waiting for Pretoria to make up their minds on the date of transfer.

Towards the end of the month Winnie was involved in a minor car crash and I heard that Nelson was, naturally, anxious about her welfare. I was unable to get across to the island to inform him of what had happened, that it was not serious and Winnie was unhurt. I also knew that such news would be deliberately kept from him when I was not there. Information about family and friends, particularly when they were involved in a serious situation such as a car crash, was invariably used by sections of the prison service as a tool to punish.

It was the evening of 31 March and I had been home for several hours. I sat watching television, when the phone rang.

It was the main switchboard at Pollsmoor. 'Greg, a message from the commander, Brigadier Munro. He asks that you meet him in the transport yard at Pollsmoor. He will be waiting for you there.'

'Yes, sir, when?'

'Now. Or as soon as you can get there.'

So this was it. I knew what lay behind the call: the transfer of Nelson and his three companions.

I took the van that had been left at my disposal and drove the twenty minutes to Pollsmoor. This time I ignored my scenic route

197

and took the M3, knowing that when Munro said 'now' he meant it. The road around the prison was unusually busy, armed guards patrolling the area. Inside the main gate, along the main road within the compound itself, were more armed guards.

Once inside the prison I headed for the main transport yard, a section fenced off with an entrance through a small Judas gate. I parked the van outside and went through the gate. I pressed the bell. Its shrillness pierced the night air. The huge gate slid silently open and I walked into the bright spotlights which flooded the entire area. I passed by the security guard, a warder I knew only as Simon. I glanced at the Uzi machine gun slung over his shoulder. The safety catch was off.

In the middle of the compound there was a cluster of people. Above the crowd I could see Nelson's head towering above the others. As I entered he turned to look at me and, as our eyes met, his face opened into a huge grin. He was surrounded by several senior officers from Pretoria and I could see Munro in earnest conversation with them. With Nelson I picked out other faces, men I knew well, Walter Sisulu, standing beside Nelson, and Raymond Mhlaba and Andrew Mlangeni. I looked further, trying to see if Kathy was there, but could not see him. I ignored Munro and the other senior officers from Pretoria and walked over to the four men, shaking each one by the hand.

Nelson turned, oblivious to the presence of the officers, and said, 'Mr Gregory, how nice to see you again. How's the leg?'

As we shook hands, I showed surprise that he had heard about my injury and Nelson joked, 'Why else would you stay away from Robben Island? I heard about what happened to you through our own communications.'

The other three crowded around me and were confused about why they had suddenly been transferred.

Walter voiced the concerns. 'Why Pollsmoor, Mr Gregory? Why here and why now?'

I was honest with them, keeping my voice low. 'Look, I have my own theories for this move, but there is not a problem. I think it may be better here for you, but I really don't know. I have known about this move now for several weeks, before I broke my leg, even. But what is behind it ... I just don't know.'

I asked them if they had been told anything at all.

Nelson chipped in, 'I realised something might be happening when I heard you were being transferred to Pollsmoor. There was talk on the island that when you went, we would follow. But we were never told anything positive, you know the way the system works. But why...' He shrugged his shoulders.

To one side boxes of books and personal equipment were being loaded and I instructed the warders to carry them up to the rooftop cell. We went to the reception office to sign the official transfers.

Nelson was given his new prison number: D220/82. He was in D section, the 220th inmate brought into Pollsmoor in 1982.

As the paperwork was being completed I was able to take better stock of the four. I could certainly understand the reasons for transferring Nelson, Walter and Raymond, but the presence of Andrew Mlangeni was surprising. While the others were all members of the High Organ, Andrew had never featured prominently in the ANC structure. I knew from my own conversations with him that he had been a driver for the organisation when he was caught at Rivonia, and had found himself being thrust into a limelight that really did not match his status. If this was, as I had suspected, an attempt by the authorities to remove the leadership section from having a heavy influence in the Robben Island 'university', then where was Govan Mbeki and Ahmed Kathrada, Kathy? It occurred to me as I stood there in the reception office that once again someone at Pretoria had miscalculated. But who was I to argue?

We went up to the third floor and I swung open the door to the large cell. Their belongings had already been carried up and had been dumped unceremoniously in a heap, some of the contents spilling out on to the floor. I apologised for the clumsiness of the warders, but we all knew this was little to do with clumsiness, more a shining example of the resentment which constantly simmered among many of them.

'Welcome to the penthouse.' I tried to be jovial. Nelson stood alongside Walter looking around. Andrew and Raymond were busy examining the far end of the room.

I continued, 'Look, it has been a sudden change and we all need time to adjust to this. I don't know what's behind it and you don't know. But together we can try and make this work. I've got everything here I thought you might need. You'll find all the toiletries down in the washroom area. If you need anything else just let me know and I'll get it. If anything doesn't work properly, the showers or the toilets, let me know and they'll be fixed.'

I think all four men were very confused about the sudden change in events in their lives. They had been on Robben Island for seventeen years and now, here, suddenly their lives were thrown

199

into total confusion. I knew they all wanted to ask questions, ensure that their families and legal advisers knew of the transfer. But I stepped in, 'Listen, there's little point us getting down to questions tonight. Let's start fresh in the morning.'

Nelson agreed and came over, again to shake my hand. He spoke for his comrades, 'Mr Gregory, at least here we have someone who understands. It's nice to see you again.'

Chapter 20

Settling in

Pollsmoor had a modern face, but its heart was as primitive and cold as any prison. Its exterior was clean and well kept. Neat, tidy lawns, bushes well tended, row upon row of comfortable new single-storey houses for the prison staff. Although the expanse of the prison was a blot on the landscape in terms of its function, it was not so incongruous that it stood out like a sore thumb. Pollsmoor was what the authorities wanted it to be, a large detention centre close to the heart of Cape Town. It was home for ordinary prisoners, and when the ANC four were transferred, they became its first political inmates.

I was still troubled by the transfer. I could not understand it and I know Nelson and the others found it equally disconcerting. The first morning I looked in briefly on them and they were busy unpacking their belongings. They said they did not need anything else, at the present time, and I left them. I could see they were disoriented after being uprooted without notice and planted in a different world. I knew it would take time for things to settle. But time was a commodity both they and I had in plentiful supply. I still believed these men were going to serve out their lives in jail. The thought of a possible release was far from my mind at that time.

From early on, when Munro had told me they were to be moved, I had started to hand pick a group of warders who would be involved in guarding the section. When word spread among the general warder staff that I was selecting people for the penthouse patrol, as it was known, there were many who approached me asking to join. Over the years I knew exactly the sort of warder I wanted to be guarding Nelson and the ANC High Organ. Men who would be fair, who could be trusted to treat them as human beings and not as the enemy. I didn't want warders who would scream abuse or resort to violence and I wanted them to show respect to Nelson and his companions as they would to ordinary prisoners. It was difficult because the resentment I myself had felt towards the ANC when I first became a censor officer on the island in 1966 remained widespread among the main population of warders, just as it did in the South African society. Changes, if they were to happen, would not take place overnight.

In those first, early days at Pollsmoor Nelson, Walter, Andrew and Raymond felt anger. They wanted answers to their questions and I was unable to give them. I was as much in the dark as they were. Every time I went to the cell, despite the improved conditions – more space, better facilities, a massive improvement in food – there was an underlying bitterness about the move.

Raymond and Walter cornered me one day and vented their anger. I had made the mistake of saying that I thought Pollsmoor was an improvement on the island.

Walter turned on me. 'These things do not matter.' His arm swept the room, taking in the new furnishings and more spacious conditions. 'These things we do not notice. We miss our comrades on Robben Island. We miss the openness of the island, we miss the camaraderie, the friendship that we had developed over two decades on the island.'

Raymond picked up the theme. 'Look, the island was bad in many ways, but we had become used to it. We were all together and we felt secure in the surroundings and with the staff. It was at least a prison where we could see the ocean and the sky, the mountains and the city, the beaches and the trees. There were flowers, animals, the sound of birds, the roar of the ocean, these things were important to us. We do not have many things that were as valuable as these little unseen gifts. Now they have been taken from us and replaced by this...'

I heard them and I knew precisely what they meant. Nelson was sitting on his bed and reading a book. He stopped and listened to the complaints of his two comrades, allowing them to put into words the feelings of the group.

Raymond continued. 'Take a look from here and tell me what you see? You see concrete. You see painted walls. You see black roof. You see the blue sky and occasionally a cloud. If you strain your eyes you can see a tip of a distant mountain. That is all. No trees, no flowers, no ocean, no birds, nothing. We sit here now and wonder if that tip of the mountain is like an iceberg to the rest of the world. We can only see that little corner and everything else is hidden. Even if I want to look out on that tip of mountain I can't see it from here. I can't even see if I stand on a chair. The only way would be to put my cupboard on top of the bed and strain on my tiptoes. Then I can see the outside world. But nothing else.'

I could hear and feel their frustration, it was palpable. I could also empathise with them. I knew exactly how they felt and yet there was little I could do. I turned and walked out.

The question of 'why Pollsmoor' had still not been resolved. But a few weeks later, the theory that this was a gathering of the High Organ, the leadership of the ANC, gained strength when Kathy arrived to join the less than happy band. Ahmed Kathrada was a constant thorn in the side of the authorities, but was also the sort of person whose enthusiasm and drive were impossible to extinguish. He was a welcome arrival. At least he was one of the comrades who was badly missed by the four. In some ways Kathy and I had never been that friendly, but I was glad to see him; I knew he would help lift the deflated spirits on the rooftop. He was a man of great principle and when they were depressed it was frequently Kathy who picked them up with his unquenchable spirit and determination to succeed. There was just one problem with this: Kathy and Andrew never got on too well together. This led to a change in the room.

Until the arrival of the fifth person, the room had been spacious and easily laid out. Nelson and Raymond had their beds lined against one wall, separated by a distance of eight feet and several boxes and cupboards. Andrew and Walter were against the opposite wall.

Now, with Kathy's arrival, Andrew decided he wanted more space, so he dragged his bed to the other end of the room, opposite the entrance door, leaving his space vacant for Kathy. This was one area I was going to stay well clear of. If they wanted to row then I wasn't going to lecture them as a father would naughty children. I knew there was disagreement and a simmering friction between Kathy and Andrew, but decided the best way was to allow the five to sort it out themselves.

Then in the middle of the year the group was joined by a sixth man. He was a stranger to the group and myself. Patrick Maqubela was a young lawyer and an ANC member from the Eastern Cape region. I knew only his name and his reputation; that he had been an articled clerk to Griffiths Mxenge, a highly respected attorney who had represented many ANC men over the years. Mxenge had been assassinated in Durban in 1982. Maqubela had been sentenced to twenty years for treason and had been in Diepkloof

Prison in Johannesburg where he had developed a reputation for organising unrest among the other prisoners.

The members of the High Organ were obviously very wary of his sudden appearance. Why should the authorities send Maqubela to Pollsmoor and not other members of the leadership group from Robben Island? It did not make a lot of sense to me and I know that the five were sceptical. The thought went through all our minds that Maqubela was a plant by the security forces, sent to spy on Nelson and the leaders, Maqubela having worked out some sort of secret deal. I knew he would be an outcast. These men had earned a lot of respect from and for one another, having spent the best part of two decades together in one another's close company. I knew that if there was a hidden agenda behind Maqubela's appearance at Pollsmoor it would take time for the truth to emerge. I decided I should take my lead from Nelson and the others. They were highly intelligent men who were likely to have a feel for anything which was untoward about his transfer.

Maqubela was given a space for his bed and belongings closest to the door. It did not take long for the group to begin to assimilate him into their lifestyle, although he was considerably younger. He was a friendly, amiable, highly intelligent man who clearly had a great respect for the men he was now with, men he considered to be the leaders of his movement. I know he spoke of his transfer to Pollsmoor with them and explained that he knew they would suspect he was a plant. His reaction was that only time could prove his innocence. Over the years he was to become a valuable asset, a man who was easy to get along with and who cared greatly for the others.

It must have been shortly before the first Christmas at Pollsmoor that I went into the cell area and was surprised to find Nelson still curled up in bed. The others were busy elsewhere, exercising, studying, working in the garden, generally getting on with their daily routine. No one had mentioned to me Nelson was still in bed.

I sat on the edge of the bed. 'Howzit, Nelson, what's up?'

He turned over and he was not well, a temperature had kept him feverish.

'I shall be all right later. This morning I decided to stay in bed a little later because of the fever. Later I shall get up.'

The group was not subject to the rules for the ordinary prisoners. They could sleep whenever they wished. I continued to sit on the bed and Nelson propped himself up. We drifted into conversation about each other's childhood, a subject where we both found great escapism. Nelson was intrigued by my friendship with Bafana and listened intently to my tales of adventure with my childhood friend.

He spoke softly. 'I knew in my heart you must have had that type of background; there is no bitterness within you to the black man or any other colour. I have watched you carefully and you treat everyone as equal.'

I nodded and said, 'In many ways you have become as close to me as Bafana, that's how I view you. Over these past years I have grown to feel as much for you as I did for him.'

Nelson said, 'But we have never done the things that you and he did together, the adventures you shared.'

'No, those things we cannot do together and in many ways our relationship is very different. You are older than me, whereas Bafana was the same age. He was my brother where you are someone I respect as an elder. Bafana and I used to be playmates, we would fool around. But I cannot be like that with you; you are my elder and you will understand just what that means to people with our upbringing. You are right, we have not shared adventures, but we have shared time together and time is a great joiner.'

Nelson nodded, understanding that in the culture of the blacks which I had experienced as a child, the elders were always the leaders and they were to be respected as a father was respected.

Although we had never spoken directly to one another about the black concept of respect, it was embedded in everything he had shown to me through his letters and in the visits he had. It was a subject we were to return to over the coming years on a number of occasions as we relaxed more in one another's company.

One of the first obvious improvements in the prisoners' conditions was in the food. Gone were the days of constant pap, in one form or another. Now, there was access to meat and vegetables. On one occasion I thought I would try it for myself. It was fish. It was tasteless. I decided to investigate further. In the kitchens the fish were all thrown into a big steel drum and boiled up. It was food for the masses, a couple of thousand prisoners. By the time it was served, the fish looked and tasted like a porridge. I went to see Munro and suggested a different course. Although the group was still subject to a diet determined by the Pretoria orders, I suggested we prepare it separately. These people were unlike the ordinary prisoners: they were in for life on a political offence and there was no reason to poison them with the ordinary slops. Munro argued that the food was better than they would have received on Robben Island. I agreed, but felt we could make it better still.

He warned me, 'Greg, this is not a blerrie hotel we are running here. It is a prison.'

'Ja, but there is no reason why we should ruin the food they are served because we don't take a bit of care. It's better that we prepare the food properly and give them a tasty meal. You know what they say: that the route to a man's heart is through his stomach.' I knew it was a weak argument, but I also knew Munro was a considerate man who would understand and probably feel much as I did.

I suggested we take their food and have it cooked in the hospital section, where it could be prepared individually. Munro agreed.

With more time on their hands study played a big role, and Nelson spent many hours every day hunched over his books in the small study on the far side of the roof area. I often looked in on him, concerned that he was spending so much time using the fluorescent strip lighting for his work. Many times I could see the tiredness and strain in his eyes.

'Why do you sit in the study? Why not come out and use the natural light?' I asked him. 'Look, your eyes are watering from the strain.'

His reply was always the same. 'It is not the strip lighting that causes that, it is a result of the days of working under the harsh sunlight in the quarry on Robben Island.'

Because of the intense study that all the group were undertaking, invariably they did not want to stop to eat at the normal meal times of 5 o'clock. Instead, they would eat only when they had come to the end of a study session. Nelson, for instance, liked to work through until around 8 o'clock before eating. Their view was that if they ate at 5 o'clock and then returned to studying, they would feel hungry again three hours later; better to eat late. This late eating caused a problem: how to keep their food hot. Initially they asked for hot plates upon which to leave the food. Every request was handled by me: I entered them in a complaints and requests book. I would attach my own recommendation to each request. On occasions, such as the hot plate request, my view that the request should be allowed was overturned by either the head of the prison or the commanding officer. Each week they would list a request for the hot plates and each week the request was refused. Eventually I said to Nelson that he was wasting time by doing so.

I told him, 'You have asked for this over and over and over again and each time they say no. Leave it now; you will not get the hot plates.'

Nelson was philosophical. 'No, just keep asking. Experience has taught me that when you ask for something like this they refuse. I keep asking and they keep refusing. Eventually they will change their minds. Both you and I know that it makes good sense to have a hot plate. They will see the sense eventually.'

I laughed and filled in the request. And, eventually, just as Nelson had predicted, the authorities agreed that a hot plate could be used. But until that time they used an urn containing hot water. The food was in a steel dixie tin and whenever they wanted it heated, they switched on the urn and boiled the water to heat the food.

Later, we agreed to allow them to have items bought on their behalf and brought in. This was a system which had been started on the island by Willemse, a man who, I thought, had a vision of the future and would improve the conditions for the ANC prisoners. Here, at Pollsmoor, I suggested to the five that, if they wished, the lists of biscuits, tobacco, soap and toothpaste could be expanded. That if they wanted, there could be packets and tinned foods, curries and spices purchased which would make the food even tastier. I could see Nelson's eyes light up and he let out two words, 'Ahhh, *biryani* ...', a curry. It was agreed that Kathy would become the custodian of the monthly shopping lists and I would purchase the items at the Pollsmoor shop.

I took the five lists to the prison shop, run by a guy called van Dyk. He said he'd have them ready the next day. I returned to find the lists covered in marks, the majority of the items scratched out.

'What have you done?' My voice was cold and angry.

He was filled with hostility. 'Mind your own damned business. I run this shop and I don't have things in this shop for fucking terrorists. If they want it, they can get their whores to bring this stuff in. They won't get it from me.'

I knew immediately I would not change van Dyk's attitude and that it was pointless arguing. I turned and stormed out. I went to see Munro. He was just as angry, and picked up the phone to call van Dyk to order him to stock the items from the shopping lists.

Before he dialled the number I held up my hand and stopped the commander.

'Sir, before you do that, perhaps I can suggest that this course will only lead to a continual conflict, because van Dyk will always be able to claim he is out of such and such an item, that it is out of stock. Believe me, he will be obstinate and will find ways of refusing to let them have items they have ordered.'

Munro was intrigued and put the phone back on its holder. 'So, Greg, what do you suggest?'

I was thinking quickly now. 'Look, sir, I'll get the five men to give me their lists at the beginning of each month, let's say the first day. We all know that sometime in the first week of each month van Dyk goes to the warehouse to stock up. I will hand the lists to van Dyk and if he doesn't have the items in stock, he will be able to buy them at the warehouse; that way he will not be able to have an excuse for being out of stock. And as long as the orders are returned by the middle of the month, no one will mind. This will cut out any nonsense.'

Munro considered this and picked up the phone again. He simply outlined the proposal to van Dyk. I could hear the splutterings from my seat and watched Munro's face breaking into a smile. He was gently emphatic. 'And by the way van Dyk, if there are any problems, anything on these lists which is not provided, you will answer to me.'

There were still minor complaints with the monthly orders. There were items, such as biscuits, which had been listed down and were not delivered. Instead of confronting van Dyk myself I decided the best method would be to take Kathy and Nelson to see him. It was a manoeuvre I had learned from Nelson himself; he said it was always easy for a person to say no to a third party or to say no on the telephone, much harder to say no to a person's face. I was fed up with having to suffer the group's complaints because van Dyk was not completing every order. I knew that behind my back he was deliberately leaving out luxury items and trying to say these things were not in stock or not at the warehouse. But, to my mind, these men had paid for the items and should have them. I arranged for van Dyk to go to the cell-block to discuss their problems with them; I went for a walk outside in the sunshine. I chuckled at the thought of these two men giving van Dyk a hard time. Half an hour later I returned and Nelson and Kathy were smiling. Van Dyk was looking less happy.

After van Dyk had left Nelson rubbed his hands and announced to Kathy and me, 'I think we'll be getting our regular supplies of Romany Creams from now on. No problems.' It was a united victory.

They began to get regular bags of fruit, bananas, oranges, guavas and apples. It was brought in from the kitchens, but it was always rotten. They were grateful in that they were at last being given fruit, but frustrated that it was left in the kitchens until it rotted. I decided to go and sort out the problem. The deliveries of fruit took place a couple of times every week, usually from the farm prisons such as Victor Verster or Brandvlei. These places produced masses of the stuff, more than enough to feed every prisoner in the Cape Province. I discovered that when the deliveries came in some of the warders were getting the pick of the crop for themselves and leaving the rest of the fruit to over-ripen before they allowed it to be given to the prisoners. This was not good enough, but if I wanted to stamp my authority on the warders in the kitchen area I could be creating problems, so I chose a different tack altogether. I went to the medical staff and got a prescription for each of the five who were under my charge. The reason I gave the medical officer, who looked at me with knowing eyes, was that these men needed vitamins. The doctor signed five prescriptions and once a week I photocopied them and sent them down to the kitchens. It meant a regular supply of fresh fruit throughout the year.

In November I had a request from one of the officers, Warrant Officer Terreblanche. Could I please go to the main cell; the prisoners wanted to see me. He did not say why, just to go. When I entered the group were sitting at the table, sombre faces, hands folded in front of them, each of them watching me. Trouble was brewing. In situations such as this I knew it was better to wait for them to start, to set the tone of such a meeting. I sat with them; a chair had been left vacant at the head of the table. Kathy got up and went to his locker. My eyes followed him as I wondered what on earth this was about. He turned and in his hands he carried a plate, piled high with biscuits of several varieties. I looked at the others as they stood and put out their hands to shake mine.

Walter was sitting beside me and he explained, 'This is for you, a birthday party. Happy birthday, and thanks.'

Kathy added, offering the plate, 'We do not have anything more than this to give you, but we would be both pleased and honoured if you joined us for biscuits.' I had long forgotten my birthday; it was just a passing moment in the calendar now to me, one I ignored. Yet this birthday was to mean more to me than any other I had before or since. This was a symbolic gesture of how they viewed me. I knew that as each of their own birthdays came around, the others would save their precious biscuits which had been hard earned. I would know each birthday and always contributed something, a packet of biscuits or something myself and would always go and give whoever was having the birthday my best wishes. My birthday fell on 7 November and with the delivery of their monthly shopping orders not due until the 15th, I knew that they had saved these biscuits for some time.

We sat eating and talking as friends and I told them all exactly how I felt; that this was the finest birthday I had ever experienced, the best present I had ever received. Years later I would look back on this moment and realise it was the occasion when I was eventually accepted by them all as a person who felt for them in many small ways that they had each understood.

As I stood to leave they all again shook my hand and said that they hoped we would not have many more parties such as this one, but if we did then they should be interspersed with good luck and good health.

One day soon after Kathy arrived, one of the other warders told me there had been trouble between Ahmed and Andrew. I went to see them both, to sort out the problem; it was silly that two men in their situation should be arguing. I knew from my years with the group that these two barely tolerated one another. The row centred on the shopping list. It was Kathy's job to collect the lists and hand them to me at the beginning of the month. Each time Kathy asked Andrew for his shopping list he turned surly and said it was not yet ready.

I walked into the cell area as the two faced up to one another.

Kathy was saying, 'Andrew, just let me have your list, it's already two days late and you are keeping everyone else waiting for their shopping. Just let me have it.'

Andrew was shouting, 'I told you, it's not ready.'

Kathy saw me entering the room and pleaded with Andrew, 'Please, just let me have what you have done.' He turned to me in despair, and I could see the anger in his face.

Andrew was unmoved and was clearly being awkward. 'No, it's not ready, I told you.'

Kathy was steaming now. 'When you're ready you can give it to the baas in person. I don't want to have anything to do with you.'

I was shocked to hear Kathy use the word *baas*. Its usage was a strict no-no, a throw-back to the bad old days when blacks were ordered to call their white masters baas, or face losing their jobs. I stopped in my tracks knowing this was now trouble. Kathy turned away from Andrew, shaking his head in exasperation.

Andrew turned angry, grabbed his metal dixie and was about to

210

launch it like a frisbee at the back of Kathy's head. I stepped in. 'Now come on, you two, that's enough.'

The tension between the two had simmered for months, even years, and each time there was an argument, I would get to hear of it. Often the peacemaker was Walter, the wise old head who had a favourite phrase. 'We are not children, we are big people.'

The times certainly were changing and where newspapers had been banned they were now a regular feature of their shopping list. The change had occurred slowly since the mid-1970s, but by 1981, while they were still on the island, many restrictions were lifted. Nelson always ensured that as well as the local Cape Town and South African publications, he ordered a copy of *Time* magazine as well as the British *Guardian*. Initially I had a problem with the delivery of the local newspapers, the *Cape Times* and the Afrikaans, *Die Burger*. Although the *Cape Times* is delivered from the city to the Tokai area, *Die Burger* is not. Eventually I found a local supermarket in Tokai which stocked both and set up a monthly account for both newspapers. But within a few months the store owner decided he was no longer bothering with accounts. I found another store, this time further away in Retreat about fifteen minutes' drive from the prison where I could get both papers, but it was a problem getting them picked up. Eventually I worked out a plan with the prison security car which patrolled the entire area at night. It was agreed the night staff should pick up the copies and leave them for me at the front gate. It led to three papers each day being left: the *Cape Times*, the *Argus*, *Die Burger* and, at weekends, the *Sunday Times*. Eventually Munro got to hear about my diversion for the security patrol and instead got one of the school bus drivers to drop the papers off. They were also permitted to purchase their own radios to be able to listen in on local news broadcasts. It was an improvement, but still not quite what they really wanted: the opportunity to get a shortwave radio which could tune into the BBC World Service. Nelson, and every one of the group, read every newspaper from page one to the back page and through again. After the years of being denied news and information they were primed to enjoy these luxuries. It was the same with the radio. Nelson could not get enough news. He listened to each and every bulletin he could tune into, be it Afrikaans radio, Springbok radio or English radio. Later still, when funds permitted, they also ordered magazines, *National Geographic*, *Farmers Weekly*. By this stage there was no censorship. It was pointless.

211

The next area where the authorities began to allow more freedom was with books and films. At first we had an eight millimetre projector which we set up in the middle of the large cell area. We covered the windows with blankets and blacked out the room for the screening, which was usually once a week. At first the only films we could get were the Rambo-style adventure films or love stories, which always drew cries of derision from the group. In a good-natured way they joked with me about getting a better class of film. Eventually I located a good source of films through one of the provincial libraries which had a stock of eight millimetre factual documentaries. I remember I set up the projector one day and announced that the film to be shown was a love story. Groans went round and the group were ready even to ignore the film. As it began to roll, they realised I had obtained a documentary on penicillin and its inventor. Their groans turned to praise; this was exactly the sort of film they wanted. These men had a voracious appetite for learning. Any and all information was absorbed as a thirsty man would drink water in the Great Karoo. Each week I would tell them it was an adventure or a cowboy film, but produce something entirely different.

Eventually when we got hold of a video machine, we were able to continue the supply of films, as their interests expanded.

It was much the same with books that were available to the five at Pollsmoor's library. The library was run by a man named Koen and he apologised that the only books he had on his shelves were what could only be described as trivial: adventure books, love stories and cowboy fiction. When they went to see Koen he promised to get a list from the main Cape Town library and they simply had to tick any they wanted, from biographies to history. The only subject they were excluded from getting was anything political, although, knowing this, they never asked for any such books.

A few months after being moved Kathy approached me with a request for a set of encyclopaedias. I was uncertain what the official response would be, but, in my opinion, they needed them. These were men who read, read and read some more. I was surprised a week later when the request came back approved, with permission to purchase a complete set of the *Encyclopaedia Britannica*.

Shortly after Kathy arrived he had a back problem and a doctor recommended he use a horizontal bar to hang from, to stretch the vertebrae. The bar was put in the area outside the cell, under cover. It was the beginning of the fitness craze which seemed to grab all five.

Nelson began to get up each morning at 4.30 and he spent an hour exercising before having a shower. The only break was when he paused to listen to the 5 o'clock news on the radio. Then it was back to his finger push-ups, jogging and various calisthenics. Later, with the arrival of more exercise bikes and rowing machines, they also asked for a tennis court to be painted on the roof area. The matches between the men were taken in deadly earnest and such was the amount that was played that within three months the complete set of four tennis rackets had to be replaced: the strings had gone. The surface on the roof was rough and although it was good in that it provided good grip for their feet, it was harsh on the tennis balls. Such was the number of new tennis balls being ordered that Munro actually asked me if they were eating them. Exercise became a big feature of each day so I decided that they should have the proper clothes with two sets of pants, vests and shoes each. The Red Cross, after one visit, also donated five track-suits and a further variety of equipment such as exercise rings and weights.

As with the newspapers, there had also been considerable relaxation on the rules governing letters. By this stage only letters which were completely political in content were censored. When that happened, I usually went to see the person due to receive the letter and told them, in my own words, what had been written and by whom. In effect I was reading them everything without handing the letter over as my own way of circumventing the system. I also ensured they replied to the letter writer to let them know their message had got through. Although the same basic rules regarding censorship had never altered, I felt that there was now greater leeway for my own interpretation of the regulations.

There was also a greater number of letters arriving for the men. One, in particular, arrived from a man in Langa, a black township just outside Cape Town. The guy wrote in perfect English and labelled Nelson 'a black bastard'. It was extremely abusive, accusing Nelson and the ANC leaders of not wanting to leave prison to face the brutal truth of township and squatter camp life. It accused him of now being in the pocket of the Boers and a willing accomplice to the government. It said that as prisoners they had three good meals of porridge every day, that they did not know what it was like to be hungry, that they had a bed, a mattress and a roof over their heads and were having an easy time. I laughed at the letter, knowing how pathetically sad and ill-informed it was. The following day I mentioned the letter to Nelson and said I was not handing it over because it was extremely abusive. We had a row when he demanded it. I refused, telling him that I had to leave it on his file because it was abusive. We came to a compromise in that I could tell him the contents, every word. The part that struck a chord was being fed porridge three times a day. When I got to that part Nelson held up his hand, stopping me.

'He says I get porridge three times a day, eh?'

'Ja, porridge, three times a day,' I confirmed.

'Okay, just make sure that this letter is left on my file. I shall want it one day.'

I was mystified. 'Ja, but why, man?'

'No, just leave it on file. I shall address this question one day.'

Years later, after being released from prison, one of Nelson's first acts was to take this letter and go to the address in Langa. Many of the ANC people were puzzled by why he was paying so much attention to this abusive letter. Was he angry? Did he wish to remonstrate with the letter writer? No, Nelson told them, he wanted to invite the man to sit down and eat some porridge with him. It was a reflection of Nelson's great sense of humour. He never forgot a thing. His mind was encyclopaedic.

Despite all the improvements in conditions at Pollsmoor, the group still agitated to get back to Robben Island. They all made verbal and written requests to Munro, who was amazed that they should want to return there. However, their attitude was one I had learned to understand and respect. These men were missing their comrades, they were missing their people and no matter that their own personal conditions had improved, they were willing to put up with privations to be with their comrades. I had grown to admire their determination to fight for what they called 'the cause'. And, as I have said, there was also an element within them that missed the openness of the island. Here, at Pollsmoor, all they saw was cement and more cement. But whatever their requests, Pretoria was not going to bend on this one.

The expanse of endless roof was broken one day when Nelson and Walter sat talking of how they would like a garden. When I went to see them in the main cell area they asked what I felt about it, how it could be achieved. We sat talking and decided the best solution was to get a number of large forty-four-gallon oil drums which would be sliced lengthways in half and filled with soil. I put it to Munro who agreed: he saw the merit of gardening. I arranged for the drums, sixteen in total, to be sliced and taken to the roof area, followed by bag after bag of rich loamy soil, out of the main prison gardens. By the time we had finished one entire area of the roof was converted into a garden with thirty-two half-drums lining the walls. Even I, who loathed doing the gardening at home, thought this was great.

Nelson became the main gardener, although all the others helped tend the plants. It became a centre of interest not only for the group, but also among the warders, and even Munro. He was a particular lover of broccoli, carrots and beetroot and gave Nelson some seeds. It was a surprising gesture from the commanding officer and an illustration of how attitudes were changing. The day Munro brought the seed packets to Nelson they stood beside the plant pots talking about how best to grow them. As I watched them I saw two men, not divided by colour and politics, but united by a common love of plants. Each morning, whatever the weather, Nelson put on his old straw hat and gardening gloves and set about planting, weeding and tending. As word spread among the other warders, they too sent him seeds. Eventually, at the height of the growing season, there was a huge variety of plants in the vegetable section: aubergines, cabbage, beans, spinach, carrots, cucumbers, onions, broccoli, lettuce, tomatoes of a number of varieties, peppers, strawberries and many types of spices. Bags of manure were carted in from the prison's small farm. At one stage there was a problem with the high winds damaging the tender plants. I got some hessian and we put it around the drums to both save the plants being burned or blown down by the wind.

In one of the newspapers Nelson had read of a new health drink consisting of boiled beetroot stems and leaves. He decided to give it a try, much to the amusement of the others, who joked with him that he was getting old and this was his way of retaining his handsome looks.

Raymond's booming voice echoed around the roof when he joked, 'Hey, Nelson, perhaps this drink will reverse the ageing process. When you drink it your years go into reverse.' It was all good-natured and Nelson smiled, determined to try it. He would not be dissuaded. So he cut the beetroots, gathering up the leaves and stems. They were sent to the kitchens with precise instructions on how to boil them. When the mix, a stinking mass of dirty green slime, was returned to Nelson, his nose turned. The others were in hysterics at this performance. I know I couldn't keep a straight face. However Nelson was now committed. He drained the liquid into a container. He offered the drink around to the others who all shook their heads. Nelson drank it himself and although he didn't immediately give his verdict, I heard that it had the effect of a good laxative. As a matter of prudence I didn't ask any more about the beetroot mix although several times Raymond offered him dirty old socks to boil up for a brew instead.

Whatever the joking that Nelson endured about his garden, it was certainly appreciated by many people at Pollsmoor. Every week he supplied a lot of fresh vegetables which were cooked in the main prison.

Chapter 21

Nelson and Winnie

It had been many months since I had last seen Winnie. Not since Robben Island, maybe four months before, when she had a Christmas visit. Now she was coming to Pollsmoor, arriving from Johannesburg. Normally visitors had to stop at the main gates, park in the visitors' park, then walk to the area where they were visiting. I left instructions at the main gate that when Winnie showed up, she was to be allowed straight through, to leave her car in front of the main building instead of the visitors' car park.

Her car pulled up outside and she was out in a flash. Beautifully dressed as usual and rushing up the steps. I knew she could not see me behind the darkened glass of the door. As she burst through I stepped out. She faced me and broke into a wide, welcoming smile.

'You again!' She burst out laughing, a deep resonant laughter that made many people in the entrance hall turn round and stare. She grabbed me by the hand and began shaking it.

'It looks like you follow my husband round wherever he goes.'

'No, you are wrong. He follows me. I was here first.' We laughed and she asked how I was. She wanted to know why I was limping a little. I explained about the leg injury and she was immediately concerned.

I was pleased to see Winnie. Her spirit was unquenchable, her constant support for Nelson an important prop. I admit I admired her courage. I'd heard and read of the rumours that were circulating about her, but in all the years she had been the one person who brought sunshine into Nelson's life.

For years, since we had first met way back on the island, I had been calling her Mrs Mandela, but it was when we met again at Pollsmoor, she insisted, 'Cut that nonsense. Just call me Winnie.'

217

At around this time, in April 1983, Raymond was the first of the group to require hospital treatment. It was the beginning of a routine which became a regular feature in our lives. On the island there was a hospital attached to the B section of the prison. Here, at Pollsmoor, the hospital section was for the entire population of something like 4000 prisoners, so it was felt that the best treatment for the group could be obtained in the public hospitals. There was also a growing number of hospital visits required by these five, not the least because all were now well into middle age and were suffering the types of illness and complaints that occur in those years. When Pretoria agreed to the outside medical and dental visits it meant a headache for me: security had to be arranged for I was mindful that at any stage an assassination attempt could be lurking around the corner. I knew only too well the hatred which raged in many quarters of South African society.

Raymond had a problem with a massive sore on his leg and we arranged for him to be taken to the Groote Schuur Hospital for specialised laser treatment. A few days later Walter had to be taken to the same hospital with a leg complaint so I arranged an ambulance. Normally I would have used an unmarked car, but because Walter was unable to walk, I called for an ambulance. The medical staff at the Groote Schuur decided Walter needed lengthy treatment, and kept him in overnight. By the time I had returned to Pollsmoor there was a call from Walter's wife, Albertina. She wanted to arrange a visit. I explained to her that Walter was in hospital, that there was a problem with a swelling on his leg which might need medical treatment and that the following day he was likely to be moved to the Woodstock Hospital. I suggested she wait a few days until we knew where he would be, either in hospital for a longer than anticipated visit or back at Pollsmoor. She agreed. A few days later, after Walter had been taken backwards and forwards between Groote Schuur, Woodstock and Pollsmoor, he stopped me outside the cell area.

'Mr Gregory, I have a complaint.'

I was puzzled because of all the group Walter was by far the most genial and easy going. I immediately could smell problems.

'Tell me about it.'

'I've just read a story in the newspaper that Albertina was refused a visit while I was in hospital. The story says that she was told I was ill but that she couldn't see me. How did that happen?'

I explained to Walter exactly what had happened, and that I suggested to Albertina that she leave the visit for a few days when we would know for certain where he was. Walter immediately saw the sense in it all, and accepted that. Once again, the newspaper had got the story entirely wrong.

I was also aware that once the story was in the newspaper, there were bound to be further problems. It would be picked up by Pretoria who would want detailed answers on what was happening. In fact, it led to a greater fuss than I ever had imagined. The alleged refusal of a visit was raised in parliament where the minister had to reply to angry opposition questions about denying visits to prisoners' families.

As a result of the story I had to write a full report on what had occurred, to be handed to the Minister of Prisons. By the time I had written the report Albertina had been in to see Walter and she had confirmed that my version of events was correct. She even thanked me for suggesting the delay in order that she did not waste time travelling from one location to another.

After the visit Walter approached me with a suggestion. He would write to both the newspaper concerned and to members of parliament explaining that the matter had been blown out of all proportion.

It was not the only time the newspapers unfortunately got it wrong. A few months later a journalist on the *Rand Daily Mail*, Benjamin Pogrund, telephoned me to let me know that Winnie had received an anonymous letter from someone claiming Nelson was very ill and was close to death. He said the story was now spreading throughout the Johannesburg papers. I knew Benjamin, both as a well-respected journalist and a long-standing friend of Nelson. I knew I was safe in talking to him. I explained that the story was simply not true, that I had been with Nelson just twenty minutes before and he was as well and healthy as ever. Together we discussed the damage this ill-founded letter could cause and Benjamin said he would call Winnie and reassure her. I said I would also call her. But first I called Munro to tell him trouble was on the way.

The frantic telephone calls, from senior prison officials in Pretoria, politicians, anyone who could get through, started about an hour later.

Pretoria was hopping mad. 'Why weren't we told he was sick? What's the problem?' I left Munro to deal with the panicking senior officers who, in turn, would handle the politicians.

I went to Nelson and explained why he was to be examined and he was, initially, amused. But this quickly turned to anger that everyone, the prison staff, the doctors, himself, had been put in this position. And he was rightly furious about the anxiety this unnecessary publicity would cause his family.

He agreed, 'Okay, Mr Gregory, let's get this sorted out as quickly as possible and we can send the doctor's results to Pretoria and they can make it public.' As ever, Nelson never remained angry for long, and he added philosophically, 'Perhaps the doctor will tell us something none of us know. Perhaps he'll tell me I really am ill and won't be with us too long.' The twinkle was back in his eye.

That evening I got two of the leading district surgeons, Dr Loubser and Dr le Roux, to attend Pollsmoor for the full examination. I explained the reason and they agreed to come as soon as possible. By the time both doctors had reached Pollsmoor there was the now familiar gathering of vultures, the media pack, at the front gate. They had heard the 'Mandela is dying' rumour and were here to report what they could.

When I spoke to Winnie she was perfectly calm. 'I know it's not true. I've spoken to Benjie and he's explained it is someone being malicious,' she explained. 'Don't worry. I've told the family the truth and tell Madiba I shall see him next week, on the 26th.' At least if Winnie was calm I should be thankful.

By the time I got back to the cell area the doctors had completed the examination of Nelson and pronounced him fit. It was certainly a case of reports of his nearness to death being greatly exaggerated. Both Dr le Roux and Dr Loubser wrote separate letters giving him a complete clean bill of health which I then faxed immediately to Pretoria.

When Winnie arrived a week later I met her as normal and handed her the original letters from the two doctors. I wanted her to read them fully before she met Nelson, rather than wasting her precious time with him having to read them then. Winnie was adamant that she was untroubled and did not need the medical reports. She was already assured that there were no problems.

But I insisted. 'Winnie, this will not be the last time something like this happens. Clearly someone is out to cause mischief. It's important that between us we have an understanding that if there is any problem at any time we have a clear line of communication.'

Later, as the visit with Nelson ended, the three of us discussed the anonymous letter. Nelson summed it up by telling Winnie, 'If you have any queries or worries about my situation here just get on the telephone to Mr Gregory. I think we can trust him by now.'

Although we had an understanding between the three of us, it did not prevent the gross exaggerations continuing. During one visit from Winnie and Zindzi, Nelson was grimacing and complained that he had just been issued with a new pair of shoes which were a size too small. He told his wife and daughter the shoes were causing a blister on his little toe. He said he would return them and get another new pair. Winnie was concerned, as she always was about Nelson's health and well-being. But then came the press reports that Nelson was having a toe amputated because the authorities had given him shoes that were two or three sizes too small. Again, as soon as I was informed about the story in the newspapers, I called Winnie to reassure her.

'Mr Gregory, please don't worry. I know the truth about it. Tell my husband that these things are getting annoying because it seems we cannot trust the press to print stories accurately without making it into a drama.'

A short time later, maybe two or three days, Helen Suzman, a member of parliament, visited Nelson and the first question she asked him was about the operation on his foot. To demonstrate its absurdity, he bent down and took off his shoe and sock. He then held up his foot to the glass and waggled his toes. 'Look, all in fine working order.'

By this time Nelson was allowed five visits each month, and he always kept two aside for Winnie. Being at Pollsmoor made her journeys from Johannesburg slightly easier, having cut out the need to travel to the island. I had personally also scrapped the permit system. It was, to my mind, absolutely pointless. Winnie was not under house arrest and it was no longer a case of needing to arrange a boat from the harbour front to the island. Just a phone call to let me know and that was it. On a few occasions Winnie would phone and say she couldn't get down from Johannesburg, so I told Nelson in time to allow for other visitors, other family members or friends to call. Through these visits I also began to get to know the family.

The visiting room at Pollsmoor was very different from the facilities on the island. It was more spacious and modern with large cubicles and larger glass partitions. The larger glassed area allowed visitors to see the entire person. There was also the benefit of a much better microphone system so that both prisoner and visitor could hear without having to continually strain.

It was in May 1984 that I received a call in my office, from Pretoria. It was one of the senior commanders. 'Gregory, you will be getting a fax in ten minutes' time. Make sure you read it, understand it, then destroy it. I shall call you back in thirty minutes.'

Well, this was all very intriguing and a number of thoughts flashed through my mind. Could another transfer be on the cards? Perhaps even a return to Robben Island because the group was still asking to go back? Perhaps more of the Robben Island leader group would join us? Certainly I had ruled out any possibility of something like a release; that would be impossible. So what was it?

The message was very short and sweet: it listed the five prisoners and said that they could now have contact visits. As simple as that. As political prisoners they had, until now, been denied the same rights as the ordinary A-category prisoners who were allowed contact visits. I knew that there had been a lot of campaigning through the Red Cross to apply pressure on Pretoria to change this arcane law. They had now succeeded. I was absolutely delighted. I looked at my visitors' list and saw that Winnie was due to arrive from Johannesburg in a few days.

When she came she was looking radiant in a beautifully coloured kaftan and head-dress. Behind her was Zindzi and Gadaffi, Nelson's grandson. I knew Zindzi was coming because I had discussed it with Winnie, but the boy was a surprise. I was even more delighted because I knew Nelson loved this child and it was to be an added bonus that he would be able to hold his wife, his daughter and grandson again. I had thought this out carefully and decided the best thing would be to tell her first. Winnie would have been used to walking into the room and finding him sitting behind the glass. If she saw him in person standing in front of her it could have been a big shock.

I was waiting for her at the front gates and I asked if she could spare me a few minutes, in the office.

There was a look of concern on her face and I could see she was worried that something was wrong.

As we walked to the office I put my hand on her arm and said softly, 'No, don't worry, there is no problem, just something we should discuss.' Zindzi barely noticed the fact we were not heading to the visiting room; she was more concerned with keeping Gadaffi in order.

Inside the office Winnie sat on the chair. Zindzi had disappeared to the toilet with Gadaffi. I took the opportunity and told her, 'From today you will be allowed contact visits. You'll be able to touch him again.' The words took some moments to sink in and I could see a mist come over her eyes.

222

I continued, 'I thought it best to tell you before you actually see him so that it was not a big shock.' She nodded, stood up and turned her back. I could see she was struggling to maintain control so I walked out of the room, ahead of her.

I had already informed Nelson and he had understood immediately. His reaction was typical. 'Mmmm, I had better get my best clothes out and pressed ready.'

There was a room I had set up next to my office, away from the main visiting area. I got some furniture, easy chairs to replace the hard-backed wooden chairs which normally would be in the rooms, side tables, a table where they could sit and talk and write if they wished. The furniture was not new, but I explained it to Munro as an area where everyone could be comfortable.

Nelson was already sitting in one of the large, easy chairs when we entered. He stood up, his long frame coming to attention. Winnie was behind me and I heard a squeal of joy and she rushed past me and leaped. Nelson caught her and held her. There was laughter and a flurry of words. They were kissing and hugging and Winnie was draped around his neck and shoulders. He lifted her off the floor. I don't think they could believe it was happening. This was their first contact visit since he had been imprisoned, nearly twenty-one years. It was the first contact he'd had with any member of his family since his daughter Zeni and her husband Muzi had come to see him on the island.

Zindzi had walked in behind Winnie, clutching her son's hand, expecting to be in a room where she would be cut off from her father. As she saw what was happening, she put her hand to her mouth and cried. Gadaffi, not understanding, tugged at her arm and demanded, 'Mummy, what is wrong, why do you cry?' She knelt down and cradled her little boy.

I was an intruder, prying into a meeting which was so intensely personal and emotional that I just wished the floor would open and swallow me up. I knew, as they did, that I had to remain in the room, but I went to the far end, to the window which faced on to the roadway where cars were parked. Through the shutters I could see other warders walking by, occasionally a voice penetrated. I concentrated my mind on what was happening outside. I tried to shut out what they were saying to one another. I switched off from this moment and tried harder to listen to what I could hear from outside. Nelson and Winnie were so taken with being able to touch one another that they had forgotten I was there. Inside the room there was no sound, yet the emotion was overwhelming. Both of

223

them knew I knew everything about their lives; by now I had read every letter they had written to one another over the past two decades. I had sat in on most of the meetings in the visiting rooms; these people were my family. I knew them and they knew me. At some stage they began talking, their voices soft and thick with emotion. I could tell Nelson was all choked up; he was barely able to speak. I knew he would be in tears. I certainly was. I felt a joy and pleasure in this moment, that they were able to hold one another again.

Nelson pulled himself away and turned to Zindzi, now a beautiful young woman. When he had last held her in his arms she was a baby. This moment was as powerful as any I have ever witnessed. Zindzi was in a mixture of laughter and tears. Winnie wept and I wiped my eyes, unable to focus on the line of cars outside. Nelson knelt down next to Gadaffi and swept him up in his powerful arms.

'And how's my little boy?'

Gadaffi was as a child would be. 'Fine thank you, Tata.' The boy did not understand this deeply significant moment, as he sat on his grandfather's lap. He looked up at his mother, Zindzi, and his grandmother, Winnie, who were both in tears. So Gadaffi wept too. The visit flew by. I had not even noticed the time. Eventually I had to separate them and explained, 'Don't worry, this is the type of visit you'll be able to have every time from now.'

As Nelson and I walked back to the cell area I knew he was remembering every moment. We talked.

'Today was the first time I had touched my wife's hand in twenty-one years.' His voice was low and solemn. 'How I have longed to feel the loveliness and sweetness of her skin.' I had learned that at these times when he was speaking like this I should keep quiet, that this was Nelson thinking aloud rather than speaking to me. There was little point in me telling him I understood, because clearly I did not. Every evening I went home to my wife and family and could not only see them, but touch them and hug them.

He continued. 'You know how I have longed for Winnie's visits, you know what they have meant to me. They have sustained me, and her beauty has always been a focus for me. Winnie has always tried hard to be at her most beautiful when she came to see me, here and on Robben Island. Yet, those visits, in a room divided by glass, were totally impersonal. They were joyful moments, but also very sad.'

I knew what he was saying because I had watched as both Nelson and Winnie kissed the glass as they departed. They would place their palms flat on the thickened glass, the power of their feelings penetrating its density.

'But now, today, to touch her and feel her, to hold her...'

As I have said, each prisoner was allowed five visits a month, and Nelson had always kept two for Winnie. That day they had used two of the visits, a total of eighty minutes. The following day Winnie, Zindzi and Gadaffi returned for a two-hour meeting. It was the entire quota of visits for the month, gone in two days.

Chapter 22

Political changes

In 1985 the entire political climate of South Africa began to change. It was a stifling summer in the Cape, but cool compared to the political heat generated by a speech from President Botha to the House of Assembly on 31 January 1985.

This was his speech:

'The government is willing to consider Mr Mandela's release in the Republic of South Africa on condition that Mr Mandela gives a full commitment that he will not make himself guilty of planning, instigating or committing acts of violence for the furtherance of political objectives, but will conduct himself in such a way that he will not again have to be arrested. It is therefore not the South African government which now stands in the way of Mr Mandela's freedom. It is he himself. The choice is his. All that is required of him now is that he should unconditionally reject violence as a political instrument. This is, after all, a norm which is respected in all civilised countries of the world.'

The speech caused more than a little anger among our group who had long discussions sitting in the cell block, deciding how best to respond, or even if a response were necessary. This was, after all, the latest in a number of release offers from the government, the previous all being linked to Nelson accepting he should live in the Transkei bantustan.

A week later Winnie arrived, accompanied by Ismael Ayob. It was a legal visit and the reason was clear: they wanted a reply to the President's offer of release. The visit led to a row. It was one of the visits during which I was working with other members of the group and so had to leave the monitoring to another warder. Within just a few minutes of the meeting starting the warder interrupted Nelson as he began to dictate his reply to Botha. As Nelson continued, the warder threatened to call the head of the prison. Nelson stood up and declared that he had every right to reply to the President in whatever manner he so wished. The row became heated and a senior officer entered, telling Nelson that he should not make any political statements; it was not allowed during visiting times. Eventually the entire situation was calmed when Munro's permission was sought, and given, for the reply. I only heard about it later and realised I should have sat in on the meeting myself, knowing that the reply was perfectly in order.

Nelson's reply to the President was read to a massive gathering at the Jabulani Stadium in Soweto two days later. It was a gathering to celebrate Bishop Desmond Tutu winning the Nobel Peace Prize. As part of the celebration Zindzi appeared on stage in front of the crowd and received rapturous applause. When she told them she had a message from her father, in reply to Botha's offer, the crowd was hushed.

She read:

'On Friday my mother and our attorney saw my father at Pollsmoor Prison to obtain his answer to Botha's offer of conditional release. The prison authorities attempted to stop this statement being made but he would have none of this and made it clear that he would make the statement to you, the people.

'Strangers, like Nicholas Bethell from England and Professor Dash from the United States have, in recent weeks, been authorised by Pretoria to see my father without restriction, yet Pretoria cannot allow you, the people, to hear what he has to say directly. He should be here himself to tell you what he thinks of this statement by Botha. He is not allowed to do so. My mother, who has also heard his words, is also not allowed to speak to you today.

'My father and his comrades at Pollsmoor Prison send their greetings to you, the freedom-loving people of this, our tragic land, in the full confidence that you will carry on the struggle for freedom. He and his comrades at Pollsmoor Prison send their very warmest greetings to Bishop Desmond Tutu. Bishop Tutu has made it clear to the world that the Nobel Peace Prize belongs to you who are the people. We salute him.

'My father and his comrades at Pollsmoor Prison are grateful to the United Democratic Front who, without hesitation, made this venue available to them so that they could speak to you today. My father and his comrades wish to make this statement to you, the people, first. They are clear they are accountable to you and you alone. And that you should hear their views directly and not through others. My father speaks not only for himself and for his comrades at Pollsmoor Prison, but he hopes he also speaks for all those in jail for their opposition to apartheid, for all those who are banished, for all those who are in exile, for all those who suffer under apartheid, for all those who are opponents of apartheid and for all those who are oppressed and exploited.

'Throughout our struggle there have been puppets who have claimed to speak for you. They have made this claim, both here and abroad. They are of no consequence. My father and his colleagues will not be like them.

'My father says, "I am a member of the African National Congress. I have always been a member of the African National Congress and I will remain a member of the African National Congress until the day I die. Oliver Tambo is much more than a brother to me. He is my greatest friend and comrade for nearly fifty years. If there is any one among you who cherishes my freedom, Oliver Tambo cherishes it more, and I know that he would give his life to see me free. There is no difference between his views and mine."

'My father says, "I am surprised at the conditions that this government wants to impose on me. I am not a violent man. My colleagues and I wrote in 1952 to Malan asking for a round table conference to find a solution to the problems of our country but that was ignored. When Strijdom was in power, we made the same offer. Again, it was ignored. When Verwoerd was in power we asked for a national convention for all the people in South Africa to decide on their future. This, too, was in vain. It was only when all other forms of resistance were no longer open to us that we turned to armed struggle. Let Botha show that he is different to Malan, Strijdom and Verwoerd. Let him renounce violence. Let him say he will dismantle apartheid.

'"Let him unban the people's organisation, the African National Congress. Let him free all those who have been imprisoned, banished or exiled for their opposition to apartheid.

Let him guarantee free political activity so that the people may decide who will govern them.

'"I cherish my own freedom dearly, but I care even more for your freedom. Too many have died since I went to prison. Too many have suffered for the love of freedom. I owe it to their widows, to their orphans, to their mothers and to their fathers who have grieved and wept for them. Not only have I suffered during these long, lonely, wasted years. I am not less life-loving than you are. But I cannot sell my birthright nor am I prepared to sell the birthright of the people to be free. I am in prison as a representative of the people and of your organisation, the African National Congress, which was banned. What freedom am I being offered while the organisation of the people remains banned? What freedom am I being offered when I may be arrested on a pass offence? What freedom am I being offered to live my life as a family with my dear wife who remains in banishment in Brandfort? What freedom am I being offered when I must ask for permission to live in an urban area? What freedom am I being offered when I need a stamp in my pass to seek work? What freedom am I being offered when my very South African citizenship is not respected?

'"Only free men can negotiate. Prisoners cannot enter into contracts. Herman Toivo ja Toivo [a founder of South West African People's Organisation (SWAPO)], when freed, never gave any undertaking, nor was he called upon to do so."

'My father says, "I cannot and will not give any undertaking at a time when I and you, the people, are not free. Your freedom and mine cannot be separated. I WILL return."'

At the end of the speech there were several seconds of silence. A moment when the crowd took its breath and took stock of Nelson's words. They absorbed the full content, and beauty of the entire speech, and of the particularly apt phrase that only free men can negotiate. It was the most significant indication his people needed of his resolve and attitude. They stood and sang *Nkosi Sikelel' iAfrika*, the anthem of black Africans before bursting into deafening applause.

The speech, and its delivery, drew condemnation from the Afrikaner press and in particular Botha, who reacted swiftly. I watched on television as he condemned what he called 'Mandela's inflexible and uncompromising rhetoric and refusal to enter into a peaceful solution'. When he was asked if his government was talking directly with Mandela, the President glowered at the camera and was emphatic. 'No, no way,' he said.

I was very surprised to hear him say that and said as much to Gloria, who was sitting beside me. She asked me whether I meant that Botha was talking to Mandela.

'No,' I replied, 'not the President directly. But I thought that one of his agents, one of his Cabinet, had been speaking to him.'

Perhaps I should not have voiced these doubts even to my own wife. This was an area which I had vowed I would not go into, even within the confines of my own home. So I said no more.

Although I had seen Coetsee, the Minister of Justice, at the hospital visiting Nelson, I had not been present when they spoke.

The message from Nelson and the other leaders had been unequivocal, as was to be expected. These men were not about to renounce their deeply held principles and beliefs. I knew, because I could see for myself, that they were not tiring of their time in prison. If anything, they were stronger, more determined now than ever. The years had only hardened their resolve. They had by now been in jail for a generation. I knew they would not throw away that time by bowing to Botha's transparent offer. What made me even more angry than the downright lie from Botha was the failure of the government to see the most obvious situation developing before their own eyes: these men were not to be broken. They were serving their cause and would continue to do so even if it ended in their ultimate deaths in custody. I had seen how Nelson had dealt with the approach from Jimmy Kruger when he was the prisons' minister in 1976, how he had responded to the offer of release to the Transkei. It made me despair that the government clearly had not learned any lessons over the past ten years. I had listened carefully to the content of the speech read by Zindzi and could see its importance. Clearly Botha's offer was an attempt to drive a wedge between Nelson and his comrades by dangling the carrot of his own freedom before him in exchange for a departure from stated ANC policy, the refusal to accept the Bantustans. I was particularly intrigued by the reference to Tambo and how Nelson took care to spell out his devotion and loyalty to his former legal partner. It showed his devotion to the cause was unswerving. I also took it as a message to the government as well

231

as all white people that although he was rejecting the offer because of the conditions which were attached to it, there was room for negotiation and that the path to ultimate peace was through discussion and negotiation, and not war.

The mention in the message from the Pollsmoor group of two visits, by Lord Bethell and Professor Dash, referred to two visits that had taken place in the preceding months. Nicholas Bethell was, at the time, a member of the British House of Lords and the European Parliament. Samuel Dash was a professor of law at Georgetown University and former counsel to the United States Senate Watergate Committee. Both had full authorisation from Kobie Coetsee for their visits.

Bethell came first, shortly before Christmas 1984, and held a meeting with Nelson in the commander's office. The discussion, which was monitored by Major Fritz van Stittert, was a friendly discussion on the aims and objectives of the ANC overall, and the imprisoned leaders specifically.

Within a few weeks Professor Dash arrived and again Nelson met his guest in Munro's office. It was a brief meeting during which Nelson outlined what he saw as the future of South Africa in multi-racial terms, with a vote for everyone, not the few, and a country that was united, rather than divided by homelands and Bantustans. Dash asked if Nelson saw the repeal of the mixed marriages legislation as an important breakthrough. But Nelson was quick to put it in context as no more than a pin-prick which had little actual effect; the real importance lay in political equality. He also admitted that the ANC would not be able to defeat the white government in a military sense, but would be able to make running the country extremely difficult.

The rest of the year saw an increase in unrest as the heat was turned up still further. On the twenty-fifth anniversary of the shootings in Sharpeville and Langa there were serious disturbances near Uitenhage when twenty people were shot dead. It resulted in further rounds of escalating violence and in July the government declared a State of Emergency, with townships and squatter camps sealed off by mass movements of military personnel.

Funeral followed funeral and anger rebounded off anger as death and destruction became a dominant factor for many. I observed Nelson and the other members of the group as they read and heard of the violence and could see the frustration in their faces. I could also hear the growing cry from outside South Africa,

232

from other countries, that demanded the government negotiate and dismantle the barriers of apartheid. All the time the statistics worsened as increasing numbers of people died. In the previous two years nearly 1000 people had been murdered for political reasons.

It all seemed to overwhelm Botha, who instead of taking the advice being showered on South Africa from abroad, chose his own course. He urged Afrikaners in a televised speech to 'stand together against the forces of darkness which had called upon foreign aid to destroy the fatherland'. It was a speech which appealed only to extremists and ignored the growing middle ground which was tiring of violence and bloodshed, and was becoming increasingly frightened by how it was now affecting their daily lives. Botha, somewhat strangely, claimed that the principle of 'one man, one vote' in a unitary system would lead to domination of one racial group over the others, which would in turn lead to chaos. It was almost as if he was describing the current situation in the country where chaos reigned with one racial group having domination, caused by a process of selective voting for whites only.

In the middle of this there came another message from Nelson to his people, this time read to a conference of the ANC in Zambia in June 1985. It was later released to the world's media.

The message, which came collectively from the leader groups in both Pollsmoor and Robben Island, but in reality was written by Nelson, said:

'We were most delighted to hear that the ANC will soon have another conference. We sincerely hope that such an occasion will constitute yet another milestone in our history. It is most satisfying, especially in our present position, to belong to a tested organisation which exercises so formidable an impact on the situation in our country, which has established itself firmly as the standard bearer of such a rich tradition, and which has brought us such coveted laurels.

'As you know, we always try to harmonise on our views and responses with those of the movement at large. For this reason, we find it rewarding indeed to know that, despite the immense distance and the years which separate us, as well as the effective communications channels, we still remain a closely knit organisation, ever conscious of the crucial

233

importance of unity, and of resisting every attempt to divide and confuse.

'We feel sure that all of those delegates who will attend will go there with one central issue uppermost in their minds: that out of the conference the ANC will emerge far stronger than ever before. Unity is the rock on which the African National Congress was founded; it is the principle which has guided us down the years as we feel our way forward.

'In the course of its history, the ANC has survived countless storms and risen to eminence partly because of the sterling qualities of its membership, and partly because each member has regarded himself or herself as the principal guardian of that unity. All discussions, contributions and criticism have generally been balanced and constructive and, above all, they have been invariably subjected to the over-riding principle of maximum unity. To lose sight of that principle is to sell our birthright, to betray those who paid the highest price so that the ANC should flourish and triumph.

'In this connection, the positions taken by Oliver Tambo on various issues and also stressed by Joe Slovo inspired us tremendously. Both drew attention to vital issues, which in our opinion are very timely. They must be highlighted and kept consciously in mind as we try to sort out the complicated problems which face the movement, and as we try to hammer out the guidelines for future progress.

'These remarks are the clearest expression of that enduring identity of approach of members of the movement wherever they may be, and a summary of achievements of which we are justly proud. In particular, we fully share the view that the ANC has raised mass political consciousness to a scale unknown in our experience. It is in this spirit that we send you our greetings and best wishes. We hold your hands firmly across the miles.'

Two months later, as the political mayhem continued unabated throughout the country, there was reaction from South Africa's business leaders who announced that they felt the government should change its attitude of non-negotiation. The Association of Chambers of Commerce, at its annual meeting, passed a resolution which called upon the government to begin negotiations with black leaders 'even if some are currently in detention in the jails'. This clear reference to people such as Nelson and Walter was a clear indication of how much out of touch certain sections of the government had become.

If the government would not listen then unusual steps were needed. Change began slowly when a group of influential business leaders went to Zambia to hold talks with Oliver Tambo and Thabo Mbeki, Govan's son, who was now playing an increasingly influential role in ANC affairs. They were soon followed by a well-publicised group of MPs from the Progressive Federal Party, the official parliamentary opposition. Following these surprise meetings a joint statement was issued with the ANC leaders in exile that 'both groups shared the urgent need to dismantle apartheid and establish a non-racial and democratic South Africa'. Central to all talks was agreement that Nelson and the other ANC prisoners should be released. The publication of such attitudes, particularly coming from influential white businessmen, convinced me more than ever that a change of government position was now just a matter of time.

But the more demands were made on the Botha government, the more the President seemed to dig his heels in. In order to stop these forays from white groups venturing outside the country to have highly publicised meetings with the ANC exiles, the government took drastic steps. First a group of eight students from Stellenbosch University, the very heartland of Afrikanerdom, wanted visas to travel abroad and visit the ANC Youth League; they wanted to talk youth to youth, face to face. Not only were they denied permission, but their passports were confiscated. Then senior clergy from the Dutch Reformed Church decided they would take a trip to Lusaka to visit the ANC's base there, but they were also denied.

The demand for change was coming from all over now, both inside and outside South Africa. From around the world came more and more reports which showed us all just how Nelson had become the modern symbol of the entire struggle of the black man.

From Britain there was story after story in the media of how street names in London and other major cities were being named after Nelson. From America came an honorary degree from the City College of New York. The Greek village of Ancient Olympia conferred honorary citizenship, with the Scottish city Glasgow awarding him freedom of the city. From Austria the Bruno Krensky Foundation gave him the country's Human Rights Award.

Pope John Paul expressed his admiration of Nelson and from West Germany, Chancellor Helmut Kohl challenged the South African government, 'Show your readiness to speak to Nelson Mandela and the other previously outlawed political forces in your country. Only then can the national dialogue you have repeatedly called for become a reality.' Poland's Communist Leader Wojciech Jaruzelski praised Nelson's principled stand against apartheid, with similar recognition coming from French President François Mitterand who said his lifelong fight for the ideals of justice, dignity and liberty were a beacon to twentieth-century statesmanship. The Scandinavian countries collectively expressed a hope that Nelson would 'soon be able to celebrate his birthdays in freedom in a country that had been liberated from all the bonds of apartheid'. The European Community's foreign ministers called for the unconditional and immediate release of all political prisoners. The World Council of Churches warned that the continued imprisonment of Nelson and all political prisoners was proof of 'the policy of repression of the South African government and its intransigence in dealing with the just demands of black people'. Mike Tyson, at the time world boxing heavyweight champion, sent Nelson his world title-winning gloves. It was a gift I know Nelson treasured. He was himself a boxer in his younger days and loved the smell of the ring.

But, somehow, President Botha refused to open his eyes and see the inevitable. Instead, he equated the continued incarceration with that of Rudolf Hess, Hitler's deputy. When he used those words I was not only shocked but outraged. Day after day the words and deeds of the government, manifested most obviously by the police and army, intensified anger at home as well as abroad. And, for the first time I could remember, the anger was now penetrating the minds of ordinary white people. Although the government kept blaming the ANC for the countrywide uprisings and troubles, it was clear the head-in-the-sand approach was as responsible as any factor.

When Winnie continued to represent Nelson's views, she almost led to a clampdown from Pretoria. In August, disregarding her banning order, she addressed a packed news conference in Johannesburg. She was typically forthright, declaring that the government's 'arrogant, insensitive manifesto was likely to have disastrous consequences'.

She added, 'If the government persists in jailing the leadership whenever they call for a national convention, the only other aspect that can be discussed by the people of this country and the ruling Afrikaner is the handing over of power.'

It provoked a stern response from Botha who interpreted Winnie's words as a political message from Nelson. He warned that the government would now reconsider the manner and extent of continued visits to those in jail.

He said, 'It is a standing policy that prisoners are not allowed to make any political statements and prisoner Mandela is no exception to that rule.'

After reading that statement I held my breath expecting to receive some heavy dictate from Pretoria. But it never came, and I began to realise these words indicated merely the public posturing which was going on. It was a case once again of empty rhetoric.

As a contrast to the politicking and sensationalism which seemed to dominate the media, there was one interesting article which appeared at the time: a letter from Reverend Dudley Moore, the Methodist minister who worked among prisoners at Pollsmoor. He wrote to the *Rand Daily Mail* in an attempt to portray a different picture of Nelson Mandela the man, the one he saw and visited in the prison. He wrote:

'I believe the people of our country ought to know something about the man. What I have written is not what is reported to me by others. It is my own personal knowledge of the man, Nelson Mandela himself. I regularly administer Holy Communion to Mandela and I did so again the day before yesterday. On that occasion, he spent some time in meditation, meditating on the tension that Jesus must have felt at Gethsemane, knowing that he was to be arrested and killed.'

I felt the letter was a welcome relief from the constant vitriol and came closer to a true picture of Nelson.

Chapter 23

Hospital visits

Censorship was still very heavy in prison at this time. If a newspaper made any mention of any of the other political personalities, such as ANC people exiled abroad, the orders from Pretoria were to cut the articles before the prisoners saw them. For many years I had been operating on my own interpretation of the rules and when, one day, there was an article on Herman Toivo ja Toivo I put it to a test. He had been one of the SWAPO men who was imprisoned on the island with the group. The rules demanded that I should cut out the entire article, but I took the view that it was a totally nonsensical rule. This man had been in prison with Nelson and the group and if they wanted to know anything about him or SWAPO all they had to do was ask him personally. I talked the situation over with Munro who agreed that I should begin to adapt the censorship rules as I saw fit.

A few days later I saw Kathy who asked if there had been a change in the censorship rules. He was surprised I had left the Toivo ja Toivo article intact. He said he had expected it to be removed. I gave him a little wink and said that times were changing faster than he realised. Later I began to leave more and more articles in without censoring them, knowing that I had to take it gradually, but that it was a way to reach the stage where there would be no censorship at all.

Studying for university exams was taking up a lot of the group's time; they were all studying for one thing or another. Improving their own education was an important part of their imprisonment. When it came to exam time I was approached by UNISA, the University of South Africa, and asked if I would be the invigilator for the exams. I agreed. All I needed was a decent room where we could have perfect quiet, but which also gave the right atmosphere to concentrate. I decided to use a room which was normally used as

239

a courtroom for departmental or internal cases. It had several wide tables which were used by the prosecution, defence and any attending attorneys. There was also a large comfortable chair which sat on a raised dais and was used by the presiding court officer. I took all the group to the room and asked if they felt it was appropriate for an exam room. They all agreed it was.

I then decided to get signs made which read 'Examinations – Quiet/Stilte'. I did not want people stumbling into the room in a crucial stage of an exam.

The exams were all sat around June. All the group were involved. Raymond, for example, was studying through the Institute of Commerce for a diploma in commerce. I told them all that even though I was a friend, I was determined to be a strict invigilator, with no favours shown. They all agreed, showing surprise that I would expect otherwise.

In the days and weeks running up to the exams I ensured that each exam was properly listed on a calendar and that they were all well aware of its approach. I also ensured they were all well prepared and did not burn the midnight oil too late in the last few days before the exam was due to be sat.

The night before the exam we all met and I read them the full set of instructions sent to me by the examining board so they were in no doubt about what I expected of them. During the exams their behaviour was impeccable. Because of the range of studies the group was taking, it was normal that they would usually sit alone, seldom having similar times for the exams. Before each exam I would shake them by the hand and wish them luck. We would enter the room fifteen minutes before the exam was due to start and I made sure they were all comfortable. Then, fifteen minutes before the end, I told them the time to allow each one to check his work.

At the conclusion of each exam I would ask how it had been and they were usually very positive although occasionally there were a few nerves jangling over questions which they considered a little tricky. I took great pride in the fact that these men passed every exam they ever sat. They showed that they were not just stronger than the prejudice that had sent them to prison in the first place, but they were determined to better themselves at every turn. They were, each and every one of them, an object lesson to every person who ever doubted the value of education.

Later, Walter gave up his studies, but only because his eyesight was failing. We knew how much Walter valued studying and the gradual loss of his sight was one of the cruellest blows of all. It was at this time I saw another side of Kathy when he took time off from his own studies to spend hours reading material to Walter. It was incredibly touching.

After agreeing to become an invigilator I received a cheque for 27 rand from UNISA, about $8. I knew they were being ultra fair in paying me, but I also knew that here I was doing this job as part of my employment as a warder. I knew I was not entitled to the cheque so I sent it back, explaining my position. I thought that was the end of the matter. I was wrong.

The following February I had to fill in my tax return forms. I did so, ignoring the cheque sent to me by UNISA, not only because I had forgotten all about it, but also because I had returned it to the university. Then a month or so later I was summonsed to appear before a woman at the revenue offices to answer questions about my income. I was mystified, but attended. The office was in the centre of Cape Town and I took a day off to sort out the matter. Clutching my letter with the details and reference number I was somewhat puzzled by what was happening, but because there was not anything to hide, I went along, wearing my prison officer's uniform because that was required of me when I was on what was considered official business.

The woman behind the desk peered from behind her half-rimmed glasses. She was like a headmistress. 'And why didn't you declare all your income, Mr Gregory?'

I was stunned. 'I have. Well, as far as I know I have. The personnel department at Pollsmoor handles all that; it isn't something I really have to deal with. I merely fill in my tax form each year and sign it.'

The old woman got angry and began shouting at me. 'I'm sick and tired of you people in uniform thinking you can get away with anything and everything.'

I was still stunned. 'Look, ma'am, would you like to explain to me what this is all about, because I have not got the slightest idea.'

She replied, 'Mr Gregory, you know exactly what this is about and I'm sure it's not the first time.' She began to wave a sheet of paper at me, explaining that she had a letter from UNISA which said I had been paid 27 rand by them. I remembered the fee for being an invigilator. I smiled and then laughed out loud.

'Oh, that?'

241

'Oh dear, Mr Gregory, we've been caught out, have we? It's not just a matter of "oh that", it's now a great deal more serious than just "that". I'm now going to turn this entire file over to the police and let them investigate you.'

Now I was getting steamed up.

'Madam, I too am getting a little sick and tired of this charade. Before you start making assumptions that I have been involved in doing anything crooked, you should, perhaps, have asked me about this so-called cheque from UNISA. If you had, I would have told you what happened to it. But, as you haven't, let's just allow your stupid procedure to take its course and we'll see who gets embarrassed by this.'

I was set to storm out of the office when another guy entered the room, attracted by the shouting between us.

He asked what the problem was about. I explained that the woman wanted to send a file to the police relating to a cheque sent to me by UNISA for acting as an invigilator, but that I'd had to return it because of my duties as a prison warder. The man was all understanding and wanted to forget the matter. I agreed. By the time I got home I had decided on another course of action and wrote to UNISA asking for the cheque to be sent to me. I cashed it and used the 27 rand to cover my expenses that day. When I told the group about how they'd got me into trouble with the tax people they roared with laughter.

'Welcome to the ranks of the law-breakers,' said Raymond as tears of mirth filled his eyes.

I was becoming more aware of world opinion towards these ANC people, particularly Nelson. They were frequently on the local news as well as worldwide news. There were times when I was bombarded with telephone calls from around the world inquiring about one aspect or another of what was happening. It was because of this massive interest I issued instructions to every warder on the section that whatever happened to any of these men, I had to have a report. If any of them had a stomach ache or needed a tablet to cure a headache I had to know and it had to be recorded in the medical book. This attitude had to prevail throughout the prison structure and whenever there was the slightest medical complaint they were taken to hospital for specialist treatment. There was also a secondary reason, one that I was coming to accept: these men were now my friends, particularly Nelson, and I was determined that if they felt anything was wrong it was the duty of the state to get them the best medical treatment. After all, the years they had suffered on Robben Island had certainly contributed to any medical complaint they had. Once a week I went to the hospital section and carefully went through the medical book, checking to see if anyone had been taking medicine or pills. If I saw a report reading, for example, 'Saw Mandela today, administered Sedunol for slight headache', I would haul up the person who had made the report. I warned them that I wanted to know everything that was happening medically. If they made the same mistake again, they would be off the section.

In January 1983 Nelson complained about a small cyst behind the ear. For weeks he had also been worried by a sore big toe, so I decided the best thing was medical treatment for both complaints. I took him to Woodstock Hospital for X-rays and it was discovered that this ear complaint was a small fat gland, inconsequential. The doctors decided that if he went into the hospital for a day they could remove both the fat gland and the toe-nail. Both minor operations.

On 2 February Nelson was taken into Woodstock for the operation on his toe and the gland which the doctor had called a lipoma. It was the first major security operation I had organised for the hospital run. With each visit to a hospital, or a dental surgery, I planned the route and security guards myself, checking the way we would travel and working out the number of armed guards we should take. I was aware then only of the need to guard Nelson and the others, rather than worry about them escaping. I had long accepted that these people did not want to escape. They better served their cause by the dignity they were showing in prison.

At the Woodstock Hospital, a small provincial unit, I arranged to have a constant armed guard on the medical wing, not just armed prison warders but also police and security guards.

One of the prison warders, a young officer, Christo Brand, was dressed in surgical gown and smock to go into the operating theatre along with Nelson and the medical team. There were armed guards outside the door to the operating theatre as well as both entrances to the hospital and patrolling its grounds. The operation was a relatively simple matter and Nelson was back at Pollsmoor by 4 February, although it provided a good exercise for later hospital visits when much more serious surgery was involved.

It was only after he returned to Pollsmoor that Nelson would allow me to telephone Winnie to let her know all was well.

We had talked about letting Winnie know before he had gone into hospital, but Nelson was adamant that his wife would worry unduly and that she would probably want to travel to Cape Town to be at the hospital.

When we had gone to the hospital I had chosen ward D1 because it was the smallest and easiest to guard. It was on the third floor and the only people who had any business on that floor were connected to Nelson. I also knew a nursing sister on that section, Sister Ferreira. She had contact with us through previous visits from Pollsmoor and we knew she was level-headed and trustworthy.

As we entered she came to me with a small problem. 'On the second floor of the operating theatre and in the passageway outside is a blackboard with numbers one to six chalked on it. This is where the day's operations, patients' and doctors' names are listed.'

I saw the problem. If we listed Nelson's name and time of operation, it could easily be seen by an outsider and news spread more widely. Only a few people knew Nelson was in the hospital and I wanted to keep it that way. The fewer people who knew the better.

I thought about it and replied, 'Sister, if we put Nelson Mandela's name on that blackboard with the time of an operation and the doctor's name we will be in for a tough time. Word will get out and we will be flooded with media people as well as people concerned about his health. They'll think the worst.'

When I called Winnie about the operations she was unconcerned, and accepted that they were both minor. She said although she could not visit that week, Zindzi would be visiting in the next few days.

The next major visit to hospital happened in August 1984 when Nelson was having difficulty in passing urine. I made an appointment with Dr Loubser, a specialist at the Medipark Clinic in Cape Town. It was set for 29 August.

I arrived early and checked through all the usual security plans; a pre-planned route as well as selected guards to follow in cars. I went up to see Nelson on the third floor of the cell block.

'Okay, Nelson, all set, let's go.'

Nelson sat on the edge of his bed and I could tell from his face there was trouble coming. He was wearing the prison garb, pants

244

and shirt. He said he wanted to be allowed to wear everyday clothes, a jersey over a pair of ordinary pants.

He explained, 'Look, the way I see it, you are trying to keep this visit all very quiet and yet you are having me walk into the hospital in the clothes of a prisoner. Anyone who sees that will know pretty soon who I am and what is happening. Then we're into the problem of dealing with the media.'

I nodded my head, understanding exactly what he was saying. 'Nelson, I agree. I'll see what the commanding officer says.'

Munro refused immediately. He would not budge. I returned to Nelson. 'Listen, man, I'm sorry. The CO says no, he will not allow you to wear ordinary clothes.'

Nelson was firm as well. 'In that case I'm not going.' His behaviour made perfectly good sense to me. I said simply, 'Okay, I'll just cancel the appointment and I'll come back and see if we can resolve this matter.'

It took a week of persuading, but Nelson got his way. He was allowed to wear his own, private clothes for hospital visits. Once again, common sense won the day. So another appointment was set for early September, with Dr Loubser.

As he walked out in his private clothes, a smart pair of well-creased grey slacks and a neat V-neck sweater, I remarked, 'You know, Nelson, you look quite good in those clothes. I think you wanted to dress like this to impress the nurses rather than for security reasons.' His eyes were twinkling.

I decided to stay close to Nelson that day. I'd suffered a similar complaint and knew what would be going through his mind. When we arrived at the hospital we were directed to a private X-ray room where an intravenous pyelogram was arranged. I'd had the same injection of iodine some years before and felt nauseous and hot as the iodine went through my veins to the kidney area. I sat on the table next to him, trying to keep his mind off the medical side of what was happening. Although he was not worried, there was a certain natural apprehension of the unknown. The IVP exam only took a short time before the two doctors, Loubser and a Dr Pienaar, returned with the results. There was a growth on his left kidney.

Nelson took the news in silence. I gripped him by the shoulder, telling him it was not a problem, something minor; they'd told me the same thing.

Dr Loubser chipped in. 'That's probably right; it is probably just something which will turn out to be of no importance; these things usually are. But we'd like to have a closer look on a CAT-scan before making any further decisions.'

The CAT-scan was explained to us as a computerised axial tomography, a full body X-ray. The nearest CAT-scan was at the Volks Hospital, and we'd have to fix another appointment for that.

Within a few minutes Dr Loubser returned and said he'd be able to get Nelson into the Volks Hospital the very next day.

We sat in silence on the drive back from the Medipark. I told the driver to take it easy; we were in no rush. I could see the worry on Nelson's face.

I must admit there were worries running through my own mind. I remember trying to make him feel easier about it, 'Don't worry, man, this CAT-scan will sort things out. It'll be able to pinpoint this thing much easier. I had a similar thing on my kidney and it turned out to be nothing.'

Nelson nodded and continued to look out of the window, down towards the ocean and out to Robben Island.

Back at the prison I let Nelson have some time alone. I knew he wanted to think quietly. Later in the evening I went to see him and sat beside him at the large table in the cell area. 'What shall we do about Winnie? Shall I call her and tell her you're going into the Volks tomorrow?'

Nelson was firm about that. 'No, let's wait until we know a little more and are more certain what it is.'

The only person I told was Munro. He had to know, but I added the caveat that it was not to be passed on to Winnie. Just yet.

The next day Nelson was still quieter than usual as we drove to the Volks Hospital. I left him with his thoughts, knowing that whatever happened, we would be nearer the truth of the problem later that day, after the full body scan.

The scan was completed and Dr Loubser came in and said straight away, 'It's diagnosed as a water blister. It will disappear of its own accord in time.' There was a conscious sigh of relief from Nelson and I admit I felt the same.

But Dr Loubser continued. 'There is, however, a problem because we have found blood in your urine. The next step is for an internal probe which will have to be conducted under general anaesthetic. It will be a full examination of the bladder, nothing to do with the kidney.' Again arrangements would have to be made, but Dr Loubser said he would call me.

Wherever we went for medical treatment there was an agreed

246

formula that as well as telling everything to Nelson, I would also be in on the discussions, to make a full report for both Munro and Pretoria. It was also agreed with every doctor that they would not hide any diagnosis or condition from us, however serious.

This was another blow. Instead of being relieved that the kidney problem had not been anything to worry about, now Nelson faced this new worry. Again, travelling back to Pollsmoor, he was very quiet.

Four days later Dr Loubser called me. Nelson could be accommodated at the Woodstock Hospital on the 12th at 3 o'clock, with the operation for the internal examination of the bladder set for the 13th. He called me so that I could make sure the security arrangements were in place.

The days leading up to the hospital visit were spent in deep study. This, I came to understand, was Nelson's own personal way of handling this type of crisis. He would bury himself in books and thought, trying to put aside what he perceived to be a personal weakness of his own body. I left him very much alone until the day before we were due to go to the Woodstock.

I'd arranged for five warders to stay inside the hospital overnight. Nelson asked me for a favour. 'Could you stay with me, please?'

I agreed. 'Of course, no problem.'

He was taken into the theatre at 8 o'clock sharp. Although I had promised to remain at his side throughout the entire operation I only stayed until he'd had the anaesthetic. I knew I could not stand the scene inside the operating theatre, so arranged for another warder to take my place, dressed in theatre gown, cap and slippers.

Just before he was anaesthetised I held him by the hand and smiled, wishing him 'good luck'. I added I would pray.

I waited in the recovery room for what seemed like hours, pacing up and down. I remember little other than praying, hoping that whatever was causing the blood would be minor and could be repaired. Suddenly they were wheeling Nelson out again. I looked at the clock and it was only 8.35. Just thirty-five minutes in the theatre. I took that as a good sign. I sat beside him as he lay on the trolley, out to the world. I took his hand and began talking to him, telling him we'd live to fight another day. The nurse who had been assigned to monitor his recovery from the anaesthetic kept giving me strange looks, unable to figure out why it was that this white man, clearly a prison warder, was sitting holding the hand of

Nelson Mandela, the most famous prisoner in the whole of South Africa. I didn't care.

Sometime around 11 o'clock Dr Loubser came into the recovery room. Nelson was still unconscious. I was anxious and wanted to know the truth.

He patted me on the shoulder. 'The problem is not as big as we feared. It is what they call in layman's language "an old person's illness". That is, part of his prostate is pressing on the bladder and that is causing the traces of blood in the urine.'

I sighed aloud and said, 'Thank you, God.'

Dr Loubser continued. 'Over a period of time Nelson will find difficulty in passing urine or he will start passing urine more frequently. As soon as that happens it must be reported to the medical officer at Pollsmoor and then we will re-evaluate the situation and consider a prostate operation.'

I again breathed a sigh of relief and added, 'At least it's not cancer, for that we can be thankful to the Almighty.'

Dr Loubser just nodded and said, 'Yes, that's true. It is a small thing that can happen to any person as they get older. It is the sort of thing that becomes unavoidable. Almost like death, I suppose.'

As we sat alone in the recovery room, I was mightily relieved, but just like the last time, still worried that ahead of us lay other medical problems. When Nelson woke, his eyes were dull and distant at first, taking time to emerge from his anaesthetic. When he came to fully I smiled and said, 'It's good news, no serious problems.' Dr Loubser came later and explained fully the diagnosis. We all knew it was just temporary relief.

It was a few weeks later that we all had a good laugh over what could have been a serious incident. At the time Walter was suffering from a heavy cough. It had followed him through the winter and was persisting. He was prescribed a mixture, a green liquid, Mistexpectsed, to soothe it. This particular day we had a new medical officer call and he picked up the liquid from the shelf and gave Walter a spoonful. Walter began to choke and splutter, spitting out the liquid. He began to foam at the mouth. I picked up the bottle and put it to my nose. It was a liquid soap.

Although it was a potentially serious incident, we all saw the funny side of the matter. The previous medical officer had used this particular bottle for a disinfectant soap and had failed to put a label on it.

When Walter got back to the cell area we all sat laughing at the incident, making up our own imaginary headlines.

Nelson: 'Government poisons ANC senior man.'

Raymond: 'Prison authorities claim Sisulu was foaming at the mouth.'

By August of the next year, 1985, the little blister the doctors had seen on Nelson's kidney had not enlarged or moved. Yet there were increasing amounts of blood in his urine. The doctors again decided to have an internal examination at the Woodstock. Again Dr Loubser conducted the examination and decided it was now time to remove the prostate. Nelson said that first he would have to discuss the matter with Winnie.

He was assured that the operation was routine, but he said, 'Yes, I am certain that is true. But I shall first speak to my wife about this because when they talk of a prostate operation the first thing that springs to mind is cancer. I shall speak to her to let her know that in this we have little worry.'

Dr Loubser confirmed this, adding, 'This is the type of operation we do every day. It is relatively minor and routine.'

So it was agreed. He would go into hospital later that year for the operation to remove the prostate.

But on 5 September the worst possible situation happened: the media got hold of the news about the operation. It was on the radio, in the newspapers. The word was 'Mandela is dying'. As usual the media was putting its own interpretation on the situation, and as usual was wrong. But that fact was not going to pacify anyone, not in the short term.

Nelson was furious that the news had leaked out. We all believed it had come out of the hospital section. This was going to cause upset for his family and problems with the media harassing Winnie. Munro went to see Nelson personally. Nelson requested his Cape Town attorney, Mr Bernard. Within a day Winnie, Zindzi and Zeni had arrived at the prison to see Nelson. I had spoken to Munro and said that these visits should be considered special visits and not taken off his monthly quota. The family group sat together for several hours that afternoon and Nelson reassured them all that the operation was minor and that it was not life-threatening.

Three days later Nelson went to see the medical officer at the prison. There was a larger amount of blood in his urine than before. There was an immediate examination and the operation which had been planned for later in the year was brought forward; it had to be done as soon as possible, it was decided.

That day I sent an official telegram to Winnie. 'The necessary authority has been granted for a private physician to examine your husband with a view to a second opinion. The necessary arrangements should be made immediately.'

Winnie's only objection had been that she did not want Dr Loubser to conduct the operation. She wanted someone of the family's choice and it would be someone from outside South Africa. At the time Nelson was happy with Dr Loubser, he trusted him, he was, after all, the top urologist in South Africa. But this was Winnie being Winnie. She was suspicious and wanted someone from outside the country brought in to conduct the operation.

Nelson stepped in and said he wanted Dr Loubser to do the operation, but he agreed that two doctors from overseas should be present as observers.

It took about a week to get the arrangements in place and once again Nelson had to attend Volks Hospital for an examination, this time for a second opinion from three specialists, Dr Gestetler from Switzerland, Mr Mzamanem from Johannesburg and Dr Motlana from Soweto. They all agreed with Dr Loubser's assessment: the prostate had to be done.

Winnie attended the clinic and it was the first time I had seen Nelson's sternness with her. When the three specialists reached their conclusion he turned to Winnie and said abruptly, 'Dr Loubser must do the operation. No question.' Winnie sniffed the air and turned away.

I noticed a change in Nelson's mood and attitude. Now he was less friendly, more introverted and worried. He was often deep in thought and occasionally ignored visitors when they entered the room. I put it all down to his own anxiety over his health. I could see the frustration in his mind: that he had survived the rigours of the state's incarceration, but he was now falling victim to his own health failing him. After several days of watching him struggle with this anxiety I stayed in the cell one day and talked to him. 'Look, Nelson, you must stop punishing yourself with worry at the moment. Dr Loubser has told you that this thing is an old man's illness, but medical technology is so advanced that the operation is routine.' He remained quiet, just nodding his head.

He forced a smile and said, 'Thank you for trying to reassure me, but no matter what is said there will be a worry in my mind until this thing is out of the way.'

Towards the end of October, on the 26th, Dr Loubser came to the prison and held a meeting with Nelson, Munro and Winnie.

Nelson Mandela's cell on Robben Island where he spent most of his eighteen years on the island (*Jürgen Schadeberg*)

Myself on Robben Island
(*Stuart Clarke*)

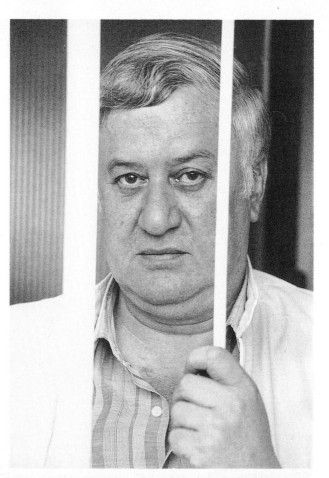

In the garden at Victor
Verster prison with Nelson
Mandela just before his
release (*Stuart Clarke*)

The note Mandela handed to me on his release (*Stuart Clarke*)

Returning to Victor Verster prison in 1994 (*Guy Hobbs*)

Nelson Mandela celebrates his release with Winnie after twenty-seven years in prison (*Associated Press*)

Govan Mbeki, Nelson Mandela and Andrew Mlangeni surrounded by journalists in the square inside the prison on Robben Island (*Jürgen Schadeberg*)

They talked through who would be present for the operation and what statement should be given out to the media. It was agreed that the date of entry into hospital should be 3 November.

Dr Loubser was insistent that the date of the operation be kept strictly private; that if the media got to hear of it, he would immediately cancel the time and date and reschedule it for a later time. It was agreed that it was in everyone's interests, Nelson, the hospital, the medical team as well as the security staff, that things be kept as quiet as possible.

Dr Loubser added, 'It only needs a hint of the operation getting out to the press and we will be inundated with media types. It will be unfair on everyone at the hospital. It will also attract many ordinary members of the public who will want to come and try and get a glimpse of Mr Mandela. For everyone's sake, let's all just keep a lid on this.' As he said this, he looked directly at Winnie, knowing she had a growing reputation for using the press for her own ends. Winnie nodded and said she would adhere to the agreement.

The Volks Hospital was an old building, one of the oldest hospitals in Cape Town. I had been there on several occasions, walking through the grounds and corridor, deciding on the security and how it could be handled. I assessed which room would be best for Nelson, how it would be protected and how we would be able to guard other areas of the hospital.

The night before he was due to enter hospital the leader group was trying hard to keep Nelson cheerful. There was a small party and they sat around the table reminiscing about what they described as 'the good old days', the times they were together on Robben Island. I came into the room and sat with them pulling their leg, accusing them of not knowing when they were having a good time.

'To listen to you guys you'd never believe the complaints and moaning that used to go on,' I told them.

'Yes, you are right, we have forgotten just how good life was on the island,' chipped in Walter, picking up the theme.

'Hey, Nelson, don't you miss those lovely lazy summer days when we used to exercise in the special gymnasium; you know, the one the authorities had us carve out of the rock.' He was referring to the limestone quarry where they had all spent many backbreaking years toiling in the blistering sun.

'Oh yes, and what about the good times when they allowed us to go paddling in the ocean when our feet got too hot, what about those wonderful days.' This from Kathy.

251

Nelson began to join in. 'Yes, but they allowed us to wade into the sea only in the winter time when it was freezing.'

'You see, you are just like all the kaffirs; you are splitting hairs, ungrateful for the kindness of the prison authorities.'

We all roared with laughter, able to enjoy the ridiculousness as well as the cruelty of the situation.

That night the other five all wished him luck. They were not to know that this would be the last evening he would spend with them.

Chapter 24

Black patient
in a white hospital

It was quiet in the hospital as I sat in the ward beside the bed, waiting for Nelson to arrive. The arrangements were unusual: I had left it to the other guards to bring him while I had gone ahead to ensure everything at the Volks Hospital was ready and in place. Once the press got wind of the operation they would be camping outside, twenty-four hours a day.

I had been in to see Nelson earlier and he was busy packing books and writing implements.

'Nelson, leave those for now. Whatever books or reading material you want or need I will fetch.'

He was concerned about his daily newspapers, having already paid for them in advance. 'I'll also make sure those are delivered to your bed.'

The stillness of the ward was disturbed by the sound of a posse of feet pounding along the wooden corridor on the second floor of the hospital. Nelson had arrived. Unlike all other patients, Nelson's registration was completed in the hospital room, rather than in the entrance hall.

Nelson took off private clothes and got into his pyjamas. He had asked Dr Loubser what he should bring with him. The doctor said he needed to bring only his body and whatever books he wished to read; everything else was provided, even the toothpaste. Nelson was always very particular about his toothpaste, so he carried his own in a small bag: a large tube of Sensodyne. He was wandering around the room, taking stock, when Dr Motlana came in. The two were old friends from way back.

Dr Motlana was a small man, all energy and vitality with a quick voice. 'Ah, the world's most famous prostate gland patient. How can we make you even more comfortable?'

Nelson frowned. 'Umtata, I am fine, comfortable enough.'

Dr Motlana replied, 'I should hope so. When someone comes in to see me for a prostate op he is in and out on the same day. Not for you this sort of treatment. You've been having the scans for weeks, blood tests, specialists from all over the world. What is all this palaver over the most simple of ops?'

I had to look twice at Dr Motlana to see if he was serious, admonishing his old friend this way. I could see he was merely putting Nelson's mind at ease.

Nelson told Dr Motlana he was not in any pain. He added, 'That's what makes it all so worrying; that I have no pain yet when I pass urine there is all this blood.'

I decided to pick up the doctor's theme. 'That was exactly what happened to me. I had blood in my urine and went into the Constantiaberg Clinic. I was in one day and out the next. No pain and no problem. It turned out to be an infection of the bladder, but the worst part was worrying about it. I was like you, worried I had cancer and wouldn't believe the doctors, no matter what they told me.'

Nelson nodded and smiled at us both. 'I know, I know what you both say is true. I also know you are trying to put my mind at ease, but consider for a moment just how difficult that is. There is blood in the urine and that is abnormal. And no matter what any doctor says, until the operation is over there will always be a little nagging doubt at the back of my mind.'

Nelson had his own room and, by chance, there was a nurse working at the hospital who had been a medical sister attached to Robben Island for a short time. Her name was Felicity Schuman. When I mentioned her name to Nelson he remembered her. We agreed that she would be a familiar face and should be attached to the medical team. I went and asked the hospital superintendent who immediately agreed that Felicity should be detached from normal duties to work solely with Nelson.

Nelson was prepared for the operation and it was carried out later that day. As the doctors stood by his bed I stayed well away, tucked into a corner. As he was laid on to the trolley to be wheeled into the pre-op room he looked over and asked, 'Please come with me.' I nodded and walked alongside the trolley. The medical staff had already given him a pre-op sedative and I could see it was taking effect. His eyes were half closed. I touched his hand and whispered, 'Remember what they said. This is nothing serious. Before you know it you'll be back on your feet playing tennis with all the old friends.' His eyes were closed but I could see him smile faintly.

I did not go into the theatre. Again I made the same arrangement as for the minor operation at the Woodstock, having a warder inside the theatre dressed in theatre clothes, the surgical mask, gown and slippers. I waited in the recovery room. In the operating theatre was a team led by Dr Loubser, Professor Chisholm from the University of Edinburgh, Scotland, Dr Gestetler from Switzerland who had previously examined Nelson, Dr Motlana, Dr Dekena, the anaesthetist and three theatre nurses, Matron Burgess as well as sisters Roussouw and Coetzee.

Again I sat in the recovery room and offered up a prayer for Nelson's safety. This time, however, I was much more confident that this was just a routine operation. I had accepted fully what the doctors and specialists had said, that it was not cancerous. Now, I was just praying for my friend. Although the prison authorities and the system had warned against forming friendships, it was inevitable that this should happen. Despite everything that had been thrust at me, through the years of indoctrination at school and then through the training at Kroonstad, it had been impossible to change my personality. From my earliest years I had accepted blacks as equals, so the basis upon which our friendship had started had been firmly set when I was a child. All that had happened was the layers of prejudice and hatred were peeled back. As I sat there I also began to realise how fortunate I had been in being given a fairly free hand within the prison system. Now the only person I reported to was the commanding officer, Brigadier Munro. And I did not believe he had a hatred of blacks. With him on my side, there were not really any problems. I recalled one day when Munro and I were walking to his car and he remarked, 'Greg, do you know just what a responsibility we have?'

I queried his question. 'Why do you say just we? Why not the whole of the maximum detention centre or the entire prison department? Why just we two?'

Munro's voice went low. 'If anything ever goes wrong with this man Mandela, it will all come down on top of you and me. They will all look for scapegoats, for someone to blame and they'll find us two. It is an awesome responsibility considering just how vulnerable he is, both in his own health and with threats from within the system.'

I nodded in agreement. 'Of course, you only have to read the newspapers and listen to the news to realise just how important Nelson Mandela is. He is a worldwide figure and if he should come to any harm within the prison all these sanctions will feel like a drop in the ocean compared with the hatred and anger that will follow.'

Munro continued. 'If he were to die it is my belief that it would plunge this country into a civil war which would make the Battle of Blood River seem like a tea party. It would be slaughter on a massive scale. That is why we have to take more care about this group, and especially this man, than with any other person or group of people within the prisons.'

Nelson's return to the recovery room disturbed my thoughts. He was still totally unconscious. I knew from the previous occasion he would remain so for several more hours. Dr Loubser came into the room and he seemed to detect my concern. 'Don't worry, it all went well. There's absolutely nothing to worry about. It was a total success and he'll make a full recovery.'

I went back to Nelson's room with him and sat listening to the creaking of the wooden floors as the medical staff walked from one room to another. Occasionally a voice penetrated the only other sound, the deep hum of the air-conditioning system. At one time Munro popped his head around the door. 'Howzit, Greg. Thought I'd look in. Is he okay?' I just gave him a silent thumbs-up sign.

There was a mumbling from Nelson beside me. He was still unconscious but I could see he was now in a dreaming phase, muttering and stirring in his sleep. Doctors came and looked in and nodded before walking out again. Nurse Schuman came in and took his blood pressure. She just said two words, 'He's fine', and left again.

Gradually he came round and asked slowly for water. I called Nurse Schuman back. She was firm. 'Just a little, to rinse out your mouth. Then spit it out again.' Nelson did as he was told and slumped back on the pillow, closing his eyes again.

It was dark and the lights from the corridor outside shone in the room. Outside I could see the lights from a distant shop glittering and shimmering. Nelson spoke clearly: 'What time is it?'

I was surprised that he was so wide awake. 'Well, here you are. It's past supper-time and I think you've missed eating today.' I added, by way of making it light-hearted, 'Just like the old days on Robben Island when you broke the rules, eh, Nelson?'

He just smiled. I told him, 'I know you are in pain but the operation has been a complete success. Dr Loubser has been in several times and I hear them all talking, saying that it was a perfect op, no complications. Just rest for now.'

I went home and was back early next day. Nelson was already

wide awake, chatting with the medical staff. Same old Nelson, awake early, bright and alert.

I walked in and grabbed his hand. 'Hey, man, what's this, still in bed? Come on, let's get up and go exercise.'

He was now smiling although there was some natural discomfort. Nurse Schuman took up my theme and added, 'Mr Gregory's right. The doctors have all said you're to get up today and start walking. So don't think you're going to lie there all day and relax. Today's the first day when the hard work begins.'

I winked at Nelson. 'Hey, a real stern one here. We should have had her on cell-block duty rather than on medical duty. In fact, she would have been good commanding the quarry; she'd have got more work out of you than the warders.' We all laughed.

Nelson's room was off to one side of a much larger ward containing ten beds. When he had struggled into his orange towelling gown, covering his green and white striped hospital-issue pyjamas, we decided to take a walk to get some fresh air out on the balcony. To get to the balcony we had to pass through the main ward which was filled with white male patients. It was most unusual at that time to see a black man as a patient in a hospital used by whites.

I asked if he wished to take my arm, or walk on his own? He said he would try it alone first, but to stay close in case he stumbled. We began to walk through the ward and Nelson stopped in the middle of the room. He looked around him, at the ten white faces looking at him. A couple of the men nodded and said a polite 'good morning'. Nelson nodded and continued to walk towards the balcony. Instead of walking on to the balcony, Nelson turned and told me he wanted to return to his room, that he was not going outside. On the way back the same thing happened. Nelson stopped in the middle of the room and the ten men stared at him. Several of them smiled and nodded a greeting. Nelson again nodded back. It was a bizarre scene almost out of a silent movie. He again continued to shuffle on and when he reached his room, Nelson sat in the chair, picking up his morning newspaper to read it.

He was half-way through the front page when he put the newspaper on his lap and began speaking. 'You know, this is all amazing.'

I knew exactly what he was referring to, but I wanted him to say. 'What is, Nelson?'

'Well, this is a whites-only hospital. Isn't that so?'

'Yes, it is.'

'Well, I just walked through the ward and not one of those men reacted to me. They stared and a couple of them actually greeted me. They actually said hello.'

'What did you expect? For them to tell you that this was for white people only and that you are a kaffir and shouldn't be here?'

'I don't know what I was expecting. This was just a surprise for me. I think I expected some degree of animosity and it just isn't there.'

'Look, Nelson, these people know who you are, they know you're Nelson Mandela and they will know all about your past. It's not so amazing that they don't ask what the hell you're doing here.'

Nelson was genuinely surprised and as he picked up his paper to continue reading he added, 'Well, it was a pleasant surprise, that's all I'm saying.'

I, too, began to contemplate the background to this little episode. This, after all, was the first time in two decades that Nelson had actually been face to face with ordinary white people, with total strangers. And they had not cursed him or shown any animosity. I smiled.

Over the next few days Nelson walked into the main ward more often and began to have lengthy conversations with these other patients, inquiring about their well-being. He was, I know, dumbfounded when they greeted him daily as 'Mr Mandela', and paid him respect. They also inquired about his health and developed a friendship, the normal type of friendship that develops between patients in hospitals all over the world. In reality, by having these daily conversations both Nelson and the other patients were all technically breaking the law which said that no member of the public could indulge in conversation with a prison inmate. I told Munro about what was happening and added, 'Look, it's human nature and I think it is having a good therapeutic effect on him.'

Occasionally, over the next few weeks while he was still in the hospital, several of the white patients wandered into Nelson's room. They enjoyed the view from his window, overlooking green fields and trees in blossom. Several times I came to the ward and heard them laughing and talking together. It was a joy to hear.

By that stage the fact Nelson was in the hospital had leaked out. It was known worldwide and there was a constant group of media-people laying siege to the hospital. They tried every devious

258

method to get inside: getting friendly with warders on guard, getting friendly with hospital staff and workers, getting friendly with police officers; all of, them trying to get in and take a picture of Nelson, the first in more than eighteen years. A small circus developed: the press men brought their portable barbecues, they began sleeping in their cars and two even erected a small tent on a patch of grass opposite the hospital. It was like a side-show. Each day they would light their barbecues and grill all types of meat, sausages and chicken on them. They offered some of the food to the warders, hoping to win a favour. One night it poured with rain, the hardest I'd seen in several years. Out came their plastic capes and hoods; the umbrellas were blown away in the wind. Out came their spare rain gear and it was handed over to the warders who were unprepared for the severe weather. A friendship was developing on both sides but I instructed every warder that the first who spoke out of turn would be sacked, no questions asked.

It was obvious Nelson was returning to his normal self when he started to ask again for his books. By the end of the first week after the operation Munro came to visit. 'How are you, Nelson?' he asked as he breezed in.

Nelson, deep in study, looked up and smiled. 'Mr Munro, I'm in finer health than even you, and you're one of the healthiest looking men I know. That's how well I am.' It was good to see Nelson back to his jovial self again.

Later that same day I had a call from Munro telling me to expect a visit from the Commissioner of Prisons, General Willie Willemse. I was surprised that the general, whom I knew from his time on Robben Island, should take time out to call. But then, I mused, perhaps it showed just how important Nelson Mandela was in the prison system.

However, I was totally unprepared for the person who accompanied Willemse. I was sitting beside the window, reading, as two nurses changed Nelson's bedclothes. Nelson himself was seated in another chair, reading the *Cape Times*. In marched the commissioner followed by Kobie Coetsee, the Minister of Justice. I stood up and saluted before Willemse nodded and introduced us.

I looked across and watched Nelson's face; this, after all, was an occasion of great importance, a meeting between a cabinet minister and Nelson Mandela.

Nelson took command quickly. 'Ah, Mr Coetsee, how nice to see you. At last. I'm sorry we have not got together before.' The polite, almost gentle criticism was perfect. I knew that months before

Nelson had written to the minister asking for a meeting to discuss formal talks between the ANC and the government. So this was quite something. I knew this was no ordinary social visit.

Nelson stood and introduced the commissioner and the minister to the nurses, ensuring they knew how well they were looking after him. It was his way of throwing both men totally off-guard. Even though I knew he had wanted to meet Coetsee for some time, I watched with admiration how he was now conducting the group to play to his tune, the moves as if on a chess board, undertaken at his pace. He was a host in his own ward and laughed about how appropriate this was because, in reality, Coetsee was his warder. It was his little joke.

My mind was racing and I knew this was the olive branch that Nelson had been seeking for many years, the great breakthrough. I caught Willemse's eye and gestured if I should leave. He nodded discreetly. I stood up and excused myself from the room. Later, when Coetsee and Willemse left, I returned and smiled at Nelson.

'What a nice man, most unlike what I had expected,' he mused.

I remained silent and he continued, 'We did not talk politics; rather we discussed general things and it was like having an acquaintance visit and ask about my health.'

As each day passed Nelson began to walk more easily, his shuffling, hunched gait replaced by the former, familiar erect carriage. He was also very polite with the nurses, always willing to pay them a special compliment. In his old-world manner he believed it important to say a few words of appreciation. To one nurse it would be a polite, 'You look nice and fresh this morning.' To another, 'How pretty your hair looks.' Small compliments. From others those same words would be flirty, but not from Nelson; they were sincerely meant to show appreciation and to be polite. It was Nelson being the perfect gentleman. With every member of staff he was always extremely courteous, understanding how they were each breaking new ground in attending to a black man in a hospital that had until then been the preserve of whites.

Gifts and get-well cards began streaming in by the sackful. They were from all over the world. Then came the fruit baskets and boxes of chocolates. These, more than anything else, caused me trouble. I was always aware of the danger of him being poisoned, so I discussed these food gifts with both Nelson and Munro and, reluctantly, had to have them destroyed. To counter the waste of these gifts Nelson took the names and addresses of each person and wrote back to the senders, thanking them. Flowers came in by the armful and after filling his room we began to distribute them around the rest of the hospital.

It was reported that a march of ANC supporters was being planned from the city centre to the hospital. To counter the march the police closed off every road near the hospital to prevent anyone who did not have business in the hospital getting close.

Twenty days after being admitted, the doctors agreed Nelson was well enough to return to prison. That day, 23 November, Munro had called me and told me that Nelson would not be going back to his comrades in the 'penthouse'. He was now going to be segregated, in another area of Pollsmoor. I asked him if he wished me to break the news. No, he said, he wished to tell him.

The next problem was creating a diversion to avoid the media. By this time they knew me and knew my car and were watching for it. It was agreed that I would act as a decoy by going out of the front entrance with two cars following me. It would make it appear Nelson was with me. At the same time, Munro took Nelson out of a side entrance and was able to drive away without being spotted.

Just before departing Nelson made his farewells to the staff and other patients. It was remarkable how, in the space of twenty days, this black man had entered the very heart of a white hospital and won them all over. It was the shape of things to come.

Chapter 25

Nelson is isolated

The new cell was as new to me as it was to Nelson. I had not been told or even consulted about it. On the drive back from Pollsmoor I considered how he would now take this move to isolate him from his friends, the other five up on the third floor. I recalled how upset they had all been at the initial move from Robben Island, away from the other ANC people. They still complained about it although asking less frequently now if they could return. Now this. This would be interesting. I knew that Kobie Coetsee's visit a couple of weeks before must have played a role in a much bigger game. Was this now the time of breakthrough? Would the government try to separate Nelson from the others to try to drive a wedge within the ANC movement? I couldn't believe even they would be so crass as to think that such a move could work. No, there was more, much more to this sudden move to put Nelson on his own. It would be fascinating to see just how he reacted to this.

I went straight to his new section, on the ground floor, three floors beneath his colleagues on a separate wing. I walked in and Nelson was not to be seen. The area was separated off from a long corridor by a set of steel bars. They had allocated him three large cells plus a large shower and toilet area. The four rooms spread either side of the corridor, a palace compared with many, but, perhaps, less inviting than the area on the third floor. Here there was less natural light and even though it was brightly painted and furnished with all the cupboard and table space he would require, it seemed less hospitable than the penthouse area. I sniffed the air and there was a mustiness about it, the sort of smell that comes from an area that has been out of use for some considerable time.

I went into one of the rooms, on the left-hand side, where they had placed a bed and bedside table. In such a large room they appeared out of place. It would need more cupboards and perhaps an armchair, I decided. No sign of Nelson. Next door was his desk and a table. It also looked empty: missing were all his personal items, the family photographs and his books. Nelson was sitting at the table, reading.

He looked up as I entered. 'Why this move?' I inquired.

'I have no idea. The commanding officer informed me on the drive back from the hospital without giving me a reason.' He shrugged.

'Believe me, I have no idea either. He only told me earlier today. It's as much a surprise to me as you.'

I continued, 'I'll get all your books and personal items brought down here in the morning. If there's anything else you need or want, just let me know and I'll fetch it as well.'

Nelson said the only thing he would need in addition to his own possessions was a hot water urn. 'I shall be busy studying and probably will not eat when the food is normally delivered. I'll want to keep it as hot as possible. That's all that I can think of needing now.'

The atmosphere was strange that first evening. Nelson was quiet, rather nonplussed by this sudden turn of events. I was also mystified. I knew then that the visit from Kobie Coetsee was not a chance happening, that in some way this change in direction had to be linked to his appearance at the hospital. Was this a way of separating him from the others to allow for one-to-one dialogue? Or to create a split within the ANC ranks? It was certainly intriguing.

A week after Nelson returned to Pollsmoor, the others – Andrew, Raymond, Walter and Kathy – were brought down from the third floor to see their old companion. It was an occasion which should have been filled with laughter and happiness, for it had been a month now since they had last seen one another, the longest they had been out of one another's sight for two decades. But this meeting was muted, almost funereal. They were cautious, verging on downright suspicious, about the split with them.

Now that he was closeted on the ground floor Nelson no longer had the opportunity to walk outside on the main roof. First they had taken away the natural beauty of Robben Island and supplanted it with Pollsmoor, now they had denied him access to the openness of the roof where, at least, he was still able to see the sky. He was now enclosed in a world of concrete and cement. I went to Munro and complained, on Nelson's behalf, that he needed somewhere to walk in the fresh air. It was agreed that he should be

264

allowed out into an area known as the courtyard, a rectangular area surrounded on all sides by the prison. The quadrangle was used during the day by regular prisoners for volleyball and was less than ideal. It was overlooked on three sides by cell windows. It was, however, the best option available.

Whenever Nelson went into the quadrangle he wore a straw hat, made for him when he was on Robben Island by Japhta Masemula (a member of the Pan-African Congress). It was a large, Mexican-style sombrero. The walls and concrete of the prison reflected the sun's harsh rays making the area like a furnace. I know it was often too hot for me to stroll around the area, so I sat on the steps leading back into the prison rather than walk with him.

It was after the first couple of days walking in the courtyard that the regular prisoners discovered who this stranger was walking in the yard. They could see him from their cells.

The first comments were innocent enough. 'Hey, amigo, where did you get the hat?' Then 'Hey, old man.' Nelson just walked on, ignoring the cat calls. Later he told me, 'I don't know what to do in a situation such as this. Should I reply or should I ignore them? If I engage them in conversation it will lead to trouble for the warders for allowing it.'

Then the nastiness started. As Nelson ignored the callers, they berated him. 'Hey, kaffir, why are you ignoring us? Hey, old man, are you too good for us now? Hey, Mandela, why are you kept in a nice cell and we are in a piss pot? Are you talking to the *Boere*? Is that it, you talk to the Boere but won't talk to us? Are you too good for us now, man? Are you one of them now?'

I heard all the calls and watched the line of faces at the cell windows. They were pouring invective down on this man who was, more than any other, fighting their cause. I knew he was hurt by the words, but he kept his words to himself, never replying. On one occasion a coke bottle, filled with urine, was thrown from a window; it fell near him and shattered. It was a large two-litre bottle and had it hit him would certainly have injured him. I went to the commanding officer and asked for help. He suggested we put louvre blinds on the outside of all the cell windows, more than thirty in all. It was a costly exercise, but effective. I could order them closed whenever Nelson was to walk in the courtyard. But this, too, brought its protest from the prisoners: they threw all their old food and rubbish out of the windows into the yard beneath. When it was time to allow Nelson into the area their louvre blinds were shut, but they could hear the gates open at the bottom to

265

allow him in. They would start shouting again. 'Hey, Mandela, clean up the shit. It's your yard so learn to keep it clean, man.'

The first time the rubbish was thrown I went to the cell block and ordered that everyone on the wing be punished: a loss of privileges and a meal. I warned them, 'If you persist with this I will stop your visits.' I also ordered that a group of the prisoners be sent into the yard before Nelson entered to ensure it was cleaned properly.

Nelson was greatly troubled by the reaction to him. I told him, 'Ignore it, man, these people are just common criminals. They are not white or black or like you and me, they are just criminals who will cause trouble wherever they are.'

It was the first time he had been exposed to the regular prisoners and I know he was a bit shocked. He said, 'You always assume that people will have some vestige of decency and understanding. When you come across people like that you realise they have a different mentality. It is not a racial or colour problem, more one of mentality.'

One day soon after this I was standing beside the entrance to the main prison when I was approached by a man I knew. He was one of the gang leaders, both inside and outside the prison walls, a gangster named Dos Santos.

He sidled up. 'Why don't you leave the door open for five minutes to allow us to get him? All we want is five minutes; no one will know.'

I turned and feigned ignorance. 'I don't know what you're talking about.'

Dos Santos continued. 'You know exactly what I mean. Give us five minutes with this bastard and your problems, the government's problems, are over.'

'Ja, man, but what's in it for you, eh?'

'Look, man, these kaffir bastards are causing all the problems in this country, and he's the main man. My people are suffering both in here and on the outside. They got no food, they got no jobs. It's because of these bastards, Mandela and the likes of him, stirring up shit.'

I could not believe what I was hearing and told him, 'Just get out of here before I put you on a charge. If I ever find you around this area again, or within spitting distance of Mandela, you'll be in more trouble than you'll ever dream of. Now just go.'

A few weeks later there was a second approach, this time from the leader of one of the most violent prison gangs. He was also in B section. He repeated almost word for word the conversation I'd had with Dos Santos. Again I reacted the same way, telling him to get lost.

I informed Nelson of these threats and warned him that wherever he was in the prison he had always to be on guard in case someone with a knife or a blade suddenly stepped out and cut him. He nodded and listened, then quietly added a thank you.

I watched carefully Nelson's overall reaction to this move from the penthouse to the ground floor. Certainly he had complained more about being moved from Robben Island, but this move was met with acceptance. At first I was uncertain why that should be. I knew he missed his comrades greatly, as well as the garden which he had so lovingly cared for. He missed the sunshine and comparative openness on the roof. But, for some reason or other, here he seemed quite content. Certainly he had his solitude, a gift I knew he valued. It gave him ample time to read, write and to think. I could also see that he knew that this separation from the others was for a reason. He believed, I was certain, that he was isolated in this way to begin secret negotiations with the government.

Chapter 26

Expanding horizons

The problem now was that although Nelson's new accommodation was spacious with plenty of facilities, it was completely enclosed. Having lost the comparative openness of the roof, it was becoming more important that he should have somewhere he could go to relax.

There was a place which had been developed by the regular prisoners, similar in size to the quadrangle. They had asked if they could start their own garden. This had been agreed and for weeks the heavy concrete was broken up and replaced by soil from the prison farm. Next came the grass, then flower and shrub beds. It was ideal for our purpose. By the time Nelson came to use it privately, to wander through and potter in the flower beds, there was a small dam and a number of hutches for chickens, turtles and rabbits. It became a focal point for wildlife and attracted pigeons and fan-tail doves. Nelson loved wandering there, as it was so unlike the rest of the concrete and brick prison. But it was not to last for long.

One of the warders found a small buck, a steenbok, injured on the road outside the prison gates and suggested it could be kept in the garden until its injured leg healed. At least once a year the prison inspectorate visited Pollsmoor to check everything from security to conditions in the cells. When they were due to inspect the prison, animals, rabbits and chickens were removed for the day. The problem was that the only place to put the steenbok was in a disused cell.

Later, when the inspector sat in the office of Lieutenant Jan Groenewald, the deputy head of the prison, he got round to the subject of the buck.

'Look, Jannie, I see you have an extra prisoner, but do you have a warrant of detention?'

Groenewald was puzzled. 'That's impossible. I've had every

prisoner checked and we have the right numbers and warrants for each of them. It's not possible.'

The inspector, a major from Pretoria, was adamant. 'I am telling you that you have a prisoner in this prison and you are holding him or her without a warrant. This is serious stuff.'

Groenewald was now turning pink with worry. A mistake had been made somewhere, perhaps.

'No, that's not possible,' he concluded.

'What about the buck?'

Groenewald was relieved and began to smile. 'Oh, that? It's just a steenbok which we're looking after until its injury has healed. It's out of the garden area started by the prisoners.'

But the major failed to see the funny side of the situation. 'Listen Jannie, I'm not laughing. Within ten minutes I want to see your permit that you have been issued with by the nature conservation people to allow you to have that animal in captivity. If you haven't got one, get rid of the blerrie thing.'

The steenbok, as well as all the other animals, had to go. The attitude of the authorities affected the mood of the prisoners who suddenly lost any interest in their garden and allowed it to lapse into a state of neglect. Within weeks the area had been returned to its former concrete state.

Now Nelson needed another place to relax in.

At the southern end of the prison were perhaps 10 acres of vegetable gardens, built around a dam. Many of the prison warders had small holdings or allotments there where they grew their own vegetables. It was an ideal place to take Nelson for a few hours of sunshine and relaxation in safety. The only concern was that it was close to the main M3 road.

The commanding officer agreed that whenever Nelson wished to get out into the fresh air he could be taken to the allotments. It was also suggested that permission should be sought from Pretoria for trips out around the countryside.

When I asked Nelson how he felt about going down to the agricultural allotments he was excited. It was agreed that the first time he should go with Lieutenant Colonel Gawie Marx, Munro's deputy, who wanted to see for himself how safe it would be. On the first visit, he arranged for armed guards to be placed around the perimeter fence at regular intervals, to ensure absolute safety for Nelson. By this time the prison authorities were as convinced as I was that there was no real reason to believe that Nelson, or indeed any of the leader group, wished to escape. Such security was designed solely for their own protection.

On that first day out, Marx drove his own car the half mile or so to the allotments. He stopped at the prison shop and asked if Nelson would like a Coca Cola. It was an indication of the complete trust which the authorities now had in Nelson and his lack of desire to escape that Marx left him alone in the car with the keys still in the ignition.

When they returned I asked Nelson how he felt. 'Man, to feel that green grass beneath my feet and to touch leaves again was a wonder. It was so, so good.'

I said to him, 'Ja, come on, Nelson, don't tell me that you'd forgotten how grass feels. We used to always walk on the grass on the island.'

His face turned serious and he rolled his eyes. 'You forget that the grass on the island wasn't real grass. In summer it turned dry and brown so there was no real grass, and everywhere was covered in the sand which was blown across the island. So to walk today on real grass for the first time was like touching it again after twenty years. I tell you it felt good.'

The trips to the allotments became a favourite for both of us. I would take him whenever I knew he had some time free from his writing or his studies, and I knew the weather was good. We would slip out of a rear door of the main building and into my car. We would drive to the end of the road, past what had once been a racing track, and into the plantation which was always kept lush by sprinklers. We would park the car beside the pathway and walk out on to the grass.

We usually headed towards the dam, where we would sit in the long, lush grass and relax.

Sometimes Nelson would wander in among the trees, touching the bark and feeling the leaves, rubbing them between his fingers. We would sit on the grass, side by side, and discuss the flights of wild geese and ducks, sometimes the elegant pelicans and the tick birds. We argued many times about the fish in the dam, I always maintaining that there was plenty of carp, Nelson laughing and telling me that was only a fisherman's tale, a wish to believe something was in the water. One day we watched a young boy, on the far side of the dam, as he pulled a fish from the water. It was the first time we had seen one and we laughed aloud at how our previous arguments had now been answered.

It was as we sat on the bank of the dam that our conversations invariably turned to our own childhoods and I would talk of Bafana and Ongemak while Nelson told me of his childhood in the Transkei.

Nelson spoke with great detail and affection of his younger days, of growing up first in the village of Mvezo, a tiny village on the banks of the Mbashe River where he was born, and later in Qunu, a larger village in the region.

I listened, fascinated by his past, comparing it constantly with my own; how he was so like Bafana.

The Transkei is some 700 miles east of Cape Town, 580 miles south of Johannesburg, and lies between the Kei River to the south and the Natal border to the north. It is bounded by the great Drakensberg Mountains and the warm, blue waters of the Indian Ocean. It is magnificent land, rich in vegetation and fertile valleys. Streams and rivers criss-cross it, bringing life and sustenance. In many ways it was very like my home in northern Natal, the one difference being it was less humid.

Nelson spoke of his own family and his background. His father, Gadla Henry Mphakanyiswa, was a chieftain by both blood and custom. He was confirmed as chief of the village of Mvezo by the king of the Thembu tribe but, under British rule, his selection had to be ratified by the government, which in Mvezo took the form of the local magistrate. As a government-appointed chief he was eligible for a stipend as well as a portion of the fees the government levied on the community for vaccination of livestock and communal grazing land.

Although the role of chief was a venerable and well-respected one, it had, even seventy-five years ago, become debased by the control of an unsympathetic white government.

The Thembu tribe stretches back for twenty generations to King Zwide. According to the traditions of the tribe, the Thembu people lived in the foothills of the Drakensberg Mountains and migrated towards the coast in the sixteenth century, where they were incorporated into the Xhosa nation. The Xhosa are part of the Nguni people who have lived, hunted and fished in the rich and temperate southern regions of South Africa, between the great interior plateau to the north and the Indian Ocean to the south and east, since at least the eleventh century. Each member of the Xhosa nation belongs to a clan that can trace its ancestry back to a specific forefather. Nelson is a member of the Madiba clan, named after the Thembu chief who ruled in the Transkei in the eighteenth century. It was why, he explained, many people often addressed him by the name Madiba, as a mark of respect for his clan name.

Nelson talked of how the village of Qunu was set in a narrow, grassy valley criss-crossed by clear streams and surrounded by green, lush hills. It consisted of no more than a few hundred people who lived in huts. His descriptions were much like the huts and kraals I had visited with Bafana as a child. Unlike the families on our farm, the families who lived in Qunu were much poorer, living off mielies, sorghum, beans and pumpkins with occasionally tea, coffee and sugar when they could be afforded. The water used for farming, cooking and washing had to be brought into the village in buckets from the streams. This was usually women's work and the village itself was mostly made up of women and children, the menfolk spending the greater part of each year working on remote farms or in the mines along the Reef, the great ridge of gold-bearing rock and shale that forms the southern boundary of Johannesburg. The men only returned twice each year, mainly to plough their fields and plant their crops. The hoeing, weeding and harvesting work was left to the women and children. Just sitting listening and talking to Nelson I could close my eyes and smell again the kraals and encampments of my childhood.

When we spoke of playing as children, Nelson and I compared how we spent our time. I spoke of the adventures I had with Bafana on the farm. Nelson said he too had spent most of his time playing in the veld and fighting with other young boys. A boy who remained at home tied to his mother's apron strings was considered a sissy. By the age of five he had become a herd-boy looking after sheep and calves in the fields. When I told him of how we too would use our knobkerries and slingshots to shoot down the birds, we found we shared a common experience. We talked with great affection and memory of the wild honey, the fruits and edible roots we would eat and how it was a delicious treat to drink warm, sweet milk straight out of the udder of a cow. On one occasion we were talking of stick fighting and to demonstrate various blows and parries, we stood, two grown men in the middle of the grass with two sticks pulled from a tree, showing one another our parries and feints.

Nelson told me of the most popular game at that time, a youthful version of war games called *thinti*. Two sticks, used as targets, would be driven firmly into the ground in an upright position about 100 feet apart. The goal of the game was for each team to hurl sticks at the opposing target and knock it down. Each side defended its own target and attempted to prevent their opponents from retrieving the sticks they had already thrown. As Nelson grew older the village organised games of thinti against neighbouring villages and those who distinguished themselves in such battles were greatly admired in the community.

As we sat talking Nelson spoke dreamily of returning to his home.

'You know, I want to go back to the river where I played as a little boy or where I would take the cattle when I was a herd-boy. I want to see if the boulders are really as big as I remember them being then.'

I spoke of my dreams. 'Ja, and I would like to return to Ongemak to see if the bluegums really were as tall as they seemed then. I can remember they were so big that if I lay down along the base of the trunk, my feet and toes would not stick out on either side, they were that wide. I want to remember if they were really as wide as I remember them.'

We spoke of the puff adder that had bitten me, and the scorpions.

Nelson suddenly became serious. 'I would like to see this place where you grew up. It sounds like the sort of home I would have loved. It would tell me so much about you and why you have turned into the person you are now.'

Our serious moments never lasted long, and we then turned to comparing notes on *kleilats*, the willowy sticks which had clay moulds on the end. We talked of hunting and of the tactics we had each employed. It was almost better than being there. We were in prison, in the midst of political upheaval, but here we were, two grown men relaxing in the quiet of a dam and a field.

Life in Nelson's kraal in the evenings sounded very similar to the life I had known with Bafana. Nelson's father would tell stories of historic Xhosa battles and tribal heroes, to contrast with his mother's enchanting recounting of Xhosa legends and fables. Each tale was designed to stimulate a child's imagination and usually contained a moral lesson.

On one of the days we sat beside the dam, leaning back in the cool grass, I asked how he acquired his English name.

'One day, when I was around the age of seven, it was decided I should go to school. On the first day my teacher, a woman called Miss Mdingane, gave each of us an English name and said that that was the name we would answer to in school. There was a custom among Africans in those days to give each child an English name.

274

Whites were either unable, or unwilling, to pronounce an African name and considered it uncivilised to have one. When Miss Mdingane gave me the name Nelson I had no idea, and I still do not, why it was. Perhaps it was related to the British sea captain Lord Nelson, but that would only be a guess.'

He continued to speak of how much of his early education had centred on British ideas, culture and institutions.

Every time we went to the allotments I always sent a car around the area to patrol it to ensure there were no other people there who would prove dangerous.

Nelson was getting virtually everything he asked for at that time. This loosening of Pretoria's attitude had a strange effect on the prison management who seemed to over-react to every small situation; they failed to get the matter into perspective. One occasion was when Helen Suzman, the member of parliament, visited. She had, by now, taken a special interest in the welfare of the group, including Nelson, and frequently visited the cells to inspect conditions.

As she came to the end of her visit, she was escorted to the cell door by Nelson who told her, 'Well, thank you for coming to see me. This is the end of my domain. I cannot go any further with you.'

As Mrs Suzman asked if there was anything he needed, Nelson stroked his chin and said there was one small item which he'd read about in the newspaper and would like to obtain.

As I stood with the commander, Munro, we wondered what he would ask for. This was something he had not mentioned before.

'What is it?' inquired Mrs Suzman.

'Well, it's Blue Pantene.'

We were all puzzled.

'Blue Pantene?'

'Yes, Blue Pantene. It's a shampoo which I've read is very good for scalp and dandruff problems.'

I stepped in here, not sure if Nelson was joking or not. 'But Nelson, you don't have dandruff or scalp problems.'

'Yes, I know, but I've read it's very good and I'd like some, if possible.'

Mrs Suzman looked at Munro in an inquiring way and they both smiled. The commanding officer turned to me and instructed, 'Greg, make sure Mr Mandela gets this shampoo.'

I went looking next day for Blue Pantene, first in all the shops in the large shopping centre in Tokai, called the Blue Route Centre.

There were three chemists and two supermarkets. There was no Blue Pantene. At each store the assistants said they could supply Red or Yellow Pantene, but Blue Pantene had been discontinued.

So I went to see Nelson and told him Blue Pantene had been discontinued.

Now I saw, once again, Nelson's iron will.

'Mr Gregory.' He stood up to his full height. 'The commander promised me in front of Mrs Helen Suzman that I could have this Blue Pantene, and now you tell me I can't have it.'

I could not understand him behaving like this, but rather than argue I agreed I would continue to look for the shampoo.

I went back to the office and began telephoning pharmacies and beauty salons in the area. There was no Blue Pantene. I asked for any place that might stock it, but found the same story: it was discontinued.

This carried on for two or three days and I sent Warder Christo Brand to Cape Town to scour the shops for Blue Pantene. I told Nelson what was happening, but he had dug in his heels and was not happy. So I wrote to the manufacturer asking if they had any supplies.

Then relief. Brand found a pharmacy where the owner had an old box in his store-room, but it was out of date. I told him to buy it immediately. All of it. When I handed it to Nelson, I told him the trouble we'd had in getting it.

When he got it he said, 'Look, I'm sorry I snapped at you, but the commanding officer cannot make promises which are not kept.'

I didn't want to argue and smoothed over any ill feeling. 'Nelson, let's not worry. We now have enough Blue Pantene to wash every head in Pollsmoor for the next year.'

Ironically, about a year later, the manufacturer again began to produce Blue Pantene because of its popularity.

Chapter 27

A world beyond

The shackles were being more than loosened when I was told by Kobie Coetsee, Minister of Justice, that we should take Nelson on a number of discreet visits around the countryside – wherever he wished to go.

The Minister took me to one side. 'Greg, if Mr Mandela wishes to be taken anywhere within reason, then you don't need anyone's permission. I've given you carte blanche to go anywhere, any time you wish. All I ask is that you make the proper arrangements and ensure safety and security are number one priorities.'

The order was, in many ways, simply unbelievable. Here we were with a man who was now considered the most high profile prisoner in the world, and yet I was being told to take him out any time, anywhere he wished. I knew there would not be a problem – not with Nelson. But the entire concept was incredible: a prisoner being taken on day trips.

I discussed the matter with Nelson, and suggested that he give me three or four days' notice if he wished to go on a visit so that I could prepare the security arrangements.

The first place he asked to visit was Langebaan, a two-hour drive north from Cape Town, close to the magnificent seaside resort of Saldanha. I was curious why he had chosen there out of all the many places in the entire province to see. He smiled and explained, 'It's very simple really. I was reading the newspaper last night and it had an article on Langebaan and the salt lakes and salt industries. I thought I would like to see it.'

I had many preparations to make. I organised two cars, Mercedes owned by the government, one as the main vehicle, the other for back-up. I spoke to the government central garage in Cape Town and ensured that the cars had tinted glass, to keep any prying eyes out, and with discreet number plates that began with the letters CA, as all Cape Town cars did. I did not want vehicles with easily recognisable government licence plates.

The garage manager had already been warned by Kobie Coetsee that any request from me was to be granted immediately. I decided that Nelson would travel with me and a driver in the first car, with the second car containing four more guards. All of the guards would be armed and two would carry Uzi sub-machine guns. In addition I also arranged with the police for two police cars with armed officers to travel with us. They would not follow in convoy, but be spaced out to check the route both in front and behind.

Langebaan Lagoon is close to a national park which stretches for mile after endless mile along the western coast. The drive north took us along the main coastal road, past Jacobs Bay through beautiful wildflower reserves. Nelson sat taking it all in, capturing the sights and views he had missed through the long years in prison. I could see him observing the passing houses, the people both black and white, the styles of the clothes they wore. His mind was like a computer, absorbing, taking it all in, reading the changes and comparing them with how he remembered it all. The heat of the day would have been overwhelming, but fortunately the car was air-conditioned, the first, I think, Nelson had ever been in.

We stopped at Langebaan, a small salt-refining town, situated at the mouth of the massive lagoon. Across the bay we could see Saldanha, one of Africa's finest harbours, a busy, bustling port.

As Nelson had wanted to see the salt refining, we drove off the road on to the heaps of dark brown, dirty salt, and got out of the car to stretch our legs. It was a bizarre sight. Two Mercedes parked on the roadside beside mountains of crusted salt, a factory billowing smoke nearby. The two police cars had pulled up and our armed escort were deployed at intervals along the roadside. We stood on the heap for a little while, examining the salt.

'I cannot believe that these mountains of dirt can be turned into salt.' Nelson was surprised.

I stood explaining how the deposits were scraped up by giant scrapers, similar to ice scrapers, and how the material was then carted into the factory where it was refined into the sort of salt he knew.

He kept saying, 'I think this will put me off eating salt for good now.'

I laughed. 'The doctors have told you that's not a bad idea. The stuff is bad for you and here is the finest example of how it can clog up the body.'

The trips out became a regular feature and on the next occasion he asked to go to Laingsburg, a small market town about 180 miles from Cape Town.

Before I could ask why Laingsburg, Nelson explained. 'I was intrigued by the flash floods which killed so many people in the area some years ago. I'm not sure why the place stayed in my mind, but I always felt I'd like to see it, to try and understand how such a tragedy occurred.'

The town is one of the few stopping places on the long road that runs north from Cape Town, the Cape-to-Cairo road. Travellers on the road see mile after mile of the wide open spaces and plains of the Great Karoo. Laingsburg itself was once the centre of the wool industry in the Karoo region until it was devastated by the floods in 1981.

When we arrived in Laingsburg we again got out to stretch our legs. Then Nelson climbed back in and we slowly toured the town, much of which had been rebuilt since the disaster. I noticed in the days before the trip, as I was making the necessary arrangements, that Nelson had been reading up on the area, its history and details of the disaster, trying to understand how it had happened.

We saw the marks made on the walls by the floods, eight, ten, twelve feet and higher.

We were genuinely surprised at the height of the water. 'It's astonishing; it just shows you the might of God,' was Nelson's verdict. 'This is a terrible thing, a natural disaster where man cannot be blamed.' We saw areas where there had once been houses and stores, but they had been swept away and replaced by new buildings.

The enormity of the disaster remained with us on our drive back to Cape Town.

One evening we were sitting in his house watching television, a programme on the tourist industry near Paternoster. The programme centred on the picturesque little fishing community where perlemoen and crayfish were in plentiful supply. The community was unusual in South Africa in that apartheid had virtually passed it by, leaving the coloured people who lived in the area to their own devices. They were similar to the Mennonites of North America, people who had remained in a different age and time, untouched by the troubles of the outside world. Nelson turned to me and I could read his mind.

'A trip?'

He nodded. 'It looks interesting.'

279

The town of Paternoster is a half-hour drive beyond the route we had taken to Langebaan. But unlike the salt-refining centre, Paternoster was tiny and very pretty. We drove into the town and along the beach front. The one small hotel was at the end of the beach, close to several houses. Past the hotel the beach was enclosed by large boulders and green vegetation, with the wild blue sea beyond. The roar of the ocean was wonderful to hear again. There were four or five fishermen's boats pulled on to the white sand, their oars still dangling from the sides.

Nelson pulled me to one side. 'Ah, got a problem. I need to urinate.'

There was the hotel, but it seemed to be busy with tourists. We could not go there with the armed guards: that could risk a scene.

'Let's take a walk along the beach and find somewhere,' I suggested.

The guards, both my own and the police, were discreetly fanning out along the roadway which followed the line of the beach, their guns well hidden.

We strolled slowly along the beach, enjoying the feeling of sand under our feet, the wind in our face. At the far end there were several large rocks the size of cars.

'Is this okay, can you go in there?' I asked, pointing behind the rocks.

Nelson smiled and replied, 'Oh, I can manage. It's what I used to do as a boy.'

As he went about his business, a group of tourists, cameras slung around their necks, began to walk towards us.

I gave him a running commentary. 'Nelson ... you'd better hurry, there's a group of tourists heading our way.'

By the time he came back the group of fifteen or so tourists were close by. I could hear them talking in German. I suggested we sit on the rock for a time.

While the tourists took pictures of the sea, the fishing boats, the rocks and virtually anything in sight, they ignored the two men in their midst, a black man and a white man.

I turned to Nelson. 'If only those people realised who you are...'

Nelson chuckled. 'Little do they know, they've just missed the scoop of the century with us sitting here together.'

We sat in the sun for some time enjoying the scenery and the atmosphere.

In the winter we saw there was snow on the distant Matroos and

Hexrivieberg Mountains, north of Cape Town. The journey we took was through the enchanting town of Ceres, in one of the most outstandingly beautiful and rich fruit-growing areas in the country.

In the distance we could see the snow covering the mountain range which disappeared into the clouds. All the way during the two-hour drive, we talked of playing snowballs, of building a snowman.

'I am looking forward just to walking in the snow, to feeling it beneath my feet.'

We were like children on an adventure. The thought that this was a prisoner of the state and we were his guards never came into our heads. However, we were to be disappointed: the road did not go high enough to take us to the snowline. Instead we stopped and looked up at the magnificent mountains.

We could feel the cold in the air as we stood looking up at the white slopes. 'We'd need to be proper mountain climbers to reach the snow today,' I volunteered.

Nelson was wistful as he looked up to the slopes. 'There is something beautiful, serene and gentle about snow, yet it can also be a quiet killer, lulling people into a false sense of security.'

We decided to drive back through the Bain's Kloof, a narrow pass which curves and winds along the steep mountain sides. The road is narrow and dangerous with the massive cliffs closing in, creating a permanent shadow that covers the entire area. At the bottom the Hex River foams white in its turbulent passage. As we returned through the town of Ceres we were held up in a traffic jam.

I turned to Nelson and joked, 'This is something you won't be used to, a traffic jam; this is now one of life's constant headaches.'

A road repair man walked along the line of cars and explained there had been a mud-slip ahead: they were having to blast it clear. There would be a two-hour delay. We were locked in, cars in front, cars behind. I ordered the car be pulled off the road, beneath the shade of a tree.

As we sat there with the doors wide open, one of the guards said he was hungry, we should get some food. Just down the road he had seen a fish and chip shop. I said I would get the police escort to fetch the food.

We sat eating fish and chips out of our paper bags. Clearly Nelson was enjoying it. 'I cannot remember the last time I had fish and chips,' he said as he screwed up his face in delight. Using our fingers to eat them seemed to make them even tastier. I stood outside the car with my meal on the bonnet. Nelson spread his meal on the back seat and began eating. Many of the people who were also trapped in the traffic jam followed our example and went to the shop to buy fish and chips.

Around Cape Town there were several drives. The one place where we frequently ended up was the botanical gardens at Kirstenbosch, a mile from the main University of Cape Town grounds. The sheer variety of plants and flowers was breathtaking: it was said there were more than 9000 varieties. Many times we sat in the car, with the windows wide open, just absorbing the beauty and smell of the entire area.

Another drive we took was along Chapman's Peak Drive, the road which follows the coastline south from the city towards Cape Point. The route hangs over the wild Atlantic as it sweeps in. On one occasion we stopped just outside the fishing village of Hout Bay to sit and watch the waves.

Nelson refused to go near the railings. 'There is no way you will get me close to the edge,' he said sternly.

I laughed and said I would hold him from behind if he wanted to take a look over.

Nelson rolled his eyes and was emphatic. 'Mr Gregory, I might trust you to hold me, but I don't think I can trust myself. I think I must have vertigo.'

Again Nelson needed the toilet, so we drove higher around the coastal road, finding a deserted picnic pull-in. As he came out of the bushes, zipping up his trousers, I smiled. 'You know, Nelson, this is becoming a habit. You're urinating all over South Africa. Where next?'

Chapter 28

Nelson's illness

Nelson was alone, but far from lonely. On occasions he would have visits from the other leaders, and I would laugh with them at the strangeness of them sitting on the other side of the room, they as visitors, Nelson as the inmate. Whenever he returned to his own cell it was straight back to his books to study, or to write about whatever he wished. The daily routine rarely varied: up before dawn, exercise, shower, breakfast, read the newspapers, listen to the news on the radio and down to his studies. I usually joined him around 7 o'clock, maybe a little later, by which time his studies would already have started. We would bid each other a good morning and I would then sit reading the papers while Nelson read. He would never miss a news bulletin through the day. Each hour he would break from whatever activity he was doing and tune in the radio for the bulletin.

One of the rare interruptions to this routine was a wedding day in Pollsmoor. It was the marriage of Raymond Mhlaba and Dideka, his common-law wife. The date was 5 April 1986. The permission for the wedding ceremony had taken weeks to obtain from Pretoria. Eventually, when it was granted, Raymond decided he wanted all those he considered to be his closest comrades to be present. I discussed it at length with Raymond and Nelson, deciding on how the ceremony should best take place. Pretoria had insisted that the ceremony take place in the prison. As well as Nelson, Walter, Kathy and Andrew, Raymond also invited the commanding officer, myself and Brand. There were also two clergy, Bishop Dwane and Reverend Molusi, and an old woman I knew only as Makasale, Dideka's mother.

On the morning of the wedding I received a telephone call from Pretoria.

'Gregory, this wedding with Mhlaba, it is going on today?'

I confirmed it was and was then told, 'You must make sure that when the ceremony takes place the front door of the building and the prison is open.'

I was flabbergasted. 'What?'

'That's right, man. Just make sure the front doors and gates are open. That's the law regarding marriages. It cannot be a legally recognised marriage if it takes place behind a locked door or a closed grille.'

I was uncertain if this was some sort of a joke being played by Pretoria, but told Munro, who felt the situation was safe enough. Whatever happened, these people were not going to be making a run for it.

The wedding was set for 10 o'clock in the prison's main conference hall. We all dressed in suits for the occasion each with a small floral buttonhole. As we stood behind Raymond and Dideka I looked at our group, the prisoners and the warders, and I could not help but smile at the picture we presented. The occasion was like any marriage ceremony, filled with happiness when the happy couple exchanged rings. We all walked to one side of the hall where a special reception, cakes, sandwiches, puddings and a wedding cake, had been laid on. We stood around laughing and joking, wishing Raymond and Dideka well, toasting them in a special drink which was non-alcoholic. Just before the end of the ceremony Raymond had to return the ring to his wife. He'd been told by Munro that all valuables had to be handed in until the time when prisoners are officially released.

'We can't have you losing that ring to one of these thieves around here,' joked Munro. 'This place is full of criminals. You can't trust them.'

The entire wedding still stays in my memory for the constant sound of Raymond's laughter, a deep booming laugh which could be heard throughout the prison.

Shortly afterwards Nelson began to complain about pains in his right hand and left knee. They were not constant, but were both of the niggling, intermittent variety. It was decided to take him to the City Park Hospital in Cape Town to see an orthopaedic specialist, Dr John May, who diagnosed both as the onset of arthritis.

My son Brent had joined the prison service in 1982 after passing matriculation exams. We had spoken often about what he planned to do when he left school. Brent felt that he wanted to follow me

284

into the job I had chosen. I spent a long time explaining all the pitfalls as well as the benefits. At the time we had moved to Pollsmoor Brent was himself transferred to Robben Island. My own experiences on the island left me with a deep worry about how he could cope with such an environment. But I need not have worried. Brent was both able to handle himself well as well as earn admiration for his ability. On Robben Island he had started work running the prison library and when a vacancy occurred at Pollsmoor I told him of it and encouraged Munro to let him join us. It was agreed and Brent was given the job. Munro also agreed that Brent could work closely with me and Nelson.

Nelson had known all about Brent virtually from the time he had been born. As we got to know one another on Robben Island he would always inquire after my family. It was not merely politeness but a genuine interest. This was a feature of Nelson's character; he was genuinely concerned for people, all people, and when he asked about their welfare, he took time to listen. It was not just a polite refrain. When Brent had decided to join the prison service I had discussed it with Nelson. It was, by then, a normal part of our conversation. We had discussed the merits and problems of working within the system, but at that time I believed it was an interim job which Brent would eventually leave. Nelson was supportive and sent his best wishes to Brent, wishing him luck and success in his working life. There was a natural paternal instinct that always came through whenever he spoke of children or to children, whatever their background. He knew all about Brent's adventures and naughtiness and all the normal things that children are involved in growing up. There was one time on the island when Brent got lost and I was worried for his safety for many hours. Nelson remembered all these adventures and seemed to enjoy watching my son grow into a man. I always put it down to the deep longings I know he felt for his own children, a longing that had intensified with the death of Thembu. It may well have been a personal feeling of guilt that he had chosen the path of pursuing equality in our country, knowing it was at the cost of neglecting his own family. Whatever it was there was certainly a link between Nelson and Brent which had stemmed from my son's childhood, even though they had never met.

They first met when Brent joined us at Pollsmoor and I sent him with the post to Nelson's cell.

Brent came back astonished. 'I could not believe it: he knew me and welcomed me as a friend. He said he had known all about me since school days. It was like meeting an uncle for the first time.'

I laughed at Brent's description and the confusion in his eyes. He had been trained as a prison warder to treat all prisoners in the same way and even though he knew Nelson and the leader group formed a special category, he was struggling to come to terms with the fact that this man Nelson Mandela probably knew more about him than any person outside our own immediate family. I had deliberately never spoken of my work when I got home and it was only when Brent joined the prison service that he began to see the relationship I had with Nelson.

Having Brent working in the library was a comfort; I knew he would display the right attitude and respect to Nelson and the others in the leader group. I arranged that Brent should take my place on visits, if I was not available to sit in with the group. It was also normal that Brent would, as part of his duties, work a night shift on a regular basis. I ensured that when he was working the night shift he was seconded to the section working with Nelson. I suppose in the back of my mind was the thought that Brent would one day succeed me in my work, but the longer he stayed working within the prison service the more he realised it was not for him. He had an interest in drawing and wanted to get a job as a city planner.

Brent was an easy-going young man, very personable and deeply religious. Whenever he sat on the night shift he did so with his Bible always close at hand. I know on several occasions Nelson leaned over his shoulder and asked what he was reading. When Brent told him it was a passage from the Bible the two would stop and discuss its merits.

Brent was with Nelson in July 1988 when there was a visit from his lawyer Mr Ayob. He had escorted Nelson to the visiting area while I was greeting Mr Ayob in the visitors' sitting-room when he suddenly burst in, his face filled with alarm.

'Come quickly, Nelson's collapsed. He's ill.'

I looked at Mr Ayob and I could see the concern on his face. I told the lawyer to wait and I would see what was happening.

Hurrying back into the visiting area Brent had explained what happened. 'He was sitting in the room as normal when out of the blue he stood up and asked me to take him back to his cell. I said that he had a visitor, Mr Ayob, but before he was able to reply he starting vomiting.'

We hurried into the visiting room and Nelson was obviously in distress. His hands were on the wall and he was struggling to stand on his feet. I grabbed him in my arms and ushered him into the seat.

'Nelson, what's up? What's happened? Talk to me, tell me what the problem is.'

The sweat was on his forehead and on his upper lip. I could feel him shaking and he just shook his head.

'Look, I'm sorry to cause you this problem,' he said, his hand pointing toward the mess on the floor, just inside the door. 'If you get me the stuff I shall clean it up, you should not do it.'

I smiled at this man's selflessness. He was embarrassed at being sick, but more than anything he was more concerned that we would have to clean up the vomit.

I knelt beside him and put an arm around his shoulders. 'Come, Nelson, let's go back to the cell and you can lie down. Don't even think about this here; there are cleaners and they won't mind cleaning it up.'

He nodded and stood up, but whatever had caused him to be sick was also causing him to be unsteady on his feet. He had trouble walking straight and had the roll of a drunken man. I held him by the arm, but he was adamant that he would walk on his own.

At first when he said brusquely, 'I am all right, I can walk on my own,' I felt snubbed, that I was being shrugged off. It was only later, when I considered the matter more closely, that I realised what lay behind his thinking. If anyone had seen him walking down the corridor being supported by me, word would have got out quickly and that would have caused more problems. Nelson could see the headlines in an instant, that he had to be supported by prison warders because he had collapsed.

Back at the cell Nelson lay down on his bed and I asked about Mr Ayob.

'Tell him I am sorry, that I cannot see him just now. I shall have to rest.'

I returned to see Mr Ayob and although he was deeply concerned, he understood and trusted my analysis of the situation, that Nelson should rest for now. He asked if Nelson had been ill recently and I racked my brain trying to recall any problems. I told him that he'd had a bad cough, which had started several months before. At first we put it down to a dampness in the cell area, but gradually I became firmly of the opinion it was caused by the overall situation of being in a place where sunlight and fresh air were in short supply. It was one of the reasons I tried to get him out to the allotments as much as possible.

As soon as Mr Ayob left I called Munro to inform him Nelson was ill and notified the district surgeon, asking him to come immediately. One of the district surgeons, a Dr Fisher, was already in the prison, visiting the Medium B facility and would be with us quickly.

Nelson was still lying on his bed when Dr Fisher arrived. The doctor conducted a thorough examination and said it was probably a 'flu bug with the added complication of a stomach virus which had caused the vomiting'. Dr Fisher suggested he rest for the next few days in bed. Before I went off duty that night I went to see Nelson and he was much better, sitting up in bed, reading.

Munro also visited and the following day General Willemse, the commissioner of prisons, came with three specialists. There was also a visit that day from Maki and Mandla and they brought the first smile I had seen in several days. I'd also had a telephone call from Mr Ayob, requesting a visit. When I told him the normal visiting hours were taken up by Mandla and Maki, he asked if he could come out of hours. I agreed, knowing Mr Ayob had travelled a long way from Cape Town and was also very concerned about Nelson's health. It was important that Mr Ayob did not suspect anything sinister or suspicious in how we were looking after Nelson, and the opportunity for the two to meet before the lawyer left for Cape Town was important.

Over the next week, I watched Nelson carefully and I knew he had still not recovered fully. His movements were slow and his eyes looked yellowish. On 2 August he was taken to the City Park Hospital to see Dr Shapiro, a specialist, and then returned to Pollsmoor. Dr Shapiro said he would be making a full report, but that he felt it might require a further examination.

Over the next two days Winnie and Zindzi visited and I could see the strain on Nelson's face. He was in pain and trying to cover it up. Although he smiled and assured his wife and daughter that all was well, I knew something more serious was going on, and he was not telling anyone.

It was a week after Winnie visited that Brand called me and said Nelson had not eaten for two days.

I was furious: I should have been told the moment he refused one meal.

Brand was contrite. 'Ah, ja, I should also have told you that he has not been exercising and has spent most of the past two days in bed.'

'Brand, you know that's not the way we agreed this should be run. I need to know immediately anything is wrong.' I went to see Nelson straight away. I knew he was ill from the moment I went into his room. His face had a yellow tinge and his eyes were set deep.

'Man, what's wrong?'

He rasped, struggling to catch his breath, 'I just don't know. I just feel lame all the time and there is trouble breathing. I feel nauseous whenever I smell food or think of food.'

'Nelson, you just stay in bed for now. I'll get the doctor in to examine you.' I shook my head at how we had missed this for two days.

Two district surgeons were with us within the hour and they said he had a fever and a problem with his blood pressure. Dr Fisher was certain there was a bronchial problem. He phoned the Tygerberg Hospital, which is situated near the campus of Stellenbosch University, and said we planned to take Nelson in immediately.

While the doctors and Munro retired to an outer office to discuss the situation, I sat with Nelson, who had still not been able to move from bed.

'You know they're planning to take you to the Tygerberg Hospital,' I told him. 'It looks as if they want to get you in there immediately.'

Nelson was lying back on the bed, his eyes closed. 'I know, I've heard them discussing it. It looks like it could be serious.'

Once again Nelson was thrown into an anxiety because of his health and I tried to reassure him. 'Come, man, you know it can't be too bad. It's your breathing they're worried about; maybe it's just a bad case of flu or maybe pneumonia.' He just nodded, but I could see the worry on his lined face.

Unlike a number of our more recent drives, this ride to Tygerberg Hospital was quick and direct. Within an hour Nelson was being examined. As soon as we arrived a specialist, Professor Rosenstrauch, and a younger doctor conducted an examination. I again stayed at his side and watched Nelson's reaction.

Rosenstrauch completed the examination and as he pulled his stethoscope from Nelson's chest he knew immediately the problem. He turned to me, ignoring Nelson, and said, 'Water on the lungs, it needs draining straight away.'

I was a bit nonplussed and asked what would happen. Rosenstrauch spluttered, 'Happen? Well, if we don't get this liquid off his lungs now he could die. The liquid could smother him, in basic layman's language.' Nelson was so exhausted that he had closed his eyes and looked to be asleep.

Rosenstrauch again addressed me. 'I need a signature now to drain this liquid. I want it done immediately.' He thrust a paper in my hand and I signed it, giving Rosenstrauch permission to do whatever was needed.

The professor said he was worried that the original problem had been caused by bronchitis, but had now turned into tuberculosis. Nelson opened his eyes and was blinking. I bent closer to his ear and explained they planned to insert a tube into him to drain the liquid. He looked at the doctor and said, 'You must go ahead, do whatever is needed.'

Professor Rosenstrauch asked Nelson to brace himself; he was going to insert a needle through his ribs and he needed to feel his way through. Nelson sat on the edge of the bed and I braced his shoulders so he would not fall forward. His head fell on to his chest and he closed his eyes as the doctor probed with the needle. Just the sight of it made me grimace, knowing it would be painful. But Nelson never uttered a word, not one moan. They drained two and a half litres of a sickly brownish fluid from the lung. Once again I felt the sort of anxiety that I would experience for a member of my own family. I was worried for his health, but also for the immediate pain he was suffering.

When the doctor had drained the liquid he said he would have to insert a drainage tube beneath the left armpit and he would need to go to theatre for a full operation.

Although I had telephoned Munro to inform him of what had happened, there was still no sign of any senior officers. Munro, in turn, had informed Pretoria and called both Mr Ayob and Winnie to explain what was going on.

Before proceeding any further Rosenstrauch said he needed forms filled in; he was only too aware of the sensitivity of the situation with Nelson, and was mindful of how things could rebound on him if there were any mistakes or complications. I sat beside Nelson as the professor gave me the forms. I looked at them and saw they required details of his entire history. I knew it all and asked Nelson if I should complete them. He turned his head and smiled. 'Please fill it in as my next of kin; you're almost that anyway.'

The operation took several hours and ensured that the lungs were cleared of the excess fluid and able to drain properly. I sat with him afterwards, looking at him and noticing fully how he had become an old man almost in front of my eyes. His eye sockets were dark pools, the lines around his face more deeply etched than ever before. As he lay asleep following the operation, I could see he had lost a lot of weight. I cursed myself for not being more observant, for having missed these tell-tale signs which should have alerted me to an impending illness.

Nelson was taken to a single room, to a ward on the G-floor, the fifth level. The room was large and airy, but now I had the curtains closed to keep it as peaceful as possible. When he came around I asked him how he felt, if he needed anything. He shook his head and stretched out his hand from beneath the covers. I held his hand and felt a weakness I'd never known before. Nelson's big boxer's hands, so gentle yet strong, were now bony and limp. I was worried for him. He said just a few words, that he was uncertain how he was feeling, he just felt pain.

The next day Winnie arrived with Mr Ayob and swept into the hospital, filled with her own importance, demanding to know what had happened to her husband.

'I want to know what's going on and who has caused this,' she said.

Professor Rosenstrauch explained the situation to Winnie and the lawyer. While Mr Ayob listened carefully to the doctor's advice and assessment, Winnie stomped around the room, clearly looking for a target to blame. I stayed outside, waiting in the corridor. Later that day the story was blasted all over the media, television, radio and the newspapers. The hospital was again under siege. Winnie was quoted repeatedly in the media as saying that the cause of her husband's illness was the prison authorities, who had neglected him and were now responsible for him having TB. Reading it just made me feel worse, knowing that the ultimate blame probably would come back to me.

I sat hunched in a corner of the corridor considering where I could have gone wrong. Certainly Nelson had complained about the new cell area being cold in winter. But then the whole of the prison was cold in winter. When Nelson had complained of being cold I had put six extra blankets in the cupboard and told him he could have as many as he wished.

The hospital room was kept dark and each day I spent hour after hour sitting watching Nelson as he slept. The doctors had told us that he would sleep a lot in the early weeks after the operation to drain his lungs. The good news was that the doctors believed the TB had been arrested in its early stages and there were no lesions or spots on the lungs which would cause long-term problems. But we all knew that the recuperation would take some time.

I was at the hospital before 7.00 each morning and each day was much the same as the next. Nelson was mostly asleep and the progress was slow. Throughout the period there a huge media contingent camped outside the hospital, and as before they all tried to trick their way in. They were swarming over all the place and I had to ensure the security was tighter than it had ever been before. Gradually Nelson began to improve, first sitting up in bed, then regaining his appetite for food before he went strolling around the ward. As his strength returned so his weight improved from the sixty-five kilos it had fallen to, nearly twenty kilos below normal. But gradually Nelson's inner strength, built up from the years of harsh prison regimen, began to return. He surprised the doctors with the speed of his recovery.

Two weeks after Nelson entered the Tygerberg he had a visit from Kobie Coetsee as well as the commissioner of prisons, General Willemse, and the commanding officer, Munro. The minister was now becoming a regular visitor and I knew both men had a high regard for one another. More than once Nelson had remarked to me that Coetsee was what he described as a 'fine gentlemen, a person who listens and understands'. I know he respected him. Within a few minutes of Coetsee arriving there was a sudden appearance of the hospital security chief, a man named Visser, who was in a lather.

'Gregory, we've got a problem. The press are climbing all over us. They know the minister is in the building and they say they must have a picture of him leaving.' Visser was sweating.

I could see Visser's concern; the very presence of Coetsee, the Minister of Justice, visiting Nelson could cause a few problems. I knocked on Nelson's door and asked Coetsee if I could see him privately. I didn't want Nelson worrying about the matter.

Again Visser explained the situation with the press. Coetsee asked, 'Can you smuggle me out without them seeing me?'

Visser scratched his chin and replied, 'Well, I can as long as you don't mind going through the mortuary and lying in the back of a Combi.'

Coetsee agreed and returned to the meeting with Nelson. The

regular meetings between the two men, to try and arrange a common ground for talks with Botha, were particularly sensitive, but unusually this visit was purely to see Nelson and to inquire about his health.

As Coetsee departed he shook Nelson by the hand and told him, 'Get well, we need you to be strong.'

When Coetsee departed along the agreed route, he took with him Munro and Willemse. It was agreed that I should take the minister's Mercedes back to Pollsmoor. As I walked out of the side door towards the Mercedes, the media, some of them standing on ladders, others on the bonnets and the roofs of their cars, began their mad scramble. The driver opened the door for me and I climbed in. The media began to scramble, thrusting microphones and cameras at the car's side windows. Suddenly they realised that I was not Coetsee and the disappointment on their faces was one of the best sights I had seen in a long time; I was beginning to take a real perverse pleasure in defeating the media.

I realised Nelson was almost back to normal when he began to complain about the standard of the hospital food. It was then he discovered fishcakes. He began to have them each morning for breakfast, with a poached egg on top.

The day after Coetsee's visit I had a call from Munro. Could I stop off at Pollsmoor, he needed to talk to me. I went, wondering what was going on. I knew that there had been developments after all the meetings with Coetsee, and wondered if I was to be told that because of the illness Nelson would be freed. It was a scenario already being speculated about in the media. As I drove back to the prison I was certain that was the thinking.

However, I was again surprised when Munro kept the meeting short.

'Greg, you understand this is just between us. Yesterday the minister met Mandela as you know, and he was told that he would not be returning to Pollsmoor.'

I nodded, expecting Munro would continue to say that once he had fully recuperated he would be released.

I was surprised when Munro continued, 'We will move him shortly from the Tygerberg. When that period of convalescing is complete we will find him a place somewhere between prison and the outside world which will prepare him fully for a return to the outside.'

So that was it. A halfway house. But where? And when?

293

I asked Munro and he was in some doubt. 'I don't really know. It has not yet been decided. All I know is that we will be moving. Or at least you will be.'

It was the use of the words 'Or at least you will be...' which were causing me so much confusion. Where Nelson went I was sure to go, that was the opinion. But where and when?

Just after I returned to the hospital Munro called again. There were further developments. Nelson was to be moved, this time to the exclusive Constantiaberg Clinic where he would recuperate. I asked when, and was told that it would be in the next few days, but I should sort out the security that would be needed.

The Constantiaberg Clinic was in Constantia, a suburb of Cape Town where the richest of the rich white elite live. Elegant homes are surrounded by acres of beautifully laid-out gardens. The private clinic was purpose-built to look after patients who could afford the best in medical care. The fact that the government planned to send Nelson to Constantiaberg to recover told me a lot about their long-term intentions.

Next morning I made my first visit to the clinic, meeting the chief executive, a man called Hofmeyer, and a security officer to be shown where Nelson would be kept and the entire surrounding area. I was startled by the luxurious feel of the clinic. It felt more like a five-star hotel than a medical centre. When I was shown where Nelson would be kept, for an estimated three months, I could hardly take in the size and scope of it all. The government had hired an entire wing, where normally twelve patients would recuperate. Nelson's wing, B-wing, was perfect, situated on the first floor with a beautiful view over towards the mountains. Security, I decided, would not be a major problem with a wing that was as self-contained as this.

I headed back to the Tygerberg to discuss the move with Nelson. He was sitting up in bed, reading the daily newspapers, as I entered.

I told him straight that he was to be moved and when I told him he was to become the first black patient to enter the Constantiaberg, his face beamed. 'I'm beginning to feel better already,' he joked.

I described the new room to him. 'It is really ultra-modern with your own radio, television and bathroom. There is plenty of room to accommodate your books and the view is spectacular.'

We moved him on 31 August, an hour after darkness fell. The media were still camped outside, but had no inkling that they had missed their target. Once again, we'd beaten them.

That first night Nelson walked around the room touching everything and saying, 'Well, well, well, this is nice.'

When he awoke, the curtains were opened and he looked out over the green fields and vineyards towards the mountains. It was a perfect morning.

'This is a little better than Pollsmoor,' I smiled.

Nelson put on his stern voice. 'Mr Gregory, let me tell you, this is certainly better than Pollsmoor, it's better than Robben Island and probably better than all the best hotels in South Africa.' We laughed.

That first morning Kobie Coetsee called, accompanied by Major Marais, a deputy commander from Pollsmoor. The minister was in his most welcoming mood. 'Anything you need, anything you desire, just ask.'

Coetsee explained the purpose of the transfer to Constantiaberg was to allow privacy and the best medical and recuperative facilities the government could provide. The minister had a twinkle in his eye and winked at me when he said, 'Mr Mandela, we can't have the media accusing us of not treating you properly.'

I almost spluttered, expecting that Nelson would throw back at him that it was a pity the government had not adopted the same approach to all political prisoners in their jails from the very start, not twenty-four years too late. But, thankfully, Nelson was too wise and was learning the art of political silence. He said simply, 'Thank you.'

Shortly after Coetsee and Major Marais arrived the nurse carried in a breakfast tray. The smell of the cooked bacon had already wafted along the corridor. Because of his recent illness and Nelson's history of relatively high blood pressure, he had been put on a strictly low-cholesterol diet. Clearly the clinic's kitchen had not yet been informed. On the breakfast tray were scrambled eggs, three rashers of bacon and a plate of hot, buttered toast. Major Marais, a stickler for rules and regulations, began to hoist the tray from the hands of the nurse, protesting, 'No, Mr Mandela is not allowed such food, it is against the orders of the doctors.'

Nelson, aghast at this turn of events, protested, reached up and placed his hands on the tray. For a moment I thought that these three people, the nurse, the major and Nelson, would be pulling each in different directions and would land the lot on top of the bed. But Nelson chipped up, 'Major, I am sorry. If this breakfast will kill me then today I am prepared to die.' We all burst into laughter, understanding his hunger, for the smell had touched all our taste buds.

The change of venue also meant more people wanted to get to see Nelson. He was fast becoming the major personality in South Africa, with a cult status now entering in to the realms of Michael Jackson's. In the first few days at the clinic we had hordes of staff who wanted to catch a glimpse of him. They would gather at the doors to the wing and several times the security staff had to shoo them away. On one occasion I got angry, accusing them of treating the place like a zoo, trying to see Nelson as if he were a caged animal. Eventually the clinic issued orders that kept all staff not working in the section strictly away from the area.

On 7 November Winnie arrived, and when Nelson explained it was my birthday, she came and wished me a happy birthday and told me, 'Right, I am awarding you a day off. You go home and enjoy the day with your family.' The mood was jovial when Winnie was told that this stage of the imprisonment, the recuperation in the clinic, was to be one of the final ones before ultimate release.

The government now publicly announced that Nelson would not be returned to Pollsmoor. The speculation that his release and that of the other ANC leaders was imminent spread like wildfire among the media. Much of the attention focused on Winnie's views. She was quoted several times as saying that she had no idea what was going on in the minds of the government. In one article she said, 'The South African Government has serious problems. It had to create the correct climate for Nelson Mandela's release and that climate does not exist. There would be no point in releasing him to the South Africa of today. He would simply be returned to prison the next day, if he was not shot dead before that.'

In another interview, published in *South*, Winnie said release for her husband was equated with liberation of all oppressed people in the country. 'He has to return to a situation where he can negotiate the transfer of power from the minority to the majority. To millions of oppressed blacks in this country and to millions of oppressed people of all colours, Nelson Mandela's name is equated with the freedom we sacrificed our lives for, for the ultimate liberation of our country.'

During the next few weeks Nelson got down to his studies, knowing that the TB had caused him to neglect them for much of the past two months. There were several meetings with Kobie Coetsee and the group of advisers I now called the secret committee, and letters to be written. At the back of Nelson's mind was the constant worry that he would be seen by the ANC executive to be working out a deal on his own, for his own benefit. I know he was anxious to dispel these thoughts and worries.

He asked permission to have a visit from Walter, who was still in Pollsmoor. It was agreed and Munro arrived with him. Walter strolled into the ward and as Nelson stood beside the window watching, Walter began to climb into the bed.

'Hey, man, I'm the old man, it's me who needs a bed like this.' This was Walter the joker, the man who knew how to break down barriers and to put people at ease. We all laughed and the two old friends who had not seen one another now for several months embraced.

'Madiba, it is wonderful to see you. We were all worried that you would be badly affected by this TB, but I can see you look better than ever.' Walter swept his arm around the room and asked when this had all become standard government issue. Again they laughed and Munro and I all left the room to allow the two friends to discuss the things they needed to talk about in private.

As each day went past I could see Nelson improving. He was putting on weight and the old sparkle was back in his eyes. The nurses who were assigned to the section, white and coloured, were spoiling him, bringing extra desserts. Even when they had time off I saw several of them in the section bringing in food they had prepared specially at home.

Shortly before he was to be moved again to our next destination, which by then I knew to be Victor Verster, one of the nurses asked Nelson if he would like to attend their Christmas party.

Nelson's eyes twinkled. He never could resist a pretty girl and he nodded in my direction and said, 'Young lady, I would love to come to your party, it would be an honour, but I have a feeling both the clinic and prison authorities might have a word to say about that.'

I agreed, explaining that while we were all enjoying the facilities at the clinic, there was still a security aspect which had to be at the forefront of everyone's mind.

That evening, shortly after tea-time, a group of young nurses, all in party frocks, descended on the section, carrying plates of cakes and gifts. Several carried bowls of punch. Their sudden appearance threw the guards into a near panic and they called me on the radio, as I had gone home. It was agreed that these young ladies hardly represented a security risk and as long as the party was kept low-key, it could go ahead.

The serious side of the security at Constantiaberg was that the team of guards were all armed and aware of the need to remain vigilant at all times. I had instructed Nelson on security and matters he had to be aware of and how to take extra care. We spoke of him not opening windows, in case of a sniper; of how, if he wanted to look out of the window, he should stand behind the curtains. On one occasion in the clinic he wanted to sit out in the sunshine, so I suggested we went up to the roof area which was entirely enclosed. He asked me if I thought it wise. I asked why and he said, 'Perhaps someone will see us and shoot us.'

We had been at Constantiaberg perhaps a month when the first telephone threats started.

'We know where he is and we'll be watching...'

'Be careful ... keep looking over your shoulder ... you haven't got long left.'

'You can't keep hiding for ever ... we know where you are at all times ... it only needs one mistake and Mandela, you are dead.'

The threats took several forms, but mostly they were either telephoned to the switchboard at Pollsmoor or to the clinic. Sometimes the person spoke in English, sometimes in Afrikaans. When the threats also included me, Munro told me to be what he described as 'extra careful'.

I told him, 'That would be impossible; we are as vigilant as is humanly possible. We are living on our nerves.'

It was agreed that the guards on duty were all uniformed as well as being heavily armed. When I discussed it with Nelson I asked if he wanted them in more discreet plain clothes with guns hidden. But he said he felt that the visible presence of so many heavily armed guards was an excellent deterrent. In total we had eight armed guards on the entrances and in the grounds. We also had men posted in the corridor and in the entrance hall.

It was this heavy security cordon which discovered a journalist who tried to get into the ward posing as a doctor. He was stopped at the first check-point and did not have any medical passes. What he did not know was as well as the normal passes for the clinic, there was also a closely guarded list of every person who had access to B-wing. The guy was quickly booted out.

The media were under orders from their editors to try to get a picture of Nelson at any cost. No photographs of him had been available since the 1960s and no one knew what he now looked like. There was one particular freelance photographer called Jack who had been dogging us for years with his stunts. He stopped me one day when I was entering Constantiaberg and asked me if I wanted to make some money.

I was immediately wary, but wanted to draw him out a little. 'Sure, who doesn't.'

Jack had with him a British journalist who said his newspaper was willing to pay a million rand, the equivalent of fifty-five years' salary for me, to obtain a picture of Nelson. I told him, 'Thanks, but no thanks.' It wasn't the first or last time a bribe had been attempted.

On my way home that evening I thought about the million rand offer and knew that it was trouble. Knowing how much the money would have meant to me I was surprised at my own reaction which had been immediate. No way. I felt rather pleased. I considered talking to Nelson about it, but realised that to do so would be an insult.

Chapter 29

Victor Verster Prison

The order given, Nelson Mandela was again on the move. Victor Verster Prison lay among the vineyards of the beautiful Franshoek Valley, a forty-minute drive north-east of Cape Town. The sprawling farming complex is a few miles outside the old Dutch settlers' community of Paarl, in the shadows of the Groot and Klein Drakenstein and Simonsberg Mountains. In the distance the taller peaks of the Holland Hottentots stand like imposing statues over the entire region. It was a prison I knew reasonably well, with a reputation as a model facility. I was convinced now more than ever that this would be his final stop before ultimately being released. It was essential that security was tighter than ever. I went round every one of the officers on duty at the hospital ensuring they were alert.

I went into Nelson's room and I could see from the sharpness in his eyes that he knew the move was imminent. 'Mr Gregory,' he said, a smile touching the corners of his mouth, 'am I right in assuming that we will soon be moving?' I nodded and said quietly that he had just to pack an overnight bag. Brent would fetch the rest of his belongings.

Mandela had been told he was to be moved to Victor Verster four days before and the need for absolute secrecy was emphasised. Although he was told he would be moved, the timing of the move and the final destination was not mentioned.

Yet there was concern on his face, not at the prospect of moving, but something else.

'A problem, Nelson?' His head was buried deep in his bag, hastily throwing together a few belongings.

There was an exasperated look on his face. He turned and defiantly placed his hands on his hips. 'This is all kind of sudden, isn't it? Do you know the place we are going to?' I told him I knew the prison, but not the house where he was to be taken.

The frustration at being moved with barely a moment's notice was shown again as he added, 'It would have been nice to have a little time to say goodbye to the doctors and nurses here. They have been loyal and I would like to have said thank you. But...'

I did not need to explain, he understood only too well the need for security and the need to move when all my preparations were in place. He shrugged his shoulders, still looking down the corridor for medical staff he knew with whom he could shake hands as a parting gesture of gratitude.

We had arranged with the security staff to leave by the rear doors to avoid the media camped outside the front door. The alarms on the rear doors were switched to 'silent', and the rear door was left open.

There were just five of us, with Nelson walking in our midst. Darkness had already fallen as we emerged through the rear door. The warmth of the evening met us like a blast from an oven as I glanced at my watch. It was 7.08.

Nelson spoke very softly as he clambered into the back seat. 'I have been well looked after here, but it will be nice not to have to return. A hospital is still a hospital wherever it is.'

The tension eased as the car joined the main N1 highway for the forty-six-mile drive to Victor Verster. I sat in the back seat alongside Nelson while Brent was in the front with the specially trained driver.

Behind us a second car with armed guards tracked our every move. I said, 'You know, I think we should not tell those media guys that you have moved for several more weeks. They seem to be having a good time and they are developing a real skill in cooking on those portable braais.'

The chuckle from the seat beside me was accompanied by, 'Mr Gregory, you should be ashamed of yourself for wanting to waste the time of these honourable gentlemen of the press.'

I felt I was being admonished until he added after several seconds' pause, 'Yes, I agree with you, let's not say a thing.'

Victor Verster is a farming prison well back from the main road, and is surrounded by fields and meadows. The farmhouse where Nelson was to be held was a mile off the main road, deep in the heart of the prison.

The drive from Cape Town had taken less than forty minutes, as we swept along at nearly 100 miles an hour. As we turned off the road into the prison boundaries, we slowed to a walking pace. We drove through a clutch of single-storey houses, warders' residences

302

and on to a dirt track. The night seemed to close in on us as we drove deep into a wood of firs. Within minutes we emerged through the wood to a brightly lit area. In the centre was a white-washed farmhouse, surrounded by exotic plants and shrubs.

Even at night the house looked the most extraordinary prison cell that could be imagined. It had previously been the home of the deputy prison governor who had been evicted to make way for this most unusual prisoner. As we stood in the spacious lounge, blinking in the bright light, it was like entering a new home and wondering what the future held.

Nelson looked in every room, through the four bedrooms, the kitchen and into the lounge. The house had been hastily furnished and it was obvious it was still not fully prepared. Everywhere there were insects, centipedes, monkey spiders and a variety of other creepy crawlies. Brent came in and placed Nelson's bag in the bedroom.

The prison commander, Brigadier Keulder, was waiting in the main lounge. He was formal and stiff. 'Welcome to Victor Verster, Mr Mandela. I hope you will be comfortable and if you need anything, just ask.'

Keulder was insistent he showed us everything in the farm-house, even though our only thought that evening was to get some rest. He also carried out the formal paperwork, giving Nelson his new prison number: 1335/88.

The master bedroom had a king-size bed, en-suite bathroom and balcony out to the garden. The room had a cool, clean look, its green thick-pile carpet matching the cream and green curtains. All along one side of the wall was a set of white wooden cupboards. The bathroom had a clinical look, tiled completely in white with a shower enclosure. There were three other bedrooms, two fully furnished and a third fitted out with medical and exercise equipment. In the winter evenings, when temperatures often dropped to near zero, Nelson would move out of the large bedroom and sleep in a smaller room, which he kept constantly heated with a small portable heater.

In the kitchen Keulder opened every cupboard to boast how everything that could be wanted was already in the house. The bar was stocked with wines, brandies, whiskies, any drink imaginable. Keulder had one key and I was given the other. Next day I handed my key over to Jack Swart because he was the person who was in charge of the kitchen and culinary matters.

Nelson was told later that the food was supplied by the prisons department and that anything he needed would be provided. The drinks were courtesy of the government and anything that was used would be replaced by the state. If, however, he had personal friends to stay then he had to replace the drinks at his own expense.

Keulder explained that there was one back-door key which was held by me, but that the keys to all other exit doors would remain in the doors so that if he wanted to open a door and, for instance, swim in the pool, it was entirely up to him. The guards, on constant patrol outside the main walls of the garden, would not be allowed inside the house enclosure.

I could see Nelson was tired and suggested we all have an early night and assess what needed to be done first thing next day. I also had to make a telephone call.

After I had been told about the move from Constantiaberg Clinic to Victor Verster, General Willemse gave me a number in Pretoria to call as soon as we had arrived and Nelson had settled in. I was told to memorise the number and, on no account, write it down. General Willemse added the telephone in Pretoria was to be monitored at all times and that I was to say simply, 'The eagle has landed.'

I went into the office outside the farmhouse and dialled the number I had memorised. It was answered on the first ring.

'Hello, this is Gregory. The eagle has landed.'

The voice at the other end of the telephone was familiar, although I had difficulty putting a name to it. He replied simply in Afrikaans 'Dankie,' thank you.

Later, in the weeks after we moved to Victor Verster, I mentioned the 'eagle' call to Nelson and we both laughed at the way the prison authorities always managed to create mystique.

Nelson laughed. 'There have been times when I wished I had the wings of an eagle.'

That evening there was one more call to be made, to Nelson's lawyer, Ismael Ayob, to tell him of the transfer and to allow him to pass the news on to Winnie.

Mandela was already up when I arrived shortly after 6 o'clock the next morning. Dawn was just coming up over the distant mountains and I found him standing outside inspecting the rose garden.

'Ah, Mr Gregory,' he said, a smile spreading over his face. 'Come, look at these beautiful blooms.' For the next fifteen minutes we inched our way around the garden sniffing the various plants.

There was a magnificent aloe bush, a fig tree, an avocado pear tree and a heavily laden lemon tree. He turned and assessed the garden before pondering, 'We will have to find a spot for a vegetable bed.'

The prison service had provided a cook to ensure anything Nelson wanted could be cooked in his own kitchen. Warrant Officer Jack Swart, a tall quiet Afrikaner, was an accomplished chef with a keen sense of humour. Soon after meeting Mandela in the house he announced to us all that he had once been a guard on Robben Island at a time when Mandela and the other ANC leaders were working in the lime quarry. Mention of the quarry put Mandela on edge and I could see him look sharply at Swart.

'Yes, I was the person who used to drive you all in the back of the truck to the quarry,' he said, chuckling at the memory. 'I used to deliberately steer the truck over the biggest bumps I could find to give you people a rocky ride.' Mandela relaxed and laughed at the thought of Swart's attitude.

'Well, Mr Swart, we will make sure you don't do any driving here, and we'll just have to trust that your cooking is better than your driving.' It was clear Swart, with his sense of humour, was going to be a good person to have around.

As we stood outside in the patio looking at the swimming pool, there was a telephone call informing us that Kobie Coetsee was calling in the afternoon.

On the verandah, beneath a tall custard apple tree, were a couple of chairs and a table. As we sat down, the full impact of the place began to hit us. This idyllic garden, surrounded by a six-foot high white wall, with an abundance of flowers, was actually a prison. The only thing that spoiled the view were two guard towers, about fifty yards away in the field beyond and the razor wire which topped the wall. I was now absolutely convinced this was the halfway house preparing Nelson for the outside world.

I kept quiet as we both sat there, soaking in the early morning sun, its heat not yet uncomfortable. Swart came out of the house carrying a tray of tea and placed it beside us.

We sat drinking our tea in absolute silence; although I'm sure both of us filled with much the same thought. Just how long would we be here before Nelson was given his freedom.

As I looked around the garden I soon realised there was a problem: the garden wall surrounding the compound was not tall enough. Anyone on the outside could see in. I knew that Nelson would spend a lot of time in the garden indulging his love of plants so I would need to get the wall raised. When I called Keulder to explain the problem he was all efficiency and promised it would be sorted out. By midnight the entire wall surrounding the house had been raised by two feet making it impossible for any outsiders to see in.

Later that day Keulder came to visit me. He was known in the prison service as 'the German' and he ruled with an iron fist. His word was law and God help any person who broke it. He was the type who did everything strictly by the book.

Yet, when he came to my small office in the farmhouse annexe, he took off his cap and started shaking my hand.

'Do you know, Greg, just what an honour this is for me?' I shook my head, caught off-guard.

'The fact the government has chosen Victor Verster out of all the prisons in the Republic shows how they trust me. To bring a man like Nelson Mandela here is such an honour. I have been given a great responsibility.'

The little speech left me wondering how he would have viewed the situation just a few years before, before this complete reversal of attitude from the authorities. But I said nothing and nodded in acknowledgement.

'I'll let Mr Mandela know of your pride,' I told him.

In the afternoon Kobie Coetsee arrived as he had promised, his arms weighed down by a case of Cape wine. 'Ah, Mr Mandela, thought you'd appreciate a housewarming gift, courtesy of the Cape.' It was the supreme irony that the man who was minister responsible for prisons, and, therefore, its inmates, was here bringing a case of best wine for his most famous guest.

Coetsee immediately got down to ensuring everyone knew what was going on, and the reason why Nelson had been brought to this house.

In typical fashion he made no bones about the fact that this was to be Nelson's final prison, if that's what it could be called, before being freed. Although he did not put a time-scale on the eventual release, he made it clear that day was not in the too distant future.

'The main reason for bringing you here to Victor Verster, and to this house in particular, was to allow you to have a place with reasonable comfort where you could hold discussions with who-ever you wish in both privacy and comfort.' In typical fashion Nelson met his gaze and thanked him, his eyes carrying with them a hint of scepticism.

Coetsee understood the look and added, 'Look, Mr Mandela, I hope you are happy here and if there is anything you wish, please don't hesitate to ask Mr Gregory. He has full authority to get it for you. Let me also assure you that any conversations you conduct in this house, or in the grounds, will be totally private.'

Even before the minister had spelled out the plan for release I knew in my heart that freedom was not far away. I also knew that the government of P. W. Botha was publicly playing one game, while privately playing a totally different one. Botha had said several times he would never speak to a man he considered to be a terrorist. From the visits and meetings Nelson had already in Pollsmoor it was clear things were moving towards release. On several occasions I could see that one day it was distinctly possible that this man whom they'd held prisoner for so long would one day end up as President. Whenever I mentioned this scenario to Nelson he would smile and typically caution me: 'Mr Gregory, it is a good idea to walk before we even consider the possibility of running.'

The next day Keulder was ordered by the minister to leave us entirely alone; that his responsibility was the main prison, everything else to do with Nelson Mandela would be handled by me at the farmhouse. He was told that we would be doing things, ordering items by fax in his name, and that he was to accept it. He was told to instruct all his officers that the area around the farmhouse was off-limits to them.

If extra officers were ever needed, he was to respond immediately, whatever the cost elsewhere in the prison. On one occasion I understood the full effects of these orders from Pretoria when I invited one officer to visit us for a coffee. He shook his head and said they were all under orders never to go near the farmhouse.

At that point I felt sorry for Keulder who would have been wounded by this order. He ostensibly had Nelson Mandela under his roof, but not under his responsibility at all.

Although the move to Victor Verster had been smooth for Nelson, it had caused me some problems. The entire business had been conducted in strictest secrecy, and now I faced the prospect of having to sell my home in Cape Town. When the prison authorities said I had to transfer to Victor Verster I resisted. By this time I had been with Nelson Mandela for more than twenty-two years. We were firm friends and, in many ways, he was like a father figure to me. However, I suggested that perhaps it was time to part Nelson and myself, that I had done as much as I could. The reply was unequivocal: they said they needed me to remain close beside him to provide a continuity which kept him comfortable.

The commanding officer was emphatic. 'Look, Greg, you 'are Mandela's personal jailer. Just stick with it now.'

I was getting angry. 'But this has nothing to do with personalities, nothing to do with the job; it has everything to do with my family. Once again you are disrupting them unfairly.'

'Greg, if you want you can try taking it up with the minister. I know you have access to him, but I'm telling you he'll refuse. I'm afraid you're now part of this whole business whether you like it or not.'

'Yes, sir, but why me?' I knew I was caving in, being irrational. I knew I was the closest person to Nelson Mandela and we had a bond.

'Look, man, you know that there are negotiations between Mandela and the government. You know those negotiations are crucial to the country's well-being. You also know that if you don't go to Victor Verster with him then he'll be in the hands of people who don't know him, who don't understand him, who will not react to his needs and moods. They will be people he will not trust. This could set back the entire process. I'm afraid it's why you have to go. They know you are now a friend and he trusts you.'

I knew the reasoning, just as the prison authorities knew that I was now too old to quit and expect to get another job. The days of heading off to somewhere else and picking up an alternative job were long gone. I was past that age.

I had one more card to play. 'Sir, I will go if I can make certain requests.' He nodded in agreement. I could see they had expected this reaction and they'd already out-guessed me.

The first request was that I would not have to sell my house in Cape Town, instead leasing it through the Public Works Department. The tenant would be one approved by myself.

The second request was that when Nelson Mandela was released I could move back again and work at Pollsmoor. He nodded again, thereby confirming my belief that the day was coming for Nelson's release.

Third, when we moved to Victor Verster I wanted to have full control over the comings and goings. I told him I wanted to do the job of protecting Mandela without having continually to consult the commanding officer. I was to be my own boss with a direct line to Pretoria.

Fourth, I wanted to take my son Brent along with me. He was also close to Mandela and an asset in the work.

Fifth, I wanted to have a house at Victor Verster. I did not want to return to the dismal life of flat-living again.

Sixth, I needed a car to commute regularly between home and Victor Verster until all these things were sorted out.

The commander said he'd get back to me on my requests. Two hours later he called me and said simply, 'All requests granted.'

I had one more obstacle to overcome: Gloria. I had not told her the situation. When I did she burst into tears, crying that she didn't want to leave her own home and the friends she had made in Cape Town. I explained it was for just a short time, although when we actually moved to Victor Verster, she sat in the car and wept, refusing to get out.

At that stage I had not discussed the matter with Nelson. It took several months for it all to come out and I explained to him what they'd told me; that they wanted someone who could be trusted by all sides. He nodded.

Once again he turned his thoughts to my family and said, 'I would like you to convey my thoughts to Gloria for causing this disruption to her life. And also to Natasha [my daughter]. I know she will be affected because she is going to university this year. Tell her to concentrate even harder on her studies, that this will help her forget the difficulties of you moving here.'

In the house there was a television and video recorder. Beside the bed Nelson placed his own radio, the same cheap one he had brought from Pollsmoor. It was one of his most cherished possessions for it allowed him to listen to every news bulletin, every hour on the hour.

Most mornings Nelson put on a pair of casual slacks and a loose-fitting shirt. In the summer when temperatures soared into the low 100s, he wore only a pair of open sandals on his feet. The house was not air-conditioned, although there were efficient shades on the windows and a number of fans placed in each of the rooms. In the corner of the room was a lovely pink Queen Anne sofa which Nelson loved to lie on. Many times I found him stretched out along the sofa, reading his papers, with a fan blowing.

The first couple of days were busy for Brent who ran a constant courier service between Pollsmoor, Constantiaberg and Victor Verster, carrying Nelson's burgeoning collection of personal items. It took four or five bakkie-loads before all his belongings were gathered at the farmhouse.

The sight of the swimming pool was irresistible, particularly in those early days when the heat was practically unbearable.

Nelson asked, 'Mr Gregory, I know I cannot swim properly, but I would like to try. It is okay?'

I laughed and told him that no matter how good a swimmer I was it was probably too late to teach him now. Because the pool went from three-feet at the shallow end to six and a half feet at the deep end, I said it was prudent to have at least one of us, either Brent or myself, around the pool if he wished to swim.

Nelson grinned. 'You are right. We cannot have the prison authorities accused of drowning me. Think of the outcry.' We both laughed although I pointed out the real danger was in him getting cramp in the deep end and struggling.

At first Nelson hardly ventured out of the shallow end, preferring to doggy-paddle his way from the edge to a few yards out. Then Brent remembered how he had learned, by using a body board. When he brought it he showed Nelson how it should be used. It led to many relaxing afternoons where he would just lie on the board and float around in the coolness of the pool.

After his daily summer swim Nelson would usually have a light snack and read a newspaper. After a short stroll through the garden he invariably had a sleep. The only time he did not sleep in the afternoon was when visitors were expected.

I knew that he was up most mornings at 4.30, so it was inevitable that he would be tired by 2 o'clock.

The second morning I picked up Swart, and I began the process of getting to know him. He, along with Major Marais and I, were virtually the only people who had direct access to Nelson through this period.

Swart was an easy-going person with a sense of fairness and honesty. Unlike so many officers in the prison service, he had no prejudices or ill feelings about blacks. He was interested in one thing only: in being a superb cook. And, in that respect, I know Nelson enjoyed his company.

As Nelson's personal cook, he was given a complete diet programme, outlined by the medical team who were supervising Nelson at that time. Each morning he arrived shortly before 7 and began cooking breakfast. Nelson's particular favourite was a little oatmeal with two fishcakes and a poached egg, accompanied by his inevitable pot of tea. Swart stayed through lunch and dinner, often leaving the evening meal in the microwave oven for Nelson to heat at his own convenience. Because he spent long hours either writing or studying, Nelson often left supper until quite late. It was a habit he had picked up at Pollsmoor and he was not about to change it now.

Remembering how he had not liked ordinary bread, I told Swart that it would be better if we had a daily supply of fresh-baked full-grain bread. Swart complied and baked his own bread, either full-grain or half-grain, always delicious.

One day I came into the kitchen to hear Swart and Nelson having a friendly row.

Nelson: 'I should do the dishes.'

Swart: 'No, I should do them.'

Nelson: 'No, you do the cooking, it is only fair that I should do them.'

Swart: 'No, that is my duty, you must return to the lounge.'

Nelson: 'But I would like to do them, let me.'

Swart: 'No, and while we're on the subject I also object to the fact that you make your own bed each morning. It is my responsibility.'

Nelson: 'But Jack, be reasonable, I have been doing it as a matter of course each morning; it is a natural reaction.'

I could not contain my mirth any longer and walked in to tell them: 'You sound like an old married couple arguing over the dishes and the making of the bed.' Both laughed and saw the funny side of it all, agreeing that Nelson could do the dishes when he wanted and could continue to make his own bed each morning.

Swart's culinary skills won many compliments from the guests who stayed, as he prepared a variety of gourmet meals.

Another time, when Nelson expected a delegation of legal advisers and friends, Dullah Omar, George Bizos and Ismael Ayob, he asked Swart about the best wine to choose for lunch. Nelson, who would only occasionally sip a white wine, and that only a sweet-tasting Nederburg, asked what he should choose.

Swart told him that the wine he usually ordered, the sweet Nederburg, was, in reality, what he considered to be pretty cheap and rough. He said that for the visit he would choose a decent dry wine as well as a Nederburg.

Nelson shook his head and disagreed, claiming, 'Mr Bizos would not be able to tell the difference.'

Swart argued the point and agreed to supply the dry white wine as an experiment. When he served the food, he brought out both bottles and asked the three guests which they preferred. All looked at the Nederburg, but chose the dry wine. At that Nelson and

311

Swart suddenly burst into laughter to the bewilderment of the guests.

Nelson told them, 'I'm sorry, gentlemen, you have let me down, you have more expensive tastes than I imagined.'

Despite the presence of alcohol in the farmhouse, Nelson seldom touched a drop, maybe the occasional sip when others had dinner with him, but then only to make them feel at ease. What he became addicted to was the special ginger beer and non-alcoholic corn beer which Swart brewed from his own recipe. Both drinks became big favourites, not just with Nelson, but everyone in the house. It got to the stage where Nelson would always help Swart whenever we had run out of supplies of the stuff. It was brewed in special containers lining the kitchen wall and Nelson was always monitoring them, tending them to ensure they were being prepared properly.

Every morning, after I had been in to greet Nelson, a doctor would come and give him a thorough ten-minute examination. At one end of the farmhouse was a room fitted with examination table, oxygen bottles, gas masks, every conceivable piece of equipment which would have allowed us to give immediate treatment in the case of an emergency, such as a heart attack. Each morning the doctor would come in, take his blood pressure and ask about any pains.

In the area around Paarl power failures were a frequent occurrence, so the farmhouse had a diesel-driven generator connected to the main electricity supply which could be turned on or off at the touch of a button.

Often after breakfast, which Nelson usually had alone sitting at the dining-room table, he would come outside on to the patio and relax. It was one of my first jobs each morning to put out the cushions for the patio furniture.

Each morning Nelson would walk around the bushes and plants, examining each one, looking for disease or fresh buds. It was as if he knew every one and tended them carefully. To one side of the house was a shrubbery which had a path running through its centre. It was covered by the overhanging branches of a fever tree. It was in here that the full range of flowers, plumbagos, pineapple lilies, bitter aloe, sour fig and pincushions grew in splendid profusion. Many times I would arrive at the farmhouse and find Nelson missing from the main house. I knew he would be in this little hideaway where he was cut off from the rest of the world. I called it Nelson's Walk.

312

From early in his stay he loved the views of the mountains, particularly the distant sight of Paarl Rock where the Afrikaans language monument was situated. Around the side of the house he came across a wild fig and as he stroked the fruit asked me if they could be eaten.

'They are not quite ripe yet, but when they are, you will want them more and more, they are delicious,' I told him.

The views of the mountains caused a hiccup in the proceedings when Nelson asked for a pair of binoculars one day. When I asked Keulder for a pair he was immediately suspicious, wanting to know why Nelson wanted them.

'Because he wants to look at the mountains and watch the wildlife,' I told him.

Keulder's mind was working overtime and he said, 'No, no, no, this man is planning an escape route or something.' I nearly laughed out aloud, knowing Nelson's attitude to escape. It was ridiculous beyond belief. When Keulder refused to send the binoculars, I contacted the commissioner, General Willemse, and explained why the binoculars were required. The next day the binoculars appeared at the front door, courtesy of Keulder.

In those early days Nelson maintained his rigid routine of getting up early every morning, exercising, showering, eating breakfast then reading the newspapers. Then he would write letters or study until someone called.

I had a special intercom system installed in the house, linking it to an office in an annexe close by. It was more for Nelson's benefit than anything else. If he required anything he would buzz and I would answer. At night the intercom was switched to the main radio control room.

One night just after we moved to Victor Verster I had an urgent call at home. I had to go to Nelson's house immediately; there was something wrong. When I arrived Nelson was in the bedroom. He said he was on edge and he heard something banging outside in the main lounge area. He was not going to take chances so pressed the intercom buzzer and asked the radio-room to contact me. I put on all the house lights and found a picture which had fallen on the floor; the adhesive holding it had failed. We both laughed, and realised our security system had worked too well.

Many evenings I simply went to the house and sat with him in the lounge, as I would a friend. It was almost as if we were lodgers sharing the same accommodation. I would walk in and say hello and just sit down.

Often I waited until after the late-night news, after 10 o'clock, before ensuring the house was closed up properly. During those evenings we would sit, sometimes reading, sometimes writing and we would be very much at ease with one another. I don't think Nelson wanted to get into great long discussions; he felt better remaining quiet, talking only when necessary. I believed the companionship of having me in the house and being with him was comfort enough.

One night I went in and the television was on. He was fast asleep in the chair. I touched him softly on the shoulder, so as not to give him a fright.

'My goodness,' he said, as he slowly opened his eyes. 'What time is it? I must have dozed off. I shall go to bed now.'

It was small incidents like this which confirmed our relationship: we were friends.

In the office I had two telephones, one directly to the Victor Verster switchboard, the other unlisted with access to anywhere outside. Not only was the area around the house considered out of bounds to other warders from the main prison, but this office was, itself, out of bounds to anyone other than those authorised by me. In the rear of the office was a small kitchen as well as the main arsenal.

I began to realise that I had to have a contingency plan to escape with Nelson in the event of a full-scale attack on the house. It was impossible to be too careful; there were madmen everywhere willing to carry out such an outrageous assassination and I knew I had always to be guarded and prepared.

I approached the commanding officer, Keulder, and asked if he could speak to the neighbouring farmer. The farmhouse where we had located Nelson was less than a quarter mile from a small dirt track which ran alongside the prison grounds. The track was on the farmer's adjoining land, and ran between the farmer's vines and peach blossoms; it was the ideal escape route should it ever be needed. The problem was the farmer was an old dyed-in-the-wool right-winger who hated blacks. He knew we were looking after Nelson Mandela in the farmhouse.

Brigadier Keulder went to the farmer's home and spoke to him about the possibility of us using the road as an escape route if trouble ever flared.

'No blerrie way,' he said. 'If they come rushing out of the prison they will spray all sorts of dust over the vines and ruin them.'

Keulder knew the man was making excuses. So the talks went

further and the farmer was visited by a number of officials who told him in no uncertain terms that unless he agreed to our occasional use of this track he would find a new provincial highway being run right through the middle of his property whether he liked it or not.

The farmer reluctantly agreed, but demanded that we should place a gate at the end of the track and keep it locked at all times. Occasionally we saw the farmer using the dirt track, driving in his tractor, throwing up far more dust than any car would. Whenever we saw him we would wave or greet him, but he merely scowled back.

Chapter 30

Death threats

The death threats started within two weeks of moving to Victor Verster. As I have said we had two telephones in the office annexe to the farmhouse, one connected to the prison main switchboard, the other an unlisted number which could be used to call anywhere.

It was early one evening the call came. The man was an Afrikaner.

'We know you are running an ANC cell in there and it is a banned organisation. We do not want your sort in here. You are a fucking bastard and we do not need you, or that kaffir bastard. We know all about you, nigger lover. We are going to shoot you as well as him. Just remember we are watching you, we will know when you go out, when you go shopping in Paarl and we will shoot you down like a dog.'

This was unlike the threats which had first been voiced to me in Pollsmoor. Those I could handle; they were coming from people already in prison and identifiable. This was more sinister.

The calls came in at different times, up to two or three times a week, but gradually tapered off to once a week. It was always the same form of abuse, but occasionally the person would add something.

'We know which house you are staying in. We know who you are. We know when you go down to the river at the weekend. We know when you go out. You won't be able to avoid us for ever. When you least expect it we'll be waiting for you and you'll be dead.'

As soon as the first call came in I knew this was a matter for Pretoria and the special security department. I had been given the names of two senior officers in the security section, Colonel Barkhuizen and Brigadier Gillingham, who would help.

The security department listed every call and instructed me to

317

listen out for tell-tale background noises. But the caller was always very careful: there was no sound at all.

When I realised there was little reason to listen to the calls I would tell the caller, 'You are wasting your time and my time,' and put the phone down.

I knew we were not welcome there in Victor Verster. I had heard various things that the other warders were saying about us. There was a lot of animosity and petty jealousy about the way we handled matters in the farmhouse, a law unto ourselves.

The first time my rules caused upset was just a few weeks after we arrived when we were informed of a visit from Brigadier Matanzima, at the time the acting head of the Transkei Army. There were rumours that Matanzima was already in trouble in his position and the Transkei elders had decided he should discuss his future with Nelson.

The system we operated was that any caller, no matter who they were, or what their position, had to leave their own car at the front gate and they would be driven to the farmhouse from there.

I went to the front gate to talk to the warders on duty. I told them I was uncertain if Brigadier Matanzima would show up in a uniform or not. If he was in uniform, as head of the Transkei defence force, he was also part of the South African government forces. As such, I said, we had to accord him full military courtesies, including saluting him. To ask a white man to salute a black at that time was unusual.

One of the warders on guard at the gate heard the conversation with Sergeant Knight, the officer in charge.

The warder asked me directly, 'Are you asking me to salute a black man?'

When I confirmed I was, he added, 'Sir, I am not prepared to do that.'

A second officer who was sitting at the back of the gatehouse, a warder named van Heerden, pitched in, 'Sir, I will do it.'

I thanked van Heerden and told him, 'Look, if you have any problems with saluting a black man, salute his uniform or salute the car.'

Van Heerden replied, 'Sir, I have no problem with saluting a black man. He is an officer and that is what I am required to do.'

After Brigadier Matanzima left I had a call from Nelson, on the intercom to the office.

'Mr Gregory, can I have a word, please?'

As I went in, he was standing. 'I just want to say thank you for what you did today.'

I was puzzled. 'For what, Nelson?'

He continued. 'Look, I know where I am here. I know I am in the Boland, I know this is Conservative Party country and I know the majority of people working here are Conservative Party members and the AWB is part of their military wing. I know only too well their feelings about black men. I know their attitudes to such matters as saluting a black man and today when the Brigadier called to see me your men saluted twice, coming in at the gate and again here outside. It was such a surprise to the Brigadier that he mentioned it to me. I must say thank you because I feel your hand in all of this.'

I began to protest that the warders were only doing their proper job, but he held up his hand to silence me.

'That incident means a lot because he will return to the Transkei and one message he will give is the absolute discipline of this place here. It means a great deal to have that message spread among black men who want to see small changes such as this.'

But the incident, although pleasing Nelson, caused further unrest among those very same right-wingers who were working in the prison. Their anger simmered.

It began to leak out that my orders superseded all others in the prison. As I was merely a warrant officer, this caused a lot of jealousy, particularly among those officers of more senior ranks.

Following the incident with the officer at the gate who refused to salute Brigadier Matanzima, I issued an instruction that that particular guard should not work in that position again.

A few weeks later the unlisted telephone in the office annexe rang. It was a young woman who wanted to speak to Pietie de Jong, one of the officers on duty patrolling the area around the farmhouse.

'I'm sorry, I think you've got the wrong number,' I told the woman.

The woman got angry. 'Look, I know he's there. I was with him last night in Paarl and he gave me this number and told me he was working with Mandela. So don't give me a lot of kak about him not being there.'

Inwardly I began to seethe. 'Look, forgive me, but I must insist you do have the wrong number and I am extremely busy. Please excuse me.'

319

I immediately summoned de Jong, and told him of the phone call from his fiancée.

'As of now you will be relieved of your duties here and returned to normal duties in the main prison. You have been instructed not to discuss your job here with anyone for security reasons. Your girlfriend has just told me you have been blabbing about looking after Mr Mandela. You know, or you should know, that loose talk can result in problems. As of now you are out of here.'

As far as I was concerned there was no compromise on this matter. It was important to maintain complete and absolute security, given the situation we were in. If one man talked to a fiancée and then someone else spoke to another relative, news of our security arrangements would leak out. And I considered that anyone planning an attack on Nelson would be looking for such leaks.

The removal of the guard from the special detail at the farmhouse was costly to him. To work at the farmhouse every warder received a special bonus. It was considered a prime job, and not because they were looking after Nelson Mandela; it meant money, almost double their normal wage.

So when I removed de Jong, word spread quickly to everyone who wanted to work there. It also had another effect. In many quarters the animosity towards me worsened to outright hatred.

I began to notice this when, on summer evenings, after returning to the warders' accommodation from the farmhouse, I took the dog out for a walk. From behind a hedge or a wall, I would hear, 'Hey, you, nigger lover. You are a kaffir boetie.' I would look around and not see anyone. It happened every time I went out. Wherever I went I was greeted with silence. A walk through the residential area would usually be expected to lead to normal conversation. But I found mostly hostile looks and people who deliberately turned their back.

On the few occasions people would stop and talk, warders I had known previously at Pollsmoor and on Robben Island, they always wanted to know about Nelson Mandela. What is going on? What is happening? What are his views? What does he want to do with the country? Will he be released? Will there be trouble? Every time someone asked me such a question I was angered. They knew I could not tell them because I would never talk about him publicly. It also showed me that they were not entering into conversation with me because they wanted to talk to me, rather they wanted to know only about the person I was looking after.

Once again it led to a situation where I had no social life. As before I became a hermit. A short time after we moved into the new house at Victor Verster 'our neighbours invited us over to a braai. They said it was to welcome us to the area. When we arrived there were about twenty couples, all gathered around the garden braai. The host introduced us and within thirty seconds the first of the questions started about Nelson Mandela. It went on for the next five or ten minutes, question after question about the man.

I turned to Gloria and she could see the anger on my face. 'Let's go home,' I said.

I explained my feelings as we walked away. 'He invited us to this braai, claiming it was to welcome us to the area. He invited a lot of the neighbours and his friends. But what did they want to know? Did they ask about how we were settling in? Did they ask about how we liked the house or the area? Did they ask about us? No, they asked only about Nelson Mandela. It was as if this guy had invited people around and told them he had a neighbour who worked with Nelson Mandela and to come and ask any question they wanted.' I was livid.

Several times when I returned home from the farmhouse there were people sitting drinking tea with Gloria. I saw them and went straight into the bedroom, had a shower, then waited until they had left before emerging.

It was hard on Gloria who is, by nature, a gregarious, easy-going person who enjoyed the company of her neighbours. But I had a rule which never varied: I would never talk about guarding Nelson Mandela to anyone outside the job.

A month or so after moving to Victor Verster I was in the garden, mowing the lawn. It was a Saturday. By the time I finished it was well into the afternoon. Too late to drive into Paarl to buy a few beers. I was filthy from gardening, but decided rather than change I would go to the warders' club and buy a six-pack.

It was mid-afternoon on a Saturday and the place was packed out not just with warders, but farmers from the surrounding area, drinking beer, playing darts and snooker. It was crowded and noisy, a typical bar-room scene. But by the time I had walked the twenty yards to the bar, silence had fallen over the entire area. Drinks were put down, snooker games halted and every head turned in my direction. The speed of the change in atmosphere was almost frightening, but I decided to ignore it, get the beer and leave as soon as possible.

Several men spat loudly on the floor. From the back I could hear the words 'kaffir boetie' and 'nigger lover'.

There was no bar as such, just a small hatch where men queued to get their drinks before taking it to another part of the room. To one side of the line-up stood a major, van der Westhuizen. He had been drinking and he stood with a smirk on his face. Turning to his group of friends behind him he jerked his head in my direction and said, 'Here he is, the arse-licking Mandela man. Who wants to ask him any questions about what the nigger is going to do with our country? Eh, come on, let's find out.'

I ignored him and went to the hatch and said quickly to the barman, 'A six-pack, please.'

Van der Westhuizen was not finished. Pointing at the mud-stained tracksuit I was wearing, he added, laying on the sarcasm, 'Nice tracksuit, Gregory. I suppose your old father down there gave it to you.' The major was indicating that I'd got the tracksuit from Nelson, but the reference to my own father got to me.

Momentarily my mind flashed back to the days in boarding-school, when the older, bigger schoolboys bullied the younger boys. I had dealt with that and I would deal with this.

I made a grab for van der Westhuizen's throat. Another officer, Agenbach, saw it coming and grabbed me, holding me back.

I hissed at van der Westhuizen. 'Listen, and listen carefully. My father has been dead for a long time now. If you have got anything to say to me or anyone about my job here we will talk about it, not in front of the commanding officer, but with the people in Pretoria. I'm sure they would like to hear your opinions. If you don't want to do that keep your cowardly mouth shut.'

I shrugged off Agenbach and stormed out. Behind me I could hear curses and laughter.

Within a few minutes of returning to our house the commanding officer Brigadier Keulder arrived, sweating and flustered.

'James, James, I'm sorry for what happened back there. It was too much drink and a bit of horse-play.'

I was furious and said to leave the matter, it was best forgotten.

A week later I was in the general shop buying cigarettes. A small boy, no more than ten years old, stood in front of me, buying sweets. He had made his selection but was ten cents short. The woman behind the counter told him to put some sweets back and to recalculate how much he had. I took a ten-cent piece out of my pocket and handed the coin to the boy.

The child shook his head and said, 'No, you are one of the spies who works down on the farm. I can't take anything from you.'

After the first death threats I was always armed. Whenever I was out I carried a point 38 calibre special in a holster slung beneath my left arm. The gun took five bullets, but in a moon-bag slung around my waist I carried an extra thirty bullets, the special soft-nosed kind that explode on impact. Whenever I took Gloria shopping I would drop her off, then cruise around the area making sure I was not being followed or watched. Every time we left the prison area, went shopping or into Cape Town, I was always conscious of the possibility of being killed.

After the first month or so, the police brought in a caravan to use as a make-shift office. They had their own communications and there were at least two officers permanently on duty. Whenever I was leaving the prison grounds I was to tell these officers my movements. On one occasion I told them I was going into Paarl, then mid-way to the town changed my mind and went into Cape Town. In the town centre I turned round suddenly to be confronted by a plain-clothes officer, about twenty yards behind me. He looked straight at me and blushed. I actually put my hand inside my jacket to the gun and walked up to him.

'Do you want to tell me what you're doing?' I asked.

The man was embarrassed. 'Look, I'm supposed to be giving you cover, guarding you in case of an attack. My bosses know about the threats, so that's why I'm here.'

Knowing he was there, following me, actually gave me comfort. I never spoke to Gloria about these threats, not wanting to alarm her. The fact I was carrying a gun was not new to her because from the early days at Pollsmoor she knew that the orders from the security people were to carry a firearm at all times.

Nelson knew about the firearms and the death threats. He was always very concerned for me.

'Mr Gregory, you have got to be careful out there. These people are serious, they play real games and they kill people.'

My reply was always the same. 'Nelson, the people who might do this do not know who I am. They don't know what car I have and they don't know what I look like.' Although I said this to him, I never actually believed it because I knew that, for anyone to get the unlisted telephone number in the office, they would also know every detail about me. I was just as certain that if they wanted to kill me, they could do so at any time. Carrying a firearm was protection, but only minimal. I knew we had armed people

323

patrolling around the warders' houses each night and that every prison house had a gun safe where firearms had to be locked when the warder was off duty. But every evening as I went to bed I placed the handgun on the cupboard beside the bed, loaded and ready to fire. On the floor next to the bed was a fully-loaded shotgun. I would not say I was living in fear, I was just fully prepared for the worst.

The result of this was to isolate me further from people. When I was not with Nelson I was alone. On weekends off I would close the front door of my home and not venture out. I was back to my schooldays when my parents had left me alone at boarding-school. It was a feeling I knew only too well.

Chapter 31

My son dies

Somewhere in the distance the telephone was ringing. I was fast asleep and the ringing of the bell pulled me out of a dream.

I reached for the phone and looked at the clock. It was 1.15 in the morning.

The voice was abrupt. 'Is that Warrant Officer Gregory?'

'Uh, oh, ja, this is he.'

'This is Klapmuts Police Station. Are you Warrant Officer Gregory?'

'Ja, I just told you I am.'

'Well, your son is dead.'

In five brief words this police officer at the end of the telephone had jerked me wide awake. I can't remember if I sat down or if I was already sitting. I do remember I was totally lame, in absolute shock.

'Look, this is no time for sick jokes; it is a quarter past one in the morning.'

'I am telling you your son is dead. He died in a car accident.'

'Can you tell me how, what happened?'

'Ja, but come to the police station.' The line went dead.

I sat on the end of the bed. Blank. Numb. Gloria had heard the phone and was still half asleep.

'James, what's wrong?'

I said simply, 'Brent has died.'

The words threw Gloria into a fit of screaming. I was confused, out of my mind. I could not think.

The first thing that flashed into my head was that he would not be able to work the next morning. I phoned Brigadier Keulder. All I could hear him saying was, 'Oh no, oh no.' Within a few minutes both Keulder and his wife were at our home. They took us to the police station to identify Brent's car. The little Toyota was smashed beyond recognition at the front. I looked at it, still unable to comprehend what had happened. That my son, our son, had been killed in that car. It was not sinking in.

The police officer was matter-of-fact. 'Come, I need to take you to the morgue to identify the boy.'

I turned, wanting support from Keulder. 'No, I can't, I can't take that.' But I knew it had to be done, however painful.

Seeing him lying there, wanting to hold him, comfort him, shake him awake. Wanting him to open his eyes and smile again. It was as painful as any moment in my entire life. Now, for the first time, I truly knew the meaning of pain.

Later we had to see a magistrate, and he needed to sign documents to certify the death. As the family involved we wanted to get to the truth of what happened. Brent had been driving home and as he came over the brow of a small incline he ran into the rear of a lorry. We had heard the truck had stopped in the road with no lights on. We wanted it fully investigated. But the magistrate called us in, Gloria, Natasha and me. He read from a police report that nobody was responsible and it was an accidental death.

He read the short police report and I asked, 'Is that all?'

He looked up, surprised at my question. 'Yes. You can go now.'

I was beginning to feel anger again. 'I want to know if the lorry had stopped. We heard this was possible.'

He looked again quickly at the report and concluded, 'There is no evidence of that. That's it, you can go.'

It was the same, impersonal harshness I had felt from the police officer.

The next moment I can remember was the following morning. The rest of the events at the police station have vanished from my memory. I sat in the lounge of our home. There were people everywhere. I went over and over the words of the policeman on the telephone. I kept replaying them, wondering why he was so cruel.

People came and spoke, shook me by the hand and offered their condolences. I heard none of them. I was in a different world.

I was back in 1967, on Robben Island, and I was telling Nelson the news about his son, Thembi. They were exactly the same age, twenty-three. Both died in car crashes. Thembi, for no apparent reason, went into the side of a road bridge. Brent went over the brow of a little incline and there was a lorry with no lights on the back. He drove into it.

I remembered riding my bike to the prison to break the news to Nelson. What had I said to him? Something like I can't tell you how deeply sorry I am because I don't know the depth of sorrow you are now feeling. But I had no real idea what I was saying then. I was merely being polite. I did not understand then, I could not. It is only now I could understand. Fully understand. It is painful. Mind-searing, heart-crushing, body-paralysing. Life-stopping.

As people came to the house I could see their mouths moving and I suppose I must have replied. I remember none of the words spoken. I knew it was important they should come because there were other members of the family, Gloria, Natasha, Zane, who needed the comfort of people. For me, I wanted to be left alone. I was retreating into the hole I had always dug for myself, the cavity where I was alone. Later I was told I had chased people out of the house, telling them I wanted to be alone. Friends, ministers, colleagues were told to get out. I remember none of it.

All the time I compared the death of Brent with the death of Thembi. I felt more sorrow then for Nelson than I had ever felt. How he must have suffered more because he was locked up, unable to find out what had happened, unable to be with the family he loved and unable to grieve properly. At least I was allowed those things.

But my mind kept returning to the first telephone call from the police officer at Klapmuts. That man should be taught a lesson in plain, common decency. To break news the way he did, was, I believed, inhuman.

Brent had died on 23 March 1989. Although he had been working with me in the prison service for some years, and was close to Nelson, he was unsettled with the job and wanted to begin a new career. As with any boy, he loved cars and he bought a Beetle which he loved. The 'Volksie', as he called it, was his and when he resprayed it and put on new wheels, it looked great.

The night of the accident he came home to Victor Verster and said he was heading into Cape Town to see his girlfriend. Was it okay to take Gloria's Toyota because the Volksie's lights were not so good; it was a long drive and he planned to be home late. It was something he did maybe once or twice every week. No problem. During the evening I slumped in front of the television, tired from a day at the farmhouse. I had been asleep maybe two hours when the phone call came.

Later, much later, I'm not sure when, Keulder told me I must do what I had to do, to organise the funeral, and not to worry about returning to work.

There were many people who attended the funeral. Keulder said Gloria was not to prepare any food, the officers' mess would handle that. Afterwards the commissioner of prisons, General Willemse, called. He had been, at one time, a commanding officer on Robben Island and had known all three children from an early age. He spoke for more than two hours and I know that he knew he was speaking to a blank wall. Just before he left his voice changed and he said something which did penetrate the fogginess.

'Greg, I am not telling you to get back to work, but I am telling you now you have to start again. You must keep busy.'

The depression was deep set. I felt like taking the gun, placing it against my head and pulling the trigger. The thoughts kept coming that if there was a God then this would not have happened. Brent had spent so much of his time bringing other young people to the church. Often, when he was working with Nelson, he would sit with his Bible and underline particularly significant passages. It is ironic that one of the last passages he underlined in pencil was 'my time on earth is over'.

Anger filled my mind. I was talking to God. 'How could you allow a person who is doing good work for you to die? What about the millions of scum in jails? The millions of scum on the streets? If you want one dead, why not take one of them? Why take one like Brent who is actually working for you?' I was certain there was no God, there could not be. I said it aloud many times.

One of those dark days an envelope arrived. I recognised the distinctive handwriting as Nelson's. It was a letter which, more than any words that had been said to me, went right to my heart. He had been there and now he was offering words that would help me.

I was deeply shocked to hear of the tragic death of your beloved son, Brent, and on behalf of myself and family I send you our sincerest sympathy. Few things are as painful as an invisible wound. But I hope you and your family will be comforted by the knowledge that Brent was loved and respected by almost all those who came into contact with him. Once again, our deepest condolences.

He used the phrase 'few things are as painful as an invisible wound'. It made sense, and I knew he understood. He suffered with Thembi.

Following the visit of General Willemse came another senior officer, Brigadier Kilder. He was more brutal. 'You can take as long as you like before you return to work, but I'm telling you now, that if you don't start doing something you will go down the drain.'

I knew he was right. That night, six days after the funeral, I said to Gloria, 'I am returning to work. You don't need me here moping around. You have your friends and family. I need to get my mind focused elsewhere.'

When I went to the farmhouse I would normally open the office annexe, then open the back door of Nelson's house and go into the kitchen and see where he was. He would have already been up for some time and would have exercised and showered. Most times he was sitting reading or writing. Occasionally he would still be in bed, and I would playfully ask him if he was getting old and lazy. This usually caused him a little annoyance because Nelson took great pride in his regime and he would jump up quickly, trying to make up for the lost hours of the morning.

That first morning back I went to the office annexe and stayed there. Jack Swart came in and was surprised to see me.

'Hello, Greg, are you coming over this morning? I've got the pot on for tea. Do you want some?'

I excused myself and said I needed to catch up on paperwork and sort out what had been happening since I left. I was anxious to keep busy.

The buzzer between the main house and the annexe sounded. It was the indication I was wanted in the house.

As I went in, Nelson was standing, his face set, his eyes looking at mine. He just stood there, examining my eyes, assessing me. The bright morning sunshine was flooding through the windows and I couldn't be certain if the glistening in his eyes was from tears or not.

'Come, my friend, let's walk in the garden.' He led me by the arm, slowly, carefully. 'Let's go to the rose garden and into our little pathway.'

If he had not spoken, if he had preferred to keep quiet, I would have gained much from his silence and his presence. As he walked he was giving me strength and beginning to open my mind. I saw the flowers again as he bent to touch them. The fragrance of the bushes began to penetrate the fog.

We walked on to the grass and he began speaking to me. 'It has happened. It is a terrible thing. I am feeling for you and I am feeling for Gloria and Zane and Natasha.'

He took my hand. It was not a handshake, more a touching, a physical contact. He held it for some time. 'Let's remember the good times we both had with Brent. He was a wonderful child and I have a picture of him sitting here reading his Bible, discussing passages with me. He cared, and in a situation like this, that is a quality that is so rare.

'If there can be any consolation from this terrible thing it is that you know where he is now.' I could not speak, my voice was choked. We sat down beneath the big tree. It was one of our favourite spots for rest and thought.

The sun was rising higher and he spoke quietly. 'People will tell you time heals. Those are empty words but empty only in a sense that those people do not know what they are talking about because they have not gone through the experience. Until the day you die, you will remember and feel this pain. At times, without even knowing it, suddenly you are thinking of him and you will be hurting again.'

He repeated the words he used in his letter. 'Time will heal physical wounds, inflicted wounds, yes, but time will not heal the invisible wounds. People will mean well when they offer kind words, but they cannot know.

'Sometimes, even now, I think of Thembi. In some ways I never stop thinking of him. I dream of him as a child when we used to play. Sometimes I dream of him and he changes, he becomes Makgatho . . .' His voice trailed off.

Over the next weeks we often sat in the garden, speaking of our children and it became a cleansing process, one of ridding the anger. At times I mentioned the callousness of the police officer and the magistrate, and we equated it with the reaction of the prison authorities who refused Nelson the opportunity of attending the funeral and being with his family. He spoke to me continuously, a therapist working to bring me back to reality. He was like a father, closer, perhaps. He spoke to me as a father would speak to a son. Each day we talked of what had happened, but gradually less and less. We talked of positive things and how important it was to return to work and keep busy.

He said, 'Remember on Robben Island you spoke to me when Thembi died.' I nodded, thinking that I had said words but I could not have understood their full meaning.

He continued. 'Well, many people are saying the same things to you now. They care now as much as you did then. It is important you remember that they mean the words even though they cannot feel them.'

I began to listen and remember the kind words that were offered. I was no longer dismissing them as empty rhetoric. There were many calls, from ANC people I had never known, from people I had known in prison, people in government. The lesson Nelson had taught me was that they all were feeling a little of my pain. It helped.

Chapter 32

The thaw

Every person who came to the farmhouse at Victor Verster remarked on its comfort and the beautiful surroundings. Except Winnie. Special arrangements were made to allow her to stay in the house whenever she wished. I personally telephoned Mr Ayob and told him, 'The minister has said that Winnie can stay in the house anytime. All she needs to do is let me know to allow us to get extra food, or anything she would like.' The advocate said this was a kind offer but he would need to discuss it. I didn't know if he was referring to the ANC or to Winnie herself.

Mr Ayob called back two or three days later and said simply, 'Winnie says she will not stay. She says that while all the other ANC people are in prison she could not stay in the house. She says the moment they are all accorded the same type of accommodation as her husband, then she will consider staying. Until then, no way.'

I informed Nelson of the conversation and he merely shrugged. When Winnie first called she was very aloof about the place, playing her role as the person who did not care about the house or its surroundings, but was more interested in the fact her husband was still being held.

She arrived with Zindzi, granddaughter Zondwa, and grandson Gadaffi. As I drove them into the farmhouse, Zindzi was looking all around, clearly impressed by the surroundings.

'Wow, look at this place, it's beautiful,' she cried. 'If you must spend time in prison then this is the place to be.'

Winnie was sitting in the back seat staring straight ahead. Determined not to be impressed. The garden gates were locked and I apologised, telling them we'd have to enter by the back door. Winnie sniffed a little. She looked straight ahead, refusing to let her eyes stray to the garden or the swimming pool. Gadaffi, who was then about six or seven, was running everywhere, thrilled by the sight of the pool.

As I led Winnie and Zindzi into the house, Gadaffi saw Nelson and rushed forward. '*Tata Omkhulu*,' he shouted as he flew into Nelson's out-stretched arms. It was the traditional greeting for a grandfather. Nelson's face was beaming.

'Come, let me show you the house they call my prison,' he said. Winnie sniffed some more and refused to say anything complimentary. I had witnessed Winnie's different faces over the years and knew that she was quietly impressed with the house and its facilities, but she was damned if she was going to praise the prison of the hated regime.

She was on her high horse and nothing, including Nelson, was going to shift her. Zindzi, however, was taken by the house, squealing at the sight of so much luxury in a prison. Gadaffi, on the other hand, wanted one thing: to leap into the pool.

Nelson asked me, 'Is it okay if he goes in?'

I was a little perplexed. 'I have to confess that I forgot to tell you something. I was told by Pretoria that when your family comes here, it does not matter who, if they hurt themselves in any way, slip, break an arm or a leg or whatever and emergency medical attention has to be given to them, or if they have to be removed to a hospital at all, the cost will be yours. You will have to pay. I'm sorry, but that's the rules they are imposing on you. So if you decide Gadaffi should be allowed into the pool he becomes your entire responsibility, the onus is on you.'

Nelson smiled, understanding the bureaucracy of Pretoria and how the rules and regulations worked. 'Let him swim, eh?' I nodded.

Whenever Gadaffi called, which was frequently as one of Nelson's favourite grandchildren, he was allowed to swim in the pool. If it was too cold, as in winter time, Swart would hire him a child's video to watch while the adults were busy discussing important decisions or family matters.

Whenever Swart knew the grandchildren were calling, he would prepare cool drinks and bake little cakes and sweets. He always left them on a plate in the kitchen, telling the children to help themselves whenever they wanted anything. The children often tried to wind Jack Swart around their fingers and would ask for his sweet goodies. Swart always obliged, until one day Nelson admonished him, complaining the children were not eating their lunch because of the sweets they had received from him.

Just before Christmas I was informed there was to be a group of special visitors that day: Walter, Raymond, Andrew and Kathy from Pollsmoor. I was uncertain whether or not to tell Nelson about their visit, rather to make it a pre-Christmas surprise. I eventually decided to let him in on the secret, knowing he would want to prepare for the visit by doing some writing.

Walter, the oldest of the ANC men held in prison, walked around the house as in a daze. 'My, my, my, this is some prison.' The four from Pollsmoor were all greeted with hugs and handshakes by Nelson, who took pride in showing them the house. They arrived at 7.40 in the morning and stayed until mid-afternoon. But this was not a meeting to admire the surroundings of the farmhouse; these men had serious talking to do. Even over the lunch prepared by Swart they were deeply engaged in strategy. At the heart of their discussions were the main areas which had prevented Nelson and the ANC moving forward with the government. There was still disagreement over the ANC's armed struggle, over the issue of majority rule and over the role that the South African Communist Party would play in any solution to the country's divisions. The discussions were often intense although never angry.

At the end of the meetings as the four Pollsmoor men were leaving Walter began playfully to pull Nelson's leg. 'My, Madiba, now you no longer stay in prison, but in a five-star hotel, complete with room service.'

Nelson, always vulnerable to criticism that he had taken the soft option, turned around to face his older, respected colleague and friend, alarm written across his face. Walter was smiling broadly and clasped him again by the hand and added, 'No, man, this is wonderful, this is the way it should be.'

The rest of that day Nelson was deeply engrossed in writing, and said he did not want an evening meal.

The next day was Christmas Eve, and Nelson asked if he could take a walk around the prison farm; it had been some time since he had seen animals. He'd heard about the orchards and gardens, and wanted to see them for himself. I took him in the car, stopping at each section, the orchards, the chicken farm, the piggery, the formal gardens, the vegetable sections, the various citrus areas. At each he became closely interested in the output and was impressed that the produce from Victor Verster was actually used to feed a number of prisons in the Cape Town area.

Christmas Day was a family affair at Victor Verster as it was in most places around the world. At the farmhouse it was the first family gathering Nelson had experienced for twenty-six years. Winnie and Zindzi and the children, Gadaffi and Zondwa, arrived for lunch, carrying their wrapped presents. In the weeks running up to Christmas Nelson had consulted Swart and me about presents for the children, insisting they receive books. For Winnie and Zindzi it was boxes of chocolates, the biggest boxes we could find. I drove into Paarl and visited a number of stores, asking which books would be suitable for children at various ages. The wrapping paper he left to me and I bought the brightest I could find.

As Winnie arrived she handed me a beautifully wrapped present. She wished me a Merry Christmas and said the present had been sent to me from Adelaide Tambo, Oliver's wife. It was a gesture so typical of Adelaide because she had heard in a letter from Nelson how Victor Verster always turned cold in June and July and how temperatures plummeted to zero. At the time, Oliver, the grand old man of the ANC, a man who held a special place in Nelson's heart, was still exiled in Switzerland. Adelaide sent the sweater, one for me and another for Nelson, telling us in a letter that they would keep us warm.

I was completely overwhelmed by the gesture. It meant more to me than anything I had received for a long time.

The sweater was a beautifully crafted Swiss type, filled with colours and Alpine scenery. Unlike previous offers of presents, such as the cars and clothes made in the preceding years, this clearly was not an attempt to bribe. This was sheer friendship, but I still had to report it to the prison authorities. Later I was to ask the commissioner of prisons, General Willemse, if I could accept the sweater, explaining to him how it had been sent to me by Adelaide Tambo.

At the time of asking, after Christmas, Willemse hesitated and said he would take advice on the matter and get back to me. Several weeks later, during a visit to the farmhouse, he pulled me to one side and said, 'Greg, about the sweater, I have taken advice from above and we'd rather you did not accept it.' I was angry that such a friendly gesture, meant in the true spirit of Christmas, had been so badly misread by Pretoria. I explained it to Nelson, who smiled and said, 'If that is the way they feel, why worry, just leave it. Adelaide will understand their intransigence.'

Early in the New Year the guards around the farmhouse asked if they could use the braai to cook meat. It was agreed. The smell of the cooking attracted Nelson outside and as he sniffed the air he wanted to know what was going on. When Swart told him he asked how it was done. Over the next few hours Swart taught Nelson how to cook chops and sausages.

Nelson's verdict was, 'This is the best meat I have tasted for many, many years. It is out of this world.' The braai was just to one side of the pool so Swart got some proper barbecuing wood and began to show Nelson how to season the meat with salt and garlic flakes to ensure the meat did not burn.

About a week later Winnie and Zindzi visited on the Sunday and Nelson announced upon their arrival that he was going to braai. The very use of the Afrikaans word caused Winnie to look at him in horror.

'What do you know about braaing?'

'This was one of my latest classes,' Nelson laughed. 'Just like the corn beer I can now brew. I have become very domesticated.'

In mid-January the four Pollsmoor members of the High Organ called again to discuss the memorandum Nelson planned to send to the State President. The group was anxious that Mr Botha be made aware of their direct views, that they were not terrorists, but were reasonable men who wanted a true democracy in South Africa.

In the memorandum eventually dispatched to Mr Botha, Nelson wrote: '*I am disturbed, as many other South Africans no doubt are, by the spectre of a South Africa split into two hostile camps, blacks on one side and whites on the other, slaughtering one another.*' He wrote that to avoid the slaughter taking place and to prepare the groundwork for negotiations, he would address the three demands made of the ANC by the government as a precondition to direct negotiations. These were the renunciation of violence, breaking with the South African Communist Party (SACP) and abandoning calls for majority rule.

On the question of violence, he said, the problem was not so much a refusal of the ANC to renounce it, rather, '*The truth is that the government is not yet ready ... for the sharing of political power with blacks.*' On the casting aside of the SACP, which he said was not under ANC control, Nelson continued, '*Which man of honour will desert a life-long friend at the insistence of a common opponent and still retain a measure of credibility with his people?*' The question of majority rule by the government was, he added, a poorly disguised attempt to preserve power and he suggested a more realistic approach should be sought. *'Majority rule and internal peace are like the two sides of a single coin, and white South Africa has to accept that there will never be peace and stability in this country until the framework is fully applied.'*

At the end of the letter Nelson also offered his views on a framework for negotiations. *'Two political issues will have to be addressed: firstly, the demand for majority rule in a unitary state; secondly, the concern of white South Africa over this demand as well as the insistence of whites on structural guarantees that majority rule will not mean domination of the white minority by blacks. The most crucial tasks which will face the government and the ANC will be to reconcile these two positions.'*

Nelson then proposed that the reconciliation be conducted in two stages, the first being a discussion to create the appropriate climate for negotiation, the second being the actual negotiations themselves. He concluded, *'I must point out that the move I have taken provides you with an opportunity to overcome the current deadlock and to normalise the country's political situation. I hope you will seize it without delay.'*

Just when it seemed, from the tone of the Nelson's letter, that much was about to change in the country, the worst possible scenario occurred: P. W. Botha suffered a stroke. While it did not entirely incapacitate the President, it did seriously weaken him, and according to the members of his own cabinet, made him even more irascible. In February Botha unexpectedly resigned as head of the National Party, but retained his position as State President. This was, therefore, a unique position in the country's history: in the South African parliamentary system, the leader of the majority party automatically becomes the Head of State. Botha was now Head of State, but not his own party. In many quarters this was seen as one of the first positive steps towards reconciliation with Botha, indicating he wanted to be above his own party politics in order to begin a negotiation process which would eventually bring about true change within the country.

In those early days of February 1989 Mr Ayob called at the house on three occasions between the 4th and the 10th and on each occasion stayed at least six hours at a time, discussing many legal implications of the negotiation process. On each occasion he stayed for lunch, although he hardly touched any of Swart's food.

At the same time as Nelson's approach to Botha the mood throughout the country began to change, fired by political violence and a campaign of defiance, as well as an increase in international pressure on the government.

Across the country a series of hunger strikes by political detainees resulted in the release of 900 people held under the harsh laws. Outside the country Oliver Tambo was working on the attitudes of major powers such as the United States, Soviet Union and Great Britain. It led to an increase in sanctions against South Africa. While these increases had little impact on the daily lives of white South Africans, it did have a psychological effect in making them feel even more isolation at a time when the world's barriers were beginning to crumble.

In late February Nelson told me he would be visited by 'a very important white man'. When I saw him making special preparations, I began to wonder who it could be. Possibly even the president?

The man was Lazar Sidelsky. This was a name that had featured in many of Nelson's stories of his younger life. Advocate Sidelsky was one of those rare breed of people who saw not the colour of a man's skin, but the tone of his commitment. He was the white lawyer who had articled Nelson at a time when, by doing so, he had put his own career and the very existence of his legal practice at risk. I knew there was an extraordinary bond of affection between these two men.

When Advocate Sidelsky arrived he was frail. Normally when visitors arrived Swart would attend to tea or coffee. But for this visit the two men, master and pupil, were left alone to remember their former days together. The visit lasted less than an hour, but as I watched Nelson's face, I could see the respect and affection he had for this old man. I could also see his own sadness because it was clear Advocate Sidelsky was close to death.

Later Nelson told me, 'It was a visit that was as marvellous as the day I was able to hold my own daughter Zeni for the first time.'

In mid-March Nelson asked me to arrange a visit from officers of the First National Bank. He was getting a monthly pension of 4000 rand paid into the First National Bank in Paarl by Mr Ayob. It was a pension which was determined by the ANC to allow Nelson to purchase anything he needed. I had signing rights over the account and the way it would work is that whenever Swart went shopping to buy extra groceries, I would accompany him and would pay whatever was extra with Nelson's cheque book. If

Nelson needed cash, often to give to his granddaughter Nandi, I would go to the bank and see a Mrs Englebrecht who knew me and she would cash a cheque. Every time I cashed money or wrote a cheque I would take an itemised bill back and insist he checked everything.

Nelson wanted to see the bank management because his money was in an account where it was failing to gain interest. So Mrs Englebrecht and a colleague visited him in the farmhouse and discussed how he could best use his money for investment purposes.

Through the next two months the visits and meetings increased to an almost daily routine at the farmhouse. From his legal advisers such as Mr Ayob and Mr Omar, to family, grandchildren Nandi, Mandla and Ndaba, to government representatives, Kobie Coetsee, head of National Intelligence Dr Niel Barnard, to Natal area ANC organisers, Harry Gwala and Linda Zama, to paramount chief Mtirara, to friends, Fatima and Ismael Meer, Yusef and Amina Cachalia and on an increasing frequency, Walter Sisulu from Pollsmoor.

On 4 July General Willemse arrived and called me into the office annexe.

'Tomorrow, Greg, will be one of the most momentous days in the history of this country.' I waited for him to continue. 'We are taking Mandela to see President Botha.'

With that he turned and went into the farmhouse to inform Nelson, asking him to be ready to depart at 5.30 in the morning. The general said the visit was a courtesy call.

Nelson was very practical about the forthcoming visit and said that while he was looking forward to it, he should have a suit for the occasion. General Willemse nodded. Just before he walked out of the door, he turned and said he needed to know Nelson's blood type. 'Just in case anything untoward should happen tomorrow.' Typically pessimistic, I thought.

This last request caused some mirth with us because we knew that Nelson's complete medical history, including his blood type, was available by a simple telephone call to Tygerberg Hospital.

I joked with Nelson, 'Perhaps *die Groot Krokodil*,' the Great Crocodile as Botha was known, 'will be after your blood.'

Within two hours of the general's departure a tailor arrived to measure Nelson for his suit. By mid-afternoon a complete outfit, suit, shirt, tie and shoes were ready. But by then Nelson was already deep in study, going through papers and his own files,

338

ensuring he was as prepared as he could be for the meeting. At times he sat in the lounge, at other times he strolled around, obviously practising what he would say, almost as if he was an attorney in a courtroom addressing a jury.

Next morning I was in the office annexe long before dawn, along with Major Marais and a driver. In the kitchen I made some tea while Marais inspected Nelson as he stood in the lounge in his new suit. He was shaking his head and joking, 'Ag, man, your tie looks like a hangman's noose.'

Nelson was calm. 'Major, I have to say that I have not had much use for ties in prison and, therefore, it might be that I have lost the art of tying them.'

Marais joked, 'Ja, and you have had no use for a hangman's noose either.'

Marais loosened the tie and took it off, then standing behind Nelson went about retying the tie in a perfect Windsor knot. He stood back and admired his handiwork.

'There. Perfect, man. If the President has any complaints about your dress you tell him at least the tie is perfect.'

We drove from Victor Verster to the home of General Willemse, who was already standing at his front door, waiting for our arrival. He ushered us all inside and was very pragmatic. 'First we must breakfast. A man cannot negotiate on an empty stomach. I don't suppose Greg or Swart have even made you a cup of tea this morning.'

The convoy to Tuynhuis, the official presidential office in Cape Town, was just three cars, but we swept straight into the underground car park without being seen. I remained behind as Nelson marched off with the general to a meeting which was to become one of the most significant in the country's history. At that time we all felt a tingle that this was, perhaps, the moment of breakthrough.

Although I was not at the meeting I heard later how 'die Groot Krokodil' had invited Nelson to sit down and enjoy tea with him. Nelson, as prepared as he could be, was also aware that he should handle this meeting with the skills of a master diplomat. P.W. had a reputation as being as stubborn, belligerent and difficult as they come. His reputation was that of an Afrikaner who would not talk to blacks, rather would lecture and instruct them.

I was told later how Nelson, far from taking the initial opportunity to discuss the many difficult matters which had engaged his mind these last few months, instead had sat down to drink tea and discuss history and culture. He spoke of an article he had recently read in an Afrikaans magazine about the 1914 Afrikaaner Rebellion and how they had occupied towns in the Free State. Nelson turned the article to an analogy of the ANC struggle. The meeting continued analysing this aspect of history before Nelson turned his mind to an issue which he wanted to raise. The tension rose as he asked the President to release unconditionally all political prisoners, including himself. It was the one moment when Botha shook his head and replied simply, 'Mr Mandela, I am afraid that is a request I cannot accede to.'

Before concluding the hour-long meeting, both Nelson and the President agreed upon a form of words which could be used publicly should their meeting become public knowledge. It was left as a bland statement which said no more than there had been a meeting over tea when the subject of promoting peace in South Africa was discussed.

When Nelson returned to the car his face was beaming, and although he said little on the drive back to Victor Verster, he had an aura which spoke volumes: he had achieved some sort of breakthrough.

On 18 July, on his seventy-first birthday, there was a birthday party which virtually made up for the twenty-six he had missed celebrating over the years of incarceration. Every member of the Mandela clan was present. It was the first gathering of all the family, from Nelson and Winnie through to the children and grandchildren. Each brought him a present, socks, toiletries, shirts and ties. Swart spent two days just preparing all the food for the forty or so people who arrived at the farmhouse. Later Nelson was to tell him, 'That was the finest meal we have ever had.'

One of Nelson's favourite grandchildren was Gadaffi, Zindzi's son. He was a boisterous child who enjoyed the farmhouse. The guards outside in the towers and in the field were a source of constant amusement. One day I heard one of the guards calling for the senior officer to 'please come quickly and sort out this child'. The guard was atop one of the towers, so I asked him to descend to explain the problem. By this time Nelson had joined us to see what the commotion was about.

I asked the guard to tell us what was wrong. The guard looked at me, glanced at Nelson and said not to bother, it was not a problem.

I insisted, telling him that if he was using his radio to summon help, he must have had a problem.

Well, the guard said, Gadaffi was baring his backside at him, slapping it and shouting rude things at him.

'I am getting fed up with this because I am here protecting him and I don't need him being rude.'

Nelson and I were struggling not to laugh out loud. As Nelson said he would speak to Gadaffi, I reassured the guard that it would not happen again.

Inside the house Nelson became the grandfather and pulled Gadaffi to his side. For the next fifteen minutes he gave him a talking to about the importance of being polite and the importance of not being rude. It was a lecture which affected Gadaffi because he never again bared his backside to a guard.

The friendship between Nelson and I became cemented through our days sitting together, either in the farmhouse or on the patio. Inevitably, we both took a closer interest in one another's children, and eventually took active roles in helping each other.

At that time my daughter Natasha was attending Stellenbosch University, and on virtually a daily basis Nelson would ask how she was progressing.

He had a constant theme. 'She must study hard because without studies you are nothing.'

On one of these days Natasha came home and complained she was having trouble with a statistics course. In conversation I mentioned it to Nelson that she hated this subject and was considering dropping it.

He became immediately aggravated. 'No, she must not, that will be entirely the wrong thing for her to do.' I was surprised at how angry this apparently small situation had made him.

He instructed me, in his now increasingly fatherly fashion. 'You go home and tell that young lady that she must stick it out. It doesn't matter how unpleasant she finds the subject, she must work at it. And if she doesn't, you tell her that one of these evenings I will come home with you and have words with her as an uncle would. She needs that advice.'

Although he finished by joking a little, I knew he was very serious about the matter.

Within a week he had arranged through the ANC to have a book sent to him for Natasha, on ways to help study statistics. When I gave it to Natasha she was stunned, that someone like Nelson had taken the trouble to consider her statistics. When she later came to take her exam she got seventy-nine per cent.

Nelson became like a godfather to Natasha; he seemed to adopt her, as he has so many who are close to him, as someone he would care for. It was a very African thing, that although he is not officially her godfather, he took it upon himself to care for her and always ask about her welfare and studies.

The entire subject of education was one which was always a hobby-horse for Nelson, one in which he fervently believed. And it was how I became even more closely involved with his family, returning the favour he had shown to Natasha.

On many occasions members of his family, perhaps Zindzi or a granddaughter, would write or call me to say they needed money for boarding-school, or needed money for books or needed money for exam fees or for one thing and another. For Nelson to reply would take time so I would initially contact Mr Ayob and arrange for money to be sent from Nelson's bank account to the child requesting the money.

There was one occasion when Makgatho wanted to get into a good boarding-school in Durban, where he could finish his education. I had to arrange all the school fees and details.

On another occasion there was a problem with Rochelle Ntirara, who was the daughter of a member of the Mandela extended family. Nelson called her his grandchild although in a strict Western sense, she was not. She was one of the children Nelson helped.

Rochelle was sent to Waterford School in Swaziland, a boarding-school where Mandla was studying. Everything was going well until one day Mandla phoned that Rochelle had left school. This shocked Nelson.

He turned to me. 'Mr Gregory, we must find out where she is and what has happened to her.'

I was perplexed. 'Nelson, how on earth can I do that? The school is in Swaziland and I am here in Cape Town. Shall I go up and sort it out?'

Nelson considered the situation for several minutes. 'Telephone Mr Dabulamanzi who is the Minister of Education in Swaziland and ask if he can help.'

I got on the phone that evening to Mr Dabulamanzi and explained what had happened, that Rochelle had vanished from school and Nelson was extremely worried about her. He said he would investigate.

By the next day he called back and said Rochelle had left school and had taken all her clothes with her. But, he added, she was still in Swaziland. He found out she was working as a croupier in the Swaziland Sun. I thanked him and said I would relay the message to Nelson.

He was furious, although a little confused. 'What is a croupier?'

I said I knew little about gambling but that it was the person who shuffled the cards.

'Man, this can't be, this can be dangerous.'

I continued, 'Mr Dabulamanzi has also asked me to tell you that for a young girl, this is a very dangerous course to take. She is only seventeen, and is vulnerable because this place attracts wealthy guys from all over. They turn up with rolls and rolls of money and for young girls this can be a big temptation. He said the danger of slipping into drugs and prostitution was high.'

Nelson was upset and asked if I could contact his old friend, Dr Nthato Motlana, in Johannesburg.

'Tell him I want Rochelle in Johannesburg by tomorrow,' he instructed. 'Even if they have to abduct her.'

The next afternoon Dr Motlana telephoned me to say they had Rochelle in Johannesburg. But before being returned to Waterford School, she was brought to Victor Verster to face Nelson.

The meeting, in mid-October, lasted all day and Nelson sat quietly in the corner talking with this very pretty young woman. Although he never raised his voice, I could see the seriousness in Nelson's face, gesturing with his hands and instructing her. He gave her the same lecture he had given Nandi on the dangers of prostitution and drugs and AIDS. The end result was Rochelle* apologised and returned to school.

There was also another problem that developed with Nandi, one of Nelson's favourite grandchildren, the daughter of his dead son Thembi. She planned to study at the University of Cape Town, but for one reason or another her marks were not quite good enough to qualify her for the social studies course and they refused to take her. One day when Nandi was visiting she told Nelson her problem.

After she left Nelson called me in and said he had a problem and he needed my help.

'Nandi's marks are not good enough to get into UCT,' he said.

---

* Note: Rochelle Ntirara was the mystery woman who was beside Mandela throughout the 1995 visit of the Queen to South Africa.

'We must find a way to get her in. She must go, I want her to go. I will pay all fees if necessary.'

Nelson and I sat deciding how we could handle it best. I decided that the most suitable course of action was for me to go and see the Rector of the University, Dr Saunders. I went and explained the situation and he said he would look at the situation. He called back and said that, although Nandi's marks had not been good enough in her matric exams, she could write a supplementary exam which could make up her marks.

I then had to arrange with Nandi for her to study for the exam and take the test. The result was that Nandi gained a very high mark and she reapplied to UCT and was admitted.

It might well have been special treatment because she was Nelson Mandela's granddaughter, but it also exposed the gap in the system, that there was a possibility of sitting a supplementary exam to get into university.

Within three weeks, in August 1989, there was a shock when Botha went on television to announce his resignation as State President. The following day F. W. de Klerk was sworn in as acting President and at the same time he affirmed his commitment to change and reform.

The appointment of Mr de Klerk was viewed in many quarters, certainly among the ANC ranks, as merely a continuation of the past. The new President was seen as a party man who had never given any hint of being a man of visionary reform. As education minister he had maintained the old apartheid stance by attempting to keep black students out of white universities. I know that from the moment he came to power, Nelson began to study the man in close detail.

In his inaugural speech the new President said his government was committed to peace and that it would negotiate with any group that was committed to peace. They were words which had been used in the past to promise a new beginning, but had proved to be empty. But within days of the new President taking office, the first breath of the wind of change was felt. A march was planned in Cape Town to protest against police brutality. It was to be led by Bishop Tutu and the Reverend Allan Boesak. Under the previous regime of President Botha the march would have been banned and anyone defying the order would be subject to arrest. As a result, violence would have been inevitable. But de Klerk lived up to his inauguration promise to ease restrictions on political gatherings and permitted the march to take place, asking only that it remain peaceful. It went ahead without any hint of trouble.

The secret meetings with the negotiating committee continued despite the change in president.

On 10 October President de Klerk announced that Walter Sisulu, Raymond Mhlaba, Ahmed Kathrada, Andrew Mlangeni, Elias Motsoaledi, Jeff Masemola, Wilton Mkwayi and Oscar Mpetha were to be released from prison.

News of the release was broken to Nelson by Kobie Coetsee who called for a fifteen-minute visit with Gerrit Viljoen, the Minister of Constitutional Development. Viljoen, an expert in constitutional matters, had long since joined the secret talks which were headed by Coetsee and seemed to be the adviser on how best to bring the talks between all sides into a constitutional framework.

Within an hour of the announcement we had a surprise call from the front gate: Walter, Kathy, Raymond and Andrew had come to visit. I knew they would be excited and watched Nelson's face closely as he greeted them, embracing each and slapping backs. The five men who had been through so much together sat talking in the garden, beneath the large tree, with laughter and shouts the predominant sound. Andrew's booming voice could be heard from every corner of the prison telling Nelson, 'Ah, Madiba, if they release us, they must release you now. These are the final days.' The sentiment was felt by all, and, as they left, it was with the assurances that Nelson's release was at hand.

Within minutes of the four prisoners heading off, there was another group at the gate, this time Albertina Sisulu, Murphy Morobo and Cyril Ramaphosa.

The new President had kept his word, and a few days later the four men who had been held with Nelson both on Robben Island and in Pollsmoor were officially released in Johannesburg. Nelson watched their release on television and I could see the emotion and strain on his face. His eyes shone and his hands were clenched tightly as he saw his old comrades walk free.

'It will be your turn next,' I told him quietly. But even as I said it to him, there was a dark look in Nelson's face, something deeper was troubling him. He was not so certain that the release would be within days, despite de Klerk's demonstration of keeping promises. He did not want to talk about it, and I did not pursue it, knowing that unless Nelson talked about it voluntarily, it was a matter he wished to keep to himself.

Over the next week, there was hardly time to catch breath, never mind think about release. There were X-rays to be taken at the Tygerberg followed by a detailed examination by Professor de Kock at the hospital. Then a series of visits by large numbers of Nelson's family, as well as a delegation of seven visitors from the Transkei.

Although the meetings continued apace, there were many afternoons when Nelson wanted to simply relax in the garden. Unless he had a meeting after breakfast, he would sit in the garden in the shade of the tree and read every word of the newspapers. I usually took the chair next to him and read my own paper or book. Sometimes we spent all morning sitting together, without having said a word; we were comfortable in one another's company, not pressured into having to make conversation. It was a relationship of which Nelson once remarked, 'We are similar in many ways. We can both dive deep into our own personalities to deal with our own thoughts and concerns, yet float on the surface and be available when need be to tend to one another.'

On other occasions we would get into debate on the news of the day, say a strike or a march. Nelson, without going deeply into ANC policy, would say that these were all part of the struggle.

On my birthday, 7 November, Swart, Major Marais and I walked in with a tray for breakfast. Nelson looked up, a little surprised. He had been expecting his normal fishcakes, but I had planned something a little different, champagne. We four stood around the table swigging champagne, toasting the future.

In the evenings I began to take a regular evening walk, and often ended up back at the farmhouse, to call in on Nelson as I would an old friend. Whatever he was doing, reading, writing, watching television or listening to a debate on the radio, he would invite me in and we would sit and chat. I had stopped being the prison guard and was now the house guest.

During this period de Klerk began a dismantling of the entire apartheid jigsaw. He opened the beaches to people of all colours and announced that the Reservation of Separate Amenities Act was to be repealed. This was the act which, since 1953, had enforced what was known to everyone as 'petty apartheid'. This was segregating parks, theatres, restaurants, buses, libraries, toilets and other public facilities according to race.

In the first week of December Winnie and Zindzi spent a day in deep discussion with Nelson, followed by a meeting with Dullah

346

Omar. Then he had a two-hour meeting with two generals from the South African police, van der Merwe and Smit.

It had reached the stage where Mohammed was not allowed to go to the mountains; they were now coming to him. The agenda was clearly set: the release of Nelson Mandela was to take place – it was merely a question of when the government felt the time was best.

When, on 5 December, he was told by Kobie Coetsee that a meeting with de Klerk was set for 12 December, there was no surprise, just a degree of expectancy.

But before that, there were a number of groups Nelson had to see to seek their opinions about progress on the streets and in the factories. There was the United Democratic Front (UDF), the body created in 1983 which blossomed into a powerful organisation that joined more than 600 anti-apartheid groups. There was the Congress of South African Trade Unions (COSATU) as well as ANC delegates from a number of regions. There was Oscar Mpetha, Christmas Tinto, Trevor Menuel, Johnny Issal and Cheryl Carolus. Cyril Ramaphosa, then the general secretary of the powerful National Mine Workers' Union, joined a delegation that included former Robben Island prisoners including Terror Lekota and Tokyo Sexwale. The fame of Nelson's lunches, or banquets as Swart turned them into, had reached far and wide. Although no one ever actually invited themselves to lunch, when asked to stay to eat, a number said with some laughter, 'We are told this is a treat to behold.'

As well as the high-powered meetings, which I saw began to take their toll, with Nelson sleeping earlier each evening, there were many visits from family. His son and daughter-in-law Makgatho and Zondi called on two consecutive days, followed by a meeting with Walter and Albertina Sisulu, now re-united and the picture of happiness.

Immediately following the meeting with Walter and Albertina, Nelson sat down to draft a letter to the President. In it he repeated much of what he had said and written to his predecessor P. W. Botha. The subject was once again the talks between the government and the ANC, that the current conflict between both sides was draining the lifeblood of South Africa and that talks were the only way forward. He emphasised that the ANC would never accept any preconditions to talks, especially not the one sought by the government, the suspension of the armed struggle. By asking for 'an honest commitment to peace', the ANC readiness to negotiate, as expressed many times in the past by Nelson, was exactly that, 'an honest commitment'. The letter stressed that talks between the ANC and the government should take place in two stages. It also endorsed the ANC Harare Declaration of 1989, putting the onus on the government to eliminate any obstacle to negotiations which had been imposed by the government themselves. That included the release of all political prisoners, the lifting of all bans on restricted organisations and persons, the ending of the State of Emergency and the removal of all troops from the townships. The letter added that a mutually agreed ceasefire to end all hostilities ought to be the first priority of the day, for without that, no business or negotiation between the ANC and government could be conducted. The letter was sent to Mr de Klerk the day before the face-to-face meeting of the two men.

The following morning Nelson went to Tuynhuis once more, this time to meet de Klerk. It was the first of three meetings between the two men at the presidential residence in Cape Town.

Later Nelson was to remark that he was struck by de Klerk's willingness to listen to what he had to say and the fact that he did not argue. He even told Nelson, 'My aim is no different to yours.'

The question of Nelson's own release was also discussed, and here there was no room for compromise.

Nelson was emphatic that if by releasing him the government expected him to go out to pasture, they were sadly mistaken. He went on to say that if he were to be released into the same conditions under which he had been arrested, he would return to doing exactly the same things for which he had been held in prison for the past twenty-six years. He made an open statement that it would be best to lift the ban on the ANC and all other political organisations, to lift the State of Emergency, to release all political prisoners and to allow exiles to return. The suggestions, I was told, did not cause a flicker of de Klerk's eyebrows. He had expected them.

That evening Nelson returned to Victor Verster and there was a mood of optimism about him. He was almost carefree in his attitude, and as we sat in the lounge, his thoughts turned not to the events that day at Tuynhuis, but once again to his childhood. I took this to be a positive sign that he felt that a return to the outside world was close. I wondered that night if it was to be a special Christmas present from the government to him.

But, instead of planning his release, the days up to Christmas seemed to be filled with more meetings at the house than ever before. Cyril Ramaphosa was prominent in a number of delegations, sometimes numbering seven or more. On one occasion there were so many delegates from COSATU that we had to divide them into two groups, one before lunch, the second after.

Nelson chided Swart about this. 'I know this is just a clever ploy to avoid having to cook meals for everyone.'

In the weeks leading up to Christmas Day I was spending more and more time simply opening mail for Nelson, examining each item in case of a letter bomb attack. There were cards and letters from virtually every corner of the globe as well as thousands from South Africa. He was getting more mail per day than the rest of the inmates at Victor Verster put together. I was always worried about abusive letters, but in the tens of thousands there was not one. Nelson insisted that every letter which had a return address needed a reply. At first he wrote personally to each, but with the increasing number of meetings at the farmhouse, he was physically unable to handle it himself. Many he still replied to, those people he knew, but others he asked Winnie and Zindzi to handle for him, asking them to write that he had received the correspondence, but that it was not possible for him to reply in person.

The mail got so heavy that I was taking it home and sorting it, going back to the farmhouse in the evening to sort it, even sitting over lunch sorting it.

One day a registered letter arrived for him from the post office in Paarl. It was a large box filled with bottles from Switzerland. According to the label it was a herbal drink which claimed to cure all ailments from cold to arthritic pains. I sent one bottle to the laboratory to be checked for contents. The chemist returned the bottle adding on a slip of paper that he was uncertain about its origin, but it was certainly herbal and harmless. When I gave Nelson the box of eleven bottles he looked at me and asked about the twelfth bottle. When I told him we had checked it for poison he burst into laughter.

One day when opening the Christmas cards there was a particularly thick envelope with an American post-mark. As I carefully opened the envelope the contents began to play a tune and in a panic I threw it across the room. Nelson, who was sitting reading in a chair, looked up in surprise. As the envelope hit the floor the musical tune stopped, so I picked it up again. Inside was a novelty card which, when opened, played a tune. Nelson virtually cried with laughter at that.

Christmas Day was spent with Winnie, Zindzi and three

349

grandchildren. Again Jack Swart out-did himself, cooking a feast for Africa: turkey, duck, mutton, the lot. Presents were spread around, chocolates, clothes, toiletries.

On New Year's Day, Nelson had planned a return surprise of my champagne birthday party. As we stood toasting one another, he wished Swart and me a happy New Year adding, 'May you both go well.'

The cleaning of the house was carried out by short-term prisoners who were in jail for a month or two at the most. On one of the days I went in to have tea with Nelson and he was sitting ruminating.

'What is wrong?'

'I have a problem with the man who is cleaning the house.'

'What, tell me what it is, has he said anything, done anything?' I was anxious because the cleaner was under Swart's supervision and I was worried that he could have been a security risk.

'No, I can't say he said or did anything. I just have a feeling about him, and I can't put my finger on it.'

I said I would talk to the cleaner and see if he was harbouring any grudges.

The man had cleaned the house and was by then working in the garden, watering the plants and vegetables. In mid-afternoon Swart called him into the house to clean up part of the kitchen.

'What, again? I have already cleaned up after that dirty kaffir. Why must I clean it again? He's a kaffir and should clean it himself.'

I heard the conversation and grabbed the prisoner telling him that he was being returned to the main prison immediately. The man spat out his hatred and said he was pleased not to have to work in the house again.

Chapter 33

'This is not goodbye...'

I knew the end was coming when I watched F. W. de Klerk stand before Parliament on 2 February 1990 and begin the process of dismantling apartheid and lay the groundwork for a truly democratic South Africa. In one swift and dramatic speech he announced lifting the bans on the ANC, the Pan-African Congress, the South African Communist Party and thirty-one other illegal organisations. He agreed to the freeing of political prisoners for non-violent activities. He suspended capital punishment and lifted restrictions imposed by the State of Emergency. In his own words:

'The time for negotiation has arrived.'

The following morning I went to see Nelson. As I arrived shortly before breakfast I was anxious to see his face, to determine how he felt about de Klerk's speech. I knew better than to ask him directly, knowing he would not commit himself to a full answer. Still, a look at his face would tell me. I know I felt excited, but I wondered if he would either show his own feelings or even say anything. When I went into the house he was sitting in his room, his back turned to me, writing vigorously.

'Good morning, Nelson, howzit man?' He turned and I could see a tiredness on his face. I made a mental note to check the log to see when he had turned out his night-light.

'Good morning, Mr Gregory. I'm fine, thank you. How's the family today? How's Natasha? Any exam results yet?'

Same old Nelson, always interested in someone else, always inquiring with that genuine concern for another person, when surely this morning of all mornings his mind would be filled with the implications of de Klerk's speech.

I checked the log and he had not turned his light out until nearly 3.00 a.m. Clearly all was not well.

Later as we sat in the lounge I probed gently, 'They say you didn't turn the light out until late. Are you okay?'

The smile was reassuring. 'Yes, thank you for asking. I'm fine. I had many things to consider last evening and I fell asleep as they raced through my brain. It was in the middle of the night I awoke again and realised I had left the light on.'

But still, in his eyes and from the constant frown that day, I could see something was troubling Nelson. I wanted to sit and ask about the president's speech, but knew it was not the right time. It was several days before I began to realise the disquiet I had detected within Nelson centred on the fact that Mr de Klerk had not completely lifted the State of Emergency or ordered the troops out of the townships.

In the days that followed it became evident that the stage was set for the release. There was increased activity at the cottage. It was clear that the freedom committee made up of Kobie Coetsee, General Willemse, Fanie van der Merwe, Director General of Justice and Dr Niel Barnard, former head of the National Intelligence Service, had been carefully chosen. The first three men were all closely associated with the prison service so if talks with Mandela foundered or leaked to the press, they had a ready-made excuse that they were merely discussing prison conditions with him. Over the past few months the meetings with the group of four had increased and it was no surprise when, on the evening of 8 February, van der Merwe again called.

The two spoke for less than fifteen minutes before van der Merwe came outside to the verandah.

He called me over and motioned Major Marais to join us. His face was deeply set and serious.

'I have something to tell you both and I'm certain you will understand both the importance of keeping it strictly to yourselves, as well as the ramifications of it. Within a few days Nelson Mandela is to be released. You already know that tomorrow he is scheduled to see Mr de Klerk. Well, as soon as that meeting is out of the way, the release will take place. Naturally this is going to place a great deal of stress upon you both and I'm confident you can handle it.'

We stood there, beside his government car, taking in the full impact of his words. Nelson Mandela was to be freed. And I would end my long association with him. To one side was a white protea bush, already blooming. I wandered to one side and picked a flower, holding the national flower of my country up to the moonlight. Van der Merwe watched me carefully.

'Greg, are you okay?'

I nodded.

'Listen, man, you knew this day would come sometime. You knew that's why we brought him here to Victor Verster. Be glad for him that he's got what he wants.'

I couldn't speak at that moment, not from emotion, more from a sense of bewilderment and confusion. My head was spinning. Van der Merwe shook my hand and said, 'Greg, you will be in charge on the day. Good luck, man.'

The car disappeared slowly into the night and I stood there for some time taking in the full meaning of what was taking place. I was confused and dazed. My feelings were a complete mixture of elation and sadness. I wanted to rush into the house and embrace Nelson, knowing that this was what he had fought for all along. The long path he had chosen to follow, for the cause, for his people, for equality, was nearly over. I wanted to celebrate with him. On the other hand I began to take in the implications of my work with him ending, that my future was, once again, thrown into turmoil. I had spent twenty-four years guarding Nelson Mandela. What the hell else was there for me to do. I was still a young man, but was I now beginning the process which would one day lead to early retirement? Certainly that was the thought that flashed through my mind.

That evening I didn't even bother to go back into the house. I knew that Nelson would want to be alone with his own thoughts. I certainly wanted to be with mine. I locked the outer office and slowly walked home. At times the elation wanted to take over. I wanted to shout out aloud that at last the strife in the country would end; that boycotts and violence would end. So much of the violence, the shootings, the stealing, looting was all done in the name of the ANC. When a thief or killer was caught he said he was doing it for a political cause or for political reasons. When Nelson got out of here, I thought, he will get a firm grip on these people and peace will come.

It began to dawn on me that by releasing Nelson Mandela and taking such steps as lifting the ban on the ANC we really were in a new era. Nelson had maintained all along, from the time they offered to release him to live in the Transkei, 'My home is in Johannesburg. I will not be released from prison to be imprisoned in the Transkei. When you release me you do so without any conditions.' I knew he would stick to those principles for as long as it took, and I knew then he was being released unconditionally. I

353

followed through this thinking. So if the government was prepared to release Nelson, to lift the ban on the ANC, what more?
Would it lead to a coalition between the National Party and the
ANC? That was some distance away: the more I considered it, the
further away it appeared. How could they unite? There had been
too much bloodshed over the years to expect both sides to live in
harmony. But why else would they release Nelson? I couldn't
figure it out without coming back to the belief that it was because
the government wanted to end South Africa's role as the world's
pariah.

I also believed that Nelson could unite the country, and this
decision by the government showed that they, too, could be
flexible. They were saying they wanted a new start for everyone.
But selfishly my mind kept asking the question: what do I do now?
Where do I go? They'll have no use for me now, and I could
probably never go back to the normal role of a prison warder. That
night I was so confused. There was a panic inside my chest, a
feeling which had been increasing for some time now. I think it had
started back in Pollsmoor. I remember one day I had been going
down to see Nelson and as I walked back one of the doors slammed
behind me. I suddenly lurched and fell against the stone wall. I
could feel the walls closing in, crushing me. I don't know how long
I was against the wall, maybe seconds, maybe minutes. When I
came out of the panic attack I was soaked in sweat. It was
claustrophobia, the doctor said. The disease of the mind which was
effectively the death knell of a prison guard. 'Often happens,' he
said nonchalantly. 'Comes from too much stress, too much
pressure.' Again, this evening, I could feel the panic coming on.

I arrived home and Gloria asked why my face was flushed. 'It
must be the heat of the night. It is blerrie hot out there,' I said. I
knew it was important to keep my emotions under control that
evening, to retain the secret. I hardly slept that night, staring at the
bedroom windows, knowing that this was almost a repeat performance of the night before Nelson and I had first met.

Over and over in my mind I recalled telling Nelson, 'One day
you will walk the passages of Tuynhuis, the president's office. I
wonder how you will feel to be the state president, the first black
man to lead South Africa.' I could still hear his chuckle.

The following morning I was at the house earlier than usual. I
had been unable to sleep. The day was as bright and crisp as any I
had ever seen. It was as if the political changes that were sweeping
our country were literally causing a breath of fresh air.

As I entered the house Nelson was in the large bedroom, dressing casually. This morning he was slipping into a sweater, the morning chill catching him unawares.

'Good morning, Nelson, sleep well?'

'Yes, I'm fine, ready for today. How about you, how are you?' He had already made his bed. It was a routine he had slipped into over the past twenty-seven years. It was second nature. I sat on the edge of the bed and watched him dress, taking time over his hair.

He turned to face me, then stepped towards the bathroom.

I continued talking. 'Well Nelson, this is it, man. This is what you have waited for.'

He stopped and turned towards me, that old reassuring smile filling his face. 'Yes, this is it, we are here at last.'

As he stood in the bathroom I continued. 'Nelson, now you are going home, what will you do? Where will you go, man? I know that this country is changing now for ever, but what about you, what will you do?'

Nelson was standing in the bathroom, flossing his teeth, I'm sure for the second or third time that morning already. There was confusion in his voice when he replied, 'I can tell from your questions that you are feeling totally unsure about the future now. Well, I feel exactly the same as you do. I am so uncertain what happens now and where we go. The only definite aspect of all this is that I have this firm belief that we must always remember that we will be led. Both you and I, we are now in similar circumstances.'

Nelson didn't speak any further about who would do the leading, but I took his words to mean that the ANC National Executive would be the body who directed his future course, just as my future course was dictated by the prison service.

As he emerged from the bathroom I still sat on the edge of the bed and he laid a hand on my shoulder. 'You know, I am feeling exactly as you. I actually feel scared of what is going to happen.'

To hear this man talk of personal fear was unusual and it jolted me. I asked, 'Nelson, do you fear you will be killed after all these threats?'

He hesitated. 'No, just for the future. It is fine to plan and dream, another matter to carry out. Now we are in the position where all the planning will have to be turned into action.'

Typically, Nelson turned the conversation to my concern, to my future. He had known for some time now of my claustrophobia and asked what I planned.

'I think that when this is all over I will have to talk to the prison service about their plans for me. If they try and put me into the maximum prison I shall be forced to resign.'

Nelson laughed and added, 'Again you resign.'

I was being serious though, and told him, 'I would prefer to become a tramp on the streets rather than go back to the maximum prison. There I would suffer a heart attack.'

There was no further time to talk. We had an early morning appointment with Dr Loubser, a final medical check-up. The drive to the hospital was conducted in total silence; his mind was elsewhere and I, too, was deep in thought. We were also in a rush because we needed to be back at the house by 9 o'clock for a meeting with the ANC National Executive: Thabo Mbeki, Cyril Ramaphosa, Frank Chicane and Dullar Omar.

We also knew that he had an appointment that evening with Mr de Klerk, when the details of the release would be sorted out.

As we arrived at the hospital in Cape Town I turned around in the seat and said quietly, 'Nelson, I know I don't really have to tell you, but please don't mention tonight's meeting to Dr Loubser. Just act as if this is another routine visit. Don't mention meeting the National Executive later this morning and certainly not the meeting with the president. Dr Loubser is an astute person and he knows you long enough now to understand the significance of the meetings. It's not that we don't trust him, merely that we have to be very careful of this leaking out to anyone.'

Nelson simply nodded. I could see his mind was elsewhere, considering the future.

Going back to Victor Verster was a rush. I was informed on the radio that the National Executive had arrived at the front gate. We decided to take the rear road, Safari Road. As we settled back at the house I told Nelson I would go and fetch them, but emphasised, 'Remember, not a word; we don't want a leak. We'll do it the way we have always done it, nice and quietly.'

The meeting with the National Executive lasted nearly six hours as they sat around the lounge. Several times Swart took in coffee, tea and sandwiches. Much of the talk centred on Nelson being geared up for his release. It was not a case of if, but when it would happen. Already the local media, particularly the *Cape Times* and local radio stations, were playing a game of guessing on the release time. 'It's Now or Never,' they proclaimed in a headline.

By the end of the meeting I could see the strain on Nelson's face. He was frowning and the lines around his mouth were deeper set than ever. Initially the meeting with de Klerk was set for 8 o'clock, then by mid-afternoon was brought forward by two hours.

Nelson chose his grey charcoal suit and a striped tie. He was in a sombre mood as we drove to Tuynhuis to see de Klerk. As the door to the President's office opened, a smiling Mr de Klerk came forward and greeted Nelson, shaking him by the hand. As the door closed on the two, I was left outside, wondering if this was the final move in the game.

As usual, I waited at the end of the terrace. It was several hours later that I saw him coming out. I watched his face intently, straining to see if there was a tell-tale clue. Kobie Coetsee came out of the office with Nelson. They walked side by side towards the car which was surrounded by police officers. Normally Nelson and Coetsee would have been walking closer, talking and sharing a joke. But there was a tension between them. Both looked straight ahead, a wide gap between them, one on one side of the wide corridor, one on the opposite, almost as if they were trying to stay as far apart from each other as possible. There was more than a hint of the mood in Nelson's walk: he was unusually striding with some purpose, not walking casually. He wanted to get away as quickly as possible. He marched straight to the car, not stopping to shake hands or speak. Normally these two men were friendly to one another and every time I had seen them together there had been conversation and animation. Normally Coetsee and Nelson would have lingered a bit over saying goodbye, there would be hand-shakes and courtesies. Tonight there were none. Coetsee bade a clipped 'good night' while Nelson merely nodded his head. No handshake. The stifling humidity of the evening seemed to close in around us and intensify the heated atmosphere between both men. Before stepping into the car Nelson slipped off his suit jacket and folded it carefully, placing it on the seat beside him. As he climbed in I could see the hardness around his mouth and the coldness in his eyes. He was in a determined mood. My heart sank. They hadn't changed the plans, had they?

As we drove back to Victor Verster in silence his head was turned to the side. I was now very confused. Had they had a serious row? Had the President changed his mind at the last minute? Were they making demands of Nelson which would have compromised him? I had always considered that possibility, that having dangled the tasty bait of release before him, the government would try one last time for a compromise deal.

I was to learn later that de Klerk had offered to release Nelson the very next day. He told Nelson that a plane was already waiting at Cape Town to fly him to Johannesburg for the release. Preparations were already in hand to inform the world's press which had been speculating for weeks that the release was imminent.

I was also to learn that Nelson was emphatic that he would not be released the next day. Although he wanted to leave prison as soon as he could, to do so at short notice was, he felt, unwise. Nelson wanted a week's notice so that his supporters and the ANC organisation, in general, could make adequate arrangements. To rush into a release would cause chaos.

I know Nelson's refusal to be released the next day had surprised de Klerk. Nelson was caught between two stools but told the President that he had waited twenty-seven years to get out of jail; a further few days would not be too long.

Another problem had cropped up: where was the release to take place? For some reason, understood only by the government, they wanted it to be in Johannesburg. Nelson was insistent that any release would be from Victor Verster. I was later to feel there was a hidden agenda, because even before Nelson met de Klerk, I had been told by van der Merwe that when the release took place I was to handle it. And I was here in Cape Town.

By the time we arrived back at the prison house, it was already close to midnight. Swart had left supper in the microwave, but Nelson was more intent on contacting the ANC Release Committee, to discuss matters with them. As he walked around the lounge I watched his face closely. The strain was beginning to show. It was a weakness in the man, that he never had the classic poker face. To understand or predict the feelings of Nelson, one only had to look at his face. His eyes and mouth spoke volumes.

As he paced the room, his mind buzzing, he turned and said, 'I think tomorrow we will have a very heavy day. Let's get some sleep now, I am tired.'

Saturday the 10th started as a normal day, and at breakfast he was as cheerful and bright as he was most days. It was as if the shadows of the night before had been wiped out by the sunshine. He was raring to go and was immediately into a day-long session with the Release Committee. They lunched and talked, had tea and talked. Then they talked some more. Everyone was now in the know; the release date was the following day, Sunday the 11th.

I was in the office when I received a telephone call from the commissioner.

'Greg, you know what is happening?'

I chuckled, wondering if he was calling to ask me or tell me. 'Yes, sir, I know about the release. Tomorrow.'

The general was now back to formalities. 'I am to tell you that he is to be released at 10 o'clock military time. Not five minutes to ten or five minutes past ten. At 10 o'clock he must walk out of those front gates a free man. I don't want there to be any hitches. The world's media will be there. The eyes of the world will be on us tomorrow. Millions upon millions of people will be examining everything that occurs.'

I couldn't help but smile at the irony of it all. Through the past twenty-seven years the eyes of the world had been on us anyway, criticising us for holding Nelson Mandela because of his beliefs. There was never any concern then. But now, now that we were actually letting him go free the government was concerned about what the world thought about how we handled it. Strange values.

Throughout the day I checked the entire security arrangements, visiting every guard, ensuring they were alert. By late afternoon when the Release Committee were leaving I went into the house to see Nelson.

He was slumped in the chair in the corner of the lounge, his eyes closed, an empty tea cup at his side.

I walked over and as he opened his eyes, I inquired, 'Is it okay?' He nodded.

We remained still for some time before I asked rhetorically, one word. 'Tomorrow?' He nodded once more and closed his eyes.

That evening I again walked to the warders' compound of houses, wondering about the scene in the morning. I knew I had to be at the prison house long before dawn. This was going to be one hell of a busy day, even if it was the last.

Long before dawn I went to the front gate and was astonished at the gathering of media people. It was as if they had all gone into the do-it-yourself business, because everyone seemed to be carrying a ladder. There were more cameras on view than in the Nikon or Canon factory. It gave me a sense of just how big this event was going to be.

Back at the house the prison governor, Brigadier Keulder, arrived, carrying a thick sheaf of papers as well as a large admission book.

The governor came into the kitchen, but when I saw the official papers and documents, I suggested he stepped into the lounge. He placed them on the main table.

Keulder, all business-like, asked, 'Where is Mr Mandela?' I was just about to tell him that he had already gone, when I thought better of it. Keulder was not known for his sense of humour.

Swart said he was in his bedroom getting dressed. I said I would fetch him.

It was then shortly after 7 o'clock and, as I went in, Nelson was in the bathroom, combing his hair. He was already dressed in casual shirt and slacks. I told him the brigadier had arrived. He said he would be ready in a moment or two.

In the lounge I offered Keulder some coffee. We sat sipping the fresh coffee, waiting for Nelson to appear. He came in, all smiles, extending his hand to Keulder. 'Good morning, Brigadier, what brings you over this way?'

Keulder, as starchy as ever, stood up. 'Good morning, Mr Mandela. I am here to release you officially. Normally, as you know, a release is done by people from the reception office. But maybe Greg here has told you that I did not, and will not, allow anyone but those authorised to come to your house here. That's why I have come here this morning.'

Nelson nodded in appreciation, signing the release form. Keulder added his name and I signed as the official witness. I looked at my watch. It was exactly 7.48.

Officially Nelson Mandela was a free man.

Keulder, a stickler to the end, continued with his little speech. 'Mr Mandela, I am giving you a copy of this release form in case someone should arrest you for escaping. You have this copy as authentic proof of release.' I watched Nelson's eyes grow at this news and he could barely contain himself from laughing out loud. In the kitchen I could hear Swart coughing to cover up his own laughter. What idiot was going to arrest Nelson Mandela and accuse him of being an escapee? And especially after the publicity that this release was going to have.

Keulder said he knew others would be coming to visit this morning, so he would leave. As Keulder walked out of the front door, the calls started from the front gate for visitors. Dullar Omar and other members of the Release Committee, including Trevor Manuel and Cyril Ramaphosa, were on their way.

I turned to Nelson. 'How does it feel, man?'

'What feel?'

'Being a free man after twenty-seven years.'

'I don't think it has sunk in yet. I feel like I felt ten minutes ago. There's no difference. It will take time to sink in. But I know I'm no longer a prisoner any more.' We shook hands.

I went to fetch Mr Omar and the other committee members. When we returned to the house Nelson was already waiting for them in the lounge. He had a folder filled with documents beside him as they entered. Tea was already being served by Swart. At the start there seemed to be an almost embarrassed silence between them all before Mr Omar stood up and walked over and embraced Nelson.

'Now you are a free man,' he told him. 'Congratulations.' The old lawyer had tears in his eyes as he turned aside. Everyone else walked over and shook Nelson by the hand.

Mr Omar interrupted, clapping his hands, and saying, 'Come on, let's drink this tea. We have a lot of hard work today to let this thing run smoothly.'

The Release Committee did not stay long, but as I drove them back to the main gate I could hear the beginnings of the political infighting which I knew would become a feature of the rest of Nelson's life. No longer was he a solitary man, the person I had grown to love during these past twenty-four years. Now, as one imprisonment was ending, he was about to become imprisoned again as public property, owned and operated by the people.

In the back of the car Mr Omar was concerned about the release. 'What on earth are we going to do with him from 10 o'clock until 6 o'clock, security-wise?'

One of the others in the back seat said, 'I don't know, but we'll make a plan; but it'd better be quick.'

I went back to the house. It was already getting towards the time for release. As the minutes ticked by so the noise seemed to increase. Overhead there had been four or five helicopters buzzing over the prison since shortly after 8 o'clock. The heat haze was already leaving the mountains shimmering and glazed.

I went back to the office, waiting for the telephone call telling me to drive Nelson to the gate. Fifteen minutes later I was still waiting. In the lounge Nelson was sitting reading. Relaxed and calm.

'Nelson, I'm told the Release Committee people are coming back again, but there's no sign of Winnie and the family,' I said.

One look at Nelson was enough to give me a sense of foreboding. 'Mr Gregory,' he said, his lecturing voice to the fore, 'I hope you remember that I will not be leaving this house and this prison without Winnie.'

What was going on? I told him, 'That's the first time I heard this. I have not been told of this until now.'

361

'I told the commissioner and he should have told you. The situation is precise. I will not leave until Winnie is here.'

'Let's hope then that she is here soon, because I was told to have you at the gate at 10 o'clock military time. Not a minute before or a minute later.'

He repeated, 'I say again, I am not leaving this house without Winnie.'

I went back to the office and sat reading the night log, waiting for the call to tell me Winnie and the family had arrived.

I knew that last night he had been restless and was up until the late hours, writing. He got up at 4.30, as usual, and had exercised, cutting his normal thirty-minute session to just fifteen. Maybe a sign of his own apprehension.

Shortly before dawn the prison doctor had arrived and inspected Nelson as he sat in his robe.

'It's a bit late for finding something wrong,' he had joked.

It was as I sat in the office that I suddenly recalled the committee's conversation in the car as I drove them back to the entrance gate. They, clearly, had a problem with security and wanted some sort of delay. How better than simply to delay Winnie's arrival, knowing Nelson would not leave without her.

The front gate telephoned me again shortly after 9.30 to say Omar and the others had returned. I went up and spoke to Omar. 'Where's Winnie?'

'In Johannesburg.'

'Don't tell me that, you know she should be here. Nelson won't leave without her.'

Omar shrugged, adding, 'Look, man, something has gone wrong with the chartered flight.'

I heard later that the South African Air Force had been put on standby to fly Winnie from Pretoria to Cape Town. The standard scheduled flights were all full.

When I took Omar, Manuel and Ramaphosa back to the house I sat listening to the politicking. Initially Nelson wanted to address the people of Paarl, to say thank you for being kind during his stay at Victor Verster. No, the committee members told him, not a good idea. It would be wrong to be seen to be speaking to a bunch of white, middle-class people, after his release from twenty-seven years in jail.

Nelson countered this by saying he wanted to spend his first night of freedom celebrating with the ordinary people of the Cape Flats, a vibrant, bustling township of squalor and deprivation on the outskirts of Cape Town. He argued that this would be his way of showing solidarity with the people who had supported him through the years in prison.

But Ramaphosa and Manuel, consummate politicians that they were, dissuaded him again. For security reasons – that hoary old chestnut – he should go to stay with Archbishop Tutu in Bishopscourt, a plush residence in white suburbia. I thought then the man of the people was certainly being drawn away from the people.

I'd heard enough of this and went back to the gate to wait for Winnie. There were thousands of people lining the roads for miles along the grass verges and spilling into the fields. They had all been told to look out for my white Nissan car, that this was the one that Nelson would leave in. As I approached the roar began and continued to swell until I stepped out and raised my hands to the heavens.

'Sorry, folks, no prize yet.'

The police were struggling to keep the crowds under control. Everywhere there was noise, from the crowds, from the shouting and screaming and from the helicopters flying overhead. This was going to be an almighty mess if I was not careful.

There was a telephone call to the guard-house. Sergeant Knight took it and handed it to me. 'General Willemse,' he said, his eyes raised to the heavens.

His words were crisp and sharp. 'Mr Gregory, it is almost 10 o'clock. Where is Mr Mandela?'

'General, I was with him just a short time ago and he told me he was not leaving without Winnie. He was emphatic.'

'So where's Winnie? Why was she not brought here?'

'Sir, I was not told about this. Mr Mandela told me only this morning. If I had been told earlier then I would have ensured she was already here in Cape Town with transport to bring her to Victor Verster. But now the Release Committee are telling me she's still in Jo'burg.'

His voice began to hiss. 'Mr Gregory, I told you 10 o'clock. I told you military time. I instructed you and you have let me down.'

I said there was nothing I could do. I wanted to ask if he wished me to arrest Nelson and have him thrown off the premises, but thought it best to keep quiet.

I put the phone down. It rang at five minutes past 10, ten minutes past, fifteen minutes past. Each time the general's voice was seething just a little more. I decided to leave.

If anything, the intensity of the noise from outside had increased. The television people had expected a 10 o'clock release and had switched on their generators to allow live broadcasts around the world. The crowd began to sing and chant, and still more helicopters flew overhead. It even drowned out the sound of the telephone.

I went back to the house and it seemed the celebrations had started. Nelson was sat in a chair sipping tea, but all around the committee members were shouting and laughing.

I was less than happy. 'Where's Winnie?' Stupid question really. I would be the first to know she had arrived with a call from the gate. Seeing the mood of the committee members I was more convinced than ever that this was all a ploy to keep Nelson inside; they simply did not know what to do with him during the day.

Nelson didn't seem to mind too greatly, so I decided to go along with everything.

Nelson patted me on the shoulder and said, 'Don't worry, she will be here in time.'

I told him, 'I was told 10 o'clock was the time of release, but I've told the commissioner, who is blerrie angry, that you were not moving until Winnie arrives.'

'Good.'

Another irony in this entire business: they'd kept Nelson for twenty-seven years, and now they couldn't get rid of him. He'd refused to leave the previous day when de Klerk wanted him out, and now here he was again, refusing to shift until Winnie arrived.

Every few minutes the phone would go, sometimes the commissioner, sometimes others. 'Gregory, what is going on? Where is that bloody woman?'

At first I was anxious, concerned that I had not followed the orders. But by mid-afternoon I had developed a mood of accepting everything that was going on. It was entirely out of my hands, and the one person who seemed less fazed than anyone was Nelson. I decided I would follow his example. Later I began to get angry with the commissioner and senior officers, not worrying about how I addressed them.

'Look, sir, I don't know. Now I don't even care. I know as much as you people know. You are waiting. I am waiting. Even if it is 12 o'clock tonight I'll be waiting, as you are waiting, as the entire world is waiting. Sir, what do you wish I do, sprout wings and fly to Jo'burg and carry Winnie here?'

'We're getting flack from the media people who are saying this show is costing them a fortune.'

'Sir, please don't burden me with that one. Just tell them that people are watching their shows whether Nelson Mandela is walking out or not. They are glued to their television, waiting. Tell them they've got the best suspense in years.'

At 2.45 the colonel in charge of the traffic police phoned to tell me that Winnie was on her way. I went to the gatehouse.

Less than half an hour later there was a roar from one end of the crowd lining the roadway. It spread along the ranks of tens of thousands like a Mexican wave. Winnie was in town. Eight cars swept in. Why on earth Winnie needed eight cars was beyond me, but right then I didn't want to ask any more.

Winnie got out and I went to her. 'Hello, Mrs Mandela, you've come to fetch your husband at last.'

'Yes, at last.' Her smile was captivating and I couldn't help but smile at her as we shook hands.

The entourage of cars went into the prison grounds. At the house Winnie was first out, leading the way, running. From outside I could hear the squeals of delight as other family members went in. It was a celebration, shouts, squeals, cries, more shouts. At the rear was a Combi driver and I told him that the boxes which belonged to Nelson were standing just inside the doorway. He should collect them and begin piling them into the back of his truck.

The phone rang. It was 3.30. It was General Willemse.

The sarcasm was not even thinly disguised. 'Mr Gregory, can you let any of us know what is going to happen? It would be so appreciated.'

'Sir, the house is filled with people and they are loading his things into the Combi. Lots of people are milling around, family and the like. It will be around 4 o'clock when we get through here. We'll be out by then.'

'Please don't make it any later.'

'Sir, I'm afraid it's out of my hands time-wise. But I'll try.'

'That would be so helpful.' The phone was slammed down on the heavy sarcasm.

The reality was that it was impossible to know how long this little party would take now. And once out of here, the roads were a mess. The main road, the N1, leading into Cape Town, I heard was blocked with traffic.

At 3.35 the phone rang again. I was standing outside in the

garden. I knew it would be General Willemse again. It was.

'Greg, a problem.' There was an urgency in his voice. Could I detect panic? 'I've just had a call from the Intelligence Services who I think have been in touch with MI5 in Britain.' He paused, wanting the effect of the overseas call to sink in. MI5, Intelligence Services, that had to be important.

'They've received information which indicates that one of the armed guards on the route to the gate has been contracted to assassinate Mr Mandela.' What the hell was happening? I froze with the phone in my hand, unable to speak.

'Greggie, Greggie, man, are you there?'

'Ja, General, I am here. What shall I do?'

'Do, man? The first thing you do is tell Mr Mandela, inform him. Then it's up to you. I'll leave it in your hands. But be careful.'

So that was it. Tell Mr Mandela and handle it myself. A passing of the kak. The release of Nelson Mandela at any time now and an assassin on my hands. And with the world's press standing on the door-step with their eyes, cameras and microphones firmly fixed on Victor Verster Prison and me. It was now in my hands. I was sweating.

Inside the house there was joy and laughter, drinks being handed around and tea cups everywhere. Nelson stood with Winnie, their arms locked together.

'Uh, Nelson, may I have a word for one second, please?' His face was puzzled as he picked out my concern. Winnie laughed and said, 'Ah, Mr Gregory, you still want to keep us apart?'

Inside the bedroom I told him of the general's telephone message. What did he want to do? Did he want to cancel the departure?

Again the hand on the shoulder. 'No, we go ahead, Mr Gregory. You do whatever you consider necessary and tell us when you are ready. I have confidence in you.'

I went into the office. I could see Nelson strolling with his family in the garden, showing them the flowers he had taken pride in tending and the vegetables he had grown.

I gave an order to the main control. 'This is Warrant Officer Gregory. I want every person along the road to the gate, including all guards, totally disarmed. I also want every officer, up to and including generals and their bodyguards, disarmed.' There was a stunned silence at the other end.

Back came a captain, Joubert was his name. 'Uh, ja, Gregory, what are you playing at, man?'

'Captain, this is an order for your people, and if it is not carried out now, then Nelson Mandela is not being released. And that will mean there will be many embarrassed prison department people who will have a lot of explaining to do. So, to repeat, I want everyone disarmed. Do I make myself clear? Now do it. I have the authority of the minister, so move, man.'

I was sweating, wondering if this was all some sort of joke. Then the phone rang. It was Keulder. 'Gregory, what the hell is going on?'

'Sir, I'm telling you because I have the authority of the minister to disarm all your guards and the people you let in today must also be disarmed. I don't know who is who or what is what; all I know is that everyone must be disarmed. Or Nelson Mandela is not leaving here.'

Keulder simply said, 'Yes, I'll get it done now.'

I don't know how Keulder did it, but within eighteen minutes every guard who lined the road to the gate had been removed. Every other person disarmed.

Outside in the office was a new face, a Brigadier Gillingham, a big-wig from Pretoria.

'I'm sorry, Brigadier,' I said, confronting him. 'I'm going to have to ask you to hand over your weapon.' I indicated the handgun in his sidearm holster. He spluttered and coughed and would have gone several shades of purple had I not continued, 'These orders are from the very top and apply to everyone.'

At exactly seven minutes to 4.00 I received a call. All was ready. I went to the house and nodded to Nelson. 'We're ready, it's up to you.' As I walked out he called me back and handed me an envelope.

Outside in the garden I opened the envelope and took out a white card. Nelson had written to me, 'The wonderful hours we spent together during the last two decades end today. But you will always be in my thoughts. Meanwhile I send you and your family fond regards and best wishes.'

The procession of cars were outside on the sandy roadway. I turned to go to the leading car to climb into the front passenger seat. As Nelson walked to his car, the third in line, he veered over and came to me.

Without saying a word he put out his hand and I put out mine. We shook firmly.

He said, 'This is goodbye.'

My throat was closed, blocked. Several times I swallowed. 'Ja, goodbye and good luck.'

He looked directly into my eyes and I could see the tears. He let go of my hand and grabbed me by the shoulders and embraced me. I hugged him back. We did not move and all around us people stood still not wishing to break us.

As he eased his grip he added, 'No, this is not goodbye. We will see each other again.'

At that moment I knew in my heart this man was going to lead my country and I bowed my head slightly and said, 'Thank you, sir.'

I climbed into the leading car, into the front passenger seat. Nelson, Winnie and members of the family were in the cars behind. Everywhere was noise, roars from the helicopters, now screaming closer and lower. Dust was everywhere. I saw little, blinking the wetness from my eyes, not caring that the other prison guards were looking at me.

The drive was slow, a procession through the ranks of, now, unarmed guards. Families of the prison guards, all of them white, stood in their gardens of the family quarters and waved. I wondered how they would have behaved just a few years before.

Down the road, lined with protea flowers, still in late season bloom, grass cut short and neat. The multi-coloured flag of the Republic fluttered from the flag-staff. Turn left, into the last 100 yards, that close to freedom. I pulled my car over to one side and stepped out. I had to stop. I could no longer see where we were going, my eyes were filled again.

I stood to one side and watched his car slide by, slowly, sedately. His face was beside the window, smiling, yet composed. I gave him the one-handed clenched fist salute, the ANC salute which would have landed me in prison a few years before. He nodded and returned the salute.

As the car passed, my mind returned to my boyhood and to the farm where I had played with Bafana all those years ago. I never had a chance to say goodbye to him. Now as my friend was leaving, my heart and mind was filled with a vision of Bafana.

No one heard me, and even if they had, they wouldn't have understood. As Nelson stepped from his car, his hand holding Winnie's, the crowd roared, the man of the people was freed. I said two words: 'Goodbye Bafana.'

Glossary of terms

assegai – wooden spear
bakkie – open-backed truck
beshu – a cow-skin loin cloth
biltong – salted uncooked meat
bioscope – cinema
braai – barbecue
impi – a battalion of Zulu warriors
kaffir boetie – nigger lover
kaffirs – blacks
kak – shit
kierie – a Zulu throwing-stick
kleilats – a throwing-stick with a piece of baked clay stuck on the end
knobkerrie – a large stick
koelies – Coloureds
kraal – enclosure for livestock
laager – military camp
maas – blend of milk and mielies
mielie – maize or corn cobs
mtecane – a time of chaos when tribes attacked other tribes
panga – broad knife
Poqo – political prisoners
rondavel – round hut
rooinek – redneck or Englishman
sangoma – with doctor
shambok – rawhide whip
sisal – straw mat
stoep – verandah
umlimo – white witch

Index

Note: Abbreviations used in the index are: JG for James Gregory; NM for Nelson Mandela; Pp for Pollsmoor prison; RIp for Robben Island prison; VV for Victor Verster prison.